This volume had its origins in the mood of disillusion and despair which followed the Third United Nations Conference on Trade and Development in Santiago in 1972. The prospects for co-operation between rich and poor nations seemed poor and new policies and instruments needed to be considered if the interests of the rich and poor nations were not to become even more unbalanced in favour of the rich. The contributors to this volume consider, analytically and carefully, what unexploited possibilities might be open to the less developed countries, both jointly and individually, in international affairs, which would generate a more equitable outcome.

The issues which are addressed in these papers are of even greater immediate relevance and public interest now following events of the last three years; the success of oil producing countries in revising prices, world-wide inflation, famine in the poorest countries, recession in industrial countries. All of these have generated enormous pressures upon the international economic system. At the same time the less developed countries have stepped up their pressure for reform at special sessions of the United Nations at which they have declared the need for a new international economic order. This volume makes an important contribution to the discussion of the new international economic order and will prove useful to policy makers in both rich and poor nations as they prepare for the Fourth United Nations Conference on Trade and Development in 1976.

Also issued as a paperback

Perspectives on Development

A WORLD DIVIDED

Perspectives on Development is organised by and
edited from the Centre for Developing Area Studies, McGill
University, Montreal, Canada. The primary focus of the series
is on economic, social and political development in third world
countries. The series includes works of a broad, comparative
and interpretive character as well as specific institutional and
empirical studies which stem from research activities of the
Centre. However, the series also includes other works judged by
the Editors to be valuable contributions to our understanding
of the development process.

Series Editors

R. Cranford Pratt, Professor of Political Science, University of Toronto,
Chairman
John A. Barnes, Professor of Sociology, University of Cambridge
Irving Brecher, Professor of Economics, McGill University
Peter C. W. Gutkind, Professor of Anthropology, McGill University
Ben Higgins, Professor of Economics, University of Montreal
Kari Levitt, Associate Professor of Economics, McGill University
Richard F. Salisbury, Professor of Anthropology, McGill University

A WORLD DIVIDED

THE LESS DEVELOPED COUNTRIES
IN THE INTERNATIONAL ECONOMY

Edited by
G. K. HELLEINER

CAMBRIDGE UNIVERSITY PRESS

CAMBRIDGE

LONDON · NEW YORK · MELBOURNE

Published by the Syndics of the Cambridge University Press
The Pitt Building, Trumpington Street, Cambridge CB2 1RP
Bentley House, 200 Euston Road, London NW1 2DB
32 East 57th Street, New York, NY 10022, USA
296 Beaconsfield Parade, Middle Park, Melbourne 3206, Australia

First published 1976

Printed in Great Britain at the
University Printing House, Cambridge
(Euan Phillips, University Printer)

Library of Congress cataloguing in Publication Data

Main entry under title:

A world divided.

(Perspectives on development; 5)

Includes index.

1. Underdeveloped areas – Addresses, essays, lectures.
I. Helleiner, Gerald K. II. Series.

HC59.7.W66   330.9'172'4   75-16606
ISBN: 0 521 20948 X hard covers
ISBN: 0 521 29006 6 paperback

Contents

[v]

Contributors

Carlos F. Diaz-Alejandro is a Professor of Economics at Yale University.

Reginald H. Green is a Fellow of the Institute of Development Studies, Sussex. At the time he wrote his paper he was Economic Advisor, The Treasury, United Republic of Tanzania.

Gerald K. Helleiner is a Professor in the Department of Political Economy, University of Toronto.

Nurul Islam is Deputy Chairman, Bangladesh Planning Commission.

Alfred Maizels is Advisor on Economic Policy and Research, Office of the Secretary-General, United Nations Conference on Trade and Development (UNCTAD).

Göran Ohlin is Professor of Economics, University of Uppsala.

Edith F. Penrose is Professor in the Department of Economic and Political Studies, School of Oriental and African Studies, University of London.

Marian Radetzki is a Fellow of the Institute of International Economic Studies of the University of Stockholm. At the time he wrote his paper, he was Head, Economic Division, Intergovernmental Council of Copper Exporting Countries (CIPEC).

Frances Stewart is a Fellow in the Institute of Commonwealth Studies, Oxford.

Paul Streeten is Warden, Queen Elizabeth House, Oxford.

Constantine V. Vaitsos is Economic Advisor, Acuerdo de Cartagena (Andean Pact), Lima, and Fellow, Institute of Development Studies, Sussex.

John White is a Fellow of the Institute of Development Studies, Sussex.

Preface

This volume had its origins in the mood of disillusion and despair which followed the Third United Nations Conference on Trade and Development in Santiago in 1972. At that time it seemed to many of those concerned with international dimensions of the world development problem that the prospects for co-operation between rich nations and poor, never very bright, had been severely dimmed. New instruments would have to be forged in the less developed countries, it was then widely felt, if they were to alter the existing international economic order so as to generate a more equitable outcome. I therefore invited a number of experienced and sympathetic authors to consider, analytically and carefully, what unexploited possibilities might be open to the less developed countries, both jointly and individually, in international economic affairs: which measures were likely to work and which were not, and why. The authors whose papers follow responded quickly and enthusiastically.

Events have moved swiftly in the meantime. The OPEC's success, world-wide inflation, famine in the poorest lands, recession in the industrialised countries, are among the factors which have generated enormous pressures upon the international economic system which had survived intact since the Second World War. The system itself is now universally seen to require repair or reconstruction. The issues which are addressed in the papers in this volume are of far greater immediate relevance and public interest than any of us had dared to hope three years ago. As will be seen, that is not to say that there can be grounds for great optimism on behalf of the less developed countries, least of all in the case of the least developed. It is my belief, however, that in this book the authors contribute significantly to informed discussion of international economic affairs as they relate to the less developed countries. It is my hope that the papers may prove useful to policy makers in both rich nations and poor who share the authors' concerns.

I am most grateful to the Dag Hammarskjöld Foundation (Uppsala) and particularly its Director, Sven Hamrell, for the support and encouragement which they have consistently given this project. The Foundation sponsored and supported a most fruitful seminar on 'The Third World and International Economic Change' in Uppsala in late August of 1974, at which the authors had an opportunity to discuss their drafts with one another and with a number of other experienced scholars and practitioners (Lars Anell, Edmar Bacha,

Jagdish Bhagwati, Eduardo Garcia d'Acuna, Dharam Ghai and Miguel Wionczek). In addition to this hospitality and support, they have provided further generous assistance in speeding the revised papers to the press. I should also like to express my thanks to my friend and colleague, R. Cranford Pratt, whose prodding led me to undertake this enterprise in the first place and whose steady encouragement has helped me to complete it. Mrs A. McMaster deserves the credit for having created order from the original typescript.

Toronto   G.K.H.
January 1975

1. Introduction

GERALD K. HELLEINER[1]

From 'partnership' to confrontation

Relationships between rich nations and poor have entered a distinctly new phase in the 1970s. For all but the poorest of the poor countries, those still persistently grappling with the reality of famine, the era in which 'development assistance' was perceived as the pivot upon which those relationships rested is over. 'Development assistance' always received more attention, both in rich countries and in poor, than it inherently deserved. Analysis of the effects upon the less developed countries of 'Northern' trade policies, technology transfers and financial policies, have long been relatively neglected by decision makers and commentators in the developed countries.

Official development assistance has been the subject of more public misunderstanding than any other aspect of the political and economic relationships between rich nations and poor. From its very beginnings in the early post Second World War period its role and likely duration were misunderstood, its objects misconceived and its measurement obfuscated by inappropriate 'targets'. Drawing on the misleading analogy of Marshall Plan assistance to war damaged Europe, foreign aid was seen as the source of the missing element – technical skill, capital or foreign exchange, at various times and various places – which would permit the acceleration of the rate of economic growth to the point where that growth would become 'self-sustaining' and the aid could gradually be phased out. Careful calculations were, therefore, undertaken both in donor and in individual recipient countries of the number of years for which foreign aid would be required. At the same time it was frequently portrayed to an anxious Western public as a guarantor of political alliances and even of political stability. Despite the relatively rapid, by historical standards, average rates of economic growth in the Third World in recent years, in relatively few less developed countries has anything resembling the expected self-sustained growth been achieved and in even fewer have recent years been characterised by the promised political stability or 'dependability' in international affairs.

The true dimensions and character of foreign aid were obscured by the introduction of aid 'targetry' which was misleadingly specified. Each developed country was, by UN resolution, adjured to devote 1 per cent of its national income (later gross national product) to foreign aid; but the 1 per cent target was defined in terms of total net capital flows – whether private or public, whether investments, loans or grants, all were lumped together within the definition. Thus private commercial flows were to be valued within

[1]

the foreign aid totals as equivalent to governmental grants. Not until the early 1970s were private commercially motivated flows and public loans at commercial rates removed from the definitions to which the official targets applied; and then, as if to demonstrate that there had never been any misunderstanding about what the target was originally intended to mean, the 'purified' aid objective was reduced to 0.7 per cent of gross national product. Even then, the aggregative targets took no account of differences in loan terms or between grants and loans (although new targets for aid *terms* were negotiated within the Development Assistance Committee of the OECD), and there were no adjustments for the reduced real value of aid flows which resulted from restrictions as to procurement and use.

In any case, not only have the targets never been attained but practice has, in fact, deviated ever more sharply from the stated aspiration. The developed countries as a group have *reduced* the share of their gross national products devoted to official development assistance in *every* single year but two (1967 and 1971, in each of which there was an increase of 0.01 per cent), since the aid targets were first proclaimed (see Table 1). In 1973, official development assistance from OECD countries totalled $9.4 billion (in current prices) – a reduction in real terms of 6 per cent from the previous year – and made up 0.30 per cent of developed countries' collective gross national products, the lowest percentage yet recorded. Adjusting for the need for repayment of loans and the costs of tying, the real value in current prices of official development assistance in 1973 (its untied grant equivalent) was no more than about $6 billion[2] – about 30 per cent less *per capita* than a decade before.

Aid could never have played the role which many thought it would. The problems were far too deep rooted and complex; the issues of development and poverty, of stability and political organisation are enduring ones which are not resolved in short bursts of international concern. Nor are alliances so easily purchased. But the dimensions of the developed countries' efforts at development assistance were always very limited. Never did the total aid flows even approach the levels of commitment undertaken by the United States in the postwar rebuilding of Europe, let alone the much larger sums which would have been required to make a significant dent in the much greater problems of the less developed countries. It is not facetious to answer those who have been disappointed with the 'results' of aid with the fact that it has never seriously been tried.

Much more fundamental than the frequent misunderstandings as to what foreign aid was, its size or its possible role, however, was the failure or unwillingness of the developed countries to place it in the proper context of *overall* economic relationships between the developed and less developed countries. Even a cursory glance at the overall balance of payments of the Third World *vis-à-vis* the developed countries reveals the relatively small importance of official development assistance in the overall scheme of things (see Table 2). Even before the recent dramatic increase in petroleum prices,

Table 1. *Official development assistance, 1962–73*

	1962	1963	1964	1965	1966	1967	1968	1969	1970	1971	1972	1973
Official (net) development assistance ($ billions)	5.4	5.8	6.0	5.9	6.0	6.5	6.3	6.6	6.8	7.8	8.7	9.4
Price deflator (1961 = 100)	101.4	102.4	109.4	105.0	109.0	110.4	113.6	115.3	120.1	129.1	141.7	180.2[a]
Official development assistance ($ billions in 1961 prices)[b]	5.4	5.6	5.4	5.6	5.5	5.9	5.6	5.7	5.7	6.0	6.1	5.2
Official development assistance as % of total donor's GNP	0.52	0.51	0.48	0.44	0.41	0.42	0.37	0.36	0.34	0.35	0.34	0.30

[a] Derived by applying the change in the new 1970 based index to the 1972 index based on 1961.
[b] Calculated from the first two lines of this table.
SOURCES: OECD, 1973, pp. 177, 181, 189. OECD, 1974, pp. 202, 209, 233.

2. *Sources of foreign exchange in the less developed countries, 1973 ($ billions)*

	1970	1973
	59.0	98.1
ich major oil exporters)	(16.3)	(33.6)
Uฺ. l development assistance (OECD only)[a]	6.8	9.4
Other official	1.2	2.6
Private capital (at market terms)–net	6.9	11.1
Direct investment (net)	3.5	6.7
Portfolio investment (net)	1.2	3.2
Export credits (net)	2.1	1.2
Eurocurrency loans (gross)	n.a.[b]	9.3
Private voluntary agencies	0.9	1.4
Total	74.7	131.8

[a] Communist countries' official development assistance has totalled annually between $1.4 and $1.6 billion in 1970–3. OPEC countries' aid has averaged $0.4–0.5 billion in the same period.
[b] Believed to be relatively small. In 1971 it amounted to $1.5 billion.
SOURCES: World Bank, 1974, p. 101: OECD, 1974, pp. 135–6, 233, 288.

Third World total exports and commercial capital imports regularly made up ten times the size of aid flows. Were the petroleum exporting countries to employ significantly more of their enormous balances for concessional loans or grants (in 1974 their total official development assistance commitments were already running at rates comparable to those of the 'traditional' OECD donors),[3] aid might become a much more important matter than ever before; but even then, aid flows would be dwarfed by commercial ones.

The less developed countries have sought for many years to widen the scope of the developed countries' stated concern with world poverty and development. Indeed, the 1960s were characterised by an acceleration in United Nations' conference and research activities in the fields of agricultural and industrial development, employment creation, technology transfer, and trade – through its various specialised agencies, the FAO, UNIDO, ILO, UNITAR, and, above all, the UNCTAD. All of these expanded efforts reflect the increased voting strength of the less developed countries in the United Nations which followed the accessions to independence of a number of former European colonies in Africa and Asia.

The first United Nations Conference on Trade and Development in Geneva in 1964 marked, it was said, 'a turning point in the evolution of international organisation' (Gardner, 1968, p. 99). It was 'the first major conference in which the lines were drawn sharply on a North-South...basis'. Its significance ranked, according to commentators of the period, with the formation of the first trade union in nineteenth-century capitalist societies. Its major accomplishment, from the standpoint of the less developed countries, was creation, over the objections of the developed countries, of a permanent

secretariat for the UNCTAD. At the two subsequent international conferences which have been held under its auspices (New Delhi, 1968, and
Santiago, 1972) a lengthy list of recommendations, requests and proposals
were presented (and passed in the form of resolutions) on subjects ranging
from international commodity agreements through tariff preferences to
foreign private investment and international monetary reform. The permanent UNCTAD staff, serving both as prophet and broker (Nye, 1973), has
undertaken research and organised countless consultative meetings on all of
these topics, which have formed the basis for informed analysis and the
creation of unified positions in many areas of Third World concern. Yet the
record of progress towards international commercial and financial arrangements, which might generate more satisfactory outcomes for the less
developed countries, has not been at all encouraging.

As has already been seen, official development assistance consistently fell
as a percentage of the developed countries' gross national product, and began
to stagnate even in real absolute terms (the improved performance of some
small donors notwithstanding). The GATT programme of action which had
called in the early 1960s for a standstill on further trade barriers against the
less developed countries, and a gradual reduction in existing ones, and
authorised non-reciprocal trade barrier reductions in favour of less developed
countries was totally ignored. At the same time, a new international textiles
agreement was authorised in which industrialised countries were to be
permitted to discriminate against low income countries, and a new instrument
of protectionist policy was introduced – the 'voluntary' export restraint, in
which poor countries were induced, through threats of import quotas, to
restrain their own exports. No significant new international commodity
agreements were negotiated. The overall terms of trade of the less developed
countries remained roughly unaltered during the decade (OECD, 1974, p. 39).

The less developed countries, nevertheless, benefited from substantial
expansion in their exports during the 1960s. This expansion was directly
related to the extended period of rapid growth in the major industrialised
countries and owed little or nothing to the introduction of any concessional
policies on the part of the developed world. The one breakthrough apparently
achieved (at the New Delhi Conference), an agreement on the part of the
developed countries to introduce preferential tariff treatment for manufactured and semi-manufactured products originating in less developed countries, proved to be of small consequence by the time each importing country
had inserted its own rules and exceptions into the 'generalised' system; and
the biggest importer, the United States, has only recently implemented it.

The explanations for this lack of success lie primarily in the structure of
international organisations and the underlying international power structure,
and, to a lesser extent, in the domestic politics and bureaucratic organisation
of individual developed countries. At the international level, it has become
clearer than ever before that resolutions carried by majority vote in the
United Nations and its specialised agencies, carry no force. The less

developed countries now have a permanent majority there, but the major industrialised powers, which continue to provide the bulk of the UN's finances, feel no compunction to comply with them. 'Confrontation by moral suasion' (Lipton, 1973, p. 32) has proven singularly unproductive for the less developed countries; indeed the incessant clamour from the poor may well have *reduced* the extent to which the developed countries felt embarrassment over their behaviour and certainly lowered their degree of commitment to, and confidence in, the agencies in which they were invariably to be outvoted. (No doubt the thaw in East-West relations has also been an important aspect of the rich countries' apparent unconcern with these issues in recent years.)

It is, therefore, hardly surprising that the developed countries should increasingly have shifted their support to institutions over which they had a greater degree of control, in particular those of the World Bank group and the OECD. (The latter, of course, is an organisation of developed countries only.) One can safely predict that in the future the major powers will continue to opt out of international institutions whose actions they can no longer control.

While the UN agencies expanded their research output and the numbers of meetings concerned with development issues, there was a substantial real increase in the development activities of the World Bank group and the International Monetary Fund. Indeed, the former led a politically unsuccessful attempt to resurrect, within the developed countries, the issues and policies which fall primarily under the UNCTAD mandate, for which support had been definitely flagging, through the Pearson Commission report.[4] (The title of this report, *Partners in Development*, was already quite inappropriate as a description either of current reality or of the prospects.) The World Bank has also been active in identifying the inadequacies of the growth 'successes' of the 1960s in terms of the alleviation of mass poverty. As far as genuine multilateralism is concerned, however, these latter agencies suffer from the major disadvantage that they are perceived by the less developed countries as agencies of the developed countries because of their location, leadership, and weighted voting and quota systems. The continued frustration of UNCTAD initiatives at the same time that these donor controlled agencies expanded their own resources, research capacity and influence, became a matter of great concern. At the Lusaka non-aligned conference in 1971, one document adopted by the meeting questioned whether 'a World Bank world' was really what was wanted (Tanzania, 1971).

At the international level, then, so far as development is concerned, there has emerged something of a split in the research and secretariat functions between those pursued under the auspices of agencies in which developed countries have most influence, and those undertaken by agencies in which their role is not so dominant, notably those of the United Nations. This does not mean that there has not been significant co-operation in development research between these agencies. On controversial issues, however, like the role of direct foreign investment, technology transfer, private property rights, and commodity agreements, the study papers, research results and background documentation for international deliberations, tend to differ in a predictable fashion depending on their origin; while power continues to rest with the major industrialised states and their policies continue to be made at national levels.

At the national level, development agencies in the developed countries have universally been created for the purpose of administering and distributing development assistance. They have carried a fairly limited political base since their principal constituencies lay outside their own countries. (Exporters have, nevertheless, been influential in affecting their behaviour.) Other aspects of international policy which might have had a bearing on the development of those countries to which development assistance was being offered typically have been within the province of other governmental departments. International monetary affairs and debt negotiations have typically been handled by finance ministries and treasuries. Trade matters – whether commodity agreements or matters of market access – have been handled by ministries of trade, commerce or industries. Neither in monetary nor in trade matters is an integrated assessment of the entire national interrelationship with the less developed countries most affected likely, therefore, to be brought to bear upon policy formation. The development implications of international trade and monetary policies are likely to remain in the background, both because of the natural bureaucratic propensities of the relevant ministries and departments whose principal concerns are domestic ones, and because of the political influences which are typically brought to bear on these branches of government by the organised representatives of the national business communities. Thus, even if suitable international forums were to be erected and universally trusted by all of the member countries, the developed countries would still probably be sending the 'wrong' representatives to them.

The international economy has thus continued to function in a manner quite unaffected by the increasing discussion of its inadequacies from the standpoint of the less developed world. It is certainly possible to argue that the international system, far from assisting the less developed countries in their development efforts, throws off effects, only some of which are the product of conscious decisions, which are detrimental to them and more particularly to their poor (Seers and Joy, 1971, pp. 37–43). Less controversial is the view that the distribution of the gains from international trade and interaction could be far more equitable than it is. The inadequate share of these gains which has been realised by the world's poor is the product of a variety of biases and asymmetries, some of which have already been mentioned, and more of which will be discussed in the essays which follow. The existing rules of international transactions – whether unregulated markets, immigration laws, conventions with regard to private property or whatever – are the product of particular social and political systems, national and international, with their particular constellations of power.

Presumably, a truly equitable distribution of the gains from international trade and investment – and from world economic activity in general – would be *possible* only with world government. But even world government, because of these same power constellations, would offer no assurance in this respect and, from the standpoint of the less developed countries, would probably carry too much 'neo-colonialist' flavour to be acceptable anyway. (The developed countries would have additional grounds for opposing it: the fear of being overwhelmed by the larger numbers in the poor countries and of the likely redistributive mechanisms which would be erected at their expense.) These attitudinal and/or interest based impediments to the achievement of an improved distribution of world income pervade all of the discussions of international reform, including those which fall far short of such utopian visions as world government. The basic difficulty is that international co-operation is *not* always in every nation's interest, even though nations *are* increasingly interdependent.

At a minimum, one must distinguish between those situations which are zero-sum, i.e. in which one nation's gain is another's loss, and those which are not, i.e. in which both of the 'interdependent' nations stand to gain through their interaction.[5] Thus, the reduction of barriers to the import of manufactured products from low income countries by the developed countries, while it may throw off internal distributional effects which will require compensatory action, is generally acknowledged to be in the interest of the developed countries as well as that of the less developed exporters. No sacrifice of national interest is involved; it is a non-zero-sum 'game'. International agreement ought to be considerably easier in these situations, provided that 'side payments' can be made to the interests which oppose such actions because of the direct effects upon their incomes and interests. It may well be that progress in these non-zero-sum cases must await the formation of the necessary interest group alliances – including those across national boundaries – to offset those which have previously dominated national governments, and drive them in the direction of their joint national interests.

In other situations, however, such as an agreement on the part of developed countries to pay higher prices for coffee, the situation is zero-sum and international conflict is more or less inevitable. In these cases, appeals are customarily made on the grounds of morality, the preservation of international order, and so forth, to persuade the governments of developed countries to pursue policies which are not in their immediate economic interest. As has been seen, these governments have not been noticeably responsive to such appeals. Nor have those domestic interest groups with the most to gain from the introduction of such national policies, e.g. machinery exporters to the less developed countries, been very effective in persuading them to act on the basis of more self-interested appeals.

All these things considered, it should not be surprising that efforts on the part of the less developed countries to persuade or shame the developed countries into altering the rules of international economic conduct should generally have been so unsuccessful. Nor can one be surprised that severe disillusion as to the utility of continued efforts to employ reason and argument should eventually have set in.

Particularly should disillusion and despair be expected at a time when the medium term international economic outlook is so bleak. Not only are the prospects for expanded real aid very sombre (there seems to be little prospect of adequately indexing aid budgets to protect them against the effects of inflation) but there are a variety of other grounds for pessimism in the medium run outlook. Export prospects look generally bleak relative to the rapid expansion of the 1960s, as the major industrialised countries head into a serious recession; even if they avert the worst cutbacks in output, most raw material prices are expected inevitably to decline (relative to the overall price level) below the levels which they enjoyed during the recent boom. According to the World Bank, less developed countries which export neither oil nor minerals can expect substantial terms of trade deterioration by 1980, with the poorest of all – those with under $200 *per capita* income which had already suffered such deterioration in the recent commodity 'boom' – projected to suffer further terms of trade deterioration of about 20 per cent (McNamara, 1974, p. 10). Protectionist pressures are also increasing in the industrialised countries in consequence not only of expanded imports of manufactures from low income countries, but also of the overall decline in business activity. At the same time, immigration from low income countries, which provided an important safety valve in the Caribbean, Southern Europe, North Africa and Asia during the 1960s – allowing about a million per year to take up temporary or permanent employment in the industrialised countries,[6] now seems to have been cut off; to the extent that it continues it seems likely to drain off only the higher level skills from the less developed countries and so, while rewarding their possessors, may actually harm the lot of those who remain behind. Interest rates on borrowed funds, while expected to decline below the extraordinary 1974 levels, which reflect both inflationary expectations and increased perceptions of risk, are still likely to remain at historically unprecedented levels for less developed country borrowers; as their debt accumulates, and particularly if there are some Third World defaults, the extent and terms of their access to commercial loans are likely to deteriorate.

Disillusion, heightened by these bleak prospects, has generated a new and angry mood in the less developed world. By the early 1970s North–South confrontations seemed to be *de rigueur* at international conferences – on the environment in Stockholm (1972), population in Bucharest (1974), food in Rome (1974) – and in the United Nations, most notably at the special session on raw materials and development in April 1974. They are only slightly muted in the annual meetings of the IMF and World Bank. But, of greater significance still, the less developed countries have developed a policy stance which moves well beyond the rhetoric of such confrontations into considered action.

New objectives, new instruments

There are two principal levels to the less developed countries' international policy stance. At the first and most fundamental level, there is the question of their objectives at the international level. One can safely assume that their general collective objectives, in the future as in the past, are to extract the maximum economic and political gains from trade and resource flows at a minimum of cost to themselves. Constant expressions of such general objectives in international forums serve an important political and educative function,[7] but as guides to specific policy and action they are not too helpful. The UNCTAD and the preparatory meetings for its general conferences have generated enormous lists of demands or requests from the less developed countries, so long and so general that the developed countries have not been required to take them too seriously. That such broad approaches are not functional is now understood; the development of that understanding has coincided with the emergence of much greater research capacity, sophistication of analysis, and political experience and determination. One can, henceforth, expect much more focused objectives based on more carefully prepared and co-ordinated positions in international discussions. Indicative of the likely pattern for the future is the work of such organisations as the so-called Group of 24 in international monetary discussions, the Andean Group in relations with transnational enterprises, and the new producers' organisations in a variety of commodity markets.

Consisting of the representatives of eight central banks from each of Africa, Asia and Latin America, the Group of 24 has formulated and agreed upon joint positions on questions of international monetary reform which reflect their joint interest. These positions extend to a level of considerable detail and, if maintained, can be expected to influence changes in the articles of agreement of the IMF where the less developed countries have sufficient collective voting strength, under the terms of its articles, to veto changes which are unsatisfactory to them. Similarly the Andean Pact countries and the member governments of organisations uniting the exporters of bauxite, copper, tin, tea, coffee, cocoa, phosphates, bananas, mercury and iron ore, have been developing very specific joint policy positions. Greater focus, and more careful and detailed preparation of joint positions, can be expected in other international deliberations as well (while the more general rhetoric no doubt continues).

Apart from this general alteration of less developed countries' approaches to the establishment of objectives, there has also been a perceptible shift in their content. The new emphases have been aptly summarised in the context of the functioning of international commerce, as: decomposability, reversibility, and unintrusiveness (or arms lengthness or standoffishness)

(Diaz-Alejandro, 1974). These characteristics are important to *all* international political and economic transactions and relationships with which the less developed countries must be concerned, and not merely the commercial ones; and they are today more frequently among the bases for their assessment. The questions now being asked with respect to specific international relationships are the following.

(1) Does the international link intrude significantly into national affairs, or might it in future? Are there more arms length alternative arrangements which would produce the same results? These questions are being asked with respect to official development assistance, relations with international organisations, direct foreign investment and concessional trading arrangements.

(2) Can the existing institutional and commercial packages of desired goods and services be broken up, so that the less developed country can acquire their components from a variety of sources and forego others altogether? This question is crucial to the development of less developed countries' relationships with transnational enterprises and may be especially important in their future acquisition of foreign technology. It is also relevant to their attempts to diversify international trade, aid and investment ties, and avoid the dangers of neo-colonialist looking 'spheres of influence'.

(3) Can international relationships, if necessary, be terminated and new policy directions thrown easily into reverse? Are there clear provisions for renegotiation where appropriate? Again, this question relates most obviously to relationships with foreign firms (particularly where ownership is involved) but it also applies to those with foreign governments in a wide range of possible issues.

At the same time, there is a continuing pressure for the *regularisation* of procedures which will generate outcomes more favourable to the less developed countries, and for *automaticity* in those matters which are already or might become favourable in this respect. Thus, if they can acquire greater influence and power in key international deliberative bodies and institutions, or if real power can be transferred to those agencies in which they already possess it, the recurrent policy struggles are likely more frequently to generate outcomes which are palatable to them. If such resource flows and trading concessions as are agreed by the developed countries could be freed from the discretionary authority of the donors, or at least from the need for frequent parliamentary approval, they would be far more valuable – because far more reliable – than they are at present.

The second level for policy analysis is that of the selection of instruments for the pursuit of these more focused and carefully formulated objectives. The approach of the less developed countries during the 1950s and 1960s has been a fairly 'passive' one. Having expressed their requests, as vigorously as they were able, they waited for the developed countries to act upon them. It was implicitly and naively assumed that their general objectives were accepted by those who were to act upon them, and that recommendations for action would eventually be followed in one form or another. Scholars and UN bodies exerted substantial energies upon the devising of targets and schemes (some would describe them unkindly as 'gimmicks') which might achieve the desired objectives – commodity reserve currencies, supplementary financing schemes, import duty rebates, international taxes, etc. To some extent such a passive stance with its concomitant supply of suggestions was influenced by the developed countries' own body of rhetoric on the subject of development and their own stated degree of commitment to it, which, if taken at its face value, fully justified it. Such naiveté became increasingly difficult to maintain in the face of the continuing failure of the developed countries not only to accept the variety of general recommendations made to them, but even to meet the modest targets they had set for themselves or fully to implement those schemes, like the generalised system of preferences, upon which they had ostensibly agreed. It was difficult not to conclude that the objectives were *not* universally agreed. It followed that new policy instruments would have to be constructed and experimented with.

At first these new perceptions were the product of disillusion with international 'partnership in development' and despair at the prospects for future such co-operation from the developed countries. They remained somewhat inchoate and ill defined; and most of those who expressed them (frequently citizens of developed countries themselves), did so with some hesitation and little confidence.

International monetary events, beginning with the first devaluation of the dollar, accelerated the growth in frustration and annoyance with the existing machinery for decision making at the international level, as they made the exclusion of the less developed countries from the relevant councils only too evident. The stalemate at the Third UNCTAD pushed it further. It was the apparent success of the OPEC and the furore surrounding the international 'energy crisis', however, which really sharpened and solidified the general consensus and the political will. Non-petroleum producers took vicarious pride in the OPEC's bargaining skill with the major oil importing countries, even when they themselves suffered severely in consequence. It seemed a clear demonstration of the possibilities from the adoption of new policy instruments and/or the shrewd and determined use of bargaining skill in relations with much more powerful international actors. The OPEC example was far more important for its galvanising of opinions in this respect than as an object lesson, which it did not really offer, in the management of commodity markets.

The less developed countries seem now, therefore, to have adopted a much more 'active' and aggressive stance in international economic relationships with richer countries than heretofore. Unilateral initiatives are being carefully considered in circumstances where the developed countries continue to refuse their co-operation, and there appears to be far less concern about the possibility of retaliation. In their increased willingness to accept risks, they can be said to have moved, implicitly, to a potentially much more self-reliant stance as well.

The new mood in the less developed countries with respect both to objectives and to instruments can be found at the national as well as the international level. *Individual* countries seem also to be more determined in their efforts to extract the maximum from their international relationships by sharpening their commercial and financial policies in areas where there existed some previous slack. These new approaches to objectives and instruments on the international level are shared by less developed countries of widely divergent political character, and seem totally unrelated to ideology. (This raises the obvious question of the possible internal distribution of the gains accruing to less developed countries in consequence of more successful international bargaining.) A watershed seems to have been reached in economic relationships between less developed and developed countries.

The instruments of the future can be grouped into three broad categories: (1) continued pleading for voluntary international co-operation from the developed countries, perhaps with more focus and more precise attention to the details of what is being sought; (2) more effective and determined bargaining with developed countries and foreign firms, both in international negotiations and in purely bilateral ones; (3) unilateral policy initiatives pursued either singly or jointly by the less developed countries themselves.

All are, of course, interrelated. Threats of unilateral initiatives, if they are credible and are likely to cause harm to the developed countries, may increase the bargaining strength of the less developed countries and/or improve the response to requests for international co-operation. On the other hand, some unilateral acts on the part of less developed countries may reduce the extent of co-operation offered by developed countries.

Whatever the new mood, one should anticipate no slackening of efforts to persuade the developed countries that they should offer more official development assistance at better terms, increase the less developed countries' power in international organisations and economic affairs, and generally undertake other policy changes unilaterally which would have similar effect. These continued efforts to employ the instruments of pleading and persuasion will be particularly important for those less developed countries which have the least with which to bargain. The 'least developed' countries have no option but to continue to seek more assistance, although they may attempt to do so in a more self-reliant manner. (See Reginald Green's paper on Tanzania below.) In some instances, it may be possible to demonstrate that changes which are important to the less developed countries involve no serious costs to the developed countries, i.e. they are not zero-sum situations. Such efforts are no longer expected, however, to generate significant aggregative change from the existing dispensation of power and resource allocation. To the extent that the 'least developed' are successful at extracting larger resource flows and commercial concessions from the developed world, they are most likely to be at the expense of the slightly more developed countries who now can, and frequently prefer to, make their way without them. One can already discern a shift in developed countries' approach to development assistance in this general direction – a shift which can only be encouraged by further 'aggressive' policy initiatives, particularly if they are successful, on the part of the 'average' less developed and semi-industrialised states.

In some policy areas the entire less developed world has little power with which to bargain: the international law of the sea, the generalised system of preferences, monetary arrangements among the major powers, immigration laws, the composition of research in the developed countries, world food consumption levels and patterns, and so forth. Only in the sense that 'everything is related to everything else' and that initiatives or concessions on one front may always be offset by those on another, do the less developed countries have any substantial capacity to influence outcomes in these areas. (When one moves to such a 'general equilibrium' level of analysis, one is, of course, beginning to deal in terms of general international economic order.)[8]

The arenas within which the second set of policy instruments will be employed are the 'traditional' ones where bargaining *can* take place. Relationships with foreign enterprises, the terms of international commodity agreements, the writing or rewriting of international conventions and agreements, debt rescheduling and the terms of international monetary reform are among the subjects which are amenable to more effective bargaining on the part of less developed countries acting either singly or in groups. Bargaining is an issue wherever the capacity of the less developed countries to say 'no' can affect the outcome of international decision making. There will, therefore, be many instances in which action is dependent upon unilateral decision on the part of the developed countries (in response to the continued appeals referred to above) but in which there remains some bargaining power in the hands of the less developed countries. Even official development assistance will be rejected by a potential recipient if it is accompanied by too much unwanted 'baggage'. The determinants of effective bargaining, within the bounds set by 'basic' bargaining strength (as determined by such factors as the possession of a scarce resource, favourable location, large market, military or diplomatic power, etc.), include the degree of unity and the extent of information possessed by the protagonists. In order that unity be achieved there must be close attention to the distribution of the gains from joint bargaining. (These issues are explored in Paul Streeten's paper below.)

The essence of successful development policy is in knowing what must be assumed constant during any particular period, and what is truly variable. This is as true in the international arena as in domestic affairs. While it must be the object of diplomacy to convert many undesirable 'constants' into variables – by clamouring or bargaining for increased official development assistance at more favourable terms, better commodity prices, access to the markets of the industrialised countries for processed exports, and so forth – strategies must, nevertheless, be constructed upon thoroughly realistic assumptions. While there has been no pause in diplomatic efforts of the above type, there has been a gradual shift in perceptions as to what it is 'realistic' to expect from the developed countries. In consequence, as has been seen, there has recently been increasing discussion of the possible resort on the part of less developed countries to policy instruments of the third type – those which do not depend upon negotiation with the developed countries but are pursued unilaterally. The new more self-reliant and self-confident mood in many less developed countries ensures that there will be increasing experimentation with such policy instruments, most of which have not been tried in any serious manner heretofore. These include all manner of agreements among the less developed countries themselves – the erection of new regional or functional institutions, negotiation of trade preferences or agreements among themselves, creation of currency agreements and payments unions, unification of fiscal conventions or technology contract provisions with respect to foreign enterprise, co-ordinated planning of industries or river basin development or research or transport networks. One can construct a strong case for a shift in the less developed countries' emphasis in international relations away from the global institutions in which, for the present, their power is insufficient to assure them satisfactory 'international' solutions towards more focused region-specific or function-specific bodies over which they have full control. (John White does so in one of the essays which follows.)[9] Such a shift may, of course, alter the relative strengths of individual less developed countries *vis-à-vis* one another. The interests of the weakest of all might conceivably be better protected in the global institutions than they would be in smaller ones dominated by a few more powerful states.

Many of these unilateral initiatives carry few implications for the developed countries and merely reflect the growing penchant and capacity for independent action. Others, however, involve direct confrontations with developed countries, transnational enterprises based in developed countries, and existing international institutions or conventions. These include such initiatives as nationalisation and/or confiscation of foreign owned assets, default on foreign debt, the co-ordinated withholding of raw materials from world markets, the abrogation or withholding of recognition of existing conventions regarding international patents and trademarks, and selective withdrawal from or refusal to join institutions which seek to maintain a degree of international economic order such as the IMF and the GATT. Examples of each of these can be found in the international experience of the post Second World War period.

Underlying such commercial and financial diplomacy rests, of course, the basic question of retaliatory power – economic, financial, military – and willingness to employ it. There are presumably limits to what the powerful developed states will tolerate when it comes to interference with their economic or strategic interests. The formulation of appropriate responses to these challenges will constitute a major responsibility of statesmen, bureaucrats and businessmen of the industrialised countries in the coming decades. One must hope that they will respond more frequently on the basis of the clear, long run world interest in peace, stability and justice than on that of the direct short run economic advantage of their most affected firms or individuals, although experience to date, and our knowledge of bureaus and lobbies, cannot leave one too sanguine about the likely future balance of their responses. It is tempting to draw an analogy between the development of reformist measures to modify the excesses of unbridled capitalism in the modern welfare state and the obvious need for parallel action at the international level; but the failure of much greater inequities at the latter level than in national affairs so far to have generated any significant response – itself primarily the result of the absence of a global government which might make and enforce such policies – suggests that there are flaws in the analogy. It may be, as Heilbroner suggests (1974, pp. 42–5), that some desperate small, weak powers, will eventually be driven to seek their objects through violence – terrorism, assassinations, kidnapping, and direct military or paramilitary threats to the cities of the developed world, made possible by the acquisition of nuclear weaponry.

Issues in trade, investment and monetary affairs: a summary

There has, by now, been quite a lot of thinking and research upon the possibilities for more effective policy initiatives on the part of the less developed countries in international economic affairs. Yet one cannot escape the conclusion that there remains a substantial imbalance in information, research output, and, therefore, bargaining capacity at the international level.

Research in the field of international economic affairs abounds in the universities, research institutions and governments of the developed world. In the North American schools of business and law, entire courses of instruction are offered in the techniques of dealing with recalcitrant and unco-operative governments in far off lands. Inevitably, such research and instruction tends to address issues from the standpoint of the rich countries; thus, the new mood in the less developed world is quickly placed into the context of the need for 'international economic order', which may be desirable enough as an end in itself, but is clearly not the prime concern of the potential 'disruptors'.

There has been very limited research of a comparable kind in the less developed countries. Despite the development of greatly increased expertise in the field of economics and the social sciences in recent years, a recent survey of the field suggests that there remain very few scholars working within the less developed countries who are addressing international policy questions (Howe *et al.* 1973, pp. 2–3). Even the international institutions which are specifically mandated to work on international development questions, despite much admirable effort, have not effectively restored the balance and probably cannot do so.

The UNCTAD, which has been a major supporter of research and source of ideas, remains, after all, an international body in which the dues are primarily paid by the developed countries. There are limits upon those matters which it can investigate, and even greater limits upon its possible recommendations; as part of the United Nations family it is committed to increasing information which may lead to more equitable international arrangements, but it is also required to avoid recommendations involving likely confrontation or conflict, or breaches of international conventions. For example, it is difficult to imagine it preparing papers on means of defaulting on debt and getting away with it, or on minimising compensation payments in cases of nationalisation. Such research is even less likely to be found, as has been seen, in the OECD Development Centre, the Research Division of the World Bank, the Overseas Development Institute, the Overseas Development Council, or the research arms of any of the national aid agencies; even if such research were to be conducted in such centres, its results and recommendations would inevitably be suspect.

An indigenous expertise and research capacity must, therefore, be developed within the Third World. In the meantime, sympathetic scholars from developed countries, particularly those with substantial experience in the less developed countries who are, therefore, not as liable to the charge that they 'lack not only the credibility but also the credentials, including, especially, a sense of what it is to be underdeveloped' (Howe *et al.* p. 3), have an important role to play. They can join their colleagues from the less developed countries in attempting to analyse the international issues from the latter's point of view. Their research and thinking, whether regarded as totally appropriate or not, may, at least, stimulate further research and thought in these areas within the less developed countries and is, in any case, probably a more helpful employment of their time and talent than most alternative uses thereof. As further research develops in the less developed countries the balance of the efforts of such scholars might gradually be redirected towards the analysis of those trade, monetary and other policies of their own countries, as they affect the less developed world.[10]

The essays which follow have been assembled for the purpose of contributing to the discussion of what it now makes sense for the less developed countries, possessed of their new self-confidence and determination, to do in the international economy. The authors were selected because of their direct experience with the topics to be discussed, and because they were each known to have something new and important to say on them. They were asked to avoid exhortation and rhetoric – their basic sympathy towards the objectives of the less developed countries in the international economy being taken as given – and to take Paul Streeten's call for 'pedantic utopianism', 'imaginative visions of alternative possibilities with close and precise attention to detail' (Streeten, 1974 *a*, p. 8), as their inspiration. Their preliminary drafts were discussed in a most fruitful meeting of the authors, together with a number of additional scholars and policymakers from less developed countries, following which, each of the papers was substantially rewritten.

Needless to say, it should not be assumed that all are in agreement on the final products. Different and even conflicting views may be found in the papers which follow. In particular, some see in the new situation a chance to achieve the objectives long pursued by international development agencies. Others, such as John White, believe that these strategies have themselves been misconceived, and that the new situation requires not only a change of strategy, but a relatively diminished role for the agencies with which strategic responsibility has previously rested.

Two further general points should be made by way of introduction to the issues which these papers raise. First, there are many very important areas of potential conflict and/or possible policy initiatives which are not discussed in the papers which follow. One cannot cover all topics in one book of this size. The focus is on export trade in primary products, relationships with transnational enterprises, financial issues, and institutional machinery. Among the many matters not seriously addressed here are: food trade, labour migration – temporary or permanent – manufactured goods exports, the environment, and the sea bed.

Secondly, one must always be conscious of the risk of generalising across the entire range of less developed countries. One cannot sensibly consider the Third World as a coherent and co-ordinated group. Among the most important 'widening gaps' of the past two decades are those among the less developed countries themselves with respect to *per capita* income and other measures of growth and development. A number of poor countries have moved significantly ahead of the remainder; and the petroleum exporting countries are not the only members of the relatively gaining group. Increasing concern is understandably, therefore, being focused upon the *least* developed countries. Apart from these differing degrees of success, the interests of particular less developed countries can be expected to diverge when specific policy issues arise. There is no adequate substitute for detailed studies of particular cases.

The papers are grouped as follows. Part I is concerned primarily with trade questions, although Paul Streeten's paper ranges rather further afield. Part II deals with relations between less developed countries and transnational enterprises. In Part III the focus is upon debt and monetary issues. The two very dissimilar papers in Part IV are concerned with international institutional change, and national economic planning in a disordered world.

The trade relationship between rich nations and poor dominates the rest in terms of its sheer dollar value. In trade matters, as in so many others, one must distinguish among less developed countries with widely varying prospects. The petroleum producers are clearly in a class of their own in this respect. The remainder of the less developed world can, perhaps, best be classified as follows: (1) the semi-industrialised, moving rapidly into manufacturing for export; (2) the primary product exporters with reasonably bright demand prospects, notably the minerals exporters; and (3) the primary product exporters with relatively weak demand prospects. As has been seen, the export outlook for the last category of less developed country is, at present, very bleak. One would like to be able to identify trade policy initiatives which could be useful particularly to these least fortunate countries; but their potential for gains through more self-reliant and determined stances is unfortunately fairly limited.

A recurring theme in discussions of trade problems of the less developed countries, whether the weaker ones or the stronger, is the potential for gains from more co-operation – through supply management, economic integration, preferential trading and payments arrangements, and so forth. In the papers of Part I, the benefits, costs and prospects of Third World economic co-operation in the field of trade are considered from some new perspectives. Marian Radetzki considers the prospects for the success of commodity supply management schemes in the light of the apparent success of the OPEC and the increased flurry of international interest in commodity cartels. Despite the calls from some developed world spokesmen for supply guarantees, and suggestions for new GATT limitations upon export restrictions, there remain severe constraints upon the potential use of supply management by the less developed countries to extract larger foreign exchange earnings from their primary products. He concludes that the number of products which might lend themselves to such management and the potential long term gains realisable through such policy are both fairly limited. Moreover, the products most likely to succeed are not generally those exported by the poorest countries. Medium term demand and supply elasticities are generally too high, and the degree of geographic concentration too low for supply restrictions to generate the desired earnings improvements. Prospects for success would increase if certain developed country exporters could be induced to collaborate with the less developed countries in supply management. Paul Streeten considers the elements of bargaining capacity and power, whatever the issues, but devotes particular attention to the problems of commodity cartels.

It may, nevertheless, be possible for the less developed countries to earn a larger *share* of the total revenues from the sale of these products and final products which use them as inputs, even if the total revenues cannot themselves be improved much. Alfred Maizels emphasises the potential gains realisable from the development of alternative marketing channels and joint sales efforts rather than continued reliance on existing foreign controlled ones; increased local processing is also a relatively unutilised source of important gains to the producing countries which he identifies. Both Radetzki and Maizels note the potential for retaining more of the economic rent deriving from the scarce resource, through joint bargaining and co-ordinated tax and incentive programmes with respect to foreign enterprise. The latter approaches have the added virtue of not penalising other less developed countries, as price increasing measures, notably in the case of oil, have done.

Frances Stewart considers the merits of developing closer trading ties with other less developed countries instead of or in addition to the traditional ones with the developed countries. Her argument relates particularly to the trade in manufactured products but there is a quite general case for working to overcome the existing biases in the infrastructure which favour trade between developed and developing countries (North–South) relative to trade between developing countries (South–South). Transport systems and freight rates, financial institutions and credit schemes, aid, investment and technology relationships are among the components of this biased infrastructure. Active discrimination in favour of trade within the Third World can certainly be justified on 'infant industry' grounds; and she offers a rationale for continued preference for such trade well beyond conceivable periods of infancy.

All of these trade initiatives are basically of the 'unilateral' type. The views and policies of the developed countries are irrelevant to their success except in so far as they seek to impede or retaliate against the initiators. Maizels also discusses some of the older style trade policy recommendations which are dependent upon developed country co-operation, such as supplementary financing or guaranteed earnings schemes. The gyrations in commodity markets of the past few years may have altered the approaches of at least some developed countries to the question of international price or earnings stabilisation schemes and commodity agreements. He notes that it may now be possible to gain international support for agreements which couple supply commitments to price guarantees.

One set of trade issues which was scarcely foreseen even five years ago is that centred on the 'world food and energy crises'. Many less developed countries have suffered severe deterioration in their terms of trade not so much because of weak demand for their exports, as was to some extent expected, but because of enormous increases in the prices of essential imports – notably food, fertiliser and fuel. These issues have been discussed primarily in forums in which developed country assistance is sought rather than in terms of unilateral initiatives. This stems, above all, from the fact that the core of the problem rests in the least developed countries, where development assistance must still be relied upon and self-reliant possibilities are limited by extreme underdevelopment. Some one must be induced to transfer resources in their direction, whatever else is done, and it should not be surprising that efforts should be made to exert maximum leverage upon the richest to do so. One must lament the fact that the Third World's apparently increased solidarity with respect to the developed countries does not extend to preferential fuel pricing arrangements between Third World producers and at least the poorest of Third World consuming countries. On the other hand, OPEC members are now extending significant amounts of development assistance to less fortunate countries, and there have already been steps toward their financing of others' commodity supply restriction agreements.

Another important area of trading relationships between developed and less developed countries which has fast become a source of potential conflicts and of potential Third World gains is manufactured and semi-processed exports from the latter to the former. These manufactured exports have been growing at unprecedented rates, averaging over 15 per cent annually over the past decade (UN, 1974 b, p. 1). To date they have been relatively concentrated in terms of countries of origin but there are indications that the future holds greater diversification in store. The development of these exports generates major adjustment difficulties for unskilled-labour-intensive industries and plants in the developed countries, and consequently has produced strong pressures for the erection of trade barriers against these products. Potential exporters of such products will, in future, have to develop sophisticated marketing strategies (and political activities) which minimise the likelihood of galvanising the injured into an effective lobby for protectionist policies. Importing firms and transnational manufacturing enterprises in the industrialised countries may well be important political allies for the exporters of less developed countries in their attempts to retain access to the developed countries' markets. Streeten emphasises the potential for such alliance formation on a North–South basis as well as a South–South one.

There is room for some considerable concern, however, that the structure of trade barriers in the developed countries against manufactured exports from the less developed world will reflect this constellation of political influences in a bias against exports which do not move through trading and distribution channels controlled by the large firms of the importing countries. In such circumstances, the potential for arms length and self-reliant international relations in development, of the type preferred by the less developed countries, may be fairly limited – perhaps more so than in most primary commodity markets. Moreover, their potential income gains may also be limited because of the large number of low income countries competing with one another for the favours of access to the relevant markets and technologies; one may think of the problem in terms of an internationalised version of the Lewis model of development (1954) with unlimited supplies of labour, where the capital is all foreign owned, and the gains to the less developed countries consist exclusively of more employment at more or less constant wage rates; or, in terms of the labour theory of value, where the surplus accrues exclusively to *foreign* capital which is itself internationally mobile while labour is not (Emmanuel, 1972). It should be evident that the less developed countries will do better for themselves in extracting gains from this type of trade by offering a unified front to foreign investors, technology salesmen and marketing firms, just as is the case in other sectors; unfortunately, the prospects for such co-operation appear less in this area than in resource industries or even than in other parts of the industrial sector, since manufacturing for export is an activity to which every less developed country aspires and for which it has the basic capacity, so that those who control markets can more readily play off one country against another. There is not a great deal that the less developed countries seem likely to be able to do in this sphere of their international economic relationships for the present; no doubt this explains the UNCTAD's recent de-emphasis of these matters following its modest success in persuading the developed countries to introduce preferential duties on many manufactured and semi-manufactured products originating in less developed countries. This is not a hopeful arena for unilateral initiatives.

The potential for extracting a larger share of the gains from trade for the raw material exporting countries, at the expense of foreign firms which have developed the relevant resource and/or control the trade, raises the broader question of relations with foreign private enterprise. A high proportion of the less developed countries' exports has always consisted of intrafirm trade; that is the 'export' involves a transfer of the product in question between two branches of the same foreign owned (or at least foreign controlled) enterprise. Minerals and petroleum are no doubt the best known examples of vertically integrated international enterprise, but similar phenomena have characterised the trade in tea, coffee, bananas, sugar, palm oil, rubber and other estate crops, and international trading oligopsonies have been important even in those countries where export crops have been grown by indigenous small holders. Today, one could conservatively estimate the share of such intrafirm trade in total Third World exports at over 50 per cent, 25 per cent excluding petroleum.[11] With the development of foreign owned import substituting industry an increasing share of Third World imports is also probably taking place on a similar intrafirm basis. To the components, machinery and equipment, and spare parts which are imported on this basis, must also be added imports of technology, capital and skill.

The prices at which intrafirm transactions take place within oligopolistic industries are not susceptible to naive market analysis of the type which is traditionally applied to arms length trade in competitive circumstances. Nor are such intrafirm transactions, in any case, likely to be governed by market criteria so much as by centrally planned decisions which are transmitted to the branches or subsidiaries of the firm directly by command. The potential role of transfer pricing in international tax minimisation is now quite widely understood; other aspects of its use, however, probably deserve more attention than they have usually received. In particular, transfer pricing can be an important instrument for foreign exchange control evasion, neutralisation of legal maxima on remittances of particular categories such as profits, and the development of a more persuasive case for tariff or other protection in feasibility studies or thereafter.

The formation of state marketing boards and state trading bodies or agencies, has had the effect of driving a wedge between the two ends of this trade, transforming it, to some extent, into an arms length relationship. Customs duties, foreign exchange controls, technology assessment boards and other legal restrictions also can drive such wedges into this trade without, however, necessarily altering its intrafirm character. The local acquisition of a share of the equity or representation on the board increases the degree of 'standoffishness' of these relationships, as, obviously enough, does nationalisation. Disclosure laws may also have such an effect on this trade, provided that they can be adequately enforced. All of these policy instruments or institutions are deployed by the governments of less developed countries with the object of improving the terms of their commercial relationships with foreign producing and trading firms. Whether any or all of them actually succeed in their objects depends upon their power, information and skill.

Constantine Vaitsos in Part II brings out the variability in these factors which is likely to be found in different sectors of productive activity and in different countries or areas. He argues that more effective, informed and co-ordinated bargaining with transnational enterprises can improve the terms of less developed countries' trade. In the case of resource based exports, as has already been seen, it is essential that host governments maximise their share of the economic rent which derives from their possession of a scarce resource. In import substituting manufacturing, there is room also for considerable tightening of fiscal provisions, including protective tariffs, and the terms of technology imports in view of the foreign firms' desire for local market access; particularly is this so where markets are large, as they will be if regional agreements can be negotiated within the less developed world. Prospects are least encouraging for manufacturing for export, which is, ironically, the fastest growing element in the Third World's total export bill, because of the limited bargaining power inherent in the sale of unskilled labour.

Edith Penrose considers the detailed elements of the bargain which must be struck between the governments of less developed countries and foreign enterprises from the standpoint of the latter. She is concerned to find a least cost (or maximum revenue) means of acquiring local (state) control; and, in the process, identifies those components of the bargain which best lend themselves to the exercise of a more determined stance and those which do not. Like Vaitsos, she concludes that improved terms can frequently be negotiated, particularly with respect to some of the detailed terms of management contracts (such as are most frequently found in Africa and parts of Asia), and technical and marketing agreements. She also argues that the attainment of majority ownership (i.e. 51 per cent of equity) is not a sensible sub-objective of a policy directed at control of foreign enterprise. Access to information and representation on the board can be purchased at far lower cost. At the same time, if there are income earning reasons for holding equity, there seems little reason to acquire any proportion short of 100 per cent.

Strikingly, neither of the papers on relations with transnational enterprises places much emphasis upon their role as sources of capital. This reduced emphasis upon what was once seen as their principal contribution reflects the 'new view' of transnational enterprise which focuses on technology and technology related issues such as management and intermediate inputs. It also probably reflects, at least in part, the increasing resort to other private sources of capital on the part of the less developed countries. Carlos Diaz-Alejandro properly emphasises in Part III the dramatic expansion in less developed countries' borrowing at arms length on Eurocurrency markets which, by increasing the borrowers' options and their capacity to decompose direct investment and foreign aid packages, has significantly raised their bargaining capacity with respect to sources of both.

This increasing resort to borrowing at commercial terms raises the difficult issue of the existing debt and the less developed countries' capacity to service what is already there, let alone additions to it. Nurul Islam and Göran Ohlin address this issue directly in Part III, although from slightly different perspectives. From the perspective of an extremely poor country with discouraging export and development prospects, and an already heavy debt burden (such as Nurul Islam's native Bangladesh), it is difficult not to advocate debt relief and an increase in the concessional element in future official development assistance. There clearly may come a point at which such countries may rationally calculate that there are no further net gains to be realised from the continued servicing of foreign debt. At that point, it would be most helpful both for the defaulting country and for the international community (particularly the borrowing members thereof) if debt default could be undertaken 'honourably' – on the basis of some internationally agreed principles.

Both Islam and Ohlin consider what such principles might be. Among the best candidates for wide acceptability as legitimately defaultable, as identified by Islam, would seem to be: loans which were clearly earmarked for consumption purposes, e.g. disaster relief; loans which were offered for projects which turned out to be mistaken, particularly where the lender was the source of the advice to proceed; that portion of outstanding loans which was absorbed in what is now universally acknowledged as having been the excess and unnecessary cost of procurement tying. If aid donors cut back their new commitments to compensate for such defaults, as they might (but, Ohlin argues, probably would not), the less developed countries would still gain in that the resources so released would be much freer than are most new aid commitments for use in accordance with the priorities of the defaulting, recipient countries. The development of such a 'code' of honourable default obviously requires the agreement of the developed countries if it is to serve its purpose, which is, above all, to free the debt relief negotiations of their bilateral character, in which each debtor is considered unique and is pitted against a united collection of creditors; and to free other borrowers of penalties which might be applied against them in anticipation of future unilateral defaults.

Ohlin makes a most persuasive argument to the effect that if the 'decks could be cleared' of the mistaken debt accumulations from the past, there is no reason why all but the poorest of the less developed countries should not continue to accumulate debt at commercial terms at roughly the same rates of growth as have typified the recent past. Diaz-Alejandro and Ohlin both note that, whatever the other disadvantages of worldwide inflation, it has produced the side effect of reducing the real burden of the less developed countries' debt; obviously, from this windfall gain it does not follow that inflation is, therefore, in their interest. Indeed, present anticipations of inflation may well be generating interest rates on new debt which exceed in real terms those which would have to be paid in less chaotic times.

Diaz-Alejandro also considers in some detail the interests of the less developed countries in a new international monetary order. He defends their expressed preference for relative stability of rates of exchange between major currencies, unlike other recent commentators, but concludes on pragmatic grounds that they would be best to settle for more flexible rates; it would be too much, he argues, to ask that the developed countries maintain both liberal trade and financial policies, and fixed exchange rates. Since, however, most less developed countries will peg their currencies' values to those of one or more of the major powers, or the new SDR, their case for a larger share of future SDR distributions is somewhat strengthened over that expressed during the period when rich countries also had fixed rates to defend. It hardly needs emphasising at this stage in the discussion that the less developed countries will and should continue to advocate an alteration in the formula which determines the distribution of special drawing rights among the members of the IMF so as directly to increase their share. Again, all of these financial matters offer limited potential for unilateral initiatives on the part of the Third World, although IMF reform could, in principle, as has been seen, be vetoed through their co-ordinated action.

Reginald Green considers means by which a determinedly self-reliant but desperately poor country like Tanzania can seek to conduct its economic affairs in the face of a most inhospitable and uncertain international environment. It may be that many more less developed countries, particularly the least developed of all, will be forced to adopt more self-reliant policies of the sort he describes, as a matter of necessity rather than of principle. This makes his description of the Tanzanian response to sharply deteriorating terms of trade of much more general interest; and the evidently very narrow error margins, upon which its policies are based, special grounds for concern. The fates of many of the poorest countries do seem at present to hang on very slender threads.

The paper which concludes this collection is one in which John White considers the implications of the new mood in the less developed countries for future international organisation. He argues persuasively that, while it is difficult to generalise as to the true roots of success or failure in efforts at Third World co-operation, other things being equal, success seems to have been greater when objectives were more narrowly focused. The United Nations agencies have played an important role in the development of the psychology and politics of the new mood, and the provision of opportunities for discussion and research support (a negative one, in White's view), but they are too comprehensive both in membership and in aspiration for very effective action of the type now sought. The future institutional instruments of change are likely to be more functionally and/or geographically restricted, less given to rhetoric and posturing, and much more technical and adept in giving 'close and precise attention to detail'. The institutional models for the future are bodies like the Andean Group or the OPEC.

Whether the new objectives and instruments of the less developed countries can be translated into the effective transfer of resources and power in their direction will depend, to a great extent, upon the successes of such newer and smaller Third World multinational institutions. Upon them and their member governments rests the prime responsibility for ensuring that the initiatives of the next decade, borne of the frustrations and disappointments of the last, involve more for the people of the less developed countries than a slight renegotiation in the terms of their poverty and dependence.

Notes

1 For comments upon an earlier draft I am grateful to Carlos F. Diaz-Alejandro, Reginald Green, Robert Matthews, Alfred Maizels, Paul Streeten and John White, none of whom are to be held responsible for the contents of this version.

2 The grant equivalent of OECD official development assistance in 1973 was 87 per cent of its value (OECD, 1974, p. 246). The cost of tying was probably between 20 and 25 per cent of the same value.

3 Total aid commitments by the OPEC countries in the first nine months of 1974 totalled $8.6 billion, exclusive of their loans of over $4 billion to the IMF's oil facility and over $1 billion to the World Bank. The largest bilateral donors have been Iran and Saudi Arabia; about one-third of these bilateral flows have gone to the countries most affected by the recent rapid deterioration in terms of trade (OECD, 1974, p. 136). So far, these development assistance flows have been characterised by depressingly familiar defects with respect to intercountry allocation and quality. For further discussion, see Nurul Islam below.

4 L. B. Pearson et al. 1969. The Pearson Commission was appointed and financed by the President of the World Bank to draw up a balance sheet on the international development effort. It made a long list of recommendations for reform and Pearson, himself, devoted considerable time and energy to their promotion but with very little effect.

5 One must also note that in reality there are situations which can only be described as negative-sum, where both parties lose or one party's losses exceed the other's gains. Aggressive acts such as inevitably cause retaliation frequently involve eventual losses for everyone. On the other hand, negative-sum games may consciously and rationally be entered into if one is sufficiently confident of one's capacity to extract positive gains at others' expense.

6   Migrants to Europe alone totalled 955,300 in 1969 (Hume, 1973, p. 3). This migration has generated severe problems both for European countries and individual migrants, which it is not the purpose of this essay to assess.

7   'Collective legitimisation' of the less developed countries' case is an important function of the United Nations, even if legitimacy does not produce change (Claude, 1967, pp. 73–103).

8   There has been growing concern in the developed countries with the maintenance of international economic order in the face of the many challenges to the post Second World War international system. For example, see Bergsten, 1973.

9   Lipton has recently made a related case for de-emphasising multilateral solutions in favour of bilateral negotiations covering a wide range of issues; this approach, he argues, is more likely to generate results useful to the less developed countries than are global approaches to single issues (Lipton, 1974).

10 The issues surrounding the establishment of research priorities are carefully considered in Streeten, 1974 b.

11 The recent UN report on multinational corporations states that 'more than one-quarter of the value of all international trade in goods appears to be of an intragroup character' (UN 1974 a, p. 88).

References

Bergsten, C. Fred (ed.), 1973. *The Future of the International Economic Order: An Agenda for Research.* Lexington: D. C. Heath.

Claude, Inis L., Jr., 1967. *The Changing United Nations.* New York: Random House.

Diaz-Alejandro, Carlos F., 1974. North–South relations: the economic component. Economic Growth Center, Yale University, Discussion paper 200, mimeo.

Emmanuel, Arghiri, 1972. *Unequal Exchange, A Study of the Imperialism of Trade.* New York and London: Monthly Review Press.

Gardner, Richard N., 1968. The United Nations conference on trade and development. In *The Global Partnership*, eds. Richard N. Gardner and Max F. Millikan, pp. 99–130. New York: Praeger.

Heilbroner, Robert, 1974. *An Inquiry into the Human Prospect.* New York: W. W. Norton.

Howe, James W. *et al.*, 1973. *The Developing Countries in a Changing International Economic Order: A Survey of Research Needs.* Overseas Development Council Occasional Paper no. 7, (reprinted from Bergsten, 1973), Washington.

Hume, Ian M., 1973. Migrant workers in Europe. *Finance and Development*, **10** (no. 1), 2–6.

Lewis, W. Arthur, 1954. Economic development with unlimited supplies of labour. *Manchester School of Economics and Social Studies*, **22**, 139–91.

Lipton, Michael, 1973. Unctad Schmunctad? *Bulletin, Institute of Development Studies (Sussex)*, **5** (no. 1) 30–41.

  1974. Confrontation versus co-operation. *Bulletin, Institute of Development Studies (Sussex)*, **6** (no. 2) 116–30.

McNamara, Robert S., 1974. Address to the Board of Governors. Washington.

Nye, Joseph S., 1973. UNCTAD: Poor nations' pressure group. In *The Anatomy of Influence, Decision Making in International Organization*, eds. Robert W. Cox and Harold K. Jacobson, pp. 334–70. New Haven and London: Yale.

OECD 1973. *Development Co-operation, Efforts and Policies of the Members of the Development Assistance Committee, 1973 Review.* Paris.

1974. *Development Co-operation, Efforts and Policies of the Members of the Development Assistance Committee, 1974 Review.* Paris.

Pearson, L. B. *et al.*, 1969. *Partners in Development, Report of the Commission on International Development.* New York, Washington and London: Praeger.

Seers, Dudley and Joy, Leonard (eds.), 1971. *Development in a Divided World.* Harmondsworth: Penguin.

Streeten, Paul, 1974 *a.* Alternatives in development. *World Development,* 2 (no. 2) 5–8.

1974 *b.* The limits of development research. *World Development,* 2 (nos. 10–12) 11–34.

Tanzania (United Republic of), 1971. *Cooperation Against Poverty.* Dar es Salaam: Government Printer.

UN (United Nations), 1974 *a. The Impact of Multinational Corporations on Development and on International Relations,* New York.

1974 *b. Trade in Manufactures of Developing Countries and Territories, 1972 Review.* New York.

World Bank, 1974. *Annual Report.*

PART I

Issues in international trading policy

2 A new international strategy for primary commodities

ALFRED MAIZELS[1]

The economic background

One of the outstanding features of postwar economic growth has been that economic prosperity has virtually by-passed all but a handful of developing countries. The problems of acute poverty, chronic unemployment and underemployment, maldistribution of incomes, urban overcrowding, high disease incidence, undernourishment and malnutrition, even famine, and many other characteristics of economic and social underdevelopment are just as widespread in Africa, Asia and Latin America today as they were a decade or two ago.

International economic policy, as enshrined in the International Development Strategy of the United Nations, was designed to remove the major constraints, both domestic and external, which limit the economic and social progress of developing countries. But the limited success of the Strategy so far and, in particular, of international policy relating to primary commodities, which still account for the bulk of export earnings of developing countries, poses an important question. This is whether a new emphasis is required for the underlying objectives of the Strategy – i.e. a substantial acceleration in the economic and social progress of developing countries during the 1970s – to be achieved. The concern of the developing countries at the unsatisfactory nature of economic relations between developed and developing countries and, more specifically, with the need for radical changes in international commodity policy, was forcibly expressed in the Declaration and the Programme of Action adopted by the sixth special session of the General Assembly in April/May 1974.

That the existing international Strategy is now largely ineffective has become abundantly clear since the sharp changes in international price relationships that have taken place since the end of 1972, the persistence of heavy inflationary pressures in the Western industrial countries and the consequent acute balance of payments difficulties of the majority of both developed and developing countries. Indeed, it would seem that the evolution of the world economy, and the changes in the relative positions of different groups of countries over the recent past, were essentially unaffected by the existence of the Strategy, and particularly by the international policy on commodities embodied therein.

What was this international commodity policy, and what were the principal reasons for its limited success? The policy itself consisted essentially of two elements, viz. (i) a consensus by governments of developed countries to reduce barriers to imports of primary commodities from developing countries, so as to allow the latter to benefit from an expansion in the production and export of products in which they possessed a comparative advantage; and (ii) a consensus by governments of both developed and developing countries to consider the negotiation of international agreements, where appropriate, to reduce instability and to achieve a level of prices remunerative to producers and equitable to consumers. This policy of improvement in market access and achievement of stable, remunerative and equitable prices for the commodity exports of developing countries was not a new one. The elements had been set out clearly in Dr Prebisch's report on 'A new trade policy for development' presented to UNCTAD I in 1964, and market access and pricing policy have been a continued preoccupation of UNCTAD discussions ever since.

In the event, very little has been achieved. Continual efforts in UNCTAD and in other international agencies have so far signally failed to produce any significant reduction in the degree of protection enjoyed by domestic producers of primary commodities in developed countries. This is particularly the case for agricultural temperate zone products, where systems of protection tend to be integrated with more general income support arrangements for the farming community.

Nor have efforts to achieve stable, remunerative and equitable prices by international action had more than very limited success. So far, international commodity agreements have been negotiated for sugar, coffee, cocoa, wheat, olive oil and tin, covering in all one-sixth of the value of primary commodity exports (other than petroleum) of developing countries. For the whole range of agricultural raw materials, which have faced severe competition from relatively stable priced synthetics, no effective international price stabilisation programme has been evolved, though certain informal arrangements under FAO auspices have been in force from time to time. Moreover, none of the agreements mentioned is now in effective control over its particular market. The agreements for coffee and sugar are at present without economic provisions as a result of disagreements between importing and exporting countries on the price range to be defended, while for both cocoa and tin, prices are considerably above the price maxima in the agreements.

As a result of the failure of governments to evolve a comprehensive programme of stabilisation measures for primary commodity markets – which would involve the extension of the principles of price support already in operation in the domestic markets of developed countries to the world markets for primary commodities – the world economy has been left virtually unprotected from the consequences of sudden and substantial shifts in the balance of world supply and demand. This underlying weakness has been dramatically demonstrated over the past two years, not only by sharp price increases for a wide range of commodities, but also in the inability of the existing system to meet the essential food requirements of food deficient developing countries.

International action to achieve 'remunerative' prices for producers of primary commodities in developing countries has also been relatively limited in scope. Successful action on these lines has been taken by the use of export quotas in the coffee and sugar agreements, and a quota mechanism exists for future use in the cocoa agreement. However, export quota agreements have covered such a small proportion of the exports of developing countries that their overall impact on these countries' export prices and on the growth in the real value of their export earnings could not have been a major one.

In addition to trade restrictions, two other factors have operated to limit the rate of growth in the real export earnings of developing countries over the past two decades. One has been essentially of a technological character, namely, a continuing increase in the relative importance in developed countries of the engineering and chemical industries (which use relatively little imported natural materials), in comparison with the textile, leather and clothing industries (which use a relatively large amount of imported materials); a secular tendency for the degree of fabrication in industrial production to increase per unit of materials used; and a tendency for the proportion of consumers' expenditure on foods which goes to meet marketing, advertising and distribution costs to rise, while the proportion spent on imports of the physical product has tended to decline.

The second factor of importance has been the mode of operation of transnational corporations. These corporations, which are owned essentially by interests in developed countries, control in one way or another a substantial proportion of the trade of developing countries. The degree of control varies considerably from one developing country to another: for some countries, virtually the entire export trade is under the effective control of foreign based transnational corporations while, at the other extreme, the foreign trade of certain other developing countries is conducted wholly or mainly by nationalised enterprises. The extent of control by the transnationals over developing countries' foreign trade has never been thoroughly investigated, though much relevant information has been made available by the governments of some developed countries, particularly the United States. Similarly, the magnitudes of the gains and losses to the economies of developing countries arising from the operations of the transnationals have never been estimated, even on an approximate basis. This is an important area in which a great deal of further research of a quantitative nature is required.

A full examination of the impact of the operations of transnational companies on the economies of developing countries would have to consider the effects of such operations on the effective mobilisation of domestic resources, on the balance of payments (making due allowance for additional royalty and other service payments), on the standard of living and on the rate of economic growth in the developing countries concerned. Here it suffices merely to point out that there are occasions on which the export earnings of individual developing countries can be restricted by the operation of transnational corporations. In some cases, this would result from restrictions on the volume of production and exports from the local subsidiary or branch of a transnational, as part of a 'market sharing' arrangement; in other cases, such restrictions might be a condition of the sale of 'knowhow' or of a technological process by a transnational to an enterprise in a developing country. Such restrictions on exports are known to be a widespread practice of the transnationals.

Probably a more important aspect of the operation of transnationals is that they can often exercise considerable bargaining power as monopsonists or oligopsonists, particularly for agricultural commodities where they are typically faced with a large number of competing sellers. Where necessary, their local bargaining power is entrenched by the use of long term contracts with individual producers. Alternatively, they may find it necessary to integrate backwards to become producers of primary commodities themselves, in order to ensure continuous supplies at costs which are under their own control. In any event, these corporations are able to transfer goods from one country to another at internal bookkeeping prices, managed so as to maximise the global profit of the multinational operation as a whole. Consequently, even when final demand in developed countries is increasing for a commodity the production and distribution of which is effectively under the control of a transnational, there may be no foreign exchange gain to the developing exporting country, any increase in price (and profit) being taken very often at a later stage in the marketing chain.

The classic example of the oligopsonistic operations of transnational corporations was the international petroleum industry up to the time when the governments of the producing countries, acting jointly through the OPEC, eventually changed the balance of bargaining power to their favour. It is now generally acknowledged that the export price for petroleum received by the producing countries was kept at an artificially low level over the entire postwar period up to 1972, and that the unprecedented economic expansion that took place in the developed market economy countries was, to a considerable extent, based on the continuous and rapid growth in the supply of cheap petroleum. What is not generally realised, however, is that cheap petroleum, by providing the raw material base for the expansion of the synthetic materials industries, was also a major factor in the relative decline in the prices of the principal natural raw materials (cotton, jute, sisal, abaca, hides and skins, and rubber), and of the real export earnings of the developing countries producing such materials.

Over the decade of the 1960s, the expansion in the production of synthetic materials offset as much as one-third of the growth in demand, in the developed market economy countries, for the principal natural raw materials exports of developing countries. As a result, prices of these exports were relatively depressed,[2] profitability was low and investment in new production capacity was generally restricted. The recent price increase for petroleum, by increasing the cost of production of synthetic materials, has to that extent improved the competitive position of the natural raw materials, though increased prices of fertilisers used in the production of natural materials are a major offsetting factor. Moreover, new technological developments which would reduce production costs of synthetics in the future cannot entirely be ruled out.

The three elements on which attention has been focused above – the network of trade barriers, the technological developments which tend to limit the growth in demand for the commodity exports of developing countries, and the structural framework of economic intercourse between developed and developing countries in so far as this is influenced by the operation of transnational corporations – obviously cannot provide a complete explanation of the changing relationship between economic growth in the developed countries and the export earnings and capacity to import of developing countries. Nonetheless, they have undoubtedly been major factors in influencing the trend in developing countries' export earnings and in their terms of trade *vis-à-vis* developed countries.

Table 1. *The terms of trade of developing countries (other than petroleum exporting countries), 1954–73*[a]

	Export prices (%)	Import prices (%)	Terms of trade (%)
1954–6 to 1968–70	−1	+12	−12
1968–70 to 1972	+12	+17	−5
1954–6 to 1972	+11	+32	−16
1972 to 1973	+29	+21	+6

[a] In terms of United States dollars.
SOURCE: UNCTAD secretariat estimates.

As Table 1 indicates, the terms of trade of developing countries (excluding the major petroleum exporting countries) deteriorated by more than 10 per cent from the mid 1950s to the end of the 1960s. The decline in these countries' export prices which occurred in the later 1950s and early 1960s was roughly offset by a price rise in the later 1960s, whereas the prices of their imports rose throughout the period, reflecting the continuing inflationary pressure in the developed market economy countries. Between the end of the 1960s and 1972 there was a further deterioration in the terms of trade of the non-oil exporting developing countries; by the latter year they had deteriorated by some 15 per cent compared with the mid 1950s, equivalent to a loss in 1972 of about $10 billion, or rather more than 20 per cent of these countries' aggregate exports, and considerably exceeding their receipts of official development aid.

The sharp rise in prices of most primary commodities, which began towards the end of 1972, reversed the previous unfavourable trend in developing countries' terms of trade. For petroleum, the price rise reflects the use of the joint bargaining power of the producing countries against a background of increasing depletion of their non-renewable natural resources. For other primary commodities, however, the price increases reflect, to a considerable extent, a conjunction of largely temporary, though acute, shortages of some commodities due to climatic and other factors, and an unusually rapid acceleration in demand, reflecting a high rate of economic expansion in the developed countries, combined with stock replenishment and a shift of short term funds into commodity markets for speculative purposes and as a hedge against inflation.

The improvement in the terms of trade of the non-oil developing countries in 1973 cannot be considered as more than a temporary reversal in the longer term deterioration that has been a dominating feature of their foreign trade position since the mid 1950s. For one thing, they face sharply increased import costs on account of higher prices for a range of essential imports, including petroleum and manufactures. For another, prices of their primary commodity exports are highly sensitive to changes in the level of economic activity in the developed countries, and an economic slowdown is likely to result in significant declines in the prices of many primary commodities, and thus in the unit value of exports from many of the non-oil developing countries.[3]

Taking a longer perspective, into the 1980s and beyond, it is also somewhat doubtful whether the past secular decline in non-oil commodity prices in terms of the prices of manufactures will necessarily be reversed as a result of persistent shortages in supply. As already indicated, part of the present difficulties of commodity supply reflect low levels of investment in productive capacity during the years of low commodity prices in the 1960s and up to 1972. The recent high levels of commodity prices, if they persist for any length of time, will inevitably result in the attraction of new investment, with consequent effects on supply in later years. Moreover, the sharp increases that have occurred in prices of many commodities are bound to stimulate research into alternatives, while as regards minerals the rise in price can be expected to result in an increase in commercially exploitable reserves. Furthermore, the prospects are for a generally slower rate of economic growth in the industrial countries than in the recent past, and this too will be a powerful influence in moderating the growth in demand for primary commodities.

Thus, the implementation of an effective international policy to safeguard developing countries against any significant deterioration of their terms of trade in the future has become an urgent necessity, whether looked at from the point of view of a possible commodity price recession in the immediate future, or from that of the prospects in the medium term.

Reasons for limited results

One reason often adduced for the limited results of past international consideration of commodity problems is that these are technically complex, differing from one commodity to another, and involve difficult issues of an economic and, in some cases, financial nature which require thorough study. However, experience has shown that even where the technical, economic and financial issues have been intensively studied, negotiations on international action become excessively protracted, usually with little concrete result.

There appears to be a deeper reason for this lack of progress. The philosophy of the Strategy is based on the assumption of a convergence of interests between developing countries exporting primary commodities and developed countries importing them. In the long run it would clearly be in the economic interest of developed countries to redeploy their resources away from the production of high cost agricultural commodities into the production of goods, such as research-intensive manufactures, in which they have a comparative advantage. But the policies pursued in these countries have tended to be based on short term perspectives, and frequently on transient and sectional interests. Experience has shown that the governments of developed countries have not so far been prepared to change their protective systems to any significant extent, even though they may have a heavy social cost in terms of misallocation of resources, as well as helping to raise prices to the consumer and to reduce the export earning potential of developing countries. As a generalisation this remains true, even though preferential entry may be allowed for the agricultural products of certain developing countries with which a particular developed country has a special political or cultural (usually post-colonial) link.

Again, developed importing countries have adopted a purely commercial self-interest approach in considering the price ranges to be defended by international commodity agreements, rather than viewing such agreements as part of a common endeavour to assist the economic development of the developing countries. Moreover, certain important developed market economy countries still oppose the idea of international commodity agreements on the ground that they would 'interfere with the free working of market forces'. It might be pointed out in this connection that a wide range of commodity prices, particularly the prices of agricultural commodities, are already subject to government controls in virtually all the developed countries, while a substantial proportion of international commodity trade consists of intrafirm transfers or transactions under long term contracts. In other words, market forces are already heavily constrained by government intervention or by private arrangements.

The general lack of support, on the part of the developed market economy countries, for the commodity policies enunciated in the International Development Strategy, can probably best be explained by the lack of bargaining power of the developing countries. This points to a major defect in the conception of the Strategy itself: the measures envisaged were to be taken within the existing institutional framework of unequal economic relations between developed and developing countries, in which the dependence of the developing on the developed nations worked to the disadvantage of the former. It now appears evident that the developing countries must strengthen their bargaining power so as to convert their relationships with developed countries from dependency into true reciprocity.

Basis for a new strategy

Two recent developments provide a basis on which a new commodity strategy might be built. The first is the enormous increase in the bargaining power of the oil exporting developing countries, combined with their rapidly growing surplus revenues. This increased bargaining power could well be used in the wider commodity context. This would set the stage for serious and realistic negotiation with the developed countries on a 'package' basis, designed to solve the major commodity market problems of the non-oil developing countries.

The second new factor is the acute concern of most developed countries about the reliability of their future supplies of essential raw materials from developing countries. This could provide a rationale for the active participation of developing countries in the evolution of a new commodity strategy. Assurance of future raw materials supply, on the part of developing producing countries could be combined with a commitment to purchase minimum quantities, on the part of developed importing countries. Such a joint approach by the main trading partners in regard to the principal primary commodity exports of developed and less developed countries would provide a basis for a rational management of the world's primary resources. A global system of commodity management would involve continuous assessments of future global needs and future global output, and international arrangements to ensure a smooth flow of supplies at agreed price levels. That such a 'managed' approach is urgently needed is all too apparent as regards the world food economy, but similar arguments also apply as regards raw materials.

Within this general context, it follows from the earlier argument that special emphasis needs to be given to the improvement of the terms of trade of developing countries. The various operational techniques that might be used are considered in some detail in the next section below, while the final section contains a discussion of possible methods of regulating the operations of transnational corporations so as to maximise the net benefit accruing to host developing countries.

Market access

These new emphases suggested in international commodity policy are not intended to diminish the importance of continuing efforts to obtain improved market access for the commodity exports of developing countries. However, as mentioned earlier, significant barriers to trade in unprocessed primary commodities exist mainly for temperate zone agricultural products. Since these trade barriers generally form an integral part of more complex systems of farm income support in developed countries, their complete abolition cannot be expected, at least for some considerable time. Recent estimates by the World Bank, assuming 'reasonable' degrees of relaxation of existing trade barriers, indicate that developed market economy countries would import by 1980 some 25 per cent more, by value, of primary commodities from developing countries on the basis of such relaxation than they are projected to import if current policies are continued.

Gains to developing countries from improved market access in developed countries would come mainly in sugar, cereals, meat, cotton, fats and oils, and timber. Such gains could be important to individual developing countries and need to be pursued but, in aggregate, are likely to fall far short of what is required to achieve a satisfactory level of export earnings in real terms.

Barriers to free entry into developed countries' markets are also important in relation to trade in processed commodities. All developed market economy countries, without exception, protect their domestic processing industries by import tariffs, often with high effective rates of protection. Such trade barriers are a major constraint on the development of commodity processing industries in developing countries, to the extent that to be commercially viable a processing industry has to produce for export markets. This constraint is generally greater for the poorer developing countries, which do not have a diversified manufacturing base, but which would be in a position to establish and expand industries which process indigenous primary commodities for export.

To some extent, this constraint has been diminished by the inclusion of certain processed commodities in the generalised system of preferences (GSP) schemes now in force in most developed countries. However, by and large, tariffs remain a major barrier to the expansion of the processed commodity exports of developing countries. The inclusion of all processed commodities in the GSP schemes of developed countries, if possible at zero rates of duty, would assist in stimulating the growth of processing industries in the developing countries, particularly in those which do not possess a diversified manufacturing sector.

An additional stimulus to the processing and manufacturing sectors of the economies of developing countries can be envisaged through more intensive co-operation among these countries themselves. A key question here is the extent to which the surplus revenues of the oil exporting countries can be used to support increased trade in processed commodities and industrial products between various groups of developing countries. It may well be that new forms of economic co-operation, such as joint industrial ventures, and triangular deals involving also the use of technology supplied by firms in developed countries, will need to be evolved.

Improving the terms of trade of the developing countries

As indicated earlier, the failure of the international economic system to transmit the benefits of postwar growth in the developed market economy countries, on any significant scale, to the majority of developing countries can be traced to a large extent to the underlying trend in the terms of trade between these two groups of countries. The essential problem is how that trend can be changed in favour of the developing countries. This way of approaching the commodity problem would represent a break with the traditional philosophy, which is based on negotiating a price for an individual commodity which is remunerative for producers and accepted as equitable by consumers.

What is now required is the acceptance by consumers (i.e. essentially the developed countries) of a more permanent improvement in the terms of trade of primary commodities *vis-à-vis* manufactures, compared at least with the position in 1972 before the commodity price boom began, as a contribution towards accelerating the economic development of developing countries. What the appropriate degree of improvement might be, and how this approach might apply to individual commodities, are matters for further consideration. There is the additional problem of those commodities which have benefited little, if at all, from the commodity price boom. Developing countries heavily dependent on such commodities urgently need international action to raise their export prices to cope with the inexorable rise in their import costs.

International action to raise commodity prices to more satisfactory levels for developing producing countries implies that the governments concerned can exercise effective control over the world markets for their commodity exports. An important question here is whether, apart from oil, there are other commodities for which the governments of developing producing countries can effectively intervene to achieve such a price objective. Certain conditions would be required for the successful intervention on these lines, the principal ones being (i) that the commodity in question is produced and exported wholly or mainly by developing countries, so that an increase in price does not attract alternative supplies from developed countries; and (ii) that demand for the commodity remains price inelastic over the price range considered, implying that an increase in price does not encourage the use of substitutes for the commodity on any significant scale, at least in the short and medium term. Agreement among producing countries might be assisted also if there are a few large producers, rather than many; and if there are substantial costs of entry (e.g. large capital expenditures), since this would restrict the ability of other potential producers to enter the market.

That these conditions are likely to obtain, to a greater or lesser extent, for a number of primary commodities, is suggested by the fact that since the sharp price rise effected for petroleum towards the end of 1973, associations of producing countries have been formed, or are under active consideration, for bauxite, mercury, bananas, iron ore, sugar and oilseeds. Moreover, the existing producers' organisations for coffee, cocoa and copper have been considering possible new pricing strategies; for coffee and copper export restriction schemes are already in operation.

Techniques of price raising

The traditional approach to price raising has been to negotiate an agreement to control the quantity of a commodity coming on the world market. Export restriction schemes can be effective in the short run, but they also create their own problems, particularly if they are not sufficiently flexible in allowing increasing market shares for newer, or low cost, producers. This was a major reason, for example, for the breakdown of the International Coffee Agreement in 1973. Market sharing conflicts have also caused great difficulties in the renegotiation of other commodity agreements based on export quotas.

There are, however, other possible techniques which can be considered which avoid the market sharing problem, at least overtly. One possibility for some commodities would be the establishment of an intergovernmental joint marketing agency, which would act as sole buyer from developing producing countries, and as sole seller to developed importing countries. The agency could maintain its own stock which could, in effect, be used in the same way as the traditional type of international buffer stock to smooth out excessive short term price variations. But, by its monopoly position, the agency would also be in a position to raise the level of prices as and when appropriate. The operational principles of such a marketing agency, and its mode of financing, would need to be elaborated in some detail.

Joint marketing agencies would be easier to operate for minerals than for agricultural commodities, since mineral output is more amenable to regulation designed to prevent the accumulation of excessive stocks, either in the hands of the marketing agency or in the producing countries themselves. In the case of an agricultural crop, if the marketing agency is obliged to purchase the entire exportable output of producing countries, it would also need the power to dispose of excess stocks either by selling the commodity (at relatively low prices) for non-traditional uses and/or by destruction. Alternatively, a ceiling on the marketing agency's stocks of an agricultural commodity could be agreed, so that producing countries would themselves have to hold or destroy some stocks in years of good harvests.

A classic example of this type of operation, in this case by a private company, is afforded by the Central Selling Agency, a subsidiary of De Beers, which has virtually a monopoly of the world supply of diamonds. The technique is probably applicable to a number of other commodities, particularly minerals.

Further alternatives arise in the field of fiscal policy. One possibility for certain commodities would be the enforcement by all producing countries of an agreed minimum price for their exports. An informal arrangement among the governments of Algeria, Italy and Spain, to take a recent example, forced up the price of mercury by about one-third between 1973 and mid 1974. A minimum export price scheme for tea is currently under active consideration by the tea producing countries, though in this case the large number of different grades and varieties may necessitate several agreed price minima.

A minimum export price scheme would have similar effects on the aggregate revenue of exporting countries as would a corresponding export quota scheme, but the distribution of gains among the exporting countries is likely to differ in so far as the enforcement of a price minimum results in a shift in the pattern of demand (e.g. away from low price varieties of the commodity).

Another fiscal approach would be the imposition of a uniform *ad valorem* export tax by all producing countries. The more elastic is the aggregate supply, and the more inelastic the aggregate demand, the greater will be the proportion of the tax borne by the consumer. The export tax approach has the advantage of simplicity in so far as it avoids the problem of classifying different varieties or grades, as well as that of negotiating export quotas. An important recent example is the decision of certain banana producing countries to impose a tax on banana exports; though strenuously resisted by the transnational corporations concerned, it seems that this would be a viable technique in suitable circumstances for achieving a fairer share of the benefits of trade for the producing countries.

Where transnational corporations are producers as well as traders, the possibility exists of increasing the net return to the producing countries from the productive activities of these corporations in developing countries by increases in local taxes and royalties. Apart from the well known OPEC case, action on these lines has recently been taken by certain developing countries (Jamaica, Guyana and Haiti) to increase their tax and royalty revenue from bauxite production. An interesting feature of these new tax arrangements is that they aim to relate government tax revenue from bauxite mining to the open market value of the end product (i.e. aluminium) where that is processed. This is a special case of the principle of 'indexation', which might well be applicable to a number of other minerals also.

Indexation, in its more general form, relates to measures designed to maintain the commodity export prices received by developing countries in terms of the prices they have to pay for their imports (or their imports of manufactures) from developed countries. Such measures clearly presuppose the evolution of effective market control techniques: once these are established, the indexation of commodity prices to the prices of, say, manufactures exported by developed countries would not be a difficult technical problem. It would, of course, have important economic effects on both the developing and the developed countries.

As regards the latter, indexation would have certain feedback effects on the rate of inflation, though this is not likely to be a major element in the whole range of inflationary pressures in the developed market economy countries. There would also be a positive element in so far as these various measures to maintain an adequate unit return, in real terms, for the exports of developing countries would be very largely balanced by a greater volume, and certainly a smoother flow, of purchases of capital equipment and other development goods from the industrialised countries.

As regards the impact on the developing countries, much would depend on national action to prevent an excessive expansion in production following an increase in the world price of a particular commodity. Without such action, a price rise could result in the accumulation of excessive stocks, as well as being a disincentive to invest in other sectors, such as in manufacturing industry. Where the monetary benefits of the price rise are channelled into government revenue (as with an export tax), it would be administratively easier to divorce the world price from the net return to the domestic producer. In other cases, internal fiscal measures may be required, according to circumstances, to regulate the growth of output, to increase the efficiency of commodity production and/or to finance diversification programmes as appropriate.

There may thus be scope for effective producer action to regulate the level of world prices of a number of important export commodities. Detailed examination of the circumstances of each commodity market will be required to determine the possibilities. In any event, producer action in one set of commodity markets would not rule out joint producer–consumer action in other markets should that prove feasible and desirable for both groups of countries. Co-operation with consumer countries would be important where such countries can improve the effectiveness of an agreement, e.g. by 'policing' the quotas under an export restriction scheme (as in the coffee and cocoa agreements), or where they are important producers of the commodity concerned (as for wheat).

However, joint producer–consumer agreements of the traditional type are likely to involve constraints on the price objective of international action, for the reasons discussed earlier. Such agreements would need to incorporate, *inter alia*, supply commitments by exporting countries at the maximum of a price range as a *quid pro quo* not only for purchasing commitments by importing countries at the minimum of the price range, but also for greater flexibility by these latter countries on the level of the price range itself.

There should, however, be increasing scope also for long term agreements between commodity importing and exporting countries, on either a bilateral or a multilateral basis. Such agreements could specify annual quantities to be traded (where this can reasonably be done), or annual quantitative targets. To the extent that prices can also be specified in such long term agreements, this would help in reducing instability in one sector of the commodity export trade of developing countries. However, price clauses in long term agreements would normally require provision for annual review in the light of changing market circumstances.

Bilateral long term agreements of this type are usual in the trade between the foreign trade enterprises of socialist countries of Eastern Europe and national trading corporations of individual developing countries. Long term agreements covering commodity trade between market economy countries are normally undertaken between private companies. The greater part of Japanese imports of iron ore, for example, are purchased under long term contracts of up to twenty years' duration from mining companies in Australia and in a number of developing countries.

The negotiation of long term contracts, on a government to government basis, would also allow for the provision of indexation clauses for the adjustment of prices of the commodities covered in line with changes in the prices of manufactured goods. In so far as such indexation is related to imports of commodities by developed countries, it would enable developing countries to import the same commodities at (lower) world market prices.

The wider use of long term contracts, both bilateral and multilateral, would allow developing countries to plan investments in new capacity with much greater assurance of profitable returns from their commodity exports than they have had hitherto.

Short term commodity market stabilisation

A comprehensive international commodity policy should include measures to reduce excessive short term price fluctuations, as well as measures to improve the price trend. For some commodities – particularly agricultural raw materials subject to displacement by synthetics – excessive price fluctuations have been an important factor in the shift of demand in favour of synthetics. To this extent, price uncertainty has contributed also to a less favourable trend in demand for, and in the prices of, these natural materials. Apart from this, sharp and unexpected price changes on world markets, in so far as they are reflected in unexpected swings in the export earnings of developing countries, can have severely adverse repercussions on economic development programmes.

A new approach to this problem could be considered in terms of a series of international buffer stocks for the principal traded commodities. The use of buffer stocks independently of export quota agreements would have two immediate advantages. First, it would avoid the difficulties of allotment of country export quotas, and could thus get away from laborious commodity by commodity negotiating conferences. Second, it would allow for stabilisation measures, based on buffer stocks, to be applied over a wide range of primary commodities. There would, of course, be technical problems to be solved and the operation would no doubt require considerable financial support, though the total finance required could be minimised by using a central pool of finance supporting a series of separate buffer stocks.

The idea of a multi-commodity international buffer stock scheme is not a new one. Indeed, a proposal on these lines was elaborated by Keynes during the last war.[4] Keynes attempted an illustrative estimate of the finance that would be required for his buffer stock scheme. He argued that a minimum stock level would need to be held of the major commodities entering world trade, equivalent to at least three months of the value of trade in these commodities. This minimum basis would have implied a stock level for eight major commodities[5] of about £240 million at 1942 prices. For 1972, the latest year for which statistics are available, the value of world exports of the same eight commodities amounted to some $20 billion. On Keynes' three month basis, the minimum stocks to be held would be equivalent to $5 billion, while if one adds cocoa, for which provision for a buffer stock already exists, and, say, copper and oils and fats, the resources required would be considerably higher, possibly as much as $7–7.5 billion. This is a sum not far short of the annual flow of official development assistance from DAC member countries to developing countries and multilateral agencies ($8.4 billion in 1972).

However, Keynes' minimum stock equivalent to three months of world trade was evidently only a very approximate guess. The optimal stock level for each commodity would need careful appraisal, based on alternative assumptions concerning the range within which the price is to be stabilised, and on estimates of the relevant elasticities of supply and demand. In this connection, it is of interest to note that the buffer stock provided for in the International Cocoa Agreement has a maximum limit of 250 thousand tons, it being anticipated that this limit would be reached only in exceptional circumstances; even so, it represents only about one-sixth of annual world exports of this commodity. The tin buffer stock established under the 1971 International Tin Agreement amounts to about one-eighth of the volume of world trade in this metal, though this has proved inadequate to prevent the price exceeding the maximum in the Agreement since mid-November 1973. Even if Keynes' 'three months minimum' proves to be too high, as a general average, clearly a reduced minimum of, say, one and a half to two months trade would also involve a large financing requirement.

The required financial support for such a comprehensive attack on the commodity instability problem should come from the international community as a whole, including contributions by OPEC countries as well as by developed countries and the international financial institutions. One possibility might be the provision of long term loans by OPEC countries to the various buffer stocks to be established. If these buffer stocks were jointly financed through a central fund, these loans would enjoy a high degree of security since they would have real assets as collateral, whose value would keep pace with world inflation and would also reflect changes in currency exchange rates.

International financial support

Direct intervention by governments in world commodity markets cannot be expected to cover more than a certain range of commodities, for which economic and technical conditions are suitable. Commodities subject to severe competition from synthetics, for example, would not be suitable for export regulation or for the imposition of an export tax. Equally, the prices of commodities produced in substantial amounts in developed countries could not be increased to any appreciable extent without the active collaboration of the governments of those countries.

Consequently, for commodities for which market intervention is not practicable, other means would have to be found – and these can be only of a financial character – if the general objectives of a new commodity strategy are to be realised. For this, some form of international financial support would seem necessary to allow developing countries to maintain their commodity export earnings even when demand and/or prices decline. An important step forward in this connection was taken at the Ministerial Conference in Jamaica, held in September 1974, between the European Economic Community and certain developing countries in Africa, the Caribbean and the Pacific. The Conference approved the principle of financial transfers from the Community to stabilise the earnings of associated developing countries from the export of primary commodities to EEC countries. Early in 1975 an agreement was reached which provided for support for the poorest of these developing countries' export earnings on twelve primary products (cotton, tea, cocoa, coffee, bananas, sisal, groundnuts, copra, hides and skins, palm produce, timber products and iron ore), when they fall 2.5 per cent below the averages of the previous four years. (The better-off of these developing countries receive support only when earnings drop 7.5 per cent below the average, and are obligated to make refunds if earnings subsequently increase.) There is a strong case for extending some such scheme to all developing countries' commodity exports to all developed countries without exception.

This type of scheme could also be extended to cover the indexation principle, if it were decided to cover by that principle a wide range of commodities not subject to international commodity agreements or other forms of effective control over individual commodity markets. Where such control does not exist, the objectives of indexation could be attained by some form of international financial transfers. In so far as such transfers were made to the governments of developing countries exporting primary commodities, the immediate balance of payments effect would be the same as for the case where effective market control is used for indexation purposes.

The longer run effects of indexation by financial transfer and indexation by market intervention would, however, be different unless the financial transfers under the latter scheme were passed on in their entirety to the commodity producers themselves. If all, or part, of the transfers were retained by governments for other uses, the production effects – and therefore the secondary effects on world prices and on demand – would be different from the case of 'direct' indexation by market intervention.

A commodity earnings stabilisation scheme, if it were universal and incorporated the principle of indexation, would go a long way in meeting the objectives of the idea of Supplementary Financing, which was originally adopted at UNCTAD I in 1964. This was that unforeseen declines in prices on world commodity markets, and in the commodity export earnings of developing countries, should not be allowed to frustrate the development plans of these countries, unforeseen shortfalls in export earnings being made good by loans from a central Supplementary Financing fund to be established. Though the Supplementary Financing concept has never been implemented, it would still be required as one element in a comprehensive international strategy for commodities, particularly if, as seems likely, an earnings stabilisation scheme covered only a limited range of commodities and applied to only certain flows of the trade of developing countries.

Regulating the operations of transnational corporations

As mentioned in the first section, transnational corporations originating in developed market economy countries control a substantial proportion of the commodity export trade of developing countries. The degree of such control varies widely among commodities and countries; it is probably greatest in minerals and metals (such as iron ore, manganese ore, copper and nickel), and in certain tropical products (particularly bananas), but transnational corporations are of importance in many other commodities also, including a number of foodstuffs and agricultural raw materials.

There are several distinct modes of operation of transnational corporations in the commodity sector. One form of operation consists of the effective control, often through majority or full ownership, over the production of affiliates or subsidiary companies in developing countries which transfer the major part of their output at internal accounting prices to parent companies and other affiliates in developed countries. An example of this form is the ownership of iron ore mines in developing countries by steel companies in developed countries. Exports from such 'captive' mines probably account for about one-third of all iron ore exports from developing countries.

A second form consists of long term contracts between a transnational corporation as buyer, and individual producers in developing countries as sellers. In some cases, such as the banana industry in certain developing countries, the transnational corporations concerned have a strong oligopsonist position, and are able to keep contract prices at levels far below the price that would obtain on a freely competitive market. Where, on the other hand, the producers also have significant bargaining power, prices in such long term contracts are usually more flexibly related to world prices, as is the case in the long term contracts between Japanese steel companies and Australian iron ore mines.

A third form of operation arises when a transnational corporation has virtually a monopsony position as buyer of a particular commodity produced in a developing country. Such a position may have originated from a legal agreement negotiated under colonial rule, but nowadays it often arises from control by the transnational of the internal marketing network or of an essential processing stage. An example of internal marketing control was the marketing system for cotton operating in Chad up to 1971, under which all the cotton grown by peasant producers was purchased by a French company (Cotonfran), which had a monopoly of processing as well as of the marketing of raw cotton in that country. The importance of control over an essential process is exemplified by the position of a transnational corporation in East Africa, which can buy the entire pyrethrum extract output because it alone has the equipment for roasting and vacuum packaging required for the export trade.[6]

Whatever the particular mode of operation, a transnational corporation which has a dominant position as a producer or purchaser of a particular primary commodity in a developing country will often have a vested interest in the processing of that commodity elsewhere, usually in its home (developed) country. To this extent, the transnational corporation can operate to restrict, or even prevent, the establishment of processing industries in the host (developing) country.

Though each case will have to be considered on its own merits, action by governments of developing countries could generally be designed to introduce a countervailing power in the market and to diminish the privileged position of the transnational corporations.

As regards transfer pricing – a manifestation of the first mode of operation of transnationals distinguished above – it has recently been suggested by the Group of Eminent Persons on the role of Multinational Corporations (United Nations, 1974) that the problems arising for developing countries could be largely overcome if both home and host countries enforced 'arm's length' pricing, harmonised their tax provisions, and arranged for the exchange of relevant information on the pricing practices of these corporations.

However, it is doubtful whether any precise or unique determination can be made of the 'arm's length' price in many cases, especially where the entire export of a commodity from a developing country is transferred to parent or affiliated concerns abroad.[7] Moreover, tax harmonisation, by itself, is not likely to meet the problem of low accounting prices for exports from developing countries which have persistent balance of payments difficulties which, in turn, act as an incentive to private capital outflows. The proposal for exchange of information is, however, clearly a useful one if it can be effectively implemented, particularly in relation to transfer prices of intermediate products as well as of primary and processed commodities, since fuller knowledge of existing pricing practices would strengthen the bargaining potential of the developing countries concerned.

An essential prerequisite to effective regulation of transnationals which operate in the production and/or export of a given commodity in several developing countries is close policy co-ordination among the governments of the developing countries concerned. Policies designed to increase export prices, or taxes and royalties on production, to improve conditions of employment, or to expand the linkages with other domestic sectors, are unlikely to be effective if applied by one developing country alone. In such cases, there will be an incentive for the transnational corporations affected to switch their operations to other host countries.

Joint action by the producing countries could take several forms. One type of action could be purely of a fiscal nature, such as, for example, the export tax on bananas or the production tax on bauxite which have been mentioned earlier. The conditions for successful action of this type have already been discussed. Fiscal action might also include, where appropriate, the withdrawal of special privileges (e.g. tax exemption) still enjoyed by transnational corporations.

A second, and more radical, type of action would involve the control of the productive and trading operations of the branches, subsidiaries or affiliates of transnational corporations operating in developing countries, and thus over their investment decisions and their transfer pricing policies. As pointed out by Professor Penrose (pp. 168–71 below), effective control over key decisions can often be obtained by the state's purchase of a minority share of the equity capital of the local transnational affiliate. However, even such state participation may have limited results, in terms of the net return to the developing country, if the international marketing of the commodity remains in the hands of the parent transnational.

A third line of action to be considered would, therefore, aim to achieve greater control over the international commodity marketing and distribution system by developing countries. Where a number of competing transnationals are operating in the production and/or marketing of the same commodity, it should be possible for marketing contracts to be given only to those offering the best terms to the producing countries. Such terms might, in appropriate cases, include the establishment of processing industries in the developing countries concerned. Where, however, there are only a few large transnationals, which together control the major part of the international marketing and distribution system, better returns for producers are likely to be obtained only by the exercise of joint bargaining power by the governments of the developing producing countries. In certain cases, this might imply participation by governments in the ownership of existing marketing and distribution facilities; in other cases, governments may even have to consider establishing new marketing and distribution facilities.

In an effort to avoid, or minimise, the degree of possible government regulation of their operations in developing countries, many of the transnational corporations – particularly those producing minerals and metals – are adapting their investments so as to expand production in areas which they believe less likely to be subject to such regulation. Mineral production from the sea bed, which is one such area, has thus become a focus of new investment by a number of large transnationals with mineral interests.[8] To the extent that alternative sources of mineral supply can be developed by the transnationals, this would correspondingly increase their bargaining power *vis-à-vis* the governments of mineral producing developing countries.[9]

A comprehensive international strategy for primary commodities cannot ignore the role played by transnational corporations in the world commodity markets, and in the net return of developing countries for their commodity exports. The strategy must, therefore, include adequate provision for regulating the operations of these transnationals, and for strengthening the bargaining power of developing countries in their dealings with them. For many commodities, this will involve changes in the existing marketing and distribution arrangements, which in most cases were developed by the principal consumer interests in the course of the nineteenth century. Inappropriate today as instruments of economic development, many of these arrangements require to be changed so that they will respond more closely to the economic needs of the developing countries.

Notes

1   This paper was presented in the author's personal capacity. The views expressed do not commit the secretariat of UNCTAD, of which the author is a staff member.
2   Over the decade from 1960–2 to 1970–2, the unit value of exports of natural materials from developing countries fell on average by 2 per cent a year, while value rose on average by only 2 per cent a year.
3   By the end of 1974, significant price declines from earlier peaks had already been recorded for a number of important primary commodities.
4   In a confidential British Government memorandum dated April 1942, Keynes advocated the establishment of a number of international buffer stocks, operating independently but subject to overall policy guidance by a General Council for Commodity Controls, elected by member States of the United Nations. The text of this memorandum has now been published (Keynes, 1974).
5   Wheat, maize, sugar, coffee, cotton, wool, rubber and tin.
6   I am indebted to Reginald H. Green for this example.
7   This is not generally an insuperable problem for most primary commodities, though it might well be an impractical approach in the case of specialised manufactured products and components.
8   Large investments have already been made in developing new techniques for processing the extensive deposits of manganese nodules (containing cobalt, nickel and copper, as well as manganese) which are known to exist on the ocean floor.
9   The governments of developed and developing countries have still to reach agreement in the Law of the Sea Conference on the nature of the international regime to be set up to administer the mineral resources of the sea bed. Broadly

speaking, the governments of developed countries want an international authority which merely issues licenses and receives royalties from the companies exploiting sea bed minerals, while the governments of developing countries want an authority with powers to control output, sales and prices, so as fully to protect the interests of existing producers.

References

Keynes, J. M., 1974. The international control of raw materials. *Journal of International Economics*, **4**, 299–315.

Prebisch, Raul, 1964. *Towards a New Trade Policy for Development*. Report of the Secretary-General of UNCTAD, United Nations.

United Nations, 1974. *Report of the Group of Eminent Persons to study the role of Multinational Corporations on development and on international relations*. United Nations document E/5500/Add.1 (Part i). New York.

3. The potential for monopolistic commodity pricing by developing countries

MARIAN RADETZKI[1]

Introduction

The ease with which the oil producing developing countries succeeded in increasing their benefits from oil exports in the early 1970s came as a surprise to many observers. Until a few years ago the members of OPEC did not exert any great influence on the development of oil prices. For a number of years their per barrel tax and royalty take had remained more or less unchanged while the oil prices were slowly falling (Adelman, 1972). From 1971 onwards, however, the situation underwent a significant change. Up to early autumn of 1973 the government take of producing countries had been raised by about 70 per cent from the levels which prevailed in 1970. Then, late in 1973, two drastic OPEC decisions increased the government revenues from about $1.75 per barrel to close to $7 with a consequent push of oil prices from $3.50 to more than $10 or by almost 200 per cent. The implications of these latest moves are overwhelming. The new price levels will provide the oil exporting countries with additional export revenues of the magnitude of some $60 billion per year. This is more than three times the global financial flows from developed to developing countries, and six times as large as overall concessional aid in 1973. The disturbing implications for the industrialised world have been widely discussed, and need not be taken up again here.

The successful price raising actions of the OPEC countries strongly boosted the morale of Third World commodity exporters. The oil cartel is widely regarded as a model for approaches to be adopted in other commodity markets. Many commodity producing countries have lost their faith in the advantages of competitive free trade. An active market intervention, sometimes combined with a policy of open confrontation with the importing countries is seen as the tool required to break the long term declining terms of trade of commodity producers. The emergence in recent years of associations among exporters of such varied commodities as bananas, bauxite, cocoa, coffee, copper, iron ore and mercury, underlines the great hopes created by the successful market intervention brought about by the oil countries.

The purpose of this paper is to scrutinise critically the developing countries' prospects of building effective and profitable cartel organisations in commodity markets other than that for petroleum. Our discussion will proceed as follows. We start out by looking at the special circumstances which have made OPEC's cartel policy so advantageous to its participating member countries. We continue by surveying a large group of commodities of importance in developing countries' exports, and apply a process of successive elimination, to arrive at the products particularly suited for producer cartel action. We finally devote more detailed attention to the international copper market, in order to determine the prospects for a successful monopolistic price policy by the developing country producers of this important commodity.

Monopolistic pricing is obviously possible for any commodity in the very short term. To be useful to producers, however, commodity market arrangements must bring about somewhat more lasting benefits. Our attention will be focused on the medium term, i.e. a period of perhaps five to seven years. This time period frequently constitutes the planning horizon in developing countries.

Monopoly power in a commodity market emerges from the buyers' dependence on the products the seller supplies. The best measure of this dependence would be obtained in our case by comparing for each commodity the net imports from developing countries to the industrialised world, with the overall consumption in the latter. But it is hard to quantify this relationship. Consumption statistics have not been systematically developed in all industrialised countries. Even where they are, their subdivisions and categories are quite different from those used in primary products imports. 'Net imports' is also a tricky concept, since it is difficult to measure the amounts of raw materials contained in processed and manufactured exports. In view of these problems I have decided to base the following multi-commodity analysis on commonly available statistics of international trade. This approach has the great advantage of being simple, and it provides an acceptable first overview of the problem we wish to study. Two important complications emerge, however, as a result of this approach. Their nature and consequences must briefly be mentioned.

The first complication is due to the fact that trade statistics provide values of gross trade flows. This will make the developing countries' commodity exports look less important than they in fact are. The Netherlands, for example, handle an important entrepôt trade in Middle East oil. Belgium functions as a transit country for more than half of Zaire's large scale copper production. It is true that some processing of these commodities is undertaken in these two countries, but the resulting value added is not very great. The substantial exports of refined oil and copper from Belgium and Netherlands to the rest of the industrialised world create a false impression of relatively less dependence on imports from developing countries. This should be kept in mind when studying the commodity trade data presented below.

The second problem which follows from our reliance on the trade statistics has to do with the wide differences between commodities as to the share of production which enters foreign trade. More than three-quarters of all natural rubber is exported, while for iron ore the proportion is less than one-fifth. *Ceteris paribus*, the exporters' ability to regulate the market ought to improve with increasing shares of production being exported. Differences between commodities in this respect do not emerge from trade statistics. To overcome this deficiency, I have attempted to measure the importance of developing countries' exports in relation to global output for those commodities which, on other counts, appear to be suitable candidates for producer price actions. The results are presented in Table 4 below.

I propose to use trade data for the last three years of the 1960s. The reasons for this are twofold. First, at the time of writing, more recent data are not available in the commodity-disaggregated form needed for our task. The second and more important reason is that the late 1960s constitute, in a sense, the 'initial conditions' from which to judge possible changes to come. The early 1970s have been characterised by upsetting commodity price changes, as a result of OPEC's actions in the case of oil, following some very bad harvest results for food products, and consequent upon the surge in demand, during the strong industrial boom in 1972–3, for a large group of agricultural raw materials, metals and minerals.

Oil market characteristics and monopolistic pricing

Before looking at other commodities, it may be instructive to summarise the set of factors which have helped the OPEC cartel to bring about such substantial benefits to its participants.

(*a*) Oil is a very large commodity in international trade, with a turnover many times larger than that of any other raw material.

(*b*) The exports of oil are strongly concentrated in a small group of countries. Several of the large exporters are sparsely populated, and their capacity to transform the oil incomes into development is limited. The large and growing foreign exchange reserves of these countries have constituted a safety buffer, permitting them to venture into daring cartel initiatives.

(*c*) Developing countries' oil exports account for a very sizeable share of overall world production.

(*d*) The demand for oil has been expanding at fast rates. This makes it easier to introduce a supply management policy. Producers will only be required to reduce output growth, without cutting their overall production volume.

(*e*) Oil has a number of very important, more or less 'indispensable' uses. Until quite recently, it was considerably cheaper in most applications than its major substitutes in the energy sector. In the price ranges which prevailed, its price elasticity of demand must, therefore, have been close to zero.

(*f*) The possibilities of substitution for oil in the short run are strictly limited by technical factors. It takes time to reopen old coal mines, to expand hydroelectric power facilities, or to accelerate the introduction of atomic power stations. The development of known oil resources outside the cartel's reach is also a time-consuming process. Witness the slow progress towards oil exploitation in the North Sea.

As will be apparent from the following analysis, oil is in many of the above respects an exceptional case. No other commodity cartel could possibly provide an equal income generating power to the developing country exporters. And few other commodities combine so many of the features required to establish and run an effective cartel organisation.

A note of doubt on the impact of the OPEC cartel, in a somewhat longer time perspective, is in place at this stage. It is widely presumed that the substantial oil price increases which occurred in 1973 were, in their entirety, the result of the OPEC producers' collective power as a cartel. We have tentatively accepted this presumption. But it is frequently forgotten that 1973 and early 1974 was a very exceptional period, during which practically all commodity prices experienced exceedingly high rises. In comparison with many other commodities, the oil price rise during the period January 1973 to March 1974 is very high, but not unique. This will be apparent from Table 1 which illustrates the US dollar price changes in the above fifteen month period for some important raw materials the prices of which rose particularly dramatically.

Table 1. *Change in monthly average US dollar prices for selected commodities between January 1973 and March 1974 (Jan. 1973 = 100)*

Zinc	424	Copper	246
Rice	330*a*	Cocoa	237
Petroleum	315	Tin	219
Sisal	301	Sugar	211
Edible seeds and oils	299	Rubber	210
Cotton	272	Wheat	184

a February 1974.
SOURCES: Petroleum: OECD estimates of average c.i.f. prices in importing countries. Others: UNCTAD, *Monthly Commodity Price Bulletin*.

The recent commodity price boom, as reflected in the table, is explained by differing factors for individual commodities. Food product prices rose in response to supply shortages, because of bad weather and meagre harvests. Industrial raw materials prices were pushed up by the expansion in demand during the very strong industrial boom of 1972–3.

Petroleum demand, too, was expanded by the industrial boom. A further important influence on the petroleum market was that the US seriously miscalculated its import needs in the early 1970s. The unexpected growth in US demand strongly contributed to the excess demand in the world oil market. With the emerging deficiency in supplies, the sharply augmented tax demands by the producer governments could easily be passed on to consumers through an increase in price, without the necessity for production cuts, export quotas or the like. At the time, it was not even necessary to cut the growth in output. The real test of OPEC's efficiency as a cartel will come only some

Table 2. *Developing countries' exports of certain primary commodities,
annual averages, 1967–9*

Commodity	SITC code no.[a]	Individual totals ($ billions)	Cumulative totals ($ billions)
Oil	331, 332	13.5	–
Copper	283.1, 682.1	2.3	2.3
Coffee	071.1	2.3	4.6
Sugar	061.1	1.5	6.1
Cotton	263.1	1.3	7.4
Rubber	231.1	1.0	8.4
Iron ore	281	0.8	9.2
Cocoa	072.1	0.7	9.9
Timber	242.3	0.6	10.5
Tin	283.6, 687.1	0.6	11.1
Tea	074.1	0.5	11.6
Bananas	051.3	0.5	12.1
Rice	042	0.5	12.6
Maize	044	0.4	13.0
Beef	011.1	0.4	13.4
Tobacco	121	0.3	13.7
Fishmeal	081.4	0.2	13.9
Phosphate rock	271.3	0.2	14.1
Wool	262.1, 262.2	0.2	14.3
Hides and skins	211	0.2	14.5
Groundnuts	221.1	0.2	14.7
Following 14 commodities		1.6	16.3

[a] Standard International Trade Classification.
SOURCE: IBRD, 1973.

time after the spectacular events late in 1973, when the particular circumstances which created the temporary excess demand have subsided. With the
benefit of hindsight, we may find that the ability of OPEC to manage supply
and to impose monopolistic prices on oil consumers is, in fact, much smaller
than was commonly presumed in 1974.

Developing countries' commodity exports compared by value

In a recent document (IBRD, 1973), the World Bank has compiled detailed
data on the thirty-five primary commodities which weigh most heavily in
developing countries' exports. These constitute a very useful starting point
for our multi-commodity analysis. We will, therefore, utilise these figures
as a basis for our own tabulations, noting that in the case of most minerals,
the figures presented are aggregates of exports at different stages of processing. Unless otherwise stated, the data in our Tables 2–4 originate from this
source.

Table 2 compares oil with a number of other important commodities in terms of export values from developing countries. Only those commodities whose exports from the Third World exceeded $200 million per year have been specified in the table.

The oil sales from developing countries were almost six times as high as the exports of the following most important products, copper and coffee. Petroleum alone accounted for a turnover which was equal to the sum total for the fifteen following commodities. The oil trade, in fact, constituted about 45 per cent of the aggregate sales value for all the thirty-five commodities together.

The value comparison seems sufficiently clear-cut to permit the conclusion that price increasing actions by developing countries in any other commodity market could not possibly have an economic impact on a scale comparable to that in oil. By its size alone, petroleum is quite exceptional. Even if other commodity producers were equally successful in their monopolistic pricing measures, the financial benefits that such action could bring to their countries would be only a small fraction of the amounts which have accrued to the members of OPEC.

A necessary condition for a producer group to be able to increase its export earnings from a product by restricting supplies and raising prices is that the absolute value of the price elasticity of demand for its output is less than unity. The lower the absolute value of that elasticity, the more advantage can be derived from collective market intervention. This price elasticity of demand can be algebraically expressed in the following way:

$$E_{Dc} = (1/m) . E_{Dw} - (1/m) . (1-m) . E_{Sr} ,$$

where E_{Dc} = price elasticity of demand for the colluding group's output, E_{Dw} = price elasticity of world demand for the product, E_{Sr} = price elasticity of supply of outside producers, and m = colluding group's share in world supply. In other words, the elasticity of demand for the output of the colluding producer group will be smaller, and hence its ability to intervene in the market will improve, the bigger their market share, the lower the price elasticity of supply of outside producers, and the lower the price elasticity of demand among consumers. We will take up each of these three factors in turn in the following discussion of developing countries' commodity exports.

Concentration and price elasticity of supply

An important precondition for successful cartel control is concentration of supply. The developing countries must account for a high proportion of world exports to be able to influence the price and the market. Table 3, below, ranks the commodities according to the share of developing countries in world exports. Only those commodities have been included where more than 50 per cent of the traded supply originates in the Third World. This notably leaves out iron ore (developing countries' share, 39.4 per cent of world exports), a commodity in which expectations have been aroused by the recent creation of a producer group. The second column of the table gives the share of world exports provided by the six largest developing country suppliers. This column is of interest because it ought to be easier to reach price and quota agreements in cases where a few countries account for a very large proportion of global trade. An additional interesting dimension would be provided by indicators of the concentration of production not only between nations, but also on an industry basis in each country. The fewer the decision units in each country, the easier it should be to control the market. This information does not emerge from the trade data we use, and it is difficult to obtain in several commodity markets. In any case, with increasing government involvement at the national level in commodity exports, for instance in the form of national marketing boards, the degree of concentration of the industry within the country loses much of its importance in this context.

Petroleum is found in the lower half of the table.[2] *Ceteris paribus*, the prospects for monopolistic pricing ought to be greater for the products at the top of the table. But everything else is not alike. As we already noted, the efficiency of the oil cartel, despite its not exceedingly high share in world exports, depends first, on a low elasticity of supply outside the cartel producers' reach, and, second, on very limited possibilities to substitute for oil consumption in the short and medium term. It is necessary to study other primary materials in these respects, to form a judgement about the prospects of cartel action in their respective markets. Such a study would have to go into the details of production, marketing and consumption conditions for each product. This is hardly possible in a general survey of many commodities. Our classification of raw materials will have to be a very rough one, based on hunches and limited bits of information. Its results should be taken as a first and highly tentative approximation which would need to be followed by more detailed studies of individual commodities along the lines we pursue later in this paper, when we scrutinise copper.

In studying the elasticities of supply, it may be useful to divide the commodities listed in Table 3 into three categories. A first group, which includes bananas, jute, groundnuts, groundnut oil, linseed oil, sugar and cotton is characterised by a wide geographical spread of potential production, and by a relatively short lag between decisions and implementation of output changes. An attempt to increase the prices of these commodities with the help of producers' cartels would probably collapse after a short time, since the higher prices would quickly induce expanded output in areas outside the cartel's control. The same is probably also true for abaca, sisal, and possibly for fishmeal. In view of my limited knowledge about the production conditions for these latter commodities, I feel hesitant in expressing a definite opinion in these cases.[3]

The remaining commodities in Table 3 are such that output can be

Table 3. *Concentration of international commodity trade, 1967–9 average*

Commodity	SITC code no.[a]	Developing countries' share of world exports (%)	Six largest developing suppliers' share of world exports (%)
Cocoa	072.1	100.0	78.7
Copra	221.2	99.1	87.2
Abaca	265.5	98.9	97.5
Sisal	265.4	96.3	88.0
Bananas	051.3	95.4	69.0
Coffee	071.1	94.4	61.8
Jute	264	93.8	93.8
Timber	242.3	87.9	64.0
Palm oil	422.2	82.6	79.8
Tea	074.1	82.6	74.9
Groundnuts	221.1	82.0	66.7
Tin	283.6, 687.1	80.7	79.8
Bauxite	283.3	79.6	74.7
Coconut oil	422.3	79.6	74.7
Groundnut oil	421.4	79.1	75.2
Oil	331, 332	76.0	58.5
Sugar	061.1	75.3	47.2
Rubber	231.1	72.3	67.6
Linseed oil	422.1	65.8	65.8
Manganese ore	283.7	60.5	51.0
Phosphate rock	271.3	60.2	53.9
Fishmeal	081.4	60.0	59.8
Cotton	263.1	57.1	36.3
Copper	283.1, 682.1	56.4	54.6

[a] Standard International Trade Classification.
SOURCE: IBRD, 1973.

increased only in the longer run. Thus, a second group consists of agricultural products from trees which must be allowed to grow for a number of years before they can be harvested. The third and last group contains the mineral commodities. The supply of these is restricted in the short and medium run by the lengthy process of defining mineral deposits and developing new mines.

The determinants of the elasticities of demand

We have already noted that inelastic supply is only one of several conditions for the organisation of effective producer cartels. It is also necessary to study the required preconditions on the demand side. Price raising producer schemes are not likely to be successful where the elasticity of demand is high in the short and medium term, e.g. where the consumer can easily abstain from consumption, or switch his demand to other products. In such cases, the diminished supply by cartel producers will result in very temporary price increases only, followed very soon by shrinking sales and revenues.

An analysis of the demand side permits us to exclude one further group of commodities from the probable candidates for effective producer actions in future. Copra, coconut oil, and palm oil can easily substitute for each other and for the edible fats already eliminated. These products also have to compete with several edible fats and oils from temperate countries. Production of the latter could easily expand if the developing countries' exports of any of the above products fell in volume or rose in price. The same is probably true for tropical timber, which competes not only with its temperate substitute, but also with such products as concrete, plastics and several metals.[4] Rubber, finally, has for some time been losing market shares to its synthetic replacement. The substitution process would be much increased if the developing country producers tried to establish a higher relative price for the natural product.

Commodities which fulfil the necessary conditions for establishing producer cartels

The primary materials which are left after these eliminations have been entered in Table 4. In addition to oil, there are eight other products which seem to possess the minimum characteristics required for effective cartel control by developing country producers. The supply and substitution elasticities of all eight are low. Third World exports in all cases exceed 50 per cent of world trade. In the second column of the table we have tried to estimate the developing countries' exports as a share in world production. This is quite significant in all cases, and very high for three of the products. The Third World does possess substantial market power in these eight commodities.

It may be instructive to make a further subdivision of the products remaining in Table 4 into two groups, viz. the three beverages and the five minerals. The developing countries account for almost all world exports of cocoa, coffee and tea. The industrialised world has no production of its own of these products. Its degree of dependence on imported supplies is much more complete with respect to the three beverages than for the five minerals. On the other hand, it is likely that the geographic location of potential new production is less restricted for the beverages than for the minerals group. It ought to be easier to relocate the production of tea than that of tin, and the tea producers' ability to manipulate price and supply will, therefore, be somewhat more restricted, if they want to retain their market intact in the longer run.[5] Although beverage consumption habits are quite stable and not very sensitive to price changes in the short and medium term, there would certainly not be any great economic hardship if consumption had to be cut, following restrictive producer actions. Decreases in the use of tin, aluminium,

Table 4. *Commodities suited for cartel action by developing countries*

Commodity	SITC code no.[a]	Developing countries' share of world exports, 1967-9 (%)	Developing countries' exports as a share of estimated world production,[b] 1967-9 (%)	Total exports from developing countries, annual average, 1967-9 ($ billions)	Growth of exports from developing countries, 1960-67/9 (%)
Cocoa	072.1	100.0	76	0.7	21
Coffee	071.1	94.4	66	2.3	26
Tea	074.1	82.6	50	0.5	-8
Tin	283.6, 687.1	80.7	74	0.6	118
Bauxite	283.3	79.6	37	0.2	69
Oil	331, 332	76.0	50	13.5	93
Manganese ore	283.7	60.5	22	0.1	-19
Phosphate rock	271.3	60.2	25 (1972)	0.2	56
Copper	283.1, 682.1	56.4	32	2.3	138

[a] Standard International Trade Classification.
[b] Obtained by valuing the world production figures with the help of prices in international trade, and then comparing the value of developing countries' exports with the value of world production.
SOURCES: IBRD, 1973. *UN Statistical Yearbook* 1971. Unpublished World Bank documents.

manganese, phosphate rock and copper, would be more difficult to bring about in the short and medium term, without harmful economic consequences to industrial growth. On this count, therefore, the mineral exporters probably have a stronger bargaining position than the producers of tropical beverages.

The beverage prices constitute a major share of the price paid for the product bought by the final consumer. This is because the beverages do not undergo any substantial processing. With the mineral commodities, however, the situation is different. The bauxite cost, for instance, constitutes only a small proportion of the cost of aluminium, and a smaller proportion still of the consumer product in which aluminium is used. Hence, the final consumers will be more affected by a given percentage rise in the unprocessed beverage price than by an equal price rise in the mineral commodities. On this ground it is reasonable to believe that the price elasticity of demand would tend to be lower for the minerals than for the beverages, thus improving the relative prospects of cartels in the minerals markets.

We noted in our discussion of oil that the organisation of price raising cartels would be facilitated by a fast expansion of the markets concerned. It is much easier to accommodate the wishes of producer members for increased production and export quotas when the overall market grows at fast rates. We have provided in Table 4 a measure of developing countries' market growth in each of the nine (including oil) remaining commodities. The last column of the table shows the percentage growth in the value of exports from the Third World between 1960 and 1967–9. On average, the mineral commodity markets have grown more than the beverage ones. This is not surprising, and is in consonance with Engel's law. The income-elasticity of demand for industrial raw materials is likely, on the whole, to be higher than that for food products. As income grows in the industrialised world, the markets for the mineral commodities remaining in our table should continue to experience faster growth than the agricultural products. This is a further indication that success is more likely for a mineral than for a beverage cartel.

For reasons already elaborated, the prospects for successful monopolistic pricing in the eight commodities are probably less good than for oil. Suppose, nevertheless, that the producers of all the eight products were equally successful as the oil exporters in controlling the market and raising prices. Since, in the initial period, their turnover was only two-thirds as large as that of oil, the benefits could also be expected to be correspondingly smaller. Given that the prospects for successful monopolistic pricing are limited to the eight commodities remaining in Table 4, we can conclude that a major proportion of the potential benefits from producers' price raising measures was achieved with the oil producers' actions late in 1973.

Some wider issues in commodity cartel arrangements

Maximisation of export revenue is only one of several possible goals which could be pursued by a price raising cartel. Other plausible objectives could be to maximise the return on capital invested in the commodity export sector, or to make the government tax take as large as possible. Each of these objectives would require a different kind of policy. This can be illustrated with the help of a simple figure.[6]

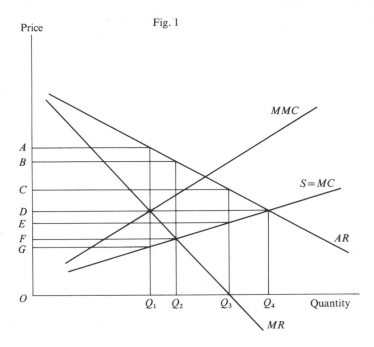

Fig. 1

In Figure 1, *AR* is the world demand curve facing the producer group. The producers' combined marginal cost curve is shown by *S*. With no market intervention, each country will produce up to the point where its marginal cost equals price. The overall supply by the group will be OQ_4, and price will be *OD*.

When the objective of the producer cartel is to maximise export revenue, production will be cut to OQ_3, where marginal revenue, *MR*, becomes negative. This is the point where the price elasticity of demand for the group's output equals unity. Price will rise to *OC* as a consequence of the production cut.

If maximum return on the capital invested in the commodity export sector is the objective of the market intervention, then production should not exceed the point at which marginal revenue, *MR*, intersects the marginal cost, *MC*. This is the ordinary monopolist's profit maximisation condition. Output should be limited to OQ_2 and price will settle at *OB*.

Assume, finally, that the policy objective is to maximise tax revenue. This could be attained by forming a joint marketing company acting on behalf of the participating governments. The company would act as a monopsonist in its relation to the individual private producing units, and as a monopolist when selling the commodity in the world market. Production would now be restricted to OQ_1, where the marginal revenue, MR, equals the marginal cost to the marketing company for purchasing the commodity, MMC (which is a curve marginal to the producers' supply curve MC). The price paid to the producers would now be OG, and the price obtained in the world market would be OA. This would maximise the participating governments' combined tax take at a level equal to $OQ_1 . GA$.

While the above analysis is important in underlining that different output policies would be required to accomplish each of the objectives specified, we should be aware that the neat results emerging from this discussion would hardly be attained in practical life. First, it would be difficult for the governments to agree on the objective to be pursued. Those with an overvalued currency would tend to opt for maximisation of export revenue; others with a stronger balance of payments might find it more interesting to pursue the maximisation of profits. In countries where the sector is in national hands, the government would probably be more cautious in implementing production cuts. Where, on the other hand, the production facilities are foreign owned, a tax maximisation objective, with more severe cuts in output, would be looked upon more favourably.

Even if agreement were reached on a joint objective, there remains the very difficult problem of allocating both the required production cuts and the benefits attained among the participating nations. Optimally, only the high cost output ought to be cut. Such a policy might be politically impossible to implement, however, especially where there are marked differences between participating countries with regard to production costs. In principle, one could conceive of various forms of redistribution of the benefits attained within the cartel group. In practice, such redistribution is likely to meet with strong opposition. One may, therefore, take it that the economic gains emerging from the cartel collaboration are likely to remain with the countries to which they accrue in the first place.

On account of all these difficulties, the real life supply management policies can be expected to be very rough and crude. Agreements to cut output will, in most cases, be scaled down to suit the convenience of the country which desires the least proportional reduction of supplies. The willingness and ability to manage supply will also depend on the commodity and on the organisation of the industry concerned. It will, for instance, be relatively easier to reduce output where such a decision does not lead to any serious employment problems, or where the ownership of production units is in foreign hands.

Before deciding even on such a rough and crude supply management policy, the participants ought to study carefully not only the benefits likely to be derived in the short and medium term, but also the hardships and costs in terms of unemployment, and the possibly permanent losses of markets in the longer run, due to substitution in demand, and emergence of competing producers attracted by the higher price levels. The necessary arrangements for policing the agreement must also be considered among the costs to be incurred. A policy of active market intervention should be entered into only if the benefits appear more important than the possible losses. Developing countries with a high time preference and/or a relatively short planning horizon may attach little importance to the longer term consequences. They may be right in doing so. Sharply expanded commodity export incomes today could enable them to diversify the economy, thus reducing their dependence on the monopolistically priced commodity by the time their market share starts to fall.

Throughout this paper, we have considered the prospects for successful commodity action by developing countries alone. This follows the whole tenor of the present book, which centres its attention on what the Third World could do to derive greater advantages from its relationships with the industrialised nations. But commodity cartels would, of course, have a much greater chance to succeed if the developing producers had tacit or overt support from industrialised exporting countries. Recent events suggest that such support might well be forthcoming. When, in 1973, the Moroccan phosphate rock exporters raised prices, their move was tacitly supported by the US producers. Despite the constraints imposed by US anti-trust legislation, the US producers increased their prices in sympathy with the Moroccan moves. And, in recent years, the governments of Canada and Australia have shown signs of becoming much more interventionist with regard to their primary materials exports. Australia's membership in the Bauxite Producers' Association is a clear sign that industrialised governments' participation in commodity cartel arrangements is a realistic possibility. Primary producers' groups would be well advised to solicit the participation of governments or private firms in industrialised exporting countries, wherever the latter account for significant shares of the overall market.

The developing country exporters can benefit substantially from successful measures to raise commodity prices. But this, of course, does not imply that the developing world as a whole will gain. The emerging evidence strongly suggests that the countries hardest hit by the rises in the price of oil were not the industrialised ones, but a group of very poor nations with little or no oil production of their own. The same is probably true for the impact of high fertiliser costs, following the price increases in phosphate rock. Poor agricultural nations, like India or Bangladesh, find it hard to afford adequate fertiliser imports at current price levels. The realisation of the hardships of the poor non-oil exporters has stimulated a discussion about the possibility of dual pricing for oil, with supplies to the poor importing countries at the lower price level. Aside from some bilateral export arrangements on favourable terms, like the one between Iran and India, the oil producers have, by and large, been unwilling to consider price concessions in exports to the Third World. A dual price system would obviously raise several complications, such as how to select the countries eligible for concessional treatment, or how to prevent re-exports. Basically, however, the problem is much more general. The newly rich oil exporters are simply unwilling to share their wealth with the have-nots. Their behaviour is in no way different from that of the old-rich industrialised nations, which, apart from such limited measures as food aid, or the system of general preferences for manufactured imports, have been quite unwilling to extend commercial concessions to the developing countries. It needs underlining that, when seen from the standpoint of the Third World as a whole, successful commodity market action may appear as a very mixed blessing.

We have centred the above discussion on the prospects for monopolistic pricing action in individual commodities in isolation. One could, of course, also conceive of cartels organised by the producers of several competing primary materials. The advantage of such arrangements would be a lesser degree of substitution at the consumer end. The edible oil market would certainly be easier to manipulate, if the producers of coconut oil, copra, groundnuts, groundnut oil, linseed oil and palm oil, co-ordinated their action through a joint organisation. A unified price policy of the bauxite and copper exporters would likewise reduce the threat to the producers of each of increased competition from the other material. But multi-commodity cartels would obviously create serious organisational problems, and raise difficult issues about the sharing of benefits between participating producers.

In assessing the prospects for price raising commodity cartels, we have relied heavily on price elasticities. While, especially in the longer run, the elasticity conditions are likely to be decisive, there are also many other factors which would influence the degree of success of a commodity cartel. Psychological measures, like dividing the buyers and bluffing, or the maintenance of idle capacity as a threat to potential new producers, are among the factors which could add to the producer group's ability to maintain prices above equilibrium.

Supply management and monopolistic pricing is not the only way through which developing nations could increase their benefits from primary commodity exports. In countries with low costs of production for a particular commodity, on account of rich mineral endowments or a favourable climate, a rent will emerge in the production and trade of that commodity. This will equal the difference between price and actual cost. In so far as this rent accrues to foreign interests, the low cost countries could improve their position by simply taxing it away. By acting in unison, the countries could prevent the transfer of production facilities to other low cost locations. So long as the tax is smaller than the rent, it can be absorbed by the foreign firms, and prices as well as quantities produced need not change. The bauxite tax increases announced by Jamaica in 1974 are a good illustration of these interrelations. Since Jamaica is a low cost producer, the bauxite it supplies will be cheaper than that from marginal high cost sources, even after addition of the new taxes. Somewhat similar circumstances prevailed in the OPEC countries in the years prior to 1971. As noted in the introduction to this chapter, the OPEC governments succeeded in increasing their share of the rent from their low cost oil sources by keeping an unchanged tax and royalty take during a period of falling oil prices. It should be obvious that the scope for extracting the rent is limited by its initial size, and that once the tax demands exceed the rent, there are bound to be repercussions on price, and, hence, on quantity demanded. With increasing government ownership of primary production facilities in developing countries, the opportunities for improving the national benefit still further with the help of rent-extracting taxes will naturally diminish.

We have concentrated our attention on 'aggregate' and global commodity markets. But each market can be divided into a number of sub-markets, for instance according to geographical areas, or with regard to qualities and stages of processing. Very substantial benefits could probably be obtained, if the developing exporting nations, individually or as a group, acquired a detailed knowledge about the characteristics of each of these sub-markets. In present circumstances there are large numbers of commodity specialists who earn monopoly profits, because they possess detailed information about the most suitable marketing arrangements for a particular commodity brand, or about the customers that demand it, and their particular requirements. The possession of market intelligence of the type referred to here would certainly greatly facilitate the efficient functioning of a price raising producer cartel.

The case of copper

It may be useful now to suggest a more detailed approach for one single commodity when considering the prospects and advantages of monopolistic pricing. I choose copper because it is the next largest commodity in developing countries' exports, because it appears in Table 4 as one of the possible candidates for monopoly pricing, and because it is the product with which I happen to be best acquainted.[7]

Table 5 provides a summary of the 1973 demand-supply balance in copper in the non-socialist world. The socialist countries have been excluded since they constitute, by and large, an isolated copper area, with little trade relations with the rest of the world,[8] and because some of their copper statistics are not easily available. The publication of scrap supply data is commonly delayed and our figures are a projection based on the 1972 values. Scrap statistics do not distinguish between old and new scrap, and our division is based on the common presumption that the two kinds of scrap are of about equal importance (McMahon, 1965). Around 40 per cent of old and new scrap originates in the US. Thus, the United States is a very marginal importer of copper.

The price elasticity figures in Table 5 are my own conjectures, based on several econometric studies of the copper market, as summarised in Takeuchi (1971).[9] Short run is intended to mean year-to-year; long run indicates the adjustment over a five year period. I do not attach a great degree of reliance

Table 5. *Non-socialist world copper balance and price elasticities, 1973*

	Demand				Supply		
			Price elasticity of demand				Price elasticity of supply
Area	Volume (thousand tons)	Short run	Long run	Source	Volume (thousand tons)	Short run	Long run
US	3,180	−0.2	−1.0	US mines	1,570	0.2	1.0
RoW[b]	6,200	−0.2	−1.0	Six major developing countries[a]	2,550		
	9,380			RoW mines[b]	1,900	0.2	1.0
				Old scrap	1,680	0.4	0.4
				New scrap	1,680	0	0
					9,380		

[a] Chile, Papua New Guinea, Peru, Philippines, Zaire and Zambia.
[b] Rest of the world.
SOURCES: *World Metal Statistics*, May 1974; Takeuchi, 1971.

to these elasticity data. In all probability, the short run values are highly unstable, both over time and over different price ranges. The long run price elasticities suggested by the econometric studies referred to by Takeuchi are so far apart as to give little definite guidance. The values used in the following analysis are probably on the conservatively low side.

In our highly simplified exercise, we will assume, for want of better information, that the elasticities given in Table 5 hold over the whole range of price levels considered. We will take it that the long run adjustment in demand is fully accomplished over five years in five adjustments of equal size. It is possible that the long run price elasticity of copper is higher than −1.0. Copper can be replaced by several other materials, and in particular by aluminium. With the gradual decrease of the aluminium/copper price ratio over the whole of this century, aluminium has taken over substantial parts of the copper market. This substitution would be speeded up by a once and for all increase in the copper price, which was believed to be permanent. A considerable time lag would be involved, however. Copper processors would have to install new equipment before they could transfer to aluminium. They would hesitate to do so before they were sure that copper prices would stay at the higher level, and before their copper processing equipment had been written off. Limiting the time horizon to five years, our assumption about a gradual reduction in copper demand, so as to correspond to a price elasticity of −1.0 at the end of the period, seems reasonable.

We will assume that the long term mining supply adjustment takes place in its entirety in year five, when the capacity expansion induced by the higher price is brought into production. The short term adjustment in supply can then be seen as the result of a more complete utilisation of existing production capacity. Economically exploitable copper resources do exist in many parts of the world, but the gestation period between the decision to invest in a new mine and the start up of production is quite considerable. It is on the basis of these conditions that we assume the price increase to lead to a small supply expansion in year one (elasticity 0.2), a large one in year five (elasticity 1.0), but none at all in the intervening years.

The availability of new scrap depends entirely on the industrial consumption of copper. New scrap supply is, therefore, not sensitive to copper prices.[10] The long run price elasticity of old scrap supply is taken to be equal to that of the short run. Intensified scrap collection, following a rise in the copper price, does not require any lengthy gestation period.

The non-socialist world copper market is divided into two parts, with differing price patterns. Outside the US the price is set by the London Metal Exchange (LME). In the US prices are determined by domestic producers; the price policy seems to be to avoid the LME extremes. When LME prices experience their trough, US domestic price levels tend to be slightly above the London market level. When LME is at its peak, US prices are commonly substantially lower. On average, over the past ten years, US prices have been some 10 per cent below those of the LME. Extending this to our exercise, we will assume that the US producers' price will be kept 10 per cent below the monopolistic price imposed by the developing country producers. The price elasticity of US demand will be taken to be related to that of the US price.

Suppose now that the Third World copper producers decide in year 0 to raise prices and to keep them on average 10 per cent above the levels which would have been attained in the unregulated market. This policy will result in reduced demand for copper sold by developing countries. The consequences for the price-raising producers can be followed in Table 6. For simplicity, we have assumed zero growth conditions in overall copper demand and supply over the period of the exercise.

The results emerging from the table suggest that the developing countries cannot improve their revenues from copper exports, even in the short term, by setting prices 10 per cent above the average level which would prevail without intervention. The same method can be used to study the impact of other intervention procedures. The conclusions for developing countries acting alone are not much reversed, when the price elasticity of demand outside the US is taken at -0.1 instead of -0.2 as suggested in one econometric study (Fisher *et al.* 1972).

To test the sensitivity of our conclusions to the market share represented by the price colluding producers, we have recalculated the results with the original elasticity values, but on the extreme assumption that all non-US producers of copper would join in the scheme. A price rise of 10 per cent would improve the revenues of this extended producer group by 6 and 2 per

Table 6. *Impact on Third World copper producers' market share and revenue from maintenance of copper prices 10 per cent above the unregulated market level*

	Year 1	Year 2	Year 3	Year 4	Year 5
Demand reduction ('000 tons)					
US	0	0	0	0	0
Europe, Japan and RoW	120	250	370	500	620
Supply increase ('000 tons)					
US mines	0	0	0	0	0
Canadian and RoW mines	40	40	40	40	190
Old scrap	70	70	70	70	70
Total market lost ('000 tons)	230	360	480	610	880
Remaining market for developing country producers ('000 tons)	2,320	2,190	2,070	1,940	1,670
Gain in revenue as compared to non-intervention (%)	0	−5	−11	−16	−28

Assumptions used in Table 6
1. Figures are derived from Table 5.
2. *Elasticities*. Demand: −0.2 in year 1, rising by equal annual adjustments to reach −1.0 in year 5; mining supply: 0.2 in years 1–4, 1.0 in year 5; old scrap supply: 0.4 over the entire period; new scrap supply: 0.
3. US price remains 10 per cent below monopolistic world price. (US price is equal to the unregulated market price level in this case.)
4. US demand is dependent on US price.
5. Demand outside US is dependent on monopolistic world price.
6. Zero growth of the world copper market is assumed over the five year period considered.

cent respectively in years one and two, but would reduce revenue by 1, 4 and 15 per cent in the three following years. With the assumptions upon which our exercise is based, it is simply not feasible for the developing countries to improve their revenues from copper by monopolistic pricing, even if they were to be supported by some developed country producers.

We have so far given consideration to foreign exchange revenue maximisation only. The objective of maximising the government's tax take is less relevant in this context, since a major and growing proportion of the copper industry in the six developing countries is already owned by the government. But it is interesting to see how our conclusions would be changed if the producing countries' goal were to maximise the return on capital invested in copper. The results of Table 6, along with a few further assumptions, can help us in illuminating the outcome in terms of this alternative goal formulation. Assume, then, that two-thirds of the developing countries' copper is produced at costs, excluding return on capital, which are 50 per cent of average unregulated market prices, while the remaining one-third is more expensive to produce, with average cost levels only 33 per cent below price. Assume, further, that any supply reductions would be attained by first taking the high cost copper out of production.

Joint action by the six producing countries to raise prices 10 per cent above the unregulated market level would increase the overall returns to capital by 13, 9 and 5 per cent respectively in the first three years, but would reduce them by 1 and 11 per cent in years four and five. (Higher price rises could reduce returns to capital from the first year.) A mild monopolistic price action by the developing country producers *could* be successful in augmenting returns to the capital invested in their copper sectors; it would simultaneously, of course, raise serious problems due to reduced export earnings and unemployment among the copper workers.

It should be underlined that the outcome of our exercise will be a reliable reflection of reality only if all the assumptions used hold true. But, in fact, each of the assumptions can be questioned. The elasticity figures, in particular, are surrounded by a high degree of uncertainty. But we have relied on the best and most recent elasticity data that are available. And even if our exercise can be criticised for an undue concentration on the elasticity approach, and for not giving sufficient consideration to 'cartel dynamics', there is no way, in my opinion, of avoiding the use of elasticities as a key factor in assessing the market power of a commodity producer group.

An interesting paradox about the elasticities can be mentioned here. The interrelationship between short and long run elasticities, underlying our exercise, is based on the assumption that all decision makers involved believe that the rise in prices will be maintained for a long time. It is because of this belief that they start preparing for a gradual reduction of demand, and for the opening of new mines. A price cartel formed by developing countries would, therefore, be more likely to succeed over a longer period of time, if consumers and non-participating producers had no faith in its ability to achieve the set objectives. This is because they would then fail to take the long run action warranted by the new price level, and consequently the long run adjustments in price elasticities would be deferred.[11]

It is true that our results, reached with the help of shaky elasticity data, remain uncertain. But their credibility is increased by the fact that other studies, using other sets of data, and sometimes approaching the problem from quite different angles, seem to reach very similar conclusions. Thus, Takeuchi concludes that 'the CIPEC countries must lose in the long run if they attempt to jack up the price of copper by cutting their supply on a long term basis' (1971). Tironi's finding (1972) that, in the short run, the elasticity of demand faced by the CIPEC countries would not be less than one indicates that revenue could not be increased even in the short run. Herfindahl's historical study (1959) suggests that competitive forces in the world copper industry have been so strong that the many attempts by producer groups to raise prices through output restrictions had been short episodes only, soon contained by the disruptive effects of unregulated supply and falling demand.

It may be worthwhile to reflect on our pessimistic conclusions by studying the main features which distinguish copper from oil in terms of the feasibility for market control by developing country producers. First, the developing world accounts for a substantially smaller share in copper than in oil in terms of world output and world exports. This is partly because of the importance of copper scrap. Second, the global price elasticity of supply of copper in the short run is increased by the speed and ease with which the output of old scrap can be expanded. The third difference is that in contradistinction to oil at the old prices, copper has several highly competitive substitutes, which have already eaten into its markets. This explains the relatively high price elasticity of its demand in the short and medium term.

Our conclusions seem to lead to the suggestion that the best longer term policy for the copper exporting developing countries could be to accept lower prices and to increase their market share through an aggressive policy of capacity expansion, which would push high cost producers out of business. Given their vast copper reserves and their comparative advantage as copper producers, on account of relatively richer mineral endowments, such a policy is certainly worth further serious consideration.

The prospects for a successful copper cartel would improve if it managed to extend its membership to exporting countries in the industrialised world, like Canada and Australia, and if it could collude in price matters with a cartel of bauxite or aluminium producers. These developments are indeed possible. Contacts have, in fact, been established and frequent discussions have been held between CIPEC on the one hand, and the governments of Canada and Australia as well as representatives of the Bauxite Producers' Association, on the other. All three attended CIPEC's Ministers' Conference in Lusaka in 1974. But there are, of course, many complications to be overcome before a tightly knit supply management policy could be agreed upon by such wider groups of primary commodity producers.

Our exercise has been exclusively concerned with the feasibility of monopolistic price action by developing country producers. Its conclusions in no way preclude that the producing countries utilise their collective powers in the market for other purposes. Much advantage could probably be obtained by a more active and forceful presence on their part in the copper market. The following instance suggests only one of a number of alternative measures which the six developing producers could enforce in order to improve their copper returns. The refined copper from Chile, Peru, Zaire and Zambia is of a quality superior to the average traded on the LME. It is commonly sold on annual contracts directly with fabricators in the industrialised world. For reasons of anachronistic historical tradition, the prices paid for this copper are somewhat below the averages of the LME. It seems both reasonable and feasible for the developing country producers to use their collective market power in order to rectify this consumer favouring bias, and to introduce a premium over LME prices for their copper, to take account of the superior quality which they supply.

Summary and conclusions

OPEC's successful policies in increasing prices and government revenues from oil have aroused wide expectations in the Third World. Developing country producers of several other commodities have formed joint bodies modelled upon OPEC, in a desire to imitate the oil producers' actions.

We start out our analysis by studying the specific features of the world oil market which have permitted the introduction and maintenance of monopolistic prices. Although oil appears to constitute an especially favourable case among commodities, it is quite possible that the monopoly powers exercised so far by the oil producers are far less than would appear from the 1973 changes in the price levels of oil.

By a process of successive elimination we arrive at eight commodities, aside from oil, which appear to fulfil the minimum conditions for establishing effective producer cartels. These eight, taken together, represented a few years ago an export revenue to developing countries about two-thirds as large as that from oil. Even if successful monopolistic price action were undertaken in all the eight markets, the benefits to the exporting countries would not match those which appear to emerge from the oil cartel.

We devote detailed attention to the prospects of establishing a successful and profitable copper cartel among the developing producing countries. On reasonable, but highly uncertain assumptions, we reach the tentative conclusion that monopolistic pricing is not likely to be successful in augmenting the foreign exchange revenues of developing country exporters. It may, however, raise the return on domestic capital in the developing countries' copper sectors.

The prospects for very substantial benefits accruing to developing countries from producer actions in materials other than oil appear to be somewhat limited. It may, nevertheless, be highly useful to establish producers' associations in primary commodity markets, as counterweights to existing monopsonistic tendencies, and as bargaining partners for more or less formal consumer groups.

The OPEC actions have increased the confidence and awakened the joint interests of primary producing countries around the world. Not only in developing countries, but also in industrialised nations like Australia, Canada or Ireland, there is a growing opinion that primary commodity production for export has, up to now, not generated adequate benefits at home. Once they become sufficiently organised and widespread, such feelings might lead to globally co-ordinated measures to increase the government take from primary commodity production and exports.

The 'oil crisis' has severely shaken many old concepts and values in the industrialised world. The developed countries, if pressed today, might be prepared to make concessions in the face of the stronger political and economic demands for a 'more just' exchange between the poor and the rich. In this situation, a high degree of bargaining skill and political collusion among the commodity exporting countries might help them to reach new long term arrangements, quite possibly rendering more benefits than purely market oriented attempts at monopolistic control.

Notes

1 I am grateful to G. K. Helleiner for comments on an earlier draft. The opinions expressed in this paper are my own and do not necessarily reflect those of CIPEC.
2 The oil figure is for both crude and products. For crude only, the developing countries' share would be higher.
3 Irrespective of their elasticities of supply, these three products would, in any case, be excluded in the next step of our analysis, on account of the ease with which their consumption can be substituted for by synthetic fibres in the case of abaca and sisal, and by soyabeans in the case of fishmeal.
4 This statement about timber has to be qualified. On the one hand, it may be true that tropical timber in general is easily replaced by several substitutes. On the other hand, there are a few much sought after species, such as teak, ebony and Brazilian rosewood, the demand for which is exceedingly insensitive to price.
5 The World Bank has ceased to finance tea projects, after realising that the very discouraging development of tea prices in the past ten years was related to the combination of very low price elasticities of demand, and earlier bank lending programmes to expand production.
6 This presentation was suggested to me by Gerald Helleiner.
7 I shall not here address the possibility, mentioned above, of increasing the producer countries' share of rent without price/quantity changes.
8 The socialist countries' (excluding Yugoslavia) net imports of all copper, amounted, as far as is known, to 62,000 tons in 1970, 95,000 tons in 1971 and 39,000 tons in 1972. (*World Metal Statistics*).
9 Two further econometric models of the copper market have appeared since Takeuchi wrote his paper, namely, Fisher et al. 1972, and, more recently, an unpublished model prepared for the Link Project by G. Adams at the University of Pennsylvania. The short run elasticity figures derived from these models are not substantially different from those in the models studied by Takeuchi.
10 The dependence of new scrap supply on the overall demand for copper implies that it has, in fact, a negative price elasticity of supply.
11 I am indebted to K. Takeuchi for directing my attention to this important point.

References

Adelman, M. A., 1972. *The World Petroleum Market*. Baltimore: Johns Hopkins.
Fisher, F. M., Cootner, P. H. and Baily, M. N., 1972. An econometric model of the world copper industry. *Bell Journal of Economics and Management Science*, **3**, 568–611.
Herfindahl, O. C., 1959. *Copper Costs and Prices, 1870–1957*. Baltimore: Johns Hopkins.
IBRD (International Bank for Reconstruction and Development), 1973. *Commodity Trade and Price Trends*, Report no. EC-166/73, mimeo.
McMahon, A. D., 1965. *Copper, a Materials Survey*. Washington: U.S. Bureau of Mines (Information circular 8225).

Takeuchi, K., 1971. An analysis of the effects of possible CIPEC actions on the copper earnings of member countries. IBRD Economics Department Working Paper 109, mimeo.

Tironi, E., 1972. Planificacion economica en las empresas del cobre nacionalizadas. *Estudios de Planificacion*, CEPLAN, Santiago, 24.

4. The dynamics of the new poor power

PAUL STREETEN[1]

Few would deny that the United Nations Conference on Trade and Development (UNCTAD) has, so far, been a failure.[2] Many reasons have been advanced for this, but the main reason is surely that, from the developed countries' point of view, it seems all give and no take. The poor countries' moral appeals and appeals to distant and uncertain national self-interest of the rich, backed by masses of facts and figures, were not enough. There must also be appeals to the clear and imminent self-interest, and backing by power.

Appeals to self-interest can be of two kinds: those that point to previously undisclosed, undiscovered or unexploited self-interest and those that create a nuisance or a threat for the removal of which concessions are extracted. An example of the first is trade liberalisation, combined with adjustment assistance to those who are displaced by the new imports. There are wide areas in which negotiations that emphasise the common interest have a better chance of success than those based solely on moral appeals.

The archetype of the second kind of appeal is the blackmailer or the kidnapper, though these expressions beg the moral question. An example is the threat to withdraw from the control of narcotics traffic by permitting the growth of opium. Ransoms demanded to correct previously committed inequities must be judged differently from those that destroy equity.

Appeals to self-interest or to the conscience of the rich must, then, be backed by power. In order to back moral appeals by power, three things are necessary: (i) solidarity among partners, (ii) fragmentation among opponents and (iii) information.

Solidarity

Solidarity between sovereign nation states is difficult to achieve. The reasons for this are best illustrated by the case of a restrictive, price-raising commodity cartel, but they apply with equal force to other exercises of joint bargaining power (see pp. 85–86). Solidarity is difficult to achieve because the more effective a cartel or a cartel-like agreement, the greater is the reward for any one member to break it. But the fear that anyone may break the agreement will induce those who would otherwise be willing to adhere to prepare for the breakup. For sticking to an agreement while others abandon it makes the loyal members worse off than they would have been without any agreement. The potential defectors cherish the *hope* of operating *outside* the agreement. But this encourages on the part of the conformers the *fear* of a situation *without* the agreement. This fear is ever present, even if there are no actual or potential defectors. The fear itself leads to actions that undermine the agreement. Action outside the agreement is an ever present hope and action without the agreement an ever present threat.

On the other hand, if buyers do not believe in the stability of the cartel, they will not take the actions they would have taken, had they expected prices to stay high (e.g. searching for substitutes or installing expensive equipment that economises in the use of the imported material).

Agreements can be renegotiated and a partner will hope that, at the next round of negotiations, he will get a better deal, a larger share. The actions necessary to secure a larger share are similar to those leading to defection or breach. Again, the knowledge that some will ask for a larger share puts others on the defensive. But defence is as disruptive as attack. Cartels are a continuation of competition by other means, as Clausewitz might well have said, and only error can arise from identifying them wholly with monopolies.

A cartel that restricts supply and raises prices must allocate quotas. (Since OPEC does not do so, it is not a cartel in the strict sense, though it is fortunate in that the exporters with large reserves, Saudi Arabia, Kuwait and Abu Dhabi, have limited absorptive capacity and an independent interest to curtail production, while those with a vociferous demand for imports have relatively small reserves.) Producers and countries have an interest in enlarging their quotas at the expense of other producers or countries. The power to negotiate for a larger quota depends, partly, on the capacity to fill it. Each country therefore has a strong interest in increasing this capacity by maintaining reserves, either in the form of productive excess capacity or in the form of stocks. In the international coffee agreement reserve stocks of coffee were feared to be ammunition of this kind. In the case of mineral agreements, the high fixed costs of mining, the equivalent of spare productive capacity, are a destabilising factor.

The incentive to hold such reserves or excess capacity and the ability to do so are diametrically opposed to the conditions on which stability in the cartel can be maintained. For the fear that these reserves will be used will tend to undermine willingness to adhere to the restrictions that are necessary to maintain the cartel. The fear that the breakdown of the cartel will make everyone worse off is not a sufficient deterrent to prevent the breakdown, for any one member, in most cases rightly, believes that the threat of breakdown comes from others. The defensive response of each member, however, has the same effect as the aggressive undermining by defectors. It explains why, in spite of the obvious rational interest of the group, successful, lasting cartels are so rare, whether in the field of commodity prices or agreements to follow common policies towards foreign companies or boycotts or sanctions.

The prevalence of reserve stocks and reserve capacity is, partly, a function of the level of demand. When world demand is high and growing, stocks and excess capacity will tend to be low, compared with the desired level, making cartel agreements workable, but there will be less incentive to form them. On the other hand, when world demand is low and falling, and reserves and excess capacity are large, the need for cartels will be more urgent, but their chances of success reduced. The situation is like a leaking roof: in good weather there is no need to repair it, in bad weather no opportunity.

The problem of adherence to a cartel agreement is that of the Prisoner's Dilemma. Peter and Paul are arrested, put in separate cells, and not permitted to communicate. The Prosecution knows that they have committed a crime but has not enough evidence for a conviction in a court. If neither confesses, they get a minor punishment on a trumped-up charge, say one year. If Peter confesses and Paul does not, Paul gets the maximum penalty, say ten years, and Peter only a light one, say three months, for turning Queen's evidence. Similarly, the other way round. If both confess, they get some remission, say eight years. Though it is clearly in their interest that neither should confess, neither can rely on the other's not confessing and the result of rational action on the part of both is that both confess.

It is this type of situation which has provided the justification for collective coercion wholly in the interest of individual preferences.[3] Only a penalty as great as that imposed by the disastrous, though fully rational, option, will ensure that they are not driven to the 'stupid' result, to avoid embarking on a negative-sum game.

An n-person analogy to the Prisoner's Dilemma is competition between sellers, where profits are eroded as a result of each trying to snatch a gain. Competition results in the erosion of monopoly profits and therefore benefits the consumers of the product. The desirable outcome depends, *inter alia*, on producers and consumers forming part of the same community, and income distribution being optimal. Clearly neither of these conditions is met in the relations between countries or between poor producers and rich consumers, and co-ordinated action can therefore improve the allocation and distribution of resources.

A cartel has, of course, greater co-ordination than the separated, non-communicating prisoners. But the penalties for defection are normally too weak to ensure adherence. Those emphasising solidarity, joint actions, common fronts, which give rise to situations in which choices of the type of the Prisoner's Dilemma have to be made should, therefore, pay attention to instituting a system of rewards and penalties that shifts the incentives so as to make the unstable optimum solution stable.

Important sources of rewards in commodity agreements are diversification funds and technical assistance to diversification. These have a double virtue. First, they compensate countries for restricting supplies and secondly, where opportunity costs are positive, they absorb resources in alternative uses, thereby reducing the danger of erosion of the cartel. Through geographical and commodity diversification countries previously dependent on one or a few markets and one or a few crops or minerals or services can thereby be made more independent and their loyalty to the cartel increased.

Another factor that will enhance the stability of the cartel is the ability of a supplier to do without any earnings, or with substantially reduced earnings, for a period. This is one of the forces that strengthens OPEC. Withholding supplies is a powerful weapon of the cartel. If a supplying country is not able to withhold supplies because it depends on earnings, the cartel can be strengthened by other members compensating the country for withholding supplies.

In order to raise the stability of cartel agreements there must exist not only rewards for adherence and penalties against defection, but also a sense of a fair distribution of the gains from the agreement between and within countries. This may require compensatory payments from large gainers to small gainers. Interest conflicts arise not only between countries but also between producers inside countries. While it is in the interest of the cartel as a whole, whenever demand is less than infinitely elastic and supply more than zero elastic, to restrict supply below the level that would be reached under competition, it is in the interest of each country to increase supply in the face of the restrictions of others, and it is in the interest of each producer within each country to raise his supply, while others restrict theirs. The reconciliation of the pressures of producers on the country's negotiating position and the pressures of countries on the agreements reached in the cartel will be possible only if each party believes it has more to lose from breaking than from keeping the agreement.

The fair distribution of gains is further complicated by differences of view as to what constitutes fairness. There may be conflicts between fairness and bargaining power, and bargaining power may change over time. Here, a sense of solidarity derived from sources other than the cartel, e.g. ethnic, religious, ideological or linguistic unity, may be a help in achieving acceptance of a system of sharing, by inducing those with greater power to make sacrifices for those with less.

Further complications arise from differences over the time distribution of gains. Some partners may prefer short term gains at the expense of longer term ones, others the reverse. Different partners may have different preferences for independently given time distributions of gains and different capacities for reserves. In addition, the time distribution of gains may itself be partly determined by the actions of the cartel. Raising prices now may encourage speedier invention of substitutes, greater economies in the use of the product or loss of goodwill and thereby reduce prices later below what they would have been had prices not been raised. On the other hand, some members of the cartel may anticipate that the supply of a non-renewable resource will have been exhausted when lower prices prevail in the future, while others may not share this view. Successful cartel agreements will have to find methods of reconciling such interest conflicts.

It is sometimes argued against cartel agreements in commodities for which the demand is more elastic in the long run than in the short run that the gains are only short term. But this is not an argument against a cartel. The short term gains can be used to strengthen the base of action at a future time when the agreement will have been eroded (for example, by promoting diversification with the aid of the short term gains from raising the price of a commodity for which short term demand is inelastic). Or they may be used to push up demand through research and development or to make it less elastic through advertising. Only to the extent to which the agreement itself is responsible for shortening the period over which benefits can be derived, e.g. by encouraging production outside the cartel or by speeding up the search for substitutes or for economies in use, or by losing 'goodwill' or by lowering future demand curves in other ways, should the longer term losses be set against the short term gains and such gains be moderated in the light of intertemporal preferences.

Illustrations of a later collapse in price, resulting from a cartel that raised prices, are the British rubber control scheme and the Brazilian attempt to raise coffee prices in the 1920s. The British rubber scheme was based on Malaya and Ceylon and succeeded, at first, spectacularly in raising the price of rubber, but investment in Indonesia was stimulated and led to a drastic fall in price. The Brazilian scheme was based on government stock holdings but the high price stimulated planting and led to a bumper crop that exceeded the government's financial capacity to hold stocks.

Division among opponents

Successful cartel action is derived from a degree of dependence on the part of the purchasers which the cartel members exploit. One-sided, permanent dependence is very rare. It is not just a question of a low elasticity of demand; for, as I have argued above, the shift of the demand curve and its elasticities in the future may themselves be a function of the present rise in price. To define dependence precisely, we should have to combine ordinary demand elasticities with intertemporal cross-elasticities. Such a cross-elasticity would be defined as the proportionate change in the quantity demanded at a given future date resulting from a small proportionate change in price now. But the precision of such a concept is a pseudo precision, for inevitably an historical element will enter into the quantity demanded at any given time at any given price. It will depend, at least partly, upon the memory of the history of prices charged in the past.

In the previous four paragraphs we explored briefly the temporal aspect, i.e. the possibility that dependence can be reduced over time. We must now turn to the question whether dependence is not mutual. If there is *inter* dependence, there is the possibility of retaliation. Not always is it the case that the victims of a cartel can say: 'anything you can do, I can do better', but, on the other hand, there is usually some countervailing power. The use of bargaining power by one group may invite retaliation by another. The recent

US Trade Act refuses preferential tariff treatment to members of an export cartel. When the knives are out, who can say who will win? To carry a gun when nobody else does, gives one extra power, but a world in which everyone carries a gun is liable to be worse than one in which nobody does.

There are four replies to this line of argument against the use of monopoly power by poor countries. First, common action by the rich already exists in many areas and joint action among the poor cannot therefore make things much worse than they are already. In the past there was always the possibility of armed intervention. Until the October 1973 War, military intervention by the big powers was improbable. In the post-Suez, post-Vietnam world of the balance of nuclear terror, the use of military power seemed ruled out. But in the new situation, in which wages, employment and standards of living are endangered and whole economies may be 'strangled', the situation has changed. It is perhaps not quite so improbable as it was before, though the super powers will probably find more effective and cheaper ways of safeguarding their supplies than armed intervention.

It is clear, therefore, that the big powers still have considerable latent bargaining power. But, military intervention apart, greater sophistication goes with better organisation for national interests. Regional groupings such as the European Community, the policies of the transnational companies, the policies pursued by the Group of Ten or by members of the General Agreement on Tariffs and Trade are, or were, to some extent, already in the nature of actions of 'rich men's clubs'. Collective action by the poor was and is needed to catch up with these established policies.

Secondly, the ability of the rich to band together can itself, to some extent, be influenced by the poor. The far-sighted cartelier must give thought to how to prevent the rallying of the forces of the opposition. Division and fragmentation of opponents is as useful to the cartel as *divide et impera!* is to the dictator. Whether by design or not, the result of discrimination against Holland and USA and in favour of France and Britain, by the oil exporting countries during the cutback in 1973–4, may have been bad economics (because it seemed to neglect substitution), but it was good politics. An Organisation of Oil Importing Countries (OPIC) could have inflicted greater damage on the oil exporters than they inflicted on importers. But powerful divisive forces were at work and were nourished by OPEC, so that it never came to joint action by importers. Such action can, of course, not be ruled out in the future.

In addition to fragmentation of opponents, the members of the cartel can weaken the power of the buyers by (i) encouraging them in the belief that the price rise is only temporary, so that they do not embark on the investment and installation costs of inventing or using alternative sources of supply or of economising in the use of the imported material; (ii) depriving them of stocks, for stocks are an important weapon in resisting the demands of the cartel.

Thirdly, if the *status quo* is quite intolerable for some countries, the result of an international free-for-all may be preferable for them, even though most countries are worse off. The balance of power and the balance of advantage may, in some instances, lie with some of the poor. However strong the organisation of buyers, they may heavily depend, at least for a time, on certain raw materials or fuels of which the exporters are monopoly suppliers, or on certain areas for locating factories requiring cheap labour. Japan is heavily dependent on imported raw materials. The United States depends almost entirely on imports of manganese, tin and chromium. All industrial countries have shown themselves vulnerable in their dependence on cheap petroleum.

Fourthly (and most important) the argument points to a non-full use of the bargaining power by all countries. As I. G. Patel has said 'once you get into a mood of warfare in trade, it is going to be difficult to keep the firing within any prescribed limits' (Patel, 1973, p. 45). The valid conclusion is that the situation calls for a new set of international rules and institutions enforcing these rules, which reflect a more even power distribution. If the rules of the game have in the past been biased in favour of the rich countries, the solution is not to abandon all rules, but to change them. For this, reference to potential, latent, power constellations and power reserves on both sides is necessary, but the powers need not be exercised. The incentive for the rich countries to avoid a breakdown of regulated international relations is that they may lose more from a situation without rules than they would lose from a set of rules that makes generous concessions to the poor. If the poor threaten to abandon the system of international rules unless their grievances are removed, a reformed system will then be preferable to breakdown of the system.

Areas for bargaining

What are the areas in which there is a prima facie case for exploring the exercise of joint bargaining power? The classical case, on which much of this discussion has focused, is joint action to raise the prices of exports in inelastic demand and to restrict supplies. Cartels will tend to be more successful in restricting the supply and raising the price of a commodity and thereby to raising total earnings, the more price inelastic the demand for the commodity, and the more price inelastic its supply in the medium and long term. Demand will be more inelastic: (i) the higher the proportion of imports to total consumption of the commodity in importing countries; (ii) the fewer substitutes there are (i.e. the lower the elasticity of substitution between the cartelised commodity and its non-cartelised nearest substitutes, including scrap and other forms of re-usable materials); and the slower the rate of innovation in substitutes in response to the price rise; (iii) the more difficult it is to economise in the use of the commodity as an input into given products; (iv) the more difficult it is to switch to products using less of the commodity in question (i.e. the lower the elasticity of substitution between products using the commodity as inputs and products using less or none of it).

The medium and long term supply of the commodity will be more inelastic: (i) the fewer the countries in which the commodity is produced and from which it is exported; (ii) the stronger the solidarity among cartel members (i.e. the greater the rewards for adhering and the penalties for defecting); agreements between governments are likely to be more successful than those between producers; and agreements between politically friendly governments more successful than between hostile ones; (iii) the more commodities that are substitutes for one another are included in the cartel (e.g. *all* metals or *all* tropical beverages).

OPEC has been the most successful institution using collective bargaining power. Its stability has been strengthened, apart from political and ideological bonds, by the fortunate and fortuitous fact that member countries with large reserves (Kuwait and Saudi Arabia) had no need for immediate earnings, while those with the strongest and most urgent needs, because of large populations and ambitious development plans (Nigeria and Iran), had small reserves.

On the other hand, price increases due to the action of the cartel may have an inflationary impact on the general price level, and therefore on the prices of the imports of cartel members. To safeguard itself against such consequences, the cartel has to fix its price increases in real terms, e.g. by indexing.

Even in this most successful case, restricting supplies and raising the price of oil is only part, and perhaps not the most significant part, of the bargain. In addition, there are the partial or total nationalisation of the oil companies and the new terms for the flow of technical knowhow from the companies to the host countries. There are also political pressures on policies towards Israel. Reducing or withholding supplies may be used for purposes other than maximising the cartel's export earnings. They may be used to achieve economic advantages in other fields, or for political purposes.

This essay is concerned mainly with the *feasibility* of exercising joint bargaining power and hence with the stability of cartels. We are not here examining the *desirability* of commodity agreements as instruments to accelerate development in low income countries and to reduce world-wide inequality. But it is worth remembering that commodity agreements, even if they could be made to work, have certain drawbacks.

First, there is the question of the internal and international distribution of gains from price increases. The beneficiaries of these cartels may be large farmers, plantation owners or mine owners who belong to the rich in poor countries and the consumers hit by price increases may be the poor in rich countries. If these plantations or mines are owned by rich foreigners, e.g. by transnational companies, the benefits take the form of aid or redistribution to the rich countries.

Secondly, many poor countries, and the largest ones among them, have few commodities that lend themselves to successful cartelisation (tea and jute are poor commodities, produced by very poor countries) and rely heavily on imports of commodities more readily cartelised and exported by relatively better off countries. Unless development aid is concentrated on these importers or unless safeguards are built into the commodity agreements, divisions within the so-called Third World would be aggravated. In addition, many rich countries are exporters of commodities that would benefit from cartels.

Thirdly, the countries most likely to benefit from commodity agreements will tend to be small countries in whose economy foreign trade plays a relatively important part. But it is precisely these countries that already get more aid per head than large countries. The so-called small-country effect of development aid would be reinforced by commodity agreements, unless the rise in import prices due to the cartelisation of imported commodities wiped out any benefits they derived from rises in their export prices.

Fourthly, while jacking up export receipts increases the *means* to diversification, industrialisation and general development, it simultaneously reduces the *incentive* to do so. Successful cartelisation may therefore delay or impede the growth of industrial exports in which the countries may have a long term comparative advantage.

Not all commodity agreements aiming at higher average export prices (contrasted with those aiming merely at stabilisation of prices) need take the form of a confrontation between exporting and importing countries. The USA used the threat of a grain cartel in an attempt to beat OPEC. But producers and consumers have co-operated on a sugar agreement, a coffee agreement and others. The main interest of consumers in remunerative prices for producers is that these ensure higher levels of investment and therefore continuing supplies. Very low prices, on the other hand, tend to discourage investment and to lead to excessive dependence on imports. They carry the seeds of future shortages and deprivation of supplies. Short term restrictions, leading to very high prices, tend to encourage the growth of substitutes and economies in the use of the product, and thereby carry the seeds of future surpluses. There is, therefore, an area in which producers' and consumers' interests coincide. Both will want to avoid setting a price that, though in their short term interest, is self-defeating in the long run. A higher average level of prices, combined with a larger volume of production, can therefore be both in the interests of consumers and producers.

So much about the desirability and the feasibility of cartels. But there are other areas than commodity agreements in which the same or similar issues arise. The following list is illustrative.

1. The threat to expropriate foreign investments.
2. The threat to default on foreign debts.
3. Limitations on the repatriation of foreign profits and capital.
4. The threat of the withdrawal of money balances or the demand of their conversion into gold.
5. Joint action to improve the terms of contracts with transnational enterprises (removal or reduction of tax concessions; demand for higher

royalties; fewer direct or indirect subsidies; stronger demands for local participation or use of local materials, etc.).
6. Refusal to admit companies dependent on cheap labour or refusal to accept polluting factories.
7. Trade discrimination against or boycott of exports from industrial countries.
8. Refusal to sign trade mark, patent or copyright conventions.
9. Demand of higher rents for granting military facilities.
10. The denial of overflying rights.
11. Non-co-operation in the control of drug-growing or drug-traffic.

Information

Solidarity and strength among protagonists and division and weakness among antagonists is not enough for the success of the cartel. Knowledge and information are also needed in order to use effective bargaining power. In the case of commodity agreements, it is important to know about alternative sources of supply, about research and development directed at the production of substitutes, about the scope for economies in the use of the material, and about the tendency to switch demand to products using less of the material. Knowledge about competition between buyers, their financial strength, their profit rates, etc. is also important. In the case of negotiations with transnational enterprises, it is important to know about accounting methods, about transfer pricing, over-invoicing of imported inputs and under-invoicing of exported outputs, about realistic figures for management fees, royalties and interest charged on inter-affiliate loans.

Several commentators have argued the case for an international agency to render assistance to low income countries in gathering this type of information and supporting them in their negotiations. Bilateral technical assistance is bound to be suspect where companies are concerned that reside in the parent country, so that this is *par excellence* an area for multilateral technical assistance or for joint agencies run for and by less developed countries. The UN has established training centres for officials from developing countries in negotiating with MNCs. The Andean Group (comprising Peru, Bolivia, Chile, Ecuador, Colombia and Venezuela) have agreed to lower tariff barriers, co-ordinate industrial development, and adopt common policies towards foreign companies, as well as to collect and pool relevant information from all members.

At present, the bulk of research is directed at problems of the rich countries and is either irrelevant or detrimental to the development efforts of poor countries. In addition, most channels of communication run from North to South and intra-Third World communications are weak or absent. An increase of relevant research and an improvement of communications between poor countries are important elements in a strategy of strengthening their bargaining power.

Interest alignments

So far, I have discussed cartel-like agreements between poor countries and explored their potential bargaining power. But a map of interest alignments should not accept the nation state as the only relevant unit. Important interest groupings run across nation states. This fact gives rise to two sets of problems. First, nation states may act 'in their own interests', which are identified with those of the ruling group and are in conflict with those of the mass of poor people in their own countries. Secondly, particular groups in the nation may take action without enlisting the power of the state.

The possibility that the governments and officials of nation states may not act in accordance with the interests of the poor of their countries, the first case, is an ever-present danger in commodity cartels (and, of course, all other negotiations in which they are involved). The producers who benefit from restrictions and price increases are often rich owners or managers of plantations or mines, sometimes allied to foreign interests, and there may not be much trickling down. Governments may, of course, form purchasing agencies or impose indirect taxes and attempt to cream off part of the monopoly gains for social benefits, but political will or administrative ability may be absent.

Similarly, the beneficiaries of negotiations with multinational enterprises may be groups of businessmen or managers in the public sector, whose interests conflict with those of the masses of the poor people. 'The host country' may benefit from certain arrangements, but the interests of the country are identified with those of a small, rich and powerful group.

The second case is where alignments of interests can be exploited in the cause of development without the assistance of the state or by exercising countervailing influence on the state. Consumers are not as well organised as producers and are therefore victims of the powerful and articulate protectionist claims of producers in rich countries. Appeals to governments to give better access to the exports of poor countries are therefore not likely to succeed. But the retail chains that are independent of the large producers or consumers' associations could be harnessed to side with the labour-intensive, low cost producers of the poor countries. The Atlantic and Pacific Stores in the USA have a commercial interest in lowering the cost of processed coffee and other food items; Sainsbury and Waitrose in Britain are interested in low cost fruit and vegetables. A department store interested in selling low-cost clothes can subcontract the making of these ('putting out' it was called in the eighteenth century) to small manufacturers or craftsmen in less developed countries.

Multinational and transnational producing firms are important advocates and pressure groups of better market access in the industrial countries. To the extent to which some of their operations take place in developing countries, this pressure is a useful ally. Trade unions and competing firms form an opposition to this access. If interest pressures like the ones described above can be combined with adjustment assistance to those displaced by the low cost imports, they are likely to be more effective, as well as more humane.

Conclusions

The conclusion of this discussion is that there must be a shift from emphasis on gaining concessions from rich nation states to using interest alignments either among poor countries or between rich and poor countries or between common interest groups across national boundaries. It is not argued that each interest group should fully exploit its bargaining power, but that these latent sources of power should be used to devise a more equitable system of international rules and institutions. In particular, greater emphasis on the common interest of groups of developing countries is a source of strength, as long as the centrifugal, disintegrating forces can be restrained. National self-interest will have to be sacrificed for greater solidarity if the developing countries wish to match the power and skills of the transnational companies, of the groupings of rich industrial countries and of the heavy bias of scientific and technical progress against the interests of the poor. There are untapped power reserves in the concerted action of developing countries if they are willing to unite. The *Communist Manifesto*, it will be remembered, ends with a call to the workers of the world to unite: they have nothing to lose but their chains; they can win a world. The exhortation, slightly adapted and allowing for the more complex network of domestic and international interest alignments, still applies.

Notes

1   I am grateful to G. K. Helleiner and Hans Singer for constructive comments on an earlier draft.
2   For a more positive view of the achievements of the UNCTAD, see Dell (1973).
3   J. S. Mill saw clearly the need for state intervention, 'not to overrule the judgement of individuals respecting their own interest, but to give effect to that judgement; they being unable to give effect to it except by concert, which concert again cannot be effectual unless it receives validity and sanction from the law'. He illustrates this by workers' restriction of their working hours (Mill, 1902, p. 581).

References

Dell, Sidney, 1973. An appraisal of UNCTAD III, *World Development*, **1** (5), 1–13.
Mill, J. S., 1902. *Principles of Political Economy*. London, New York and Bombay: Longmans.
Patel, I. G., 1973. Some reflections on trade and development. In *Trade Strategies for Development*, Papers of the Ninth Cambridge Conference on Development Problems, (ed.) Paul Streeten. London: Macmillan.

5. The direction of international trade: gains and losses for the Third World

FRANCES STEWART[1]

Alternative trading arrangements open to Third World countries are manifold. Some options – those involving mutual arrangements between more than one country – are only open to countries as a group, while others depend solely on the unilateral decision of the individual country. Group trading arrangements – just because they are group arrangements – are more difficult to negotiate and maintain than individual arrangements, but they also potentially offer more, by extending the options, than individual arrangements which are limited by the necessary assumption that they must take the arrangements of the rest of the world as given. Group arrangements may range in coverage from those involving only two countries to world agreements.

The purpose of this essay is to look at different types of trading arrangements for Third World countries, both from the point of view of theoretical advantages and disadvantages and from that of current trading practices. First, it considers general arguments relating to the quantity and direction of trade. In the last section, it considers possible institutional changes in the light of the preceding argument.

Free trade versus protection: underlying assumptions

Very broadly, in the sphere of trading arrangements, there are two schools of thought – free trade and protectionist; the same, in fact, as in nineteenth-century (or even eighteenth-century) Europe, when the current disputes were rehearsed by the Mercantilists, and Adam Smith, Ricardo, John Stuart Mill and List. The free traders emphasise the gains from trade via improving the efficiency of resource allocation, while the protectionists emphasise the dynamic advantages of protection, economies of scale, learning by doing and other external economies which, they argue, can only arise if domestic industry is protected, initially at least, from competition from goods produced by more industrially advanced countries.

The free traders[2] seem to have the upper hand at the moment – at least in terms of the weight of advice given, if not in terms of advice taken – because they can point to the inefficiencies resulting from protection introduced by underdeveloped economies in the 1950s and 1960s, the high cost of protection sometimes even involving negative value added at world prices (Little *et al.* 1970, p. 195). In many economies, the expected (by protec-

4-2

tionists) external economies do not seem to have materialised; import protection has been associated with imported capital-intensive techniques of production (see e.g. Islam, 1967), slow growth of employment, and a dualistic form of development with very little overspill from the small protected industrial sector to the rest of the economy. Indeed, it has been argued that the majority of the population in many economies has actually suffered, with a deterioration of its terms of trade with the industrial sector and the outside world, as a result of the policy of protection combined with overvalued exchange rates. In contrast, it is argued (by free traders), free trade economies have visibly benefited by international exchange (Little *et al.* 1970).

While it is true that most of the countries which experienced rapid growth rates in GNP *per capita* between 1960 and 1969, experienced rapid growth in manufactured exports, it is also true that many of the slow growing countries also experienced rapid growth in manufactured exports, as Table 1 shows.

Table 1. *Manufactured export and per capita GNP growth, 1960–9*

Growth rate in GNP *per capita* (%)	No. of countries with growth rate in non-resource based manufactured exports	
	Above 20% per annum	Below 20% per annum
Over 6	4	1
3–6	5	12
1–3	7	8
Under 1	3	4

SOURCE: Chenery and Hughes, 1973, pp. 26–7.

There are, of course, numerous conditions making for rapid growth in such exports (including the small base from which they start). But it does seem that growth in exports is certainly not a sufficient condition for general economic growth; it may, nevertheless, during this period, have been a necessary condition. Thus the protectionist case is much more on the defensive than in the days when it could point to countries such as Germany, which had successfully developed under the protectionist mantle, and which, it could plausibly be argued, would never have developed without it.

The argument, as summarised above, is much too simple. First, as Fei and Ranis have pointed out (1975), the appropriate policy may differ according to the stage of development. Without protection, many economies would never start to develop industrially, but would remain forever specialists in primary products, their livelihood depending on uncertain market prospects and terms of trade, unable to provide the employment that they require and forever completely dependent on other (mainly developed) economies. But at a later stage of development, a more open economy may allow advantage to be taken of economies of scale, of returns to specialisation and of comparative advantage. Fei and Ranis point to the economies of Japan, Taiwan and South Korea as examples. Thus the appropriate question, according to them, is not free trade *or* protection, but free trade *when*, or free trade *and* protection.

The second way in which the argument is simplistic is in assuming that there are only two alternatives – free trade or protection – as if the unit in which there should be free movement of goods must either be the individual country or the world. Clearly, if these are the alternatives, unless we assume constant costs for all industries, irrespective of scale (an assumption, of course, which many free traders do make), then the answer to the question – free trade or protection – must differ according to the size of the country concerned. Very small countries cannot follow a protectionist policy without experiencing extremely high costs of production; large countries can. The individual country is, in terms of economics, an arbitrary unit: there is no rationale for supposing that it is correct that there should be free movement of goods within it, but not outside. It is equally arbitrary to assume, as free traders do, that the world is the correct size for a trading unit. Some of the many intermediate arrangements may give the best combination of benefit from trade via economies of scale and specialisation combined with sufficient protection from the outside world to secure the dynamic/development effects of protection.

While it is true that neither theory (Lipsey, 1970; Meade, 1955; Viner, 1950; Robson, 1971) nor practice – as shown by the many trading arrangements made by groups of countries – have stuck to the rigid dichotomy between free trade and protection, there has been a tendency to regard such arrangements as second best. Viner's classic work on customs unions, for example, regards such unions as desirable in so far as they are a step towards the freeing of international trade; the net balance between trade creation and trade diversion which he regarded as the test of the virtue of such unions (in which, with various qualifications about measurement and effects, he has been followed by most other theorists) was essentially a test of the extent to which a union contributed towards freeing trade, as against freezing it. Since so much of the theoretical analysis of customs unions has been *allocative*, rather than *dynamic*, in its concern it has not, in general, provided sufficiently for the possibility that a customs union (or other less than free trade trading arrangement among partners) may have dynamic benefits for the countries concerned, which might justify the arrangements even if free trade were an option.

There has been ambiguity in the assumptions made about the policies of other countries in much of the theoretical discussion. The free trade argument rests firmly on the assumption of unchanging conditions – technological, economic and policy. That is to say, current costs and opportunities can be assumed to continue irrespective of policy. The most obvious respect in which this may be wrong is where demand or supply of traded goods is not perfectly price elastic with respect to the quantity traded by the country in question. The case for an 'optimum' tariff rests on this possibility, which only arises where the country is large enough, or the commodity it is trading has a sufficiently large share of world trade, for the country to be in a monopolistic or monopsonistic position with respect to the commodity, so that the quantity it buys or sells influences the price. In such a situation, like a good rational monopolist, a country should ensure that the trading price represents the true marginal cost through the use of tariffs and taxes. The reaction of other countries can be analysed by taking the possibility of tariff retaliation into account.

For the most part, however, unchanging conditions are assumed. There are a number of respects in which this assumption may lead to wrong policy conclusions, particularly where developing country trade policy is concerned.

(a) Consider the usual assumption (apart from the analysis of retaliation to an optimum tariff, just discussed) that the trading policy of other importing countries remains unchanged, irrespective of the quantities involved. The experience of developed country (DC) reactions to successful and large scale exports of labour-intensive manufactures suggests that this is both untrue, and a very risky assumption on which to base policy. For example, the history of British policy towards textile imports from less developed countries (LDCs) (WDM, 1972), and that of the EEC restrictions on their 'generalised' system of preferences (Tulloch, 1972) show that DC policies do react to LDC trade performance.

(b) A different aspect of policy reaction which is inconsistent with the assumption that there is no change in trading conditions derives from the fact that while individually LDCs may have little market power, together they have considerable power over a number of commodities. The OPEC appears to have exploited this power.

(c) On the demand side, the assumption of unchanging conditions also ignores marketing costs and uncertainties. The introduction of such costs which are often not proportional to total quantity, but increasing and discontinuous functions as new markets are tapped, may justify bilateral trading arrangements which eliminate many of the marketing costs and the risks associated with breaking into new markets. In the absence of uncertainty and marketing costs, such arrangements can easily be shown to be inferior.

(d) Nor is the unchanging conditions assumption consistent with the existence of increasing returns to scale for which there is considerable evidence in manufacturing (Pratten, 1971; UN, 1964).

Increasing returns give an advantage to the firstcomer. This, of course, has been one of the justifications of infant industry protection, but while it is a justification it also contributes to the inefficiency of protection, since a protectionist policy tends to confine the market to that of the home market, which in the case of many LDCs may be too small to exploit the economies of scale. There thus appears to be an impossible dilemma. On the one hand, free trade appears to justify the continued hegemony of the firstcomer, because of increasing returns; on the other hand, the protectionist policy which appears, therefore, to be justified is doomed to failure because markets are too small in view of these same increasing returns. Both free trade and protectionist cases need modification in the light of increasing returns: free trade has to be accompanied by selective subsidisation of exports; protectionist arrangements need to extend to a number of countries to ensure adequate 'home' markets.

(e) While the theoretical argument for free trade has been adapted to allow for technological change (Black and Streeten, 1957; Johnson, 1958; Meier, 1968), it has, on the whole, been done only in a very formal way. The usual assumption made is that of unchanging technology. The biased source and nature of technological change has particular implications for LDCs' trade policy. This is discussed further below.

(f) Along with the assumption of unchanging technology goes that of instant and painless adjustment (Haberler, 1950). Of course, in the absence of technological change, not much adjustment is needed, which makes this assumption easier to accept, though even here the move towards free trade requires some adjustment, which may be particularly costly for LDCs (indeed in some cases impossibly costly).[3] But once technological change is intro-duced, adjustment possibilities and costs are of key importance.

There are other unrealistic assumptions (e.g. that of full employment). In general, relaxation of the assumptions (a) to (f) favours neither the free trade nor the protectionist argument; rather it suggests, as has been argued above, that these are false alternatives, and some intermediate trading arrangements may be preferable. In particular, it will be argued that different arguments apply towards trade between developed and developing countries as com-pared with trade between developing countries. It will be argued that North–South (a shorthand for developed–developing country) trade may inhibit development, while South–South trade (trade between developing countries) may extend it. It will also be argued that current and historical trading arrangements favour North–South trade and discourage South–South trade. Finally, possible institutional arrangements to offset this bias (and indeed extend an opposite bias) will be discussed.

Different approaches to international trade

Different theories of international trade conflict both as to the predicted direction of trade, and to the gains from such trade. Most of the discussion centres on manufactures rather than primary products. This is mainly because there appears to be less choice about the direction of trade for primary products, since location of production is largely determined by natural factors, and location of consumption depends largely on income levels. Consequently, however it is organised, there is likely to continue to be a net flow of primary products from the South to the North. In what follows we shall be mainly concerned with trade in manufactured products, where choices about location of production and consumption are much greater.

The neo-classical approach to international trade – commonly described as the Heckscher-Ohlin approach – which is based on the theory of comparative advantage, predicts that trade will be most likely between *unlike* economies, and that the gains from trade will be greatest where conditions are most dissimilar. This means that trade will be greatest, and the gains largest, between North and South, where factor endowments and consequently costs of production differ most. The theory predicts that the advanced countries will export capital-intensive goods to the underdeveloped countries, which in return will export labour-intensive goods to them.

However, the theory has been shown to be factually wrong in two important respects.

Table 2. *Direction of exports, by value, 1970*[a]

Exports from	To North (%)	To South (%)	Total
World	79.8	20.2	100.0
North	80.2	19.8	100.0
South	78.2	21.7	100.0

[a] Market economies only.
SOURCE: UN *Monthly Bulletin of Statistics*, December 1971.

(1) Trade flows are greater, and they have increased faster, between rich countries and regions (North–North) than between rich and poor countries (North–South). As Table 2 shows, the developed countries account for about four-fifths of total trade (roughly the same proportion as that of income). There is no tendency for trade between countries with dissimilar factor endowments (North–South) to be greater than trade between similar countries. In fact the proportion of trade accounted for by North and South countries is very similar for both North and South, with a slight tendency for greater trade between *similar* groups than dissimilar groups. Over time, trade has increased fastest between *North* countries, and least fast between South countries; this is particularly marked for manufactured goods (see Table 3). The trends over time may, in part, be due to relaxation of restrictions between rich countries and the imposition of restrictions between rich and poor countries. But they are too strong for this to be the whole explanation. Evidently, given the increasing trade and specialisation between advanced countries, differences in factor endowment leading to differences

in comparative advantage cannot be the whole explanation of trade. Other explanations involving increasing returns, similarity of demand and technology must be introduced.

Table 3. *Export growth rates, by direction, by value,[a] 1960–70*

Direction of exports	Total (%)	Manufactures (%)
World	2.5	3.0
North to North	2.9	3.4
South to North	2.0	3.2
North to South	1.9	2.1
South to South	1.8	1.3

[a] Market economies only.
SOURCE: UN *Monthly Bulletin of Statistics*, December 1971.

(2) Leontief, in a famous 'paradox' showed that US exports were labour-intensive relatively to her imports. This paradox has been 'explained' by the heavy human capital content of US exports. This explanation, which takes us far from the simple factor endowment view, tends to turn the theory into a tautology.[4] There is a further difficulty about using factor endowment as an independent explanation of trade. In its use to describe natural resources – e.g. climate, and, therefore, agricultural production potential, or mineral resource availability – endowment may be taken as largely independent of economic development and trade. But once one uses it to describe man made factors, like capital goods, educated manpower, etc., then the endowment is itself a product of the economic development of the region, and may, therefore, be a product of past trade developments; current policies cannot, therefore, take factor endowment as given but must regard it as one of the variables which may be affected by policy.

Myrdal's theory of cumulative causation (1957) makes an economy's current efficiency a product of its past history. It is argued that advantages are cumulative, so that any initial competitive edge results in further increases in efficiency leading to a cumulatively greater advantage: similar economies at a competitive disadvantage may contract cumulatively. Cumulative advantages arise from different types of economies of scale. While some types of economy of scale may be offset by subsidies, those which relate to the size of the economy as a whole may be impossible to offset in this way. This is true of most of the dynamic economies – i.e. advantages accruing from a rapid rate of growth. Dynamic economies of scale arise from positive association between growth and resource accumulation (of domestic and foreign savings and skills), and growth and technical progress, particularly the introduction of new and improved products and methods of production.

Cumulative causation means that even where economies start equal they are unlikely to remain so since if one or other gains a competitive edge it will become cumulative. But if economies start from a position of inequality, then cumulative causation may work to prevent the less developed economy developing. This, broadly, is how many see the relations between North and South (Griffin, 1974) and the main reason why most South countries are anxious to protect their economics against more advanced countries. The theory explains why, with free trade, far from factor price equalisation, factor price divergence tends to occur, as in the first half of the twentieth century. The dangers – for the less developed – of cumulative causation working to their disadvantage are greater, the more unequal the initial position. Within the South, countries start much more nearly equal. (Nonetheless, as will be seen, there are large divergencies in efficiency between South countries, and there is a danger that these would increase with freer trade between South countries.)

Myrdal does not question the direction of trade suggested by the classical approach, but the predicted consequences from such trade. However, Burenstam-Linder (1961) has argued that the direction of trade for manufactured products is likely to be the opposite of the classical predictions, being greatest between similar countries and least for dissimilar countries. He argues that the nature of products consumed varies with income level and will be most similar for countries at an equal stage of development. Innovation and production are undertaken first for the home market; exports follow once the home market is established. These exports will find a market in countries with patterns of consumption similar to those of the home market – that is, countries at a similar stage of development. The evidence of the rapid growth in North–North trade supports his contention. However, as shown above, South–South trade has grown less fast than the other categories of trade. Factors which, for the most part, he ignores, help explain this.

First, during the colonial era North–South channels of trade – communications, transport and trading arrangements – were developed, while restrictions were imposed on South–South communications and trade.[5] With some recent exceptions, trading arrangements since the colonial era have followed this pattern. Hence, trade has not been left to follow natural channels but has had a sort of North–South straitjacket imposed on it.

Secondly, the Linder thesis does not allow for the transfer of technology, and in particular multinational firms' investment. The transfer means that technology developed for the home market in one country may be transferred abroad and the products not only produced and consumed abroad, but actually exported back to the home country. While there are all sorts of market difficulties that make this process very unusual for local South firms, multinational firms may transfer production location overseas without meeting market difficulties in their home country. The product cycle theory (Hirsch, 1967; Vernon, 1966) predicts that location of production will be transferred overseas in this way for 'mature' products, to take advantage of lower labour costs, especially in poor countries; advanced countries will produce and export new products. The flow of trade will thus be North–South for new ('technological gap') products (Hufbauer, 1966; Posner, 1961), and South–North for mature products. Export of labour-intensive parts from South to North also occurs mainly via the multinationals (Helleiner, 1973). North–North trade occurs as different advanced countries innovate and exploit economies of scale in different products, exporting those in which they have gained a technological advantage. According to this type of analysis, South–South trade is least likely to occur, since South countries are not innovators and, with roughly equally low labour costs and a desire to protect their own employment, do not benefit from importing low cost products from each other.

The concentration of innovation in the North is very important in explaining the nature and consequences of international trade. The virtual absence of innovation among South countries, particularly in product development, means that North products are at a great advantage in all markets. Innovations – in both products and techniques – have had, simultaneously, two consequences. On the one hand, they have increased output in relation to resource use, economising on inputs and improving the efficiency of products. On the other hand, they have been associated with changed factor use and increased income levels of consumers. More recent product innovations have tended to be labour-saving and investment-using in production, and have been designed for richer consumers; indeed, a good deal of what constitutes a higher level of income is this improvement in product nature and quality (Stewart, 1972 and 1974 b). These trends in innovation reflect the resource availability and income levels of consumers in the countries in which the innovations occur. The difficulty, for South countries, is that the two tendencies go together. While it is clearly to the advantage of poor countries to make use of developments that economise in resource use, they are unable to do so without also being affected by the changed pattern of resource use and income level. The dominance of North products in South consumption thus means that the products consumed are designed for higher income levels than those typical in the South. The consequence is a distortion in the pattern of consumption in the South. This distortion is partly a question of income distribution, with inequality of income distribution producing consumers with income levels similar to those typical in the North, despite the very large differences in average *per capita* incomes. The Linder thesis fails to allow for differences in income distribution. Distortions also occur in the balance of consumption by individual consumers, with disproportionately large amounts spent on the consumption of some items to the detriment of others, often to the detriment of balance in nutrition and, more generally, in living.

Technological linkages reinforce the dominance of North products. If one North product is selected, because, for example, it is more efficient than the alternatives, it tends to require the consumption of many other North products which are linked to it as complementary items for inputs or consumption. These, in turn, generate further requirements for North products. For example, suppose an underdeveloped country decides to use modern tractors because of the high productivity so engendered. As a result the country may also need skilled drivers, high class mechanics, high grade petrol; modern fertilisers may be required as a complementary input, as well as large scale methods of processing, storing and packing the resulting product. If it is decided to manufacture any of these items, then modern quality materials and methods will be required. Each of the requirements for other North products leads to further linkages with other advanced country products. These linkages mean that it is very difficult to confine the choice of advanced country products to a few essential items. The process of trade itself also imposes requirements; for example, docks appropriate to advanced country ships, airports to receive advanced country planes, communications networks which their firms require.

The combination of concentration of innovation in the North and the linkages between products, largely explains the dominance of North products. Income distribution plays a part, as a consequence as well as cause. The link between products and income distribution can be seen most clearly in public goods, where the provision of high income type goods, e.g. modern hospitals, is at the expense of low income services, such as rural clinics, which would reach much greater numbers of people.

Production techniques for innovations in the North are designed mainly to suit conditions there, using relatively much investment, skill, and modern management technique per unskilled employee. So long as North products are imported this need not directly affect production styles in the South. But once import substitution occurs and North products are reproduced in the South, the production techniques have to be adopted. Similarly, with the product cycle, if the South attempts to export North products back to the North, it needs to use the techniques developed in the North which are often inappropriate to the South.

Concentration of innovation in the North is thus a major explanation of why Linder is wrong in believing that trade is greatest among similar countries – when those countries are the poor countries. However, this same concentration is also the main reason why South–South trade *ought* to be developed, and North–South trade inhibited: in other words, Linder's thesis ought to be made true. Consumption patterns among South countries should be much more similar to each other than those of North countries: the sort of goods – for consumption and investment – developed for one country in the South should be more appropriate, both for production and consumption, to other South countries than the North products they currently import. However, so long as innovation in the South remains potential rather than actual, then such trade will also remain potential and the North will continue its dominance. The issue then turns on why there is so little innovation in the South.

There are, of course, many reasons but important among them are trade patterns. The long dominance of North products has established patterns of production and consumption that make it difficult to displace. Innovation in low income (which often also means low standard) goods needs protection against competition from established products and established innovators, particularly as a market structure has been developed which favours high income products. Historically, it has been shown that innovation responds to restraints and shortages (Rosenberg, 1969). The free import of goods from the North thus inhibits innovations in the South. Ironically, the protection policy established by many South countries has also inhibited these innovations, because while the policy has restricted the import of some goods it has been based on the import of North technology – products, machinery, parts and knowhow. The dominance of North technology has tended to be cumulative, through the links between products, resource accumulation and the build up of contacts and markets by those using this technology. Firms who have attempted to use their own technology have found that competition from other producers using the latest advanced technology and keeping abreast with the later product developments was impossible to deal with, and have often given up the attempt (Sercovich, 1974). Export of manufactures to the North tends to require the use of North technology to secure the standard appropriate to the high income of the North's consumers. Producing goods to the required standards tends to demand the use of sophisticated methods of production to ensure standardisation, strength, etc. In addition, it is often difficult to isolate export activities so that the items produced are confined to export and do not influence local consumption patterns (Stewart, 1974 b).

The need to export 'high' standard goods is, at present, just as great for South–South as South–North trade because all the difficulties faced by local South innovators on their home market are multiplied in other South countries, where they face competition from the North. A co-ordinated policy to encourage South–South trade would provide the South innovators with the markets they require, and hence, in the end, would be likely to prove self-justifying. Developing countries individually are too small to be successful innovators across-the-board. But it is across-the-board innovation that is required to develop a system of appropriate products and techniques, to prevent the continued domination of North products, with their continuing changes in increasingly inappropriate directions. Quite apart from the adjustment costs so imposed, this means that the pattern of development will become increasingly inappropriate over time. While international trade is only one dimension of a complex problem,[6] possibly even a subordinate dimension, its redirection may well be a necessary condition and a starting point for more appropriate patterns of development.

The recent discussion of 'unequal exchange' (Emmanuel, 1972) provides support, many would say 'metaphysical' support, for a redirection towards South–South trade. Unequal exchange arises in trade between North and South, basically, from unequal wage rates, so that one hour's labour in the North receives substantially more return than one hour's labour in the South from the production of goods and services which are traded between North and South. This does not mean that reorientation need produce greater absolute gains for anyone. But it does mean that reorientation would reduce this aspect of North–South inequality.

The case for South–South trade

In part, the case for a reorientation of trade towards South–South patterns and against North–South ones is a matter of offsetting historic biases in the opposite direction. But there is also a case for positive bias. The process of cumulative causation benefits the North and may harm the South: inappropriate and expensive technology seems to be an inevitable feature of continued emphasis on North–South trade. But autarky is not possible for most underdeveloped countries because of their small size. Developing an appropriate technology is not a possibility for individual countries. South–South trade appears to provide an answer in extending the market and thus enabling countries to exploit the gains from economies of trade and specialisation, providing conditions in which innovations towards appropriate technology are more likely. South–South trade may also help insulate the South against fluctuations in the North and, by reducing dependence, may increase the bargaining power of the South. The best counter to the colonial and neo-colonial policy of *divide and rule* is *unite and fight*.

There are, however, some difficulties. First, initially a switch to South trade from North trade may involve a switch to less efficient products and processes, because of the technological dominance of the North and its ability to exploit economies of scale. Any resulting cost is likely to be short run, because the switch should enable the South to develop efficient and more appropriate products and processes. In any case, for many countries there may be short run gains to offset the short run losses, in the form of market outlets for their products in other underdeveloped countries. This, of course, assumes (an assumption for which there is abundant evidence) spare capacity in industries in the South. But, given the similarity of patterns of development in many countries, spare capacity is often present in identical and not complementary industries. The more developed countries are likely to gain most from short run market extension because they are most likely to have spare capacity in industries (e.g. capital goods industries) for which there is a net import demand from other underdeveloped countries.

The different stages of development of underdeveloped countries present the second major difficulty. The tendency for development to polarise, discussed above in terms of North–South development, is likely to occur between different underdeveloped countries if the more backward areas have no way of protecting themselves against the faster developing areas. The gains from more South–South trade may be unfairly distributed initially, and the dynamic gains may be cumulatively unfairly distributed. Therefore, any system for promoting South–South trade needs to incorporate some means through which the losing areas can protect themselves against the gaining areas, and of securing a fair distribution of gains. Although fair distribution of gains is obviously an important aim, the essential feature of any arrangement must be that no area loses *absolutely*: this is consistent with an unfair distribution of gains.

Thirdly, historical trading conditions have been responsible for the growth of North–South transport, communications and marketing arrangements that do not exist on a South–South basis. It is well known that until recently in order to travel from West to East Africa one had to pass through London or Paris. Communications are even worse between different continents. Such trade as there is on a South–South basis is thus mostly confined to one region, and is not interregional, as is shown in Table 4. The absence of transport and communications imposes a major obstacle to trading ties. This is a vicious circle because until trading ties are formed, improved transport and communications will not appear justified.

Table 4. *Direction of exports from developing economies to other developing economies, 1969* [a]

Exports from	To Latin America (%)	To Developing Africa (%)	To Middle East (%)	To Asia (%)
A. Total exports				
Latin America	56.9	1.9	2.3	5.0
Developing Africa	5.9	57.8	12.5	19.4
Middle East	7.6	20.1	34.4	33.9
Asia	3.6	9.5	8.6	76.6
B. Manufactured exports				
Latin America	96.1	0.8	0.6	1.1
Developing Africa	5.6	73.2	12.7	8.2
Middle East	3.8	18.9	56.1	22.0
Asia	4.2	13.9	11.5	67.6

[a] Totals do not add up to 100 because of the exclusion of 'Rest of the World'.
SOURCE: UN *Monthly Bulletin of Statistics*, March 1971, Special Table E.

Fourthly, the economies of countries in the South have been (and are) dominated by the North–South connection to such an extent that it is extremely difficult for them to break out. For example, marketing and production franchises have been given to firms from the advanced countries. Technology purchase agreements include clauses restricting exports to third countries and tying imports to the advanced country.[7] Export credits are available for imports from the North. Tied aid requires purchases from the North. Links with advanced country firms have created powerful vested interests in the South among politicians, civil servants, businessmen, and the army, which are likely to resist any change in direction. Apart from the specific vested interests, the pattern of development arising from trade, capital and technology flows with the advanced countries has been responsible for an oligopolistic market structure and an inegalitarian income distribution which together reinforce North–South ties. Thus, to establish a market for advanced country products it was helpful to establish an unequal income distribution; such an income distribution in any case tended to emerge from the type of technology adopted. Any major change in the pattern of development towards more appropriate products would require a major change in income distribution, which will naturally be resisted. The existing market structure and income distribution generate demands for the latest products and technology from the North, all of which makes any appropriate, local technology difficult to establish. Thus, even in those countries which have technological resources and which have developed some viable technologies, foreign technology continues to be imported (Sercovich, 1974; Subrahmanian, 1972).

All this means that even in one country, let alone the whole of the Third World, a policy of orientation away from North–South to South–South trade, with associated changes in products and income distribution, would be difficult both to introduce and to carry out. But the problem is that the policy needs to be adhered to quite widely and rigorously for the major gains to be realised. For example, suppose one country did reorient exports and imports towards other Third World countries. If the other countries continued to use the latest technology and produce the latest products, the change in policy would change neither the nature of imported products nor that of imported technology. Similarly, if the other countries continued to import freely from the North, then the country which had readjusted trade would have to compete with goods from the North, in a consumer market that generated demand primarily for the latest North type products. Hence, to be successful, the country would have to import North technology, and would not be able to use appropriate technology or sell appropriate products.

The above arguments again are primarily concerned with trade in manufactures. Neither the cumulative causation argument nor the inappropriate technology argument applies to a significant extent to primary products. Even for manufactured goods there are exceptions, where continued export to or import from the North is obviously the best policy; for example, processing of primary products for export. Institutional change needs to be sufficiently flexible to allow for exceptions.

Institutional arrangements

The earlier parts of this paper consider the arguments for changing the direction of trade from North–South towards South–South for developing countries. It was concluded that there were considerable advantages for the underdeveloped countries for, at the least, offsetting existing biases in favour of North–South trade, by institutional arrangements which favour South–

South trade. This section briefly considers some institutional arrangements that might achieve this. Possible arrangements include: (a) trade negotiations involving reduced tariffs on inter-South trade; these could range from arrangements confined to tariffs, to those involving overall co-ordination of economic policy; (b) monetary reforms which effectively favour South–South as against North–South trade; these include formal monetary unions, exchange rate policy, and the issue of special South international money to finance South–South trade.

In theory, one can devise a variety of arrangements, classified under either of these headings, which would have equivalent effects (e.g. a change in tariffs can be devised which is theoretically equivalent to a change in exchange rates). In practice, there tend to be important differences between the different policies in terms of negotiating problems presented, administrative problems, the likelihood of countries breaking away from the arrangements, and the ease with which countries may safeguard their special interests. The divisive tendencies within the Third World are probably as strong as any other divisions in the world. Although originally fostered by the influence of colonial powers, there are now substantial vested interests within the various Third World countries that gain by the divisions. What is needed is to create actual, not just potential, interests who would benefit by greater unity. Paradoxically, at present it is the multinational firms who press for more unity in some parts of the world (e.g. LAFTA) as they gain by the rationalisation of their production facilities. Once South–South trade begins to take off, interests which favour it will accumulate and further moves towards relaxation of restrictions will become easier. It is the initial change which is the most difficult to achieve.

From the point of view of the earlier discussion, there are certain features which we should look for in the institutional arrangements. These are as follows.

(i) The arrangements should cover as many South countries as possible, and not be confined to countries in a particular region. From this it follows that policies requiring too much political co-operation of a long term nature are not suitable. This rules out, for example, fully fledged customs unions, at least initially.

(ii) The arrangements should, if necessary, permit the least developed countries to safeguard their industries and their terms of trade against the more developed. Thus, if the arrangements involve multilateral abandonment of trade restrictions (tariff and non-tariff), the less developed should be permitted either to proceed more slowly with these policies, or to have the effects in part offset by special financial arrangements (e.g. direct subsidies).

(iii) The arrangements should allow countries which consider that the benefits outweigh the costs to continue to put their main efforts into North–South trade; this applies particularly to countries which are and will remain mainly sellers of primary commodities.

These conditions effectively rule out most trading arrangements. Some, simply confined to preferences on tariffs (and non-tariff barriers) and not involving any step towards full economic union, have been tried, to a small extent, on an overall South–South basis,[8] but they neither make provision for the weaker areas to safeguard their developments, nor do they include provision for inter-country subsidies. Hence, they might tend to weaken the least developed areas, and for this reason are unlikely to be effectively introduced, or, if introduced, adhered to. On the other hand, more fully fledged customs unions do normally include some provision for protection of the weaker areas; but they require a degree of political cohesion that makes them difficult to extend beyond a relatively small politically cohesive area.[9]

Trading arrangements have been treated as *alternatives* to monetary arrangements. They are alternatives in the sense that one can achieve what the other could, if properly designed and executed. But they are also potential *complements* in the sense that one may support and encourage the other, and the use of one by no means rules out the other. This complementarity is recognised in many economic unions between countries, which normally require both tariff and monetary co-operation. Trading and monetary arrangements may also be in conflict, one offsetting the effects of the other. For example, exchange rate changes may induce trade of a certain kind, but this can be offset by tariffs or other trade restrictions. Similarly, tariff concessions may be effectively negated by monetary arrangements. Consequently, one should not treat monetary and trade arrangements as independent, but consider them together. (Industrial plan co-ordination is another vital area where policies may complement and support trading arrangements or may conflict with them. Where they conflict the trading policies can be rendered useless.)

Monetary reforms which would favour South–South trade include: (i) credit or payments unions between underdeveloped countries, so that payments between the countries are eased administratively, and credit extended between the countries; (ii) the issue of a form of international paper money, Rocnabs, to be used in (part) payment for goods and services from developing countries (Stewart and Stewart, 1972); (iii) exchange rate policy such that the South as a whole acts as a bloc with a joint devaluation against the North.

Formally, each of these alternatives can be designed to achieve the same effects, in terms of incentives for trade expansion among South countries. They need not be alternatives, but may be combined. We shall examine each in somewhat more detail.

(i) The first purpose of credit or payments unions is normally the easing of payments between the different countries, where lack of convertibility of currencies is inhibiting trade. This was the main feature of the European Payments Union. Lack of convertibility is not a major problem among South countries, as it was in postwar Europe;[10] in so far as it is a problem among South countries, such a union would ease it. The second purpose of payments unions is to extend credit among the members enabling them to expand trade among themselves without risking the loss of (scarce) convertible currencies. Many variations are possible: 100 per cent credit, up to some limit, may be extended; or some maximum proportion of debts may be met by credit. The net effect is to provide a considerable incentive for countries who are likely to be in deficit with other South countries, to expand their purchases from them, and meet the deficit with credit. But other countries, who are likely to be in surplus with South countries, but in deficit with the North, may not wish to sell their goods in exchange for such credit. They require North currency to finance their North deficit. Insofar, however, as their total sales are limited by lack of markets, any additional sales to the South need not reduce their earnings of North currencies; and they will be able to buy more South goods replacing North goods and diminishing their North deficit. If the credit is only allowed in part payment for the deficit with South countries, then sales to the South will earn these countries some convertible currencies, usable in the North. In addition, there may be arrangements whereby unused credits may be sold (to the central organisation or to deficit countries) in exchange for convertible currencies, at a market clearing rate.

(ii) The proposed scheme for the issue of international money, Rocnabs, for use among South countries is very similar in its operation to a credit union. In fact, if we call credit with the union, Rocnabs, then the effects of the two schemes may be identical. Rocnabs are to be issued in fixed quantities, distributed among the countries in accordance with some formula (trade, or income, for example) to be accepted in part payment for goods and services from other South countries. The part payment aspect means that countries do earn some convertible currency if they run up a surplus with the other South countries. Again, some system of selling Rocnabs from countries which have accumulated them, to countries which have sold theirs in exchange for convertible currency, is required to prevent the scheme seizing up, if there are some countries who are in permanent surplus with the other countries. This reselling or recycling operation is similar to the market clearing operation of the credit union.

(iii) A joint devaluation by all South countries against the North would have the effect of increasing the relative prices of North as against South goods, thus presenting an incentive for the South countries to buy from each other, rather than the North. They would, at the same time, have an increased incentive to *sell* to the North. The scheme resembles the other schemes in that the North currency content of any given sales to other South countries would decrease relatively to that of sales to the North.

Despite the similarities, there are significant differences between the three schemes. In the first place, the problems of administration differ. A credit union involves continuous administration, whereas Rocnabs may be issued once and for all, and the market clearing sales of Rocnabs can be conducted through normal market channels without any special machinery. The joint devaluation scheme is once and for all, like the Rocnab scheme. But there are administrative problems – in particular effective mass devaluation against North currencies can only be achieved with the co-operation of the North, whose buying and selling of currencies may determine the exchange rates. There is a second major difference between the credit/Rocnab schemes and the devaluation scheme. The latter operates directly on prices paid and received by traders. The former only operates on the incentives of those responsible for monetary and economic management. Hence, the devaluation scheme would not require any further change in policy to encourage a redirection of trade. The credit/Rocnab schemes would have no immediate effect on prices traders face, and would, therefore, only affect trading patterns to the extent that governments pursued tariff, direct purchase, and bilateral trading policies favourable to inter-South trade, as encouraged by the scheme. In a sense, the main incentive effect of the schemes would be on the economic managers; the managed would only be affected via subsequent changes in policy. This has advantages as well as disadvantages. The advantages are that the governments could operate the incentive towards South trade selectively – picking out, for example, manufactures, where the main arguments for trade expansion arise, and leaving the export of primary commodities unaffected. In contrast, across-the-board devaluation could mean that the primary producers suffer possibly undesirable deterioration in the terms of trade. The disadvantage is that the scheme might be ineffective in encouraging redirection of trade.

As argued above, the schemes need not be alternatives; the most desirable solution might be a combined scheme. A credit union could be accompanied by the issue of paper money, Rocnabs; and both could better achieve their effect with exchange rate (and/or tariff) changes.

It has been argued that the factors that inhibit South–South trade are not monetary at all but tradition, lack of market contacts, lack of transport links, and poor quality goods. In part, clearly, all these factors are responsible for the small amount of South–South trade. Also, as argued earlier, technological backwardness means that the North captures all the 'technological gap' trade. Monetary reforms may nonetheless be effective in producing an expansion of South–South trade, even if the explanation of low levels of trade is not to be found in monetary institutions, since financial incentives can compensate for other disadvantages – poor quality goods may be a best buy if they are cheap enough. Expensive and cumbersome transport routes may also be compensated for. What cannot be compensated for is the total absence of a crucial link; e.g. where there is *no* method of getting the goods from *A* to *B* then financial incentives will not make a difference. But the way this has been posed shows that it is not a likelihood. If goods can be transported from *A* (South country) to *C* (North country) and from *C* to *B* (South country), then goods *can* go from *A* to *B* via *C*, and given sufficient financial incentive, they will do so. In any case, factors such as transport cannot be taken as given, except in the very short run. They are the outcome of trading ties. This is an externality of trading, which means that there is a tendency for trade to expand in traditional channels. Routes between A and B will only be developed if there is seen to be potential trade between A and B. If the absence of routes is taken as an argument against developing trading ties, then the *status quo* trading situation will always be seen to be justified, even though an assessment of the relative advantages of A–B and A–C trade, allowing for the transport and other links that will develop with the trade, would argue for the creation of A–B routes and trade.

Monetary incentives for the creation of new trading ties will therefore: (i) compensate for other trade inhibiting effects; (ii) by so doing, and by initiating or increasing trade, lead to the development of other factors, the absence of which may have been primarily responsible for the lack of trade; and (iii) provide an incentive for governments to act directly in removing other impediments to trade.

One question that arises, for all these schemes, is how far they can accommodate opting out countries. Countries may opt out because of various pressures from North ties; or because they are surplus foreign exchange countries and therefore have little incentive to come in. The latter applies most obviously to the oil exporters. In fact, many of the arguments in favour of South–South trade have little to do with foreign exchange shortage and apply equally to the surplus foreign exchange countries. Nonetheless, the schemes must clearly be consistent with opting out or they would come to nothing. Any of the schemes *would*, in fact, be perfectly manageable with provisions for opting out, so that only some South countries were participants; but their point and effectiveness would diminish with increasing numbers of non-participating countries. The main advantages to any one country come from the action taken by others, rather than from its own action: e.g. the agreement of others to accept Rocnabs, for which its own agreement is a return.

Countries may wish to isolate 'hard currency' commodities from the schemes – that is, confine Rocnab payments and receipts to those commodities for which there is no 'hard currency' market – probably mainly manufactures. They may achieve this isolation, if they wish, by selling all such 'hard currency' commodities to the North (including some for resale to the South)[11] or by increasing their price when sold direct to the South. The point is that the price of these commodities is determined by world demand and supply, in terms of North currencies, and it is unnecessary, therefore, for countries to accept reduced hard currency returns for them, *unless* they believe they will gain still more in earnings from their manufactures, by the extension of markets brought about by the schemes. In contrast, such schemes may *extend* markets for 'soft currency' products, as well as bringing about the advantages discussed earlier, of a redirection of given quantities of trade.

It was argued above that a necessary feature of any scheme was that it protected the weaker areas. Some trading schemes do not do this. But the monetary schemes do, insofar as they allow the weaker areas to protect themselves, by tariff and other forms of protection, and by action on the exchange rate. The joint devaluation scheme, though in theory it permits countries to vary their exchange rates relative to one another, would, in practice, be difficult to combine with the kind of freedom over exchange rate changes that countries prefer and need. For this reason, the other schemes seem more likely to be adopted. This is particularly likely to be true for countries with long ties with particular North countries, who might refuse to devalue against these currencies, but for whom extension and receipt of credit with other South countries would be acceptable.

In conclusion, it must be emphasised that whichever approach is adopted initially should not be regarded as exclusive. It may fruitfully be combined with other aggregative approaches to greater South–South trade – whether monetary, trading or institutional (e.g. new transport links). Aggregative approaches to South–South trade are perfectly consistent with further moves towards regional economic groups. In fact, the more successful the regional economic groupings, the easier such schemes would be to introduce, since the smaller would be the number of independent parties concerned.

Notes

1 I am grateful to Paul Streeten for comments on an earlier draft, and to the participants in the Uppsala meeting (which I was unable to attend) whose comments were reported to me by G. K. Helleiner.

2 Many who advocate *freer* trade do not advocate unqualified free trade – the term 'free traders' should, therefore, be regarded as shorthand for a (sometimes) more qualified position.

3 Hufbauer and Chilas (1973, p. 13), looking at trade within the US conclude 'the analysis illustrates the very substantial *continuing* adjustment process which accompanies free commodity trade. The elimination of trade barriers not only creates an *initial* adjustment burden, as industries relocate to areas where specific factors are most favourable; there is also an on-going movement of capital and labor in response to changing circumstances. By the yardstick of international experience, the continuing adjustment process is formidable in magnitude, quite apart from the initial burden of industrial relocation.'

4 'The introduction of factor categories, such as "technical labor", i.e. capital-intensive labor, is a gimmick which, when its superficial advantages are more closely examined, turns out to rob the factor proportions theory of all meaningfulness.' Burenstam-Linder, 1961, p. 86.

5 Some evidence of this for West Africa is offered by Amin (1973) and Hopkins (1973). Robana (1973) describes how the orientation of all the Maghreb States is with European countries, particularly France. Transport has been developed so that it is cheaper between the States and South Europe than among the States themselves. Insurance, banking and other commercial ties have all been developed with France.

6 Other aspects, particularly the relationship between technology and income distribution and employment are discussed in Stewart, 1974 a.

7 There is abundant (and growing) evidence of such restrictive practices, much of which has been established in the Andean Pact and in the UNCTAD, see e.g. UNCTAD, 1971.

8   In 1971 a GATT protocol established mutual trade preferences among sixteen developing countries.
9   Customs unions even among such similar countries as the East African Common Market countries have met with formidable obstacles – political and economic. For a general discussion of the difficulties involved see Dell (1963) and Maritano (1973).
10 Though it does undoubtedly impose some obstacles to trade. Thus trade among the Maghreb States has to be financed in francs because of the inconvertibility of the States' currencies (Robana, 1973).
11 In many commodity markets this happens anyway.

References

Amin, Samir, 1973. *Economic Development in West Africa*. Harmondsworth: Penguin.

Black, J. and Streeten, P. P., 1957. La balance commerciale, les termes de l'échange et la croissance cconomique. *Economie Appliquée*. Reprinted (in English) as Appendix 1 in Streeten, P.P., *Economic Integration Aspects and Problems*, Sythoff, Leyden, 1964.

Burenstam-Linder, S., 1961. *An Essay on Trade and Transformation*. Stockholm: Almqvist and Wikesell.

Chenery, Hollis B. and Hughes, Helen, 1973. Industrialization and trade trends: some issues for the 1970s. In *Prospects for Partnership, Industrialization and Trade Policies in the 1970s*, (ed.) Helen Hughes, pp. 3–31. Baltimore and London: Johns Hopkins.

Dell, Sidney, 1963. *Trade Blocs and Common Markets*. New York: Knopf.

Emmanuel, Arghiri, 1972. *Unequal Exchange, A Study of the Imperialism of Trade*. New York and London: Monthly Review Press.

Fei, J. and Ranis, G., 1975. A model of growth and employment in the open dualistic economy, the case of Korea and Taiwan. *Journal of Development Studies*, forthcoming.

Griffin, K., 1974. The international transmission of inequality. *World Development*, 2 (no. 3) 3–14.

Haberler, G., 1950. Some problems in the pure theory of foreign trade. *Economic Journal*, 60, 223–60.

Helleiner, G. K., 1973. Manufactured exports from less developed countries and multinational firms. *Economic Journal*, 83, 21–47.

Hirsch, Seev, 1967. *Location of Industry and International Competitiveness*. Oxford: Clarendon Press.

Hopkins, A. G., 1973. *An Economic History of West Africa*. London: Longman.

Hufbauer, G. C., 1966. *Synthetic Materials and the Theory of International Trade*. London: Duckworth.

Hufbauer, G. C. and Chilas, J. G., 1973. Specialisation by industrial countries: extent and consequences. In *The International Division of Labour, Problems and Perspectives*, (ed.) Herbert Giersch, pp. 3–38. Kiel: Institut für Weltwirtschaft.

Islam, N., 1967. Comparative costs, factor proportions and industrial efficiency in Pakistan. *Pakistan Development Review*, 7, 213–46.

Johnson, H. G., 1958. *International Trade and Economic Growth*. London: Allen and Unwin.

Lipsey, R. G., 1970. *The Theory of Customs Unions: A General Equilibrium Analysis*. London: Weidenfeld and Nicolson.

Little, Ian, Scitovsky, Tibor, Scott, Maurice, 1970. *Industry and Trade in Some Developing Countries*. London, New York and Bombay: Oxford University Press.

Maritano, Nino, 1970. *A Latin American Common Economic Community: history, policy and problems*. Notre Dame, Indiana: University of Notre Dame.

Meade, J., 1955. *The Theory of Customs Unions*. Amsterdam: North Holland Publishing Co.

Meier, G. M., 1968. *The International Economics of Development, Theory and Policy*. New York, Evanston and London: Harper and Row.

Myrdal, Gunnar, 1957. *Economic Theory and Under-developed Regions*. London: Duckworth.

Posner, M. V., 1961. International trade and technical change. *Oxford Economic Papers*, **13**, 323–41.

Pratten, C. F., 1971. *Economies of Scale in Manufacturing Industry*. Cambridge, London and New York: Cambridge University Press.

Robana, Abdurahman, 1973. *The Prospects for an Economic Community in North Africa: Managing Economic Integration in the Maghreb States*. New York: Praeger.

Robson, P. (ed.), 1971. *International Economic Integration*. Harmondsworth: Penguin.

Rosenberg, N., 1969. The direction of technological change: inducement mechanisms and focussing devices. *Economic Development and Cultural Change*, **18**, 1–24.

Sercovich, Francisco, 1974. Foreign Enterprise in the Transfer of Technology to Argentina. D.Phil. thesis, University of Sussex, unpublished.

Stewart, Frances, 1972. Choice of techniques in developing countries. *Journal of Development Studies*, **9**, 99–121.

1974 *a*. Technology and employment in less developed countries. *World Development*, **2** (no. 3) 17–46.

1974 *b*. Trade and technology. In *Trade Strategies for Development*, (ed.) P. P. Streeten, pp. 231–63. London: Macmillan.

Stewart, Frances and Stewart, M., 1972. Developing countries, trade and liquidity: a new approach. *The Banker*, **122**, 310–18.

Subrahmanian, K. K., 1972. *Imports of Capital and Technology, A Study of foreign collaborations in Indian Industry*. Bombay: People's Publishing House.

Tulloch, Peter, 1972. Developing countries and the enlargement of the EEC. *ODI Review*, **5**, 92–115, 133.

UN (United Nations, Department of Economic and Social Affairs), 1964. Plant size and economies of scale. *Industrialization and Productivity*, no. 8, 53–61.

UNCTAD (United Nations Conference on Trade and Development), 1971. *Restrictive business practices, Interim report by the UNCTAD secretariat*. New York: United Nations.

Vernon, R., 1966. International investment and international trade in the product cycle. *Quarterly Journal of Economics*, **80**, 190–207.

Viner, Jacob, 1950. *The Customs Union Issue*. New York: Carnegie Endowment for International Peace.

WDM (World Development Movement), 1972. *Textiles – A Protection Racket*.

PART II

Relations with transnational enterprises

6. Power, knowledge and development policy: relations between transnational enterprises and developing countries

CONSTANTINE V. VAITSOS

The structure of relations between countries and foreign controlled transnational enterprises is interpreted in traditional economic analysis as, fundamentally, one involving a harmony of interests. Traditional analysis concludes that mutual benefits can arise from the promotion of new economic activities induced by or originating from the flow of factors of production, goods and services across national boundaries. Such analysis has served as a convenient instrument for rationalising private or country interests as they are expressed in positions or government policies towards private direct investments abroad.

Alternative conclusions are reached if economic analysis is enriched to allow for imperfect world markets, distortions induced by certain government policies, costly and inequitably distributed productive knowledge, concentration of resources, and the effects of transnational enterprises on unequal exchange between and within countries as well as classes. Additional considerations arise if one also takes into account the effects of transnational enterprises on (i) the political composition and developmental objectives of the host economies; (ii) the resulting income distribution and the inducement of particular consumption patterns that are in accord with the market origin and product standardisation of such enterprises; and (iii) the displacement of domestically controlled economic activities and the limits that are created on economic and political self-reliance.

In the pages that follow we will discuss two underlying factors, that of *power* and its use and that of *knowledge*, as they affect the diverse considerations raised above with respect to transnational enterprises. With respect to power we will first consider the relationship that exists between government policies or the power position of the home countries of transnational enterprises and the international spread of such firms. Then we will explore certain power elements and their effects as they originate from: (*a*) the global activities of transnationals; (*b*) their centralised control in decision making; and (*c*) certain institutional considerations. With respect to knowledge, as related to power, we will discuss its significance in three areas where foreign firms concentrate their operations in the Third World, namely: (*a*) import substituting manufacturing activities; (*b*) the extractive and other commodities sectors; and (*c*) manufacturing activities for the purpose of exporting from developing countries. Our analysis will be directed so as to draw policy conclusions for the Third World countries.

Issues of power in the foreign investment model

A proper understanding of relations between developing countries and transnational enterprises needs to begin with an appreciation of three underlying and interrelated issues: first, the origin and manipulation of *power* among the parties involved; secondly, the manipulation of *risks* stemming from the potential exercise of power; and thirdly, the manipulation of *institutions* to reinforce certain power structures. We will start by treating the case of power and of risk as they apply in foreign investments and then deal with the case of institutions.

Power and official government policies

Economic reasoning often ascribes to markets a spontaneity in origin and a determinism in operations that originate from economic necessity which is itself related to scarcity and the behavioural propensities of economic actors. Thus the implications of government policies, as they relate to the foreign investment model, are only seen within the context of their effects upon the basic elements of scarcity and economic behaviour. Central are such considerations as tariff policies, exchange controls, tax systems, monetary instruments and liquidity, etc. Outside of these economic policies it is assumed that 'official policy has a rather limited direct role in determining the volume of private investment abroad' (Tripartite Report, 1972, p. 21). Yet, if markets are viewed as creatures of social and political systems, then their operations, given certain economic parameters and technical constraints, can be understood as being induced or suppressed through political decisions and institutional mechanisms both at the national and international level (Diaz-Alejandro, 1974, p. 2; Keynes, 1924, p. 585). Such an interpretation is particularly applicable to the phenomenon of foreign direct investments, especially as they take place in developing countries. Official policies and political decisions, both by home and host countries, have a direct bearing on the flow and the presence of direct investments. Hence, the effects of the latter and their treatment cannot be separated from the power relations that prompt such official policies.

Available statistics indicate that for many developing nations the country of origin of foreign investors is very closely linked to special political relations, spheres of economic influence and old colonial ties.[1] Table 1, showing participation in the total foreign investments received by various developing countries by major countries of origin, indicates a marked division of the Third World map into areas of economic influence. The figures presented in this table do not distinguish the manufacturing and service sectors from the extractive activities. The latter (which constitute about 50 per cent of the reported book value of foreign investments in developing countries) are much more linked to old colonial ties (for European nations) and to strong political control or military influence (in the case of the US),

Table 1. *Book value of US and European direct investments as a percentage of total investments reported by selected developing countries, end 1967*

United States	United Kingdom	France	Belgium	Italy
Africa	*Africa*	*Africa*	*Africa*	*Africa*
Libyan Arab Rep. 77.7	Nigeria 53.8	Algeria 71.7	Zaire 87.8	Somalia 83.3
Liberia 57.8	Zambia 79.6	Gabon 73.4	Rwanda 86.8	Tunisia 28.5
	Ghana 59.1	Senegal 87.4	Burundi 84.5	Dahomey 25.7
	(Rhodesia 83.3)	Cameroun 75.1		
	Kenya 78.8	Central African Rep. 91.8		
	Sudan 74.9	Niger 95.7		
	Malawi 92.7	Chad 80.4		
	Swaziland 96.6	Mali 76.9		
	Botswana 88.0			
Asia	*Asia*	*Asia*		
Philippines 88.4	India 64.6	South Vietnam 65.7		
Indonesia 73.2	Malaysia 74.3	Rep. of Khmer 88.2		
South Korea 92.3	Pakistan 59.5	New Caledonia 91.4		
Afghanistan 54.2	Sri Lanka 95.1	French Polynesia 72.7		
	Burma 92.8			
Middle East				
Kuwait 54.4				
Bahrein 91.8				
Israel 59.8				
Jordan 75.0				
Western Hemisphere	*Western Hemisphere*	*Western Hemisphere*		
Venezuela 73.0	British Honduras 70.2	French Antilles 71.7		
Mexico 76.4		French Guyana 100.0		
Panama 90.8				
Peru 84.4				
Colombia 86.2				
Honduras 97.7				
Dominican Rep. 81.1				
Guatemala 84.4				
Bolivia 82.9				
Costa Rica 89.3				
Chile 91.3				

SOURCE: OECD, 1972.

given their strategic importance for the economies of the developed countries. The manufacturing and service sectors show more diversity in investment patterns. Yet, even in this case, investment flows to developing countries are very strongly linked to overall political and economic links and historical ties such as those involving colonial domination. For example, as of 1971, approximately 60 per cent of the manufacturing subsidiaries of UK-based parent firms were in ex-colonies. (About 40 per cent of them were in less developed countries) (Vaupel and Curhan, 1973, pp. 104ff.). Similarly, more than half of foreign controlled manufacturing subsidiaries in ex-French colonies belonged to French enterprises, as of 1971 (Franko, 1975, p. V−9).[2] Also, as of 1967, more than two-thirds of foreign investments in Colombian manufacturing industry were of US origin. In the case of the Chilean manufacturing sector, for seven out of eleven industry groups, the US alone or with one other country accounted for more than 95 per cent of profit remissions, royalty earnings, and trade flows linked to foreign investment and technology imports (Vaitsos, 1974a, pp. 17, 81).[3]

Table 2. *Numbers of foreign manufacturing subsidiaries established, by country of parent, 1953–5 to 1968–70*

| | Nationality of parent firms | | | |
	US	UK	Continental Europe	Japan
1953–5	283	55	117	5
1956–8	439	94	131	14
1959–61	901	333	232	93
1962–4	959	319	229	160
1965–7	889	459	532	235
1968–70	n.a.	729	1,032	532

SOURCE: Tsurumi, 1974, p. 11. Data for all but Japan are from Vaupel and Curhan, 1973.

In the postwar era two phases of direct investment activity can be distinguished. During the 1950s and early 1960s the expanded presence and power (political and economic) of the United States in the world scene meant an increasing participation of US private interests in areas that previously were almost exclusively under European or Japanese influence.[4] By the late 1960s and early 1970s, however, with the recovery from the war completed and the expansion of the Western European and Japanese economies well under way, inroads were made by the latter in some areas where the US presence was previously predominant. The rate of increase in European and Japanese investments in the rest of the world was significantly greater than that of the US from the middle of the 1960s onwards (see Table 2).

The changes that have occurred in the last five to ten years have introduced a relatively wider distribution, with respect to the nationality of parent firms, in the world-wide operations of subsidiaries. They also reflect leader–follower behaviour on the part of transnational firms, with lagged participation by the followers within oligopolistic market structures. Finally, they reflect the firms' search for cheaper inputs, especially cheap and low-skilled labour, in developing countries, and a shift from a predominant concentration on import substitution towards world-wide sourcing and trade promotion (Helleiner, 1973; Adam, 1971).

The relatively more diversified share of the nationality of parent firms reflects the new multipolar structure of the world economy after the middle of the 1960s with the decline of the US hegemony (at least before the recent oil crisis). The activities of non-US enterprises are thus linked with the political economy of their home countries just as the US firms' expansion was linked to the predominant role of US political and economic interests in world affairs in previous years. During subsequent years the international spread of subsidiaries serves, in turn, to reinforce the economic interests of the home country of the parent.

Yet, certain important differences that reflect the inertia of world power relations from past decades still persist between parent firms of distinct national origin. One of these is the relatively very limited foreign investment activity of Japanese firms in North America and Europe as compared to firms from other developed countries. For example, as of January 1971, the major Japanese transnational enterprises had only 8 per cent of their manufacturing subsidiaries located in Europe and North America, while the rest were located in other parts of the world, predominantly in developing countries. The corresponding figure for US based transnationals (as of January 1968) was 52 per cent, that for the UK 42 per cent, for Germany 63 per cent, for France 58 per cent, and for Switzerland 64 per cent, all of them as of January 1971. (This situation might change from the mid 1970s onward as a result of political developments and the changing business strategy of Japanese firms.)[5]

Another persistent difference relates to the distinct geographic preferences for manufacturing investments in the Third World of parent firms from different developed countries. Japanese investments are predominantly concentrated in Asia while US and German subsidiaries are basically located in Latin America where the UK presence is small. The latter has a divided preference between Asia and Africa. All such preferences demonstrate historical ties of a political nature, expressed in economic relations. The distribution of foreign owned subsidiaries in the Third World is shown in Table 3.

The data presented on investment patterns by geographic area could be seriously understating the actual concentration for two reasons. First, the percentages have as base the total investments originating from various developed countries. If, instead, the table were inverted to show the percentage concentration in developing countries of subsidiaries originating

Table 3. *Geographic concentration of manufacturing subsidiaries in the Third World, 1968–71*

Origin of investments	Location of subsidiaries in the Third World			
	Latin America (%)	Asia and Oceania (%)	Africa and Middle East (%)	Total (%)
U.S.A.[a]	56	31	13	100
Japan[b]	19	70	11	100
U.K.[b]	10	47	43	100
Germany[b]	47	26	26	100
France[b]	40	15	45	100

[a] January 1968.
[b] January 1971.
SOURCE: calculated from data in Vaupel and Curhan, 1973, p. 122.

in particular investing centres in the industrialised world, then the concentration indices might increase considerably.[6] Secondly, the percentages shown refer to the number of subsidiaries and not to the level of activities, size of firms, etc. In oligopolistic and segmented markets, with leader-follower behaviour on the part of firms which monitor their competitors' activities in some markets while concentrating their own in others, the number of subsidiaries could grossly understate the true concentration of operations. On the other hand, the figures presented indicate total investments as of the end of the 1960s and do not separate out those of the last five to ten years when important changes in investment patterns took place in the world economy.

The above data and analysis serve to indicate that attitudes and policies towards foreign investment in developing countries cannot be separated from their overall relations with a specific country (or a few particular countries) in the industrialised world with which certain political and economic ties exist affecting the rest of the developmental process. Policies affecting foreign investments on the part of developed countries' governments are present in the rules applied by multilateral lending agencies (Tripartite Report, 1972, p. 20), retaliatory acts on trade relations,[7] links with foreign aid policies (such as the application of the Hickenlooper amendment), direct diplomatic pressures,[8] etc. Furthermore, foreign private interests often take advantage of the multiple links that tie developing countries with the rest of the world so as to enhance their own private interests. Non-equity external financing and certain trade relations, although external to particular foreign firms, become internalised in their power relations and conflicts with host countries. For example,

the Latin American countries have a long experience in the sense that in the majority of cases when any one of them tried to modify, to its advantage, the conditions under which an extractive industry operates, adversary propaganda campaigns have been started, resistance has arisen in foreign banking circles, and distortion of the image of the government and of the country have been attempted, all of which result in an adversary climate of foreign cooperation with national development. (Mayobre, 1972, p. 278.)

Similar cases have been noted in the manufacturing and service sectors (Wionczek, 1971, pp. 406–8).

The previous analysis indicates that, from the point of view of each developing country, the issues of power relations with foreign firms and the perceived risks from certain actions constitute a 'macro' and not a 'micro' problem. This is not just the result of the relative size of such firms in the local economy but stems more from the firms' links with their home country. It is for this reason that relations with foreign firms involve, directly or indirectly, the leadership and its orientation at the highest political level in the developing world. The perceived or actual risks are further influenced by the mounting of various international institutional arrangements that we will discuss below.

Two qualifying notes should be introduced at this stage. First, the figures and trends presented above should be interpreted in the light of the facts that essentially four Latin American countries (Mexico, Brazil, Argentina, Venezuela, plus some Caribbean Islands), one Asian (India), and one African (Nigeria) accounted in 1967 for 43 per cent of total foreign investments reported by the Third World. Thirteen more countries (basically in the Middle East and in Latin America) account for another 30 per cent (United Nations, 1973, p. 19). Second, in the pre Second World War period, business history indicates that individual industrialists or groups of them were able directly to affect the direction of foreign policy of their governments in various areas that enhanced their private interests. In more recent times, however, the *power* rests basically in the hands of the state while firms exert *influence*, directly (e.g. lobbying) or indirectly (through the conduct of their business), in the shaping and direction of policy. The extent of such influences depends on the presence and strength of other developed country interests in the same area (Barnet, 1971, p. 186).

It is precisely that 'presence and strength of other developed country interests' that seriously affects the scope and possibility for exercising the power available in the hands of the host governments in their dealings with foreign investors and the risks they run in undertaking such policies. For example, in the 1970s, important developed countries' interests centred on the energy question and their access to oil. Venezuela, by making a sharp distinction between the continuing supply of oil to the United States and the ownership of the oil producing firms, was able to announce its plans for nationalising foreign firms in that industry (as well as in the steel industry and in banking) without major external risks. Such external risks were further discounted in view of Venezuela's foreign exchange capacity. Had the situation been different, the influence of the affected foreign firms on their

5

home government as well as on international credit and other institutions, might have made the host government actions difficult to undertake. It pays to be small (or, in the case of Venezuela, not to touch the major country interests of the US) as long as the influence and power of the affected foreign private interests are not sufficient to overthrow a weak internal political structure that could stem from (economic) smallness.

We have talked above about the policies and power of the host governments as if they represented a cohesive national interest conceived, if not expressed, in an independent manner. Obviously this is not the case since both foreign firms and national interest groups associated with them affect and are part of host government policies. A proper understanding of the attitudes and policies of governments towards foreign investors needs to be integrated into a political theory of the sources of policy (Streeten, 1971, p. 245). In developing countries the often overwhelming presence of foreign enterprises in the host economies brings them into direct involvement with the forces of internal political power,[9] establishes intricate structures of relations with local groups (including the state), affects directly and indirectly the distribution of income and the allocation of resources, and thus influences the affairs of the states (Ferrer, 1971, p. 157). Furthermore, certain local groups not only relate their own prosperity to the presence of foreign firms but also ascribe to them values similar to their own orientation with respect to the political structure and form of their society. Thus the established bonds are much stronger than simple pecuniary ones. As a result, when one talks about power and risk in the relations between developing countries and foreign enterprises, one has to take into account that there exist two interrelated 'fronts': an external and an internal one.

Global activities, comparative advantage and power implications

Transnational enterprises, because of their size and particularly because of their accumulation of productive knowledge, demonstrate certain distinctive comparative advantages which are ascribed to the whole organisation rather than to the individualised activities of a branch or a subsidiary (Vaitsos, 1973, p. 624). These include 'the ability to attract and deploy high-calibre personnel, world-wide procurement facilities and marketing networks, a financial reputation that can be used to obtain large quantities of capital and immediate access to the parent company's accumulated and continually expanding store of research and development' (Gabriel, 1972, p. 120). Such advantages imply economic power and access to them commands a price. At the same time, though, most of these advantages have a cost structure for their development that is heavily skewed towards fixed expenditures and relatively small or, as in the case of technology, minimal additional costs for their incremental use. (The only important cost is management time in the employment of already developed assets.) As a result, there exist significant opportunities for bargaining in the acquisition of such inputs.

The countervailing power possessed by developing countries stems from the ability of the governments to control access to local markets (as in the case of import-substituting activities) or access to local natural resources (as in the extractive sector). In the first case, the risk of loss of a market, through government policies and the presence of competitors in an oligopolistic market structure, has proven paramount in the decision making of transnational firms to undertake investments and/or to sell other inputs (Wells, 1972). A non-automatic, negotiated entrance to the host's market is thus an indispensable element of government policy to increase bargaining power. Such power is generally not available to the national private sector, except in specific cases such as patent monopolies. Access to market should thus be considered by governments of less developed countries as a more important negotiating element than rules or treatment for foreign investments in the bargaining process. Furthermore, although costs associated with such investments are of lesser importance to foreign investors as compared to market access, costs to the local economy from inappropriate government policies (such as high tariff and other protection) are critical. What governments should pursue is obviously not the simple acquisition of investment *per se* or the sharing in the advantages that transnational firms have to offer, but their use for the net social benefit of the local economy. Hence, industrial planning and overall policies on market protection should be concomitant government policies to those on access to market through local production.

In the case of extractive industry the focus of government policy often rests in diverse forms of co-operation with other governments whose countries possess similar resources. Despite industry and market differences, it is indicative of the limited application of government policies that only the demonstration effect of the OPEC countries in recent years has prompted serious consideration (some claim an inflated one) for combining the interests of the producers of a variety of other primary commodities. In this sector, in previous years, the focus was basically limited to *individual* government negotiations with foreign enterprises and governments rather than to the possibility for combined action on terms of trade.

Centralised control in decision making and power

The application of centralised control in decision making by transnational enterprises, coupled with their size and global operations, transforms them into one of the most important non-market forces in the world economy. This is a result of their ability to shape the demand facing their products and to influence their economic environment through central planning and the exercise of their power. Furthermore, it is the result of the increasing share of world trade and production which is exchanged or planned among affiliated firms in the absence of arms length relationships, thus by-passing direct market considerations. The importance of this inter-affiliate trade of goods and services is paramount for many economies where foreign investors operate. For example, in 1969 about 75 per cent of the exports of US subsidiaries based in Canada were to their affiliates (United Nations, 1973, p. 54). For developing countries the importance of such tied trade in the whole industrial sector is considerable; it exceeds that of the trade with transnational enterprises by the latter's subsidiaries in the host economies. This is because the acquisition of technology by nationally owned firms or joint ventures in developing countries is frequently tied to the purchase of intermediate products and capital goods the prices of which are set by the transnational enterprises. These serve as suppliers for such inputs which are sold collectively in a packaged form.

A structure of production and trade controlled by parent firms of transnational enterprises enables decisions on the location of physical output (and their consequences) to be divorced from the question of the output's valuation through administrative price setting. This, in turn, affects income generation and its distribution both within and between countries. The pricing of such goods and services exchanged among affiliates constitutes a critical element in business behaviour, and it relates to such diverse objectives as: global tax minimisation or tax avoidance; reduction of tariff payments for goods imported by foreign subsidiaries and increase of tariffs and/or price levels for those produced by them in the host country; maintenance of market captivity and price barriers of entry against competitors; hedging against changes in currency values; reduction of political and business risk from high rates of declared profitability which might be susceptible to host government reactions, trade union pressures and antitrust actions, etc. The multiple channels of effective income remission that such inter-affiliate trade permits can, and often do, result in significant fiscal losses for the host governments. They also increase the cost bases upon which tariff and price levels are negotiated and set, since many of the earnings items of the parents appear as costs in the income statements of the subsidiaries.

Such a structure (which includes oligopolistic markets for 'final' products and administrative, non-market operations for inputs) implies a need for particular government policies. These should be oriented so as to regulate the operations of transnational enterprises in their local economies as well as to promote action at the international level with countries sharing the same interests or having similar concerns. However, the necessity for such policies should not preempt an evaluation of their efficacy and completeness so as to ensure that they do not become counterproductive for the interests of the countries that establish them.[10] Centralised control in decision making and world-wide operations offer several degrees of freedom to the enterprises involved enabling them to offset certain government policies. An indispensable aid to governments in this respect is the training of personnel who can understand the internal functioning of transnational enterprises, administer the policies and be able to negotiate with foreign factor suppliers. The characteristics of foreign investments and technology sales within the context of transnational enterprises are such that a country cannot simply legislate rules on their behaviour. Such legislation is necessary but not sufficient, and cannot replace competent local personnel and information to deal with foreign investors.

Some institutional considerations

Power relations and the pursuit of the participants' objectives do not exist in an institutional vacuum. Rather, particular organisational structures are fostered which reflect and reinforce the prevailing power relations and serve as the social environment within which power is being exercised. With foreign direct investment a particular international institutional framework has been constructed which tends, in various instances, to reflect and foment the interests of transnational enterprises while often reducing the potential application of national power and the interests of the host economies as well as the role of their governments. Not infrequently this international institutional framework contradicts policies and institutions pursued or created at the national level by the host countries. Recently, though, through efforts within the United Nations, the initiatives of Third World representatives, and also through the encouragement of a few relatively small industrialised countries, such as Sweden and Canada, there have been advances towards new forms of international co-operation. The power is still determined to a large extent, however, by the already existing institutional arrangements and their supporting entities.

The prevailing bias in the international institutional structure can be seen at five different levels.

(*a*) Institutional arrangements which have a *manifestly negative effect* for the interests of developing countries. This category refers to institutions such as the international patent system, stemming from the Paris Convention of 1883, the secretariat of which has recently become a specialised United Nations body. Also in this category are special lobbying groups created by transnational enterprises (such as the Council of the Americas), the function of which is the promotion of the private interests of the firms involved.

(*b*) Institutional arrangements which *facilitate the existing international specialisation of productive activities*. This category includes policies and norms of official multilateral financial institutions which orient their operations so as not to 'compete' with the presence of private capital. They thus limit the options of developing countries with respect to potential alternative sources of finance and reinforce existing channels for relations between nations and foreign enterprises.

(*c*) Institutional mechanisms which *facilitate existing relations of transnational enterprises with host governments*. Such mechanisms include international insurance schemes to cover properties of foreign investors in developing countries and mechanisms for the resolution of conflicts between foreign private investors and states. The control over the functioning of these multilateral insurance schemes,[11] the proposed subrogation of private property rights by international institutions,[12] and the history of arbitration and international resolution of controversies (Vaitsos, 1975) are all examples of how an institutional superstructure is created to fit and assist the interests of transnational enterprises. The basis of power is maintained in their hands through the influence they can exert on such institutions directly (through their own activities) or indirectly (through the policies of their home governments), while the conflict of interests and power confrontations are shifted to the international level.

(*d*) Institutional efforts with *limited effect in favour of developing countries' interests*. Such efforts include the preparation of 'codes of conduct' or internationally sanctioned 'rules of behaviour' for the operations of transnational enterprises. These efforts will highlight certain problem areas and as such they can be of use to some 'late-comers' in the efforts to restructure relations with foreign factor suppliers. Yet those least affected by such rules will be the enterprises involved. For this reason they will be among the strongest supporters of such 'codes of conduct', the adoption of which could be interpreted as having settled and satisfied the preoccupations of the Third World in its relations with transnational enterprises (Vaitsos, 1975, pp. 18–24).

(*e*) *Missing institutional requirements and efforts*. There exist obvious gaps in what would be a minimum institutional framework for satisfactory relations between transnational enterprises and host country governments. Among the most important are (i) the absence of internationally agreed provisions for the disclosure of information and accountability with respect to the activities of transnational enterprises, and (ii) the inadequate facilities for training of appropriate personnel for or the provision of negotiating assistance to developing countries in their dealings with foreign firms.[13]

Issues of knowledge in the foreign investment model

The benefits that accrue to developed countries through international investments and the operations of their enterprises in the less developed countries have rarely found their way into the empirical literature. Attention is focused on the contributions that such operations make to the Third World.[14] It is of interest to note that official, country-wide studies for developed economies on the home-country effect of transnational enterprises have tended to be undertaken and to be made public only after, and as an answer to, internal criticism about the repercussions on the home economy of such activities; witness the recent experience in the US.[15] The Europeans and the Japanese, both at the company and at the country level, have followed a low profile strategy, severely limiting the disclosure of information on the effects on their economies of the international activities of their own enterprises.

Two general propositions about developed countries' interest in the foreign investment process can be stated. First, the smaller the domestic market of the home economy the more important the foreign investment operations become. Through the latter, high standards of living can be achieved for the home economy both through returns to capital invested abroad and through the high remuneration of skilled labour, professional or managerial services, research and development activities, etc., all of which are made possible by the sale of goods and services tied to foreign investments and technology sales. The achievement of similar results for an exporting country through simple trade relations is not always attainable in view of market segmentation, specific imperfections in inputs trade, and host government policies on import substitution.

Secondly, the larger the domestic market relative to the country's resources, the more important foreign operations become to assure the availability of inputs as well as their supply at prices which permit rising real incomes at home. Both elements (availability and prices) are affected by direct investments abroad.

These two propositions about the size (absolute and relative) of the home economy of a developed country stress the importance of the foreign investment and technology sales processes as compared to untied trade relations. For corresponding reasons, from the point of view of developing countries, there can be negative effects from trade relations which are tied to foreign factor flows for their real income. Declared and explicit payments for foreign capital and technology are not the most significant aspect of their relationships with supplying firms.

Before moving to discuss the specific economic interests of developing countries in the foreign investment model, we need to add that the world-wide investment activities of transnational enterprises, particularly in the manufacturing sector, are primarily financed from savings that do not originate from their home economies. In many cases, the most important financial contribution comes from the domestic resources of the host economies. For example, less than 15 per cent of the total financial needs of US-based manufacturing subsidiaries abroad originated from US sources (United States Senate, 1973, p. 38). Even this 15 per cent is an overestimate of the actual financial contribution in view of the common practices of capitalising intangibles and secondhand machinery, the revaluation of assets affecting equity accounts, etc. In this sense the term 'foreign *investments*' constitutes a misnomer. A more correct term would be 'foreign *controlled* firms' financed basically from local savings.

How about the specific interests of developing countries? Investments in these countries accounted in 1968 for about one-third of the total book value of foreign investments in the whole world outside of the centrally planned economies. This contrasts with their participation in the global GNP (one-sixth) and their participation in world exports (one-fifth, excluding again the centrally planned economies) (United Nations, 1973, p. 16). The basic economic reasons explaining why transnational enterprises pursue investment activities in the Third World can be grouped into three broad categories: (*a*) threats or opportunities appearing in the markets of developing countries concerning the products and services of foreign firms; (*b*) the need to secure *sources of supply* of critical inputs, such as mineral resources, or other commodities that are present in developing countries; and (*c*) cost opportunities, particularly *low-wage labour*, available in the economies of the Third World that are critical for the competitive position of certain industries in markets mainly other than those of the host economy. We shall analyse each of these cases (i.e. markets, natural resources, labour). In all of them we will stress the critical importance of the *terms of trade* of developing countries as they are affected by the presence (or absence) of foreign controlled enterprises through equity and/or technology contracts.

Import substituting activities and foreign investments: the case of markets

There are at least two levels for analysing the economic effects of foreign investments on the interests of developing countries. The first involves an evaluation of different economic indicators (e.g. income effects, balance of payments, employment, etc.) as they relate to the host developing countries alone. The second includes the total benefits obtained from such investments by both participants, the foreign investor and the host economy, and the way they are distributed between them.

With respect to income measurements one of the most complete intercountry and inter-industry analyses to measure the full effects[16] of foreign subsidiaries in the 1960s was undertaken by a team of Oxford economists for UNCTAD in a study of 156 manufacturing firms in six countries of the Third World (UNCTAD, 1973). Using the Little–Mirrlees (1969) project evaluation methodology it was concluded that 'on a fairly reasonable set of assumptions nearly 40 per cent of the firms in the six countries taken together have negative effects on the overall social income of the host economies' (p. 59). In another 30 per cent of the firms studied, the full social, rather than private, positive income generated for the host economy (including government revenues) amounted to less than 10 per cent of their sales (p. 62), that is less than the margins that wholesalers or distributors usually get.

The existence, in import substitution, of a large number of foreign investments with negative social income effects for the host economy or small positive ones, tends to be explained by two trade effects as well as by the use of local scarce resources (such as local savings) by the foreign firms.

First, inappropriate government policies, partly induced and influenced by the foreign firms, permit substitution for imports under very high tariff and non-tariff protection. This creates extra income gains for the producers which are then transferred abroad (hence involving income loss for the local economy) as payment to foreign factors of production.

Secondly, income gains (through higher efficiency of foreign firms) or income redistribution effects (through monopolistic practices and market protection) generate transfers abroad through the high pricing of imported inputs that are induced by the 'final' product import substitution. This, in turn, results in foregone fiscal earnings for the host governments. Such fiscal effects could perhaps constitute the most important potential direct income gain of the host economy in view of the relatively high capital-intensity which characterises such activities, even in capital poor countries, and the diverse payments made abroad for imported technology. With respect to trade effects it has been argued that, since intermediate and other input markets tied to foreign investments tend to be more imperfect than final ones (for the goods produced by developing countries), the terms of trade worsen for such countries through import substitution cum foreign investments cum protectionist policies (Vaitsos, 1969).

In other cases, even with more appropriate government policies, the full effects could still be negative because of intrafirm market segmentation for the activities of affiliates, inter-firm technology contract cross-licensing and market divisions, patent monopolies, usage of local scarce resources, displacement of local activities, marketing practices and product differentiation, etc. On such occasions developing countries need to have the evaluation capabilities, the regulatory powers and the political will to refuse the entrance of such investments.

A further element of knowledge concerning the activities of foreign investors in the manufacturing sector of developing countries needs to be stressed. Such investors have specialised primarily in catering to the needs of high income consumers. Their original markets in rich industrialised countries and the kind of standardisation employed to achieve production efficiency, imply products and technologies which do not meet the needs or financial possibilities of the majority of the population in the Third World. Their activities *require* dual structures and unequal income distribution in developing countries (Stewart, 1974). Thus, in many cases, basic human necessities are unserved by the operations of transnational enterprises. Elementary health requirements, nutrition and housing for low income earners are not areas in which such firms tend to dedicate their resources or use their capabilities. Nationally owned firms in developing countries pursuing similar productive activities and producing the same goods and services do not behave differently. In some cases, like labour utilisation, they have been known to make more inappropriate selection of technologies than foreign firms (Vaitsos, 1974 b).

Until now transnational companies have indicated that they are not interested in or that they are not equipped to enter into these areas of activity. This lack of interest stems essentially from the fact that social benefits in these fields exceed and are not reflected in terms of private profitability. Their lack of capability for meeting such basic human needs is related to the complexity of diverse social organisations, cultural orientations and other problems of a heterogeneous nature inherent in economic backwardness. These factors create demands which are not subject to standardisation or uniform consumption patterns, which norm of behaviour is implied in many of the activities of transnational firms. To a great extent, the efforts necessary to satisfy the needs of the majority of the population in developing countries are outside the sphere of activities of foreign investors at least in the manufacturing sector. Rather, they are the subject of policies and efforts by governments and other economic actors at the national level.

Transnational firms, nevertheless, do have a direct impact on the necessary policies at the national level; but this is often negative. First, directly or indirectly, foreign investors attract local scarce technological capabilities and other resources into areas distinct from those meeting the basic needs of the developing countries. This constitutes an important internal 'brain drain' of equal or greater importance than the external one. Secondly, their activities often accentuate the existing unequal income distribution. Thirdly, since efforts by governments to pursue policies and introduce structural changes which imply a more equitable income distribution can be interpreted as having a negative effect on at least the short term interests of foreign investors, and since such changes affect local concerns who associate a part of their activities with and/or serve as spokesmen for transnational enterprises, the latter can constitute an impediment to the introduction of such necessary changes which promote greater equity in the Third World.

Commodities and foreign investments: the case of resources

After a long and turbulent history in the extractive industries, by the end of the 1960s there had been certain significant redistributions in favour of host developing countries as compared to earlier agreements with foreign investors. For example, for its copper activities in Chile the Braden Company was paying the Chilean government taxes that amounted to less than 1 per cent of gross sales value over the period 1913–24. The corresponding figure was less than 6 per cent for 1930–9 and it reached 64 per cent in 1953 (Mamalakis, 1971).

Yet, such host country gains, achieved basically through changes in fiscal rates and (some) through changes in ownership and control of natural resources, were circumscribed by the low price ranges in markets controlled by transnational enterprises and affected by developed countries' government policies. As a result, despite the gains achieved, the distribution of total returns between producing countries and consuming ones or their enterprises was often still unequal. For example, the principal oil producing countries before the Teheran negotiations of 1971 earned in terms of royalties and taxes something around $1 per barrel of refined oil. Yet, tax collectors in Western Europe (the oil importing countries) averaged about $4.50 out of each barrel. The same barrel of oil was selling in Europe for about $8.00. Although the figures cited do not distinguish between intercountry balance of payments considerations and intracountry income distribution effects, they are indicative of the wide scope within which income transfers could have taken place between countries. (*Fortune*, March 1971, p. 30).

By the middle of the 1960s and particularly in the 1970s certain significant changes in the attitudes and policies of producing countries began to appear. Such changes extended the sphere of host government actions beyond the simple tax collections which take as given the prices and the location of activities as defined by the foreign firms. Instead more serious attention began to be paid and policies were directed towards the issues of (i) the terms of sales through the organisation and manipulation of overall demand and supply conditions; and (ii) the location and control of multiple activities that are involved in vertically integrated production and marketing operations. The major impetus in this transformation, whose roots in various industries can be found in host government preoccupations in the 1960s, was given by the oil producers in the early 1970s. The actions in the latter industry broke the political and institutional inertia that can restrict initiative and limit the credibility of certain government policies.

The multiple forms of action by producing countries in the 1970s can be summarised in four categories which have interrelated repercussions: (*a*) the trend towards nationalisation and control over natural resources; (*b*) organisation of the supply, collectively or individually, to affect terms of sales (output and export controls, common price of sales or minimum export prices, export taxes, etc.); (*c*) tying of levies on exports to the prices of 'final' products in vertically integrated industries rather than to those of raw material exports; (*d*) forward linkages and location of activities.

We proceed, first, to analyse the case of national control in various sectors and then refer to the remaining three categories mentioned above by distinguishing the characteristics of each natural resource involved.

Nationalisation. Prior to 1960, with the exception of centrally planned economies and the policies pursued by countries during the Second World War years on 'enemy properties', relatively few cases of nationalisation could be found.[17] A compilation undertaken by the United Nations on occurrences of nationalisation or takeovers for the 1960 to mid-1974 period, however, came up with 875 cases in all sectors in sixty-two different countries (United Nations, 1974). The natural resources sector accounted for 38 per cent of the nationalisation incidents and for a much larger share of assets nationalised.[18]

This relatively recent world-wide trend towards nationalisation merits specific analysis within the context of the overall evolution of host country policies in the extractive sector. Obviously, nationalisation and control over natural resources involves multiple economic and political objectives, various short term conflicts over the terms of takeovers, and a host of medium and long range effects. From the various relevant issues we will consider here three propositions of direct interest to our analysis. First, nationalisation in itself is not a sufficient and in some cases, in the short run, it is not even a necessary condition for altering the terms of sales (except by eliminating transfer pricing) or for significantly modifying the location of other productive activities as between countries. Yet, secondly, in the medium run, nationalisation in the extractive sector turns out to be a necessary element in the attempts of a (developing) country to administer its resources in its best interests. This is so both because of the effects of nationalisation on the learning process and the introduction of nationals in key controlling, managerial and technical positions, and because of the political and institutional pressure it produces on the host government to carry out other complementary activities and necessary policies. Thirdly, nationalisation generates countervailing behaviour by transnational enterprises and their home governments which attempt to prevent the attainment of the objectives of the takeover process in the natural resources sector.

The validity of the above three general propositions can be discussed in the light of the following experiences in the extractive industries. By 1974, the members of the organisation of copper exporting countries (CIPEC) had completed nationalisation in most of their exploited copper resources and controlled, through their governments, almost all of their export trade.[19] Copper prices continue, nevertheless, to fluctuate widely and CIPEC, in its June 1974 meeting in Lusaka, did not produce an agreement regarding the floor price of copper; nor did it reach an accord on the establishment and financing of a buffer stock.[20]

In contrast, Jamaica, with all its bauxite production under foreign control (as is that of its Caribbean neighbours with the exception of Guyana) achieved, in the spring of 1974, significant improvements in the terms of its sales of the metal by levying an export tax proportionate to the price of aluminium ingot instead of that of bauxite itself. Similarly, the OPEC countries achieved in the 1970s the well known increases in oil prices prior to, or concomitant with, their efforts at nationalising oil production.[21] (The dynamics of the nationalisation process and the exercise of power in the oil industry in the 1970s were as follows. Some companies rejected the terms set by the host governments – like Nelson Bunker Hunt in Libya – while others reached an agreement. Those that did not accept the proposed terms and insisted on maintaining their existing operations were nationalised. Finally, oil companies were offering to be nationalised – like the big oil firms in Abu Dhabi which offered a 60 per cent participation to the government – in an attempt to achieve better terms in an inevitable outcome.)

Nevertheless, actions undertaken by developing countries exclusively on the terms of sales without the presence of nationalisation did not prove to be totally successful unless the characteristics of the industry or the support of other producers were sufficient to bestow the warranted (market) power to enable them to impose new terms. For example, countries in the oil industry that tried in the past unilaterally to increase taxes on foreign firms often found actual or threatened cutbacks in company operations, with the companies shifting production and overall activities to countries with lower taxes. (Similar phenomena were noted recently in the banana producing Central American countries.) Yet, the threat of nationalisation from the tax imposing oil producers has more recently led firms to increase their investments and production after the tax increase in the countries concerned (Mikesell, 1974). Thus, nationalisation, either as a threat or as an actual outcome, becomes an integral part of the restructuring of the power relations that affect market and productive performance.

Furthermore, nationalisation prompts institutional efforts (e.g. creation of national state enterprises) which permit the takeover of some or all of the operations of the foreign firms. It also progressively brings national expertise into key and responsible positions, in a way which might not always be attainable through contractual agreements. Successful negotiations, including those involving personnel management, involving the multiple facets of vertically integrated and internationally spread activities related to the extractive sector require detailed knowledge about the content of the elements under bargaining. Such knowledge is achieved, in certain cases, only if one controls and exercises power over the negotiated activities. (If, through covenants, such exercise of power and control is withheld from the equity participants then ownership is reduced to a simple financial proposition rendering only dividends if any.)

Finally, the act of nationalisation not only involves economic considerations but also represents a political commitment which galvanises the government as well as the country in question into further actions of self-reliance. Both at the political and the economic level such actions affect the location of activities between countries over time and the resulting income distribution. Thus, the importance of nationalisation does not rest simply on the issue of ownership but, more so, on the knowledge that it can create and on the political commitment that it generates. It is with respect to these two criteria that the success of a nationalisation should be judged.

After nationalising foreign firms developing countries often are confronted by limitations in their knowledge and, hence, in their capacity to manage the multiple aspects of the relevant sector. They thus conclude management, sales and technology agreements with the parent firms of the enterprises taken over[22] or with other specialised firms.[23] Some of these agreements can prove to be not only necessary but also helpful in training nationals of the developing country in question, thus leading to effective national control over a period of time.[24] Others, however, serve as means for preserving control in the hands of the foreign parent firms even after the takeover of their subsidiaries.[25]

There are three other means by which foreign firms attempt to counteract the effects of nationalisation in their overall operations. First, they may try to strengthen their control over other activities, such as in international marketing, thus still maintaining the nationalising countries' dependency upon them.[26] Second, they may sign future procurement contracts that secure availability for raw materials while leaving certain elements unspecified so as to be able to influence future prices or costs of delivery.[27] Third, firms may move to close substitutes[28] or diversify into related activities that permit increases in prices of raw materials to be passed on to the consumers or that enable them again to minimise the risks of nationalisation by increasing the host country's dependence upon outsiders (Moran, 1973).

Supply organisation, levies on exports and forward linkages. The capacity of a group of countries to organise the supply of a particular commodity and thus affect its terms of sales in the world market depends on a host of elements, both economic and political. Among the most important ones, we can cite the following:

(i) the share of the countries' exports in the total market (both in exports and in total production);

(ii) the growth of demand for the commodity *versus* supply expansion, including substitutes and easiness of entry of 'non-member' countries;

(iii) the number of countries involved and degree of their cohesiveness or discipline;

(iv) the structure of the market, which includes the number of purchasers, the availability of stocks, the possibility of withholding production or storing output, the cost structure of the industry, etc.;

(v) the financial capacity of members and credibility of retaliatory acts on both sides;

(vi) the political orientation, economic links and type of dependence (or relations) between the countries in spheres outside of the commodity in question.

The initiatives and characteristics of the OPEC countries in their efforts to increase the posted prices of 'bench-mark' oil from $1.80 per barrel at the beginning of 1971 to $11.65 as of 1 January 1974 with further increases during the subsequent year have been extensively documented. In the pages that follow we will explore, in some detail, how certain of the above enumerated elements apply to three other commodities, bauxite, copper and bananas; and how differences between them account for variations in the requisite policies of the producing countries. One of our objectives is to demonstrate that there is no exclusive formula for action by producers' associations. Rather, the warranted policy tools will depend on the characteristics of each sector.

Bauxite. The particular characteristics of the bauxite industry are such that it is most likely to be one of those that attains similar successes as the oil industry. The reasons are the following. First, present bauxite production is concentrated in a relatively small number of countries (Jamaica, Surinam, Guinea, Australia, Guyana, Sierra Leone). The International Bauxite Producers' Association, which was established in March 1974, accounts for a high percentage (75 per cent) of all exports to market economies. Also, major consumers depend on imports for most of their consumption. (In 1972, the US counted on imports for about 96 per cent of its needs for bauxite, alumina and related products (Howe, *et al.* 1974, p. 184).) Furthermore, major consuming countries, like the US, do not presently hold reserve stocks as is the case for other metals (e.g. tin). Secondly, the bauxite content represents a relatively small percentage of the total cost of aluminium ingot. (Four tons of bauxite that cost a total of $36 to $60 are needed to produce one ton of aluminium ingot which presently is worth more than $600. In contrast, crude oil accounts for more than half of the value of refined petroleum products (Mikesell, 1974, p. 30).) Thus, a given percentage increase in bauxite prices will be reflected in a much smaller increase in the price of the final product, which could be absorbed in a relatively easy manner. Thirdly, demand for aluminium is projected to rise at about 7 per cent per year, one of the highest rates among minerals (United States, 1970). The major risks for bauxite producers rest with the existence of close substitutes (hence the importance of co-operation between copper and bauxite associations) and on the relative economic weakness of the producing countries which could thus be subject to economic and other pressures from abroad.

The form that future actions by bauxite exporters will take will greatly depend on the present productive structure and economics of the industry. A key characteristic of the present structure relates to the fact that while most of the bauxite output is concentrated in developing countries and Australia, practically all the aluminium metal is produced in the developed countries. Thus, there are two most likely first steps (that were also part of the Jamaican strategy of last year).

(a) Relating initial export levies or minimum bauxite export prices to the price level of aluminium ingot rather than to the cost (or market price) of bauxite production. This will enable bauxite exporters to negotiate participation in the value added of the different stages involved in obtaining the final metal. (Jamaica increased its earnings in 1974 through the introduction of such a scheme from $25 million to $160 million. Guyana in its negotiations with Reynolds and the Dominican Republic with Alcoa both have opted for the Jamaican formula.)

(b) Establishment of forward linked activities so as to avoid oligopsonistic pressures from transnational firms affecting export levies. Forward linked activities could also increase domestic value added accruing to the producers. (Caribbean bauxite producing countries are advancing with the establishment of joint smelting facilities in their territories.)

Finally, the general trend towards nationalisation and sovereignty over natural resources is also bound to affect the bauxite producers.[29]

Copper. Despite the substitutability between bauxite and copper, the industry characteristics differ, leading to distinct policy requirements and policy potentials. Among the key characteristics of the copper industry one can cite the following four.

First, among copper producers no one country controls a sufficient proportion of the world market to be able to affect the price of the metal unilaterally. Thus, common action by a producers' association is essential. (In bauxite, Jamaica succeeded in increasing unilaterally export levies which then generated a demonstration effect on the other producers.) In 1971 the four CIPEC members controlled 38 per cent of the world production excluding non-market economies, and 53 per cent of exports. To reach an export market share of 70 per cent (which is still less than the bauxite association's) CIPEC will need to incorporate Papua New Guinea, the Philippines, Mexico and Algeria. Under present or enlarged membership, joint action by CIPEC could certainly exercise an important influence on the world copper market; yet, certain limitations will exist in view of domestic production in consuming countries. For example, net US imports of copper amounted to 18 per cent of domestic consumption in 1972 (Howe, *et al.* 1974, p. 184). This contrasts with 96 per cent which was the corresponding figure in the case of bauxite and alumina. Thus, CIPEC's success will also depend on the conditions affecting importing countries' domestic output (e.g. trade union action on the part of US copper workers).

Secondly, the copper trade is practically in its totality in the hands of the producing countries' governments. Thus, contrary to the case of bauxite or to OPEC's past history, CIPEC's action will not involve a fiscal arrangement but will need to establish common or minimum export price levels. Also, the absence of inter-affiliate trade precludes the type of individual company captivity by producing countries that is present in the bauxite industry. Such captivity can prove important in inducing certain initial changes in overall country-company relations, as in the case of relations between Libya and certain oil firms.

Thirdly, copper supplies are expanding. Known reserves are quite substantial and all CIPEC countries have plans to expand production. For example, Peru which is reported as having the largest underdeveloped reserves is presently producing about one-fourth as much as Chile and Zambia. Zaire has announced output expansion and Chile is planning to double its production by 1980 (Mikesell, 1974, pp. 28–9). At the same time, relatively recent technological developments (especially in the hydrometallurgy of copper for commercially exploiting low content ore) could significantly further expand capacity. Moreover, scrap has constituted in several cases about one-third or more of the material used. Such recycling is not present in oil, though it is in the case of aluminium. The supply of scrap is quite price-elastic even in the short run as contrasted with ore production which requires lump sum investments over longer periods.

Fourthly, projections for the average growth of demand for copper place the annual rate at 3.8–5.8 per cent (United States, 1970). Although this is higher than for several other metals[30] it is still not sufficient to offset the likely supply increases. An important form of co-operation among copper producers will, therefore, involve activities that will induce technological advancement and promotion of alternative uses of copper.

Thus, the success of CIPEC will greatly depend on production controls over time as well as on the existence of a buffer stock. The latter implies the necessity of substantial financial capacity, something that is not present in the CIPEC members who are all short of foreign exchange. Hence, any collaboration between various producers' associations will, from the point of view of copper exporters, rest on possible financial assistance from oil producers (and price agreements with the bauxite ones).[31]

Bananas.[32] The characteristics of the banana industry are quite distinct from those explored above in the case of bauxite and copper. As a result the strategic elements for common action of the fruit's producers are different.

The value of banana exports amounts to about 0.2 per cent of world trade and of this amount less than one-half to less than one-third accrues to the producing countries. Hence, contrary to the often cited experience of petroleum, any effort to redistribute returns in favour of banana producers will imply minor repercussions at the country level between consuming and producing nations. Rather, the conflict of interest rests between exporting countries and a small number of transnational firms. Three such enterprises control about 70 per cent of world banana trade. (One of them is the United Fruit Company, the growth of which involved the merging of some twenty-one once independent banana concerns (May and Plaza, 1958, p. 15).) Yet, the banana industry is a key one for the exporting countries' economies. For example in Ecuador, which is the world's largest producer/exporter, banana activities accounted for 20 per cent of the economy's demand for labour and 50 per cent of export earnings in 1971.[33] Thus, for such countries their performance in this industry is critical for their developmental objectives.

There are four additional key characteristics of the banana sector which have important policy implications. The first relates to supply considerations. Although only ten countries account for 80 per cent of the world banana trade, forty-five countries actually produce them. Given comparable climatic and land characteristics the potential for future expansion is, thus, significant if returns stimulate new entrants in exports[34] or if transnational firms shift (with certain important costs) sources of procurement to counteract pressures from an exporters' association. Furthermore, because of the perishability of the fruit no possibility exists for organising a buffer stock as in the case of minerals. In the 1973–7 period export availability is expected to grow by 8 per cent per year while import demand increases by 2 per cent annually. Thus, unless major changes occur in demand patterns or unless major new markets (like those of the socialist countries) are tapped, efforts simply to organise the total supply of bananas will most likely have limited success.[35] The areas for concentrated action by the newly created Union of Banana Exporting Countries (UPEB) lie elsewhere, as will be seen below.

The second key characteristic of the banana industry relates to its cost structure. In 1971, only about 12 per cent of the retail price went to the producing countries while the remaining 88 per cent accrued basically to developed countries' firms and their fiscal authorities. The average export tax in the producing countries was 0.8 per cent of the final retail price while import duties in the consuming nations were 6.9 per cent, that is more than eight times larger. Export levies collectively established could, thus, prove to be an important source of earnings for the producing countries. This is particularly so since (i) present fiscal rates for such countries are so small, in relation to retail prices, that increases can be passed on to the consumer with relative ease; and (ii) the price-elasticity of the demand for bananas is quite low within existing retail price ranges as the experience of brand named bananas has indicated. Within certain ranges of fiscal rates transnational firms might not be able to shift to new production sites in view of the heavy infrastructural investment requirements for establishing and maintaining appropriate farms. (A modern banana division of 20,000 acres amounting to four farms, needed for adequate production, required in the mid 1950s an investment of $20–25 million, excluding the value of the land.) Because of special tariff preferences offered by consuming countries there also exists considerable concentration in the world banana trade between origin and destination of the fruit's sales.

Another fundamental policy area for action by banana producers depends on understanding of the combined effect of two additional characteristics of the industry. The first stems from the cost structure and unequal returns referred to above. The ripeners' gross margin that accrues to specialised firms from developed countries amounts, alone, to almost double the total payments obtained by the producing countries. The packing outlays for transport from the exporting country amount to about forty times (!) the producers' gross margin. Thus, entrance into forward linked activities by exporting nations appears to be a mandatory move if increased returns are sought. The concept of 'nationalisation' here takes the form of national participation in new activities previously controlled by foreign firms. The other characteristic relates to the increasing concentration at the retail level in the developed countries by interests distinct from those of the banana trading transnational enterprises (e.g. supermarket chains). This phenomenon could facilitate a more direct contact by producing countries with the retailers, preempting the participation of the transnationals in various activities.

Under such circumstances collective action by UPEB could include joint advertising budgets (to counteract the brand name promotion of the big transnational firms),[36] financial arrangements for storage and ripening facilities, quality control standards, discounts in transport and packaging through oligopsonistic activities, and other such non-conventional forms of co-operation among countries.

Concluding remarks on natural resources. The recent actions of OPEC countries and their success has prompted the development of various producers' associations. Our previous discussion indicates some of the very different characteristics involved in each of the three products analysed and the resulting distinct policy requirements. There appears to be no uniform and exclusive prescription for improving the terms of trade of countries endowed with different natural resources. The OPEC experience demonstrated the potential of applying collective economic *power* by developing countries and the need for explicit political commitment and market intervention to convert such power into economic gains.[37] In the case of other commodities, the realisation of equivalent redistributive possibilities requires specific *knowledge* of the relevant industries and distinct policy instruments (even if the potential gains are nowhere comparable, in quantitative terms, to those in petroleum).

Export promoting activities and foreign investments: the case of labour

As noted earlier, a particular shift in investment flows and operations has taken place in the last five to ten years that relates to export promoting activities. The interest of the foreign controlled enterprises in the Third World originates, in this instance, from their strategy with respect to world-wide sourcing where attention is focused on cheap labour. The opportunities available to transnational enterprises are due to differences among countries between labour productivity differentials (for comparable investments) and wage differentials. The latter are much larger than the former.

The case of Third World labour resources and their direct or indirect usage by transnational enterprises in recent periods can be examined in terms of the stages at which they affected relations between nations. The first stage involved the actual emigration of labour from developing nations to the industrialised world, such as occurred in the early 1960s in Europe. It has been pointed out that 'it is instructive to compare actual Western European treatment [and US treatment in the case of Mexico] of immigrant labour with the treatment some LDC's have tried to impose on immigrant capital' (Diaz-Alejandro, 1974, p. 10). The actions of the less developed countries have met strong opposition from official representatives of developed countries and have been criticised as 'irrational' and inefficient by economists. Yet, with respect to treatment of labour, industrialised countries have applied, as noted by Diaz-Alejandro: fade-out rules and rotation schemes; discrimination between nationals and foreigners; discrimination among foreigners according to nationality; the Calvo doctrine (that is the competence of local laws and of local courts and the absence or non-acceptance of international tribunals on conflicts or disputes with guest workers); lack of consultation regarding the establishment or change of regulations affecting immigrant workers.

The costs for societies in the industrialised world of labour migration from developing countries could prove, however, quite substantial. Such costs could include national considerations of the type that Switzerland faced when foreign workers came to constitute a very substantial proportion of blue-collar wage earners. They could also raise issues of racial discrimination with repercussions on internal politics, as in the UK, or of important social problems in the cities, as in West Germany. In consequence, unskilled labour proves in many cases to be the least mobile factor of production. An alternative strategy has thus been followed within which vertically integrated enterprises at the international level established subsidiaries and allocated part of their activities in areas or countries where cheap and unskilled labour was abundantly available.

This phenomenon, based on inter-affiliate trade by transnational enterprises, increased substantially the inter-country flow of goods and services in certain parts of the international production structure, particularly the flow from the Third World.[38] Such operations by transnational firms have been compared, however, to the earlier cases of enclave investments leading to 'shallow development'. The technology, skilled labour, marketing and managerial services, etc., are provided from abroad with minimal spillover effects for the host economies. Through the usage of transfer pricing by foreign firms, the surplus of the product of labour above the wage payments is transferred abroad. As a result, the net effect consists in the exportation of labour rather than the product of labour (Streeten, 1973, p. 6), while, at the same time, industrialised countries avoid the costs that foreign labour immigration implies for them. In view of inappropriate government policies in the less developed countries the net balance of payments effects or the social income can even be negative. Such inappropriate policies include the offer of tax holidays and payment of subsidies to attract such investments.[39]

Since the end of the 1960s, transnational enterprises have been deepening their world-wide sourcing activities, particularly in certain developing countries, by increasing the value added accruing to their host economies. They have extended their operations, from the simple use of cheap unskilled (particularly female) labour, to more sophisticated activities that generate spillover effects for the countries involved. Nevertheless, the basic generation of productive knowledge, managerial control, marketing decisions and other key elements of the corporate overhead are still concentrated in the home economies of the parent firms. Similarly, the direct income effects are conditioned by the transfer pricing policies of the enterprises.

Such a development will lead towards a new form of international specialisation where (a) capital is raised internationally but controlled at the equity level by transnational enterprises based in the developed countries; (b) labour is provided by the Third World which will proceed on a dependent industrialisation path; and (c) developed countries specialise in highly skilled professions that generate various forms of productive knowledge, and in the decision making (and power) which shape the specialisation, activities and rewards of the rest of the world.

The gains for developing countries from such dependent industrialisation are likely to mirror their performance in the extractive sector during the 1940–60 period. They will tend to bargain for higher local content of manufacturing activities including some fiscal gains, higher participation in joint ventures at the subsidiary level, more exports (yet not necessarily an improved net balance of payments position), etc. All such moves can generate benefits though not all of them are congruent with developmental goals (e.g. higher local content in certain industries could imply increased capital-intensity and inappropriate employment policies). In terms of North–South relations such performance, although potentially beneficial if adequately managed, will still be circumscribed within the above described international specialisation. It will not, that is, confront the nature of uneven development and uneven rewards. An alternative strategy, which will not exclude increased bargaining with respect to existing opportunities, would need, in this context, to include two radical changes in international relations.

First, in selected productive sectors or geographic regions, developing countries will need to develop their own companies with international operations *and* the advancement (including copying and assimilation) of productive knowledge. Some of the petroleum producing countries appear to be moving in this direction in the field of petrochemicals and fertilisers. Similar cases might be presented in forward linked activities in other commodities. Brazil, Argentina and Mexico could advance in the capital goods industries if they could apply more 'nationalistic' treatment in their local economies as India has done in some instances. (The case of Czechoslovakia is an instructive example of a small country with world-wide exports in a particular sector. Switzerland and Holland are others.) The Andean Pact countries, through a combination of treatment of foreign investments and technology *coupled* with joint industrial planning, could achieve similar results at least within their own markets. Yet, all such actions are likely to emanate from the more developed or resource richer countries of the Third World and their effects will tend to concentrate within particular classes of their societies.

A second, much more complicated change will involve the role of developing countries' labour resources in international specialisation and the distribution of rewards. If developed countries in the 'post industrial' period shift their labour utilisation more towards service and skill-intensive activities, and if in the coming decades the Third World will increasingly provide the pool of labour for industrial expansion, can the less developed countries negotiate *jointly* for the usage of such a resource to achieve income gains above the existing wage earnings?[40] The level of unemployment in the Third World will always put pressure for rewards to be based on the internal conditions of such countries rather than on the needs of the transnational enterprises for their global activities or the preferences of the already industrialised countries with respect to their employment orientation. Clearly, collaboration by developing countries in this matter will be quite difficult in view of their sheer number and the variety of conditions found in each of them. Also, capital-intensive technological change will put certain limits on developed countries' dependence on Third World labour. Yet, the rewards could be substantial and the scheme might merit particular consideration if production structures are transnationalised and the developed countries' population becomes an ever smaller part of world employment. The evolution and degree of international income redistribution and the institutional mechanisms erected in the commodities markets during the 1970s will tend to have effects for such co-operation in the Third World on labour rewards in the 1980s.

It is important to note that such a scheme, in order to have serious repercussions on international income distribution, will need a political commitment at the highest level and cannot simply be implemented through international trade union action. Furthermore, in order to achieve internal income redistribution in the Third World (rather than creating pockets of labour aristocracy incorporated in transnational production structures) there will be added need for government participation in such negotiations, with fiscal earnings accruing to the host countries above the direct wage earnings and taxes on profits of the subsidiaries. Such a policy would be a complete reversal from present practices with respect to tax holidays and free industrial zones for the attraction of export oriented foreign investments. Also, it need not interfere with trade unionism in developing countries, since the host government's fiscal earnings can be based on 'physical' quantities (e.g. number of cars produced) rather than on the number of workers employed.

Concluding remarks

There are very few developing countries of sufficient size and resources to be able to undertake fundamental changes, structure their societies, and advance development through exclusively inward-oriented policies and relative or complete isolation from the rest of the world. China was able to achieve it and many consider it as a warranted policy for India. Yet, most of the other Third World countries will find it necessary to take into account their relation (dependence) with the industrialised world.

Transnational enterprises constitute an intrinsic element of the developed countries' political economy. As such, their multiple operations affect 'North–South' relations in a critical manner, even if such operations do not often meet the developmental needs confronted by the majority of the population in the 'South'. Power, stemming from the home country economy of transnationals, some intrinsic properties of such enterprises, and the institutional arrangements that have been created to support them, constitutes an element explicitly to be reckoned with in assessing and responding to the firms' activities in developing countries. Productive knowledge as well as knowledge about the key interests involved in the operations of transnational enterprises will affect the exercise of power, while capital is becoming a progressively less important element in the operations of such firms.

The joint objectives of power formation and of enhancement of knowledge to achieve a more equitable international economic structure necessitate the presence of a set of conditions in the Third World. These conditions include: the political will and commitment to achieve such a change; a certain degree of unity of action (including exchange of information) leading to new non-spatial forms of economic integration; the development of expertise so as to advance knowledge and promote self-reliance; and the elaboration of 'stages' in a country's capacity to bargain effectively as well as recognition of the variant characteristics and possibilities at each stage.

An important reminder needs though to be added. A restructuring of power relations between developing countries and the transnational enterprises (or their home countries) will not necessarily and by itself lead to a restructuring of power relations within the Third World. The gains obtained could benefit only a small part of the population in developing countries unless internal changes take place in policies and hence in the interest and powers that promote them. Nevertheless, the two issues are not unrelated: external dependence affects internal inequality and hence policies which redress such external relations are necessary, even if not sufficient, for social and economic development.

Notes

1   Some of the ideas in this section have also been discussed in Vaitsos, 1975.
2   For the case of France, whose manufacturing subsidiaries have greatly expanded in territories outside her ex-colonies, Franko indicates that 'manufacturing in colonies and ex-colonies by large French firms was virtually non-existent prior to 1950. The first major move into manufacturing in former colonies came as part of the effort to ward off the threat of Algerian independence in 1950–61 During that period, 12 of the 13 manufacturing subsidiaries entered in French Africa by continental companies were owned by French firms. In the three years following Algeria's independence, French entries into manufacturing in Africa dropped to nearly nothing. Subsequently, the rate of establishment rose markedly... [together with companies of non-French origin]' (Franko, 1975, p. V-8).
3   The US share of the book value of total direct investments in the Third World in 1967 was about 50 per cent; that of the United Kingdom was 20 per cent and that of France was 8 per cent (OECD, 1972).
4   For comments on the relative shift in Saudi Arabia from British to US oil companies, see Barnet, 1971, pp. 199ff.
5   Y. Tsurumi predicts such an evolution in the behaviour of Japanese firms in view of (a) the political reaction of Asian countries against Japanese investments; (b) the underlying political and economic reasons that led the US to force the revaluation of the yen in 1971; and (c) the need of Japanese firms to monitor the activities of US and European firms in their home countries and discourage disruptive competition through a strategy of 'hostage exchange'. See Tsumuri, 1974, pp. 16–17 for discussion on these matters as well as for the sources of the figures given on p. 116.
6   For the divergent conclusions, depending on the base employed for interpreting the statistics, in the case of French investments abroad and total investments in the ex-French colonies, see Franko, 1975, pp. V–8–9.
7   See the recommendation by Jack Behrman on the linking of trade pressures

on developing countries with the treatment applied by the latter to foreign investors, in Overseas Development Council, 1973, p. 46.

8   For such pressures applied against Peru, Colombia and other Andean countries, see Vaitsos, 1973.

9   For references to the financing of political campaigns by foreign companies in Venezuela, see Perez, 1972.

10   For discussion of warranted policies in this area and their limitations, see Vaitsos, 1974 *a*.

11   The United States position on the IBRD associated project on multilateral insurance stipulated that the voting participation in the Council and Board of Directors should be linked to the financial participation of the member countries in a similar form as votes have been distributed in IBRD or the IDA. Thus, a supranational 'legislative' authority could be created controlled by majority votes from developed countries with 'self executing' provisions applicable to developing countries (CEMLA, 1971).

12   In contrast see Article 51 of Decision 24 of the Commission of the Andean Pact.

13   Efforts have recently been undertaken in this area by the Economic and Social Council of the United Nations.

14   'Since the end of World War II the U.S. Government has asserted that a major element of its programmes for assistance to developing countries would be reliance on the contributions of private foreign investment' (Overseas Development Council, 1973, p. 39).

15   Recent publications by the United States Senate indicate that the US has obtained significant overall benefits in the late 1960s from the world-wide operations of US based transnational enterprises. Such firms, whose share amounted to 62 per cent of total US exports in manufactured goods, had an overall direct increase of net exports to the rest of the world (exports minus imports) of $3.4 billion for the 1966–70 period. (Important variances, though, were noted among industries.) During the same years 'non-transnational' firms had a negative net trade balance of $3.6 billion. The indirect effects on net exports of the transnationals (after taking into account, that is, the most probable substitution of foreign affiliates' production for US exports in foreign markets) indicated a net gain of $400 million over the same period.

In terms of overall basic balance of payments (current account and long term capital movements), US based transnational firms improved their position by $2.8 billion in 1966–70. During the same period non-transnationals experienced a deterioration in their basic balance by $3.3 billion while the US accounts as a whole also deteriorated. The US Senate study indicated that 'the most consistent of the conclusions is that the U.S. based transnational enterprises in their transactions with the United States, exert a uniformly large, negative impact on the current accounts of balances of payments of the host countries. (Conversely, of course, they have a favourable impact on the corresponding account of the U.S. balance of payments.)' (United States Senate, 1973, pp. 5, 7, 29.)

16   The full quantifiable effects should include: (*a*) the net (after payments abroad of dividends, royalties, interests, etc.) and direct income effects of the activities of foreign investors; (*b*) the indirect effects through imports, investments, etc. induced by the operations of foreign investments; (*c*) the usage of local scarce resources by foreign enterprises thus preventing income contributions elsewhere in the local economy; and (*d*) the preemption of local activities (e.g. acquisition of national firms) or the exclusion of alternative ownership or production schemes that could be available to undertake similar activities.

17 Mexico (1937), Iran (1950–2), India (1956), Egypt (1956).

18 Companies whose parent firms were in the UK accounted for 84 per cent of the number of nationalisations in the agricultural sector and 58 per cent in banking and insurance, while US based firms accounted for 45 per cent of the number of nationalisations in mining and 40 per cent in petroleum (United Nations, 1974, Annex p. 15).

In the 1960–74 period, the peak in the number of takeovers occurs consistently every three years (1961, 1964, 1967, 1970, 1973) with much smaller occurrences in the remaining ones. This phenomenon may be reflecting a demonstration effect among developing countries with a resulting easing in certain political obstacles (during the months of each peak year). Also, it may reflect the pressures that mount from the developed countries to stop the trend of nationalisations (leading to the troughs).

19 Zaire nationalised in 1966–7 the Union Minière du Haute Katanga. Zambia took over 51 per cent of its copper production in 1969–70. Chile achieved majority control in 1967 and completely nationalised large scale copper mining in 1971. In 1974 Peru took over Cerro de Pasco, one of the country's major copper producers.

20 Also, on 19 September 1974 the CIPEC countries agreed in Paris to reduce their exports by 10 per cent in an attempt to control prices in the world market. Yet prices dropped after the CIPEC announcement since the export reduction was not accompanied by a production control or a decrease in output. Such performance induced consumers to expect an accumulation of stocks by the producers in quantities that were interpreted as leading to further reductions in copper prices in the future. Reuters reported that immediately after the CIPEC meeting the Minister of Mines of Zaire announced that his country planned to continue with its projects for expanding the capacity of copper production in Zaire.

21 Joint action by some of the OPEC countries towards nationalisation commenced on 2 October 1972 through an accord in New York between Saudi Arabia, Kuwait, Qatar, Abu Dhabi, Iraq and the major oil companies. The performance of the OPEC countries in 1973 exceeded the terms of the New York agreement both with respect to the percentage of nationalisation (above 50 per cent instead of the 25 per cent agreed) as well as with respect to the level of compensation ('net book value' instead of 'updated book value').

22 For example, the government of Venezuela signed such agreements with US Steel and Bethlehem Steel in the recent nationalisation of the iron ore industry on 31 December 1974 (*Business Latin America*, 15 January 1975).

23 For example, Peru after nationalising IPC has been using the services of a relatively small specialised firm in oil prospecting.

24 See the experience of Guyana in signing marketing and purchasing contracts with built-in clauses for local personnel training in *Guybau, Annual Report*, 1972.

25 Zambia, after taking over 51 per cent of its copper production in 1969–70, signed a sales and management agreement with the parent of the foreign enterprise it partially nationalised. Yet, this resulted in effective control resting in the hands of the minority holders and necessitated further 'Zambianisation' measures in 1973 (United Nations, 1974, p. 11).

26 The strategy of the three transnational enterprises that dominate the world banana trade has included strong expenditures on brand name product differentiation and control of distribution outlets while divesting in banana plantations (UNCTAD, forthcoming).

27 The Japanese instead of undertaking direct investments have shown a preference for long run financing in developing countries tied to procurement contracts. Such arrangements guarantee availability of inputs for the materials-short Japanese economy. Yet, the contracts signed may not always include specific provisions as to the purity of the materials purchased or the transport and delivery facilities to be employed, all of which might lead to additional costs incurred by the exporting country in future negotiations.

28 Oil firms are entering into alternative energy sources in the 1970s.

29 The Jamaican Prime Minister's statement to the Parliament on 15 May 1974 included, in addition to the export levies, the following policies for the future: (a) reversion of lands owned by foreign companies to Jamaican hands; (b) re-acquisition of control of bauxite ore by the government; (c) national partici- pation in the ownership of the bauxite and alumina operations in Jamaica.

30 The average annual growth rate of various metals is projected as follows: chromium, 2 to 3.3 per cent; tin, 0 to 2.3 per cent; manganese, 2.4 to 3.5 per cent; mercury, 2.2 to 3.1 per cent; nickel, 2.8 to 4.0 per cent; tungsten, 2.1 to 2.9 per cent; zinc, 2.5 to 3.3 per cent (United States, 1970).

31 Venezuela is at present financing with part of its oil earnings a coffee buffer stock in Central America.

32 The information on the banana industry that is presented here is based on an excellent report prepared by the UNCTAD (forthcoming).

33 After the oil discovery in Ecuador, the share of export earnings declined but that of labour demand remained about the same.

34 The exports of the Philippines were negligible less than ten years ago. By 1973 the Philippines accounted for one-third of the banana imports of Japan.

35 The past history of export (as distinct from retail) prices of bananas has been quite poor for the producers. In the 1954–73 period the aggregate index of fruit prices increased by 22 per cent while banana prices declined by 30 per cent. Also, according to UNCTAD's estimates the terms of trade of bananas in relation to manufacturing products deteriorated by 61 per cent between 1954 and 1973.

36 In 1964 the advertising budget for the promotion of Chiquita bananas amounted to $6 million.

37 The increase in petroleum prices in the early 1970s was prompted by a host of fears that included (a) the increase in global demand for energy as a result of the world-wide economic expansion during those years, (b) the continuous reduction in US production of petroleum in recent periods and (c) the repercussions of the last Arab–Israeli war. The power of the OPEC countries has not yet been put to a real test. Its function has been more a catalytic one and it was not the determinant factor in the joint increase in the price of petroleum.

38 For example, articles imported under the terms of items 806.30 and 807.00 of the US Tariff Schedule (in which tariffs are paid on the foreign value added for goods that originated from the US rather than on the total value of the imports) increased from $593 million in 1966 to $1,842 million in 1969. The share of developing countries in such imports jumped from 7 per cent to 22 per cent during the same period with a sixfold increase in absolute terms (Helleiner, 1973 and Adam, 1972, p. 310).

39 For the case of Ireland, see Cooper, 1973.

40 I thank Celso Furtado for suggesting this idea to me.

References

Adam, G., 1971. New trends in international business: world-wide sourcing and dedomiciling. *Acta Oeconomica*, **7**, 349–67.
 1972. Some implications and concomitants of world-wide sourcing. *Acta Oeconomica*, **8**, 309–22.
Barnet, R. S., 1971. *Roots of War: The Men and Institutions Behind U.S. Foreign Policy*. Harmondsworth: Penguin.
CEMLA, 1971. Proyecto del BIRF de creacion de un organismo internacional de seguros sobre las inversiones extranjeras. *Boletin Mensual*, Mexico, March.
Cooper, Charles, 1973. Science, technology and industry in Ireland, diagnosis and policy proposals. Science Policy Research Unit, Sussex University, mimeo.
Diaz-Alejandro, Carlos F., 1974. North–South relations: the economic component. Economic Growth Center, Yale University, Discussion paper 200.
Ferrer, Aldo, 1971. El capital extranjero en la economia Argentina. *El Trimestre Economico*, **38** (no. 2) 301–23.
Franko, L. G., 1975. *The Other Multinationals* (forthcoming).
Gabriel, P. P., 1972. The multinational corporations on the defensive (if not at bay). *Fortune*, January.
Helleiner, G. K., 1973. Manufactured exports from less developed countries and multinational firms. *Economic Journal*, **83**, 21–47.
Howe, James W., *et al.* 1974. *The United States and the Developing World: Agenda for Action*. New York: Praeger.
Keynes, J. M., 1924. Foreign investment and national advantage. *The Nation and Athenaeum*, 9 August.
Little, I. M. D. and Mirrlees, J. A., 1969. *Manual of Industrial Project Analysis in Developing Countries*, Volume II. Paris: OECD.
Mamalakis, M., 1971. Contribution of copper to Chilean economic development, 1920–1967: profile of a foreign-owned export sector. In *Foreign Investment in the Petroleum and Mineral Industries*, (ed.) R. F. Mikesell, pp. 387–420. Baltimore: Johns Hopkins.
May, Stacy and Plaza, Galo, 1958. *The United Fruit Company in Latin America*. Washington: National Planning Association.
Mayobre, Jose Antonio, 1972. Politica sobre inversion extranjera en materia de recursos naturales: el regimen del petroleo y su futuro. In *Inversiones Extranjeras y Transferencia de Tecnologia en America Latina*, (ed.) K. H. Stanick and H. H. Godoy. Santiago: ILDIS.
Mikesell, Raymond F., 1974. More Third World cartels ahead? *Challenge*, **17** (no. 5) 24–31.
Moran, Theodore H., 1973. Transnational strategies of protection and defense by multinational corporations: spreading the risk and raising the cost for nationalization in natural resources. *International Organization*, **27**, 273–87.
OECD, 1972. *Stock of Private Direct Investment by DAC Countries in Developing Countries, end-1967*. Paris: OECD.
Overseas Development Council, 1973. *The United States and the Developing World: Agenda for Action*. Washington: Overseas Development Council.
Perez, Ruben Sader, 1972. La inversion extranjera y petroleo; reversion de concesiones y nacionalizacion de la industria petrolera en Venezuela. In *Inversiones Extranjeras y Transferencia de Tecnologia en America Latina*, (ed.) K. H. Stanick and H. H. Godoy. Santiago: ILDIS.

Stewart, Frances, 1974. Technology and employment in less developed countries. *World Development*, 2 (no. 3) 17–46.

Streeten, Paul, 1971. Costs and benefits of multinational enterprises in less developed countries. In *The Multinational Enterprise*, (ed.) J. H. Dunning, pp. 240–58. London: Allen & Unwin.

1973. The multinational enterprise and the theory of development policy. *World Development*, 1 (no. 10) 1–14.

Tsurumi, Yoshihiro, 1974. Multinational spread of Japanese firms and Asian neighbours' reactions. Paper presented to the conference on The Multinational Corporations as an Instrument of Development–Political Considerations, Yale University (unpublished).

Tripartite Report, 1972. *Reassessing North–South Economic Relations, a Tripartite Report by Thirteen Experts*. Washington: The Brookings Institution.

United Nations, 1973. *Multinational Corporations in World Development*. New York.

1974. *Permanent Sovereignty over Natural Resources*. Report of the Economic and Social Council, A/9716.

UNCTAD (P. Streeten and S. Lall), 1973. *Evaluation of Methods and Main Findings of UNCTAD Study of Private Overseas Investment in Selected Less Developed Countries*. United Nations TD/B/C.3/111.

Marketing and Distribution System for Bananas (forthcoming).

United States (Bureau of Mines), 1970. *Mineral Facts and Problems*. Washington.

United States Senate (Committee on Finance), 1973. *Implications of Multinational Firms for World Trade and Investment and for U.S. Trade and Labor*. Washington.

Vaitsos, Constantine V., 1969. Transfer of resources and preservation of monopoly rents. Development report no. 168, Center for International Affairs, Harvard University, Cambridge, Mass.

1973. Policies on foreign direct investments and economic development in Latin America. *Journal of World Trade Law*, 7 (no. 6) 616–55.

1974 a. *Intercountry Income Distribution and Transnational Enterprises*. Oxford.

1974 b. Efectos de las inversiones extranjeras directas sobre la ocupacion en los paises en via de desarrollo. *El Trimestre Economico*, 41 (no. 2) 377–406.

1975. North–South economic relations: the case of foreign investments and productive knowledge. In *Beyond Dependency*, (ed.) Guy Erb. Overseas Development Council (forthcoming).

Vaupel, James W. and Curhan, Joan P., 1973. *The World's Multinational Enterprises*. Boston: Division of Research, Harvard Business School.

Wells, Louis, Jr. (ed.), 1972. *The Product Life Cycle and International Trade*. Boston: Division of Research, Harvard Business School.

Wionczek, M. S., 1971. La reaccion Norteamericana ante el tratado comun a los capitales extranjeras en el Grupo Andino. *Comercio Exterior*, 17 (no. 6) 27–30.

7. 'Ownership and control': multinational firms in less developed countries

EDITH PENROSE

In a number of less developed countries, or groups of countries (such as the Andean Group, the Caribbean Community, the East African Community) and in international organisations, much academic discussion, official attention, political pronouncement and international consultation are devoted to the general problem of the ways in which a host government can establish control over the activities of multinational corporations in its country. Very often the question of obtaining ownership, or equity participation, in the local subsidiaries of such corporations moves to the centre of the stage, and an inordinate emphasis is often placed on the necessity of obtaining a majority of the equity. Thus, the magic figure of 51 per cent emerges as the primary target, and ways and costs of obtaining it tend then to preempt attention.

Some sort of special government control over the operations of foreign firms is widely held to be necessary because the objectives and operations of such firms may not be consistent with the objectives of the host countries, and their methods of operation may be disadvantageous in some respects for the economic development of these countries. To the extent that such inconsistencies and disadvantages are believed to exist, the host country will want to be in a position to exercise sufficient control over the firms to ensure that it maximises its own gains.

There is no need here once again to discuss the ways in which the operations of multinational corporations may adversely affect the host countries, both economically and politically. Apart from the general objection that decisions affecting the local economy are 'made in New York' without specific concern for local development, there are particular areas where serious divergencies of interests often arise. These include the costs of foreign investment and especially the foreign exchange cost (profit remittances, technological and managerial payments, excessive transfer pricing, etc.); restrictive practices affecting exports or domestic markets; inadequate localisation of skilled and managerial personnel and inadequate training of workers; and the introduction and use of inappropriate technology, both in consumption and in production.

In addition, a particular subsidiary of a foreign firm may sometimes simply be incompetent or unenterprising, failing to take advantage of opportunities in local or even world markets which could benefit the host country (and perhaps even the international firm itself). Such a situation may remain unnoticed or even be tolerated by the head offices of the firm, especially if the market of the host country is small or the subsidiary is of little consequence in the total operations of the firm. A failure of a subsidiary to take initiatives which could widen its market, for example, through increased processing of a raw material, or effective response to changes in demand, might also be the product of constraints imposed by the international plants of the foreign parent. Thus, actions which would benefit the host country may be possible only if the government can influence, or even control, the decisions of the local subsidiary.

Some of the costs to the local economy, for example, certain of the foreign exchange costs, could be eliminated or reduced by the transfer of all or part of the foreign equity to local hands; and localisation of managerial direction could also probably be increased. But the transfer of control over foreign enterprises to local private interests is likely to have very different consequences from that of such a transfer to government. If the primary purpose of a move to secure an increase in local ownership is to decrease foreign influence and control in the economy, then a transfer to local private investors will probably promote this end, although there is always the danger that a foreign company will use local people as a 'front' or 'façade' to satisfy local aspirations while itself retaining effective control. On the other hand, often the demand for government equity control is primarily ideological – that is to say, is based on a desire to move towards a socialist organisation of the economy which requires that the government own the means of production. If this is the case, then a transfer of ownership of foreign firms to local private hands may actually hinder the 'transition to socialism' by creating a stronger political base for the private sector which is likely to oppose state ownership. It is often politically easier to expropriate foreigners than local entrepreneurs.

In any case, as will be seen, the problem to which this paper is chiefly devoted relates primarily to poor countries in which the supply of managerial and entrepreneurial resources is extremely limited, or to countries which are attempting to expand much faster than such resources permit. This is not true of all less developed countries. But where it is true, the important question arises as to how far the acquisition of equity control over the subsidiaries of a multinational corporation by the host government is likely to be the most economic and effective means of controlling the operations of such firms in the directions desired. In particular we shall be interested in examining the types of arrangements made for the acquisition of effective management and other services, and in discussing ways in which costs may be reduced. This will involve a detailed discussion of the nature of the agreements for the supply of management and other services which are often negotiated between a government and its foreign partner.

Finally, I shall discuss briefly the role of minority equity participation in the subsidiaries of foreign firms and of the circumstances in which full ownership is likely to be both necessary and effective. Briefly, my conclusion will be that 51 per cent control will usually achieve little more in less developed countries with very limited managerial resources than could be achieved with a much smaller proportion of the equity, especially if the government is prepared to adopt appropriate financial and commercial legislation. In a number of circumstances, however, full ownership is appropriately sought. Government may achieve its ends sometimes with 10 per cent ownership or less, sometimes only with 100 per cent; 51 per cent is very often unnecessarily expensive and sometimes useless if the primary purpose is to obtain government control in order to ensure that the firms operate in accordance with government policy. Insofar, however, as the demand for a controlling equity is simply part of a general attempt to establish a government-run socialist economy, the present analysis is not relevant except to the extent that it points to some of the difficulties and indicates ways in which the costs of transitional arrangements may be reduced.

Whether they operate through wholly owned subsidiaries, or as partners in a joint venture with government, the overall objectives of foreign parents are likely to be much the same. We assume that prominent among these objectives is the desire to make and retain as much money after taxes from its worldwide operations as seems practicable, where 'practicable' includes the parents' judgement about the importance of local goodwill, 'good citizenship' generally, and the relation between present behaviour and longer run prospects. Hence we do not assume that the motivation of a foreign firm will be changed by its participation in a joint venture, but we can ask whether the judgements it makes of its long run interests will be modified to the advantage of the host country, or whether its power to obtain its own objectives will be reduced if the government acquires a majority of the ownership in its subsidiaries in host countries. We need not quarrel with the assumption, well supported by experience, that in many respects the power of multinational corporations is superior to that of the governments of host countries and that they will not gratuitously use their power in such a way as to maximise the gains to their hosts. It is appropriate, therefore, for the latter to exert their own power in order to obtain a greater gain than they otherwise would get – in other words, to use the power of the state to control the behaviour of multinational corporations.

The areas in which governments want to curb the activities of foreign firms or to reduce the cost of their operations are essentially those mentioned above where divergencies of interest arise, and such divergencies exist in developed as well as in less developed economies. In industrialised, private enterprise economies governments normally establish and enforce certain rules governing and restraining the activities of private firms. The rules are designed to protect various groups of people who might be adversely affected by unethical or unfair practices of business. It is common, to give some examples, to find rules regulating the provision of information for shareholders, the behaviour of firms so far as it might affect stock markets, the quality of products, the nature of advertising and warranties, permissible competitive practices, labour policies and practices, sometimes regulations governing foreign transactions, etc. Corporate charters impose obligations as well as confer rights, as do patent grants and other legal privileges.

The extent and nature of such regulations vary widely among countries but, whatever they are, business firms are generally free within the rules to run their own affairs and to make their own business decisions independently of government intervention. Thus, those who command a majority on the board of directors can indeed exert considerable control over the policies and, within limits, over the practices of the enterprise. It must be remembered, however, that the independent power of management is also very great even in these countries; for management has a detailed knowledge of business operations which is often difficult for directors representing shareholders to obtain. Apart from companies which are treated as public utilities, where regulations governing business decisions, notably pricing, are more extensive, the principles which are accepted as the basis of such economies will lead governments that want to obtain reasonably detailed control over the business decisions of a firm to acquire a controlling equity interest in it – in other words to nationalise wholly or in part the relevant enterprise.

Total or partial nationalisation (as distinct from the establishment of state enterprises) is, sometimes, adopted in industrialised capitalist countries as a means of forcing firms to act in the public interest as contrasted to their commercial interest, but there are often special problems so far as foreign firms are concerned. Nevertheless, in many developed countries there is much concern over the possible adverse effects of the operations of foreign firms in their economies and special measures are not infrequently adopted to mitigate such effects. Nationalisation is, however, especially difficult if for no other reason than that any country doing so would be extremely vulnerable to retaliation, especially if the country is itself the home of multinational enterprises. These have given hostages to fortune in the form of subsidiaries operating abroad which they would not like to imperil. Fear of retaliation often gives rise to a great reluctance even to impose general regulations which might adversely affect the profitability of foreign along with domestic firms and would be strongly resisted by them.

In Britain, for example, one of the most effective arguments against government proposals to limit patent protection and the use of brand names in the pharmaceutical industry is that such measures would not only interfere with exports and contravene international agreements, but would also invite retaliation against the subsidiaries of British pharmaceutical firms which operate abroad, especially in the United States. The dependence of industrialised countries on the goodwill of other industrialised countries arising from the interest of each country in its own foreign subsidiaries may place greater restraints on the domestic policy of each, than the dependence of the countries of the Third World on the technology and expertise of industrialised countries places on their own freedom of action.

In general, and contrary to received opinion, I am inclined to think that less developed countries often have *more* scope to take independent and radical action with regard to multinational corporations than do governments of the larger industrialised countries. Retaliation is more difficult since it cannot go much further than restricting access to technology, capital, markets, etc., which is hard to enforce whenever private firms believe that it is still profitable to invest in the country or to provide their services for a fee. True there can be restrictions placed on the flow of aid, even from international organisations, but it is becoming more difficult for industrial countries openly to take even this kind of action to defend the interests of private enterprise except in the case of expropriation without compensation, while 'gun boats' as a form of intervention have become quite rare.

Secondly, the less developed countries are often less inhibited by their own attitudes and by respect for the prevailing traditions and rules of international economic behaviour, holding either that those traditions and rules were made in the interest of the industrial powers and have no moral claim to international acceptance, or that their own history of deprivation justifies exceptions in their favour. Hence they have been prepared to repudiate contracts and unilaterally (and sometimes even retrospectively) change the rules when they felt that it was in their interest to do so, inhibited only by their appraisal of the risks and costs that they might have to accept. Already they have had a marked impact in changing the accepted rules. Finally, because there are so many of them, poor countries have a strong voice in international organisations, and precisely because they are poor their arguments have a strong moral appeal, which, given the present political rivalries among the more industrialised countries, places them in a good psychological position at least to squeeze foreign interests, and especially 'capitalist' interests, to their own advantage.

Yet all of this does not mean that governments of the Third World have unlimited bargaining power and can do what they like without a cost to themselves. For most practical purposes it is impossible to force foreign firms or governments to invest, to provide technology and the knowhow for its use, to open their markets or to give financial assistance, either as aid or commercially. The very concept of 'bargaining power' implies a bargain – both sides receive and both give. Its use assumes, therefore, that any government that engages in bargaining with multinational enterprises wants to receive something that it can obtain only by giving something. For this reason, nationalisation or expropriation embarked upon unilaterally, without agreement on compensation and other conditions, is not, I think, appropriately looked on as an exercise in 'bargaining power' since what is obtained is not the result of a give-and-take process. Equally, if the aggrieved party, or its government, takes unilateral action in response, this is not appropriately treated as part of a bargaining process, for it is a straightforward retaliation. At the same time, however, the fact that the host country has the political power to expropriate and the home country the economic power to retaliate,

6

may induce the two sides to bargain, or negotiate, and the cost to each of unilateral action by the other may influence the extent to which the one or the other is prepared to make concessions in the process. But the framework of relationships is not usually so stark. When it is one tends to speak of a 'confrontation', and confrontations can occur at various points even when the overall bargaining process is reasonably peaceful.[1]

At a number of points in this paper I shall refer to the bargaining power of the host countries, which, I think, is often greater than is commonly assumed. The fact that multinational corporations are very often wealthier and more experienced, have easier access to finance, technology and markets, as well as a wider range of alternative courses of action, than the individual less developed countries in which they operate, is often taken as *prima facie* evidence that they necessarily have an advantage over such countries in negotiations. But such generalisations are of little use, for clearly very much depends on individual circumstances. This is not the place to embark on a full discussion of the meaning of 'bargaining power', but from the point of view of the kind of negotiations considered in this paper, two very different elements should be distinguished.

The first is what I might call 'bargaining skill', which includes not only competence in making a case and persuasiveness in discussion, but also the ability to probe intelligently and perceptively into the minimum and maximum positions of the negotiating partners – the skill to push as far as possible but no further. There is little inherent reason why the bargaining skill of negotiators for less developed countries should be significantly less than that of foreign firms, since it is always possible for a government to acquire the services of knowledgeable individuals from outside the country. Clearly, also, as time passes and the government gains experience as well as a larger supply of competent local negotiators, its bargaining power in this respect may be expected to increase.

The second, very different, component of bargaining power relates to the strength of a government's desire for what the foreign firm has to offer in relation to the willingness of the firm to supply it, for this not only determines the range over which agreement is likely to be possible, but also indicates towards which side any agreement is likely to be weighted. A government that is known to have a very strong desire for a factory in a particular field, for example, may find itself in a weak negotiating position *vis-à-vis* foreign firms if there is little or no competition among them for the contract. Conversely, when it is known that there is a strong foreign demand for, say, a particular raw material, countries possessing that material may find themselves in a strong position to extract a high price in return for granting foreign firms permission to produce it.

Similar remarks apply to negotiations over government policies affecting existing enterprises as contrasted to negotiations over the entry of new-comers. Existing foreign enterprises can always withdraw or contract their activities or refuse to supply all the services desired. If a government wants to reduce the scope for independent action by existing firms, and to exercise greater control over their investment policy, their foreign payments, their industrial relations and personnel policies, or to restrict their existing property rights (e.g. patent rights), it must recognise that such actions may reduce the incentive for the firms to continue or expand activities which are desired by the government. On the other hand, if firms have already committed themselves to existing activities in a country they may stand to lose a great deal if agreement is not reached. The bargaining power of the government in negotiating with an existing individual firm may be greater than it is with respect to newcomers, but when the policies it adopts, or attempts to enforce, affect a considerable number of foreign firms, then it may want to move slowly in order not to induce a general reaction among foreign investors which might adversely affect its economic activity. This is especially important for countries in which there are many foreign firms which collectively make a significant contribution to particular industrial sectors of the economy or to the industrial sector generally. Moreover, as Vaitsos points out elsewhere in this volume, there often tends to be an association between political and other historical tries between countries and the flow of direct investment. As a result numerous economic and political relationships have developed of a kind that may enable the country from which investments come to bring a wide variety of pressures on host countries which take measures adversely affecting the interests of the foreign investors (pp. 118–9). This type of pressure is perhaps most important in Latin America whose relations with, and dependence on, the United States have long been a source of tension.

It is easy to understand not only that less developed countries should take a special interest in examining carefully the relation between foreign and domestic gains from the operations of multinational corporations, and that they would often show little compunction in adopting any measures they felt they could afford, after taking into account the probable costs arising from adverse reactions of the foreigners. But it is also easy to understand that many of them would proceed slowly in attempting to control them. Their economic objective is to advance their own development; their political objective is to assert control over their own affairs, which they see as an attribute of political independence. But there are different views regarding the role of foreign investment in promoting economic development. Some countries welcome it with the minimum degree of control. For others, as much government ownership of the means of production as possible is seen as a step towards the creation of a socialist society which they consider to be not only more equitable but also more efficient in meeting the needs of their people and less subject to exploitation by external as well as by internal groups. For still others, government control is considered essential to ensure that foreign firms operate in the public interest, and government ownership is looked on as the most effective means of asserting such control and reinforcing political with economic independence. 'Now Zambia is ours', exulted Kenneth Kaunda on the nationalisation of 51 per cent of the assets of the copper companies. A majority ownership was looked upon as the equivalent of effective control.

But ownership, wholly or in part, is not a *sufficient* condition to assure control of a foreign enterprise. Stated in this bald form there will probably be few who would not agree that the mere acquisition of shares is of little economic consequence without the ability and willingness to take advantage of the powers that ownership confers. If we assume that governments acquiring ownership interests in foreign companies want to exercise some effective control (as distinct from merely receiving their share of the distributed profits), we have then to inquire into their capacity to do so. Further, we have also to ask whether the cost of this means of exercising control and of achieving the ends sought is likely to be less than that of other methods.[2]

Clearly if a government nationalises an enterprise *and* takes over the management it will, by definition, be in control of it. But it is common for a government of a less developed country to acquire a majority control (often 51 per cent) and thus a *de jure* controlling voice on the board of directors, but to refrain from taking over management because it does not have enough qualified people to run the enterprise. In these circumstances they must obtain the necessary managerial and other services, usually through the negotiation of management contracts which often include technological and marketing agreements as well. In the following section we examine the nature of these contracts and discuss some of the problems met in negotiating them.

Ownership with foreign management: comprehensive management agreements

There are many types of arrangements which can be adopted when a government takes over equity control but has not the resources at its disposal to undertake the management of the company. In these circumstances governments often negotiate a comprehensive management/technical/marketing agreement with the foreign partner, either in the form of a single comprehensive agreement or in the form of several linked agreements. The chief characteristic of comprehensive agreements is that they place the responsibility on the foreign partner for organising and managing the domestic operations of the enterprise and often its foreign trade and purchasing operations as well. Such agreements will lay out the rights and obligations of both parties in considerable detail as well as the financial terms of their association. The broad purpose is to make available to, or in the case of newly nationalised industries to retain for, the local company the skills, knowledge, equipment and facilities that it lacks and that can be supplied by the foreign partner.

But since the purpose of acquiring ownership control is to assert national control over the enterprise, the agreement will provide that the foreign partner as a managing agent will operate under the control of the board of directors on which, of course, the government representatives are a majority. Sometimes the duties of the board are specified in considerable detail. But the approval of the board and thus of the government directors will be required for all major actions of the firm including its investment, pricing, sales, employment and financial policies and practices. By these means it is hoped to ensure that the firm operates to maximise the benefit to the host country, subject to a 'fair' or acceptable return to the foreign partner on its investment and for its services. 'Control' over the decisions of the board is deemed to be achieved if the government takes 51 per cent of the equity and thus has a majority vote on the board.

In management contracts of this broad kind it is recognised that when the managing agent is given responsibilities he must also be given the authority necessary to discharge his responsibilities. Hence sufficient control over the relevant aspects of operations is normally granted to enable him to fulfil his obligations under the agreement without interference from the board in the delegated areas. Such responsibilities, which must be conducted within the budgets approved by the board, include the running of the factories, the organisation of marketing and the co-ordination of production, the purchase and installation of machinery and the acquisition of the materials appropriate for the operation and control of production processes. The managing agent will typically have the right – and the obligation – to provide key personnel (a condition often specified in the contract on the insistence of the agent), and the right to make the decisions and take the action respecting equipment, materials and operations, that are necessary to discharge his responsibilities. It will often be formally agreed that such decisions will not be interfered with by the board without full consultation.

In addition to these direct responsibilities and the exercise of the complementary powers, the agent usually agrees to provide a variety of specified services to the local company. He will ordinarily agree to make available patent licenses and trademarks and information about processes, formulae, new technology, knowhow, etc., both from his own organisation and as available elsewhere; he may advise on and act as the company's agent in purchasing; he will ensure the availability of the necessary specialist staff; and he may agree to provide a market for the company's products, either by direct purchase or as selling agent in world markets. He will normally agree to train local people and promote them as rapidly as possible in the firm. The services supplied naturally vary from industry to industry but, in general, the resources of the foreign company are put at the disposal of the local company within the framework of the contract. Such agreements may also be concluded before the start of operations of a joint venture and include not only the establishment of the plant but also all aspects of the creation of a new industry. They usually last for a defined period of years, renewable at the pleasure of either party. Sometimes they may be cancelled without penalty with due notice.

Often there will also be provisions restricting exports, granting exclusive marketing rights or rights respecting the source of purchases, and similar matters. Tariff protection may be ensured and certain types of financial arrangements insisted on.

The level and form of payment for the services rendered will be specified. These are likely to reflect the bargaining strength of the parties as discussed above, and, in particular, the skill of the negotiators for the host government, their understanding of the terms agreed to, and their knowledge of the terms similar companies have obtained elsewhere. In general there are six broad forms of payment, each of which may be used singly or in combination with one or more of the others depending on the position of the company and the type and extent of the services provided. The foreign managing partner may receive a percentage of the profit earned, a percentage of sales value, a fixed fee for specific services, a percentage of the purchase price of equipment for his purchasing services, a lump sum or a fixed annual fee for specific services, or a fixed fee per unit of sales volume. The first two may be subject to minimum or maximum totals or both and be calculated on a sliding scale which decreases as profit or sales increase. Any of these may appear in combination with any of the others – for example, a percentage of profit plus a percentage of sales, both subject to a minimum and maximum, plus fixed fees for the purchase and installation of plant and equipment. In addition it is often provided that the salaries of personnel supplied by the foreign partner acting as managing agent be paid by the local enterprise.

Let us now consider in more detail the provisions often found in such agreements with respect to the types of costs incurred. We shall first discuss the methods of remunerating the foreign partner undertaking to supply management and other services, and some of the problems involved in keeping such costs as reasonable as possible. We shall also note the existence of other types of costs, such as inadequate localisation and monopolistic restraints.

Broadly speaking there are four issues raised in connection with the methods of remunerating the foreign partners in management, technical and other general consultancy agreements: (1) the need for management and other fees for the foreign partner when a company is a joint venture; (2) the forms of payment and the desirability of negotiating one overall fee instead of a variety of fees each attached to particular services, including the use of fees as an incentive to improve performance as contrasted to simple remuneration for services rendered; (3) implicit remuneration when agents are also suppliers; and (4) the appropriateness of payment for certain kinds of services, notably salaries of personnel supplied by the foreign partner as managing agent and fees for patent licenses, trademarks, etc.

1. *Fees in joint ventures*

In view of his equity interest and the return obtained from it should the foreign shareholder be separately remunerated for the services he renders to advance the efficiency of the company? After all, he gains from any increased efficiency through his share of the increased profits. *Per contra*, if losses are made should he not bear his share of the losses?

Let us look first at the theory of the problem. A limited liability company is a separate entity from its shareholders. Profit for the company is the difference between its receipts and the sum of its costs, including the cost of capital and all expenses. 'Profit' on investment for shareholders is the return on their capital investment in the firm. A simple shareholder, taking no part in the operation of the firm itself, obtains a share of the profit in proportion to his holding, either in the form of dividends or of an increase in the capital value of his shares.

If a shareholder provides services to the firm without payment he receives no special benefit in relation to other shareholders who share proportionately in any increases in profits attributable to the services. The value of the services provided are, in principle, equal to the increase in profits (or decrease in losses) that can be attributed to them. If the company were wholly-owned by a single shareholder who also provided managerial, organisational or technological services, the shareholder would expect to capture the full value of his services in the form of increased profits or reduced losses except insofar as the government took a proportion in taxes. If he is only a part owner, however, he obtains only a part of this value in proportion to his equity in the company. The other shareholders also benefit in proportion to their equity.

At the same time the provision of the services involved the 'managing' partner in costs which are not shared by the local partner and he will feel entitled to be reimbursed for these costs. But such a reimbursement would then appear as a charge on the company and thus a deduction from total receipts when profits are calculated. In effect, therefore, the managing partner would still bear a portion of the costs for which he had, in principle, been reimbursed. Hence, at a minimum, a partner providing services to the company is not unreasonable in asking for fees to cover his costs plus a reasonable margin.

Whether a managing shareholder would accept less than this or ask for more depends on a number of circumstances. If, for example, the investment has already been made and the company is already operating when agreements are being negotiated (the company might have been partly taken over by the government), the foreign shareholder might give his services free in order to ensure the profitability of his remaining investment; or, at the opposite extreme, he might be paid a great deal as an implicit part of compensation arrangements, especially if the remaining equity held by him is so small that his share of the profit would be negligible and the return from providing managing services too small to make it worth his while if only his costs were covered.

Nevertheless, even accepting that it is appropriate for a partner providing services to be recompensed for his costs, including the opportunity costs of services supplied, this is no reason why a host country should go out of its way to incur such expenditures by insisting on the negotiation of formal agreements. Local shareholders will clearly gain financially if the foreign partner is willing to give services free, providing that the powers of the local members of the board of directors are not affected, and it is difficult to see why their powers would be diminished by the mere absence of a formal agreement. In principle, therefore, from the point of view of the host country, management agreements should not be entered into for joint ventures with foreign corporations whenever the foreign partner can be persuaded to render the services required without them, provided that the absence of such agreements does not impair the degree to which *in practice* the host country can monitor the behaviour of the firm and exert its control.

2. *Type of payment*

As indicated above, the agreements may provide for remuneration by some combination of the following: fixed sums per unit of time, lump sums, percentage of sales, percentage of profits, percentage of purchase price, fixed amount per unit of sales and special payments or agreements to purchase.

In practice contracts that provide for payments under a variety of these headings may turn out to be more expensive than if only one type of fee had been negotiated, although in principle this need not be the case. Hence critics of comprehensive management agreements often argue that only a single fee related to profits should be agreed to, and that a schedule should be adopted which provides for a decline after a point in the percentage of profits paid as total profits increase. This has the advantage of simplicity, and to some extent may make it easier to calculate the total obligations that may arise and thus to ensure that excessive payments are not incurred.

Ideally, of course, the different elements of the services rendered should be costed and priced separately so that it would be as clear as possible exactly how much is being paid under each heading. In practice this may give the foreign negotiator an advantage and make it easier for him to inflate his total remuneration; but if the government negotiators are not aware in reasonably precise terms of the nature, scope and value of the services they require they would be at a disadvantage in any circumstances. Moreover, again in principle, the foreign company in drawing up its own position would have made calculations of the cost of the several types of services involved based on its own past experience, and would take into account the terms accepted in similar contracts elsewhere. These would form the bases for its estimate of the overall payment it would require. If this were the case, the minimum acceptable overall payment would not be much different from the minimum acceptable calculated from a set of separately specified payments. The overriding determinant in the end would be the relative bargaining power and expertise of the two sides.

A major difficulty with the notion of a single type of fee for a comprehensive managerial contract arises from the fact that such a fee, by its very nature, must be either fixed per unit of time or related to a single aspect of the performance of the firm, while the services rendered relate to different aspects which may continue to be provided and required in spite of a disappointing performance in other directions. Fixed fees are unrelated to any aspect of performance; fees expressed as a percentage of profits, production, sales or purchases vary with the relevant value or volume, and a case can be made for paying separately for each of these services when required and for relating the fees to some measure of performance in each case.

Obviously, for any type of payment other than one related to profits, the foreign supplier may be profiting while the company is making losses, the extent of which will be aggravated by the size of the fees paid out. Moreover, if fees are related to sales, there is an incentive to maximise sales at the expense of profits, while if they are related to value of purchases there is an incentive to inflate this value.

On the other hand, losses may be made through no fault of the management and even in spite of his most competent and diligent attention to the affairs of the company; indeed, because of this attention losses may have been very much reduced over what they would have been. Losses for a considerable period are not uncommon, for example, when reorganisation of an ailing company is required or when an entirely new industry is being established. For any company where the risk of making losses, or very small profits, is high due to circumstances beyond the control of management, fees related only to profitability will not be acceptable unless a minimum is specified. But if special services to increase sales, introduce new technology, improve quality, etc., are required, it may be necessary, and occasionally desirable, to make special payments for the purpose in order to provide adequate inducement for the supply of the desired services.

Let us consider briefly the types of services often required and some general principles which may be considered in negotiating fees in comprehensive management/technical contracts.

Remuneration for management. If foreign equity is substantial *and* if for some reason it is considered necessary or desirable to draw up formal contractual arrangements with the foreign partner, a fixed fee per year based on the estimated costs of the managing services to be rendered may be the most desirable method of remuneration. The interest of the foreign partner in the profits of the firm as a consequence of his shareholding should provide an incentive to good performance providing that there is an assurance that the remittance of dividends on an acceptable basis is agreed. A limit to dividend repatriation in these circumstances is equivalent to a change in the method of remuneration to a percentage of profit subject to a maximum, which may, in effect, mean that it becomes a fixed annual fee at the maximum. Incentive to improve profits further is then removed.

Such contracts should not run for long periods (say over six to eight years) unless there are special circumstances (e.g. they may be linked to compensation arrangements after a nationalisation). As the management of joint ventures becomes increasingly localised, the strictly managerial functions of the foreign partner will decline, although they will probably not disappear entirely in view of the continuing advice and new 'management technology' that the foreign partner may be able to provide.

If the foreign partner has such a small equity in the venture that the prospect of profit is of negligible interest to him, fees as a percentage of total profit, subject to a minimum sum, may be appropriate. A guaranteed minimum, whether or not profits are made, will probably be required whenever the risk of loss, or of very small profits for a considerable period, is high.

Special management fees, preferably a fixed sum, may also be appropriate as payment for the planning and development of management organisation in the pre-production stage of a new company. Wherever possible, however, the senior management personnel who are expected to run the factory after it begins production should be associated with the development, and, if possible, with the planning of the layout and construction of the plant. There is sometimes a tendency for management taking over a new plant to put the blame for poor performance on those who were responsible for the original construction and planning. This tendency can be lessened if the operating management is associated with the plant from the beginning. At the same time management, on taking over the plant, should be in a position to appraise the work done and insist on any alterations required. It will be willing and able to do this most effectively if it is independent of the plant contractor. Hence, for a new plant it is preferable, if possible, to make the technical consultancy agreement for the construction of the plant with one company and the management arrangements with another while associating the future management with the planning of the plant. Often, however, this is an impracticable policy to pursue because of the difficulties in getting separate international groups to operate in this way.

Remuneration for technology. Royalties as a percentage of sales value are the usual form of paying for technology, whether it be secret knowhow or the use of patented equipment, processes or products. For the most part when a company makes existing knowledge available to others it incurs little or no additional cost unless it also provides the personal services of technical personnel to assist and advise. Certainly the cost does not increase with the value of sales. For these reasons fees for such services cannot be based on costs to the supplier. Non-industrial countries which are of marginal importance to a multinational corporation may, by hard bargaining, often obtain existing technology on favourable terms when the risk that similar terms would have to be offered to the more important industrial countries is low. In any event, on this issue, special efforts should be made to keep the percentage on sales as low as possible and subject to a maximum sum, or even to persuade the supplier to accept a fixed fee. Unless technical assistance is required, all payments are simply contributions to overhead expenditure already incurred and to on-going research and development expenditures. Attempts should be made to relate the royalties to the specific technology supplied where this is practicable since it is often easier to build a case for limited royalties on this basis and to avoid the open-ended commitment which is implied by payments as a percentage of sales. To protect its position elsewhere a foreign company will often insist that the fees paid be kept secret.

Again, of course, it may not be necessary to pay for the technology if the foreign agent has an extensive equity stake in the local company. One of the effects of partial nationalisation of the subsidiary of a multinational firm, however, is likely to be a demand by the foreign parent for payment for the technical services it had formerly supplied free of charge to the subsidiary.

Remuneration for marketing services. Unless it is necessary to establish or reorganise a complete marketing network there seems to be no special reason why local sales should not be part of the general managerial functions performed by the foreign managing group. For many companies local sales do not pose particularly difficult problems apart from the question of the general efficiency of management. Where this is the case, payment for marketing services should be resisted. If, on the other hand, the development and promotion of local sales is a major problem, then fees as a percentage of sales, up to a viable maximum, may have to be paid. The scale and maximum for such fees should be based, as closely as possible, on the degree of initial difficulty.

Export sales pose an entirely different problem. In the first place, the contribution of the foreign company may be largely related to the services provided by an already established marketing organisation, the use of which may be an important, and even necessary, condition for the successful promotion of exports of the commodity concerned. Some incentive and remuneration will often be necessary to ensure optimum performance by the exporting firm if it is acting as an export sales agent. This appropriately takes the form of a straight commission on the value of sales. If, however, the foreign partner buys the product as a principal, either for his own use or for resale, any remuneration should be related to world prices for the product purchased or for the finished product of which it is a major ingredient. A small discount off such world prices is a usual commission.

The question of payments for trademarks and trade names is particularly difficult. Their value is directly related to sales, and if the foreign company as part of its managerial and technical agreements or by virtue of its shareholding, receives dividends, a percentage of profits, or a percentage of sales, it automatically receives an implicit payment for the use of trademarks. It incurs no cost whatsoever in making them available and in principle, therefore, no further payment should be made. On the other hand, the foreign firm may, in conformity with its own established principles, insist on some payment. If so, the payment should take the form of a lump sum or at most a fixed sum per year. Trademarks can be very expensive indeed, especially if paid for with a percentage of the value of sales, but the use of an established trademark is often extremely valuable, especially for manu-factured goods in export markets. For the local market they are of less importance and may even be dispensed with if the cost is high and if they are not embedded in the manufacturing process or associated with the technology or packaging (e.g. moulds for tyres or Coca-Cola bottles for Coca-Cola) and if imports of competitive commodities whose trade names have a widespread appeal can be controlled.

If foreign trademarks have to be paid for, it is desirable, whenever possible, to make provision in agreements for the possibility of introducing local trademarks, especially for goods largely consumed in the local market. This has been done in a number of countries for such things as beer, spirits and cigarettes.

Purchasing services. The only reason for paying separately for purchasing services provided by the foreign managing partner would be to cover costs he may incur in purchasing and in making available the services of his purchasing organisation. But both of these services are, like sales, a neces-sary aspect of the obligations of general management and, unless there are special costs, should not have to be paid for. Sometimes, however, skilled advice needs to be especially hired or other unusual costs incurred which may justify special remuneration.

Plant construction and associated services. Both technical and managerial services are required in the construction of a plant and preparations for production, and fixed fees are an appropriate type of remuneration for such services. In general, fees based on the value of capital equipment, though common everywhere, should be avoided in order to avoid creating incentives for the agent to maximise the costs of acquisition and installation. 'Cost plus' contracts have built-in disadvantages.

3. *Implicit remuneration of suppliers*

A difficult problem for which there is no entirely satisfactory solution arises when the foreign partner is also the supplier of equipment or materials which do not have reasonably unambiguous international market prices, or of which he is the sole international producer. This is the notorious problem of 'transfer pricing' which has been widely discussed in the literature. Whenever there are international prices relating to such equipment or materials, the agreement need only provide that the prices paid shall be 'competitive', that is, not higher than known international prices. But very often no such prices exist, or if they do and the agent is either the sole international supplier or is linked with other suppliers in a cartel, the prices charged may, and indeed are likely to, be very much higher than costs of production plus reasonable margins for development costs and profits. International prices will not exist if the parent of the partner itself produces specially designed machinery (and the corresponding technical knowhow and services) only for his own subsidiaries or associated companies; and obviously international prices will not be 'competitive' if the supplier is the sole producer (or is careful to avoid price competition with other producers) of machinery, equipment or materials for which there are no close substitutes. This is frequently the case when machinery or products are patented or associated closely with secret knowhow. It is also true when trademarks have come to be so accepted as a guarantee of quality that the owner of the trademark can command a significant price premium.

In all of the above circumstances, the supplier may make a considerable profit from a management agreement which is unknown to the purchaser. If, in addition, the supplier receives fees as a percentage of purchases or of capital expenditures for plant, or has been permitted to obtain an equity holding through the capitalisation of equipment, he clearly is likely to do very well indeed out of it. Such arrangements may be necessary at times, but they need very careful evaluation and monitoring.

As already noted, there is no completely satisfactory resolution of these difficulties and careful (and sophisticated) bargaining is required. If international prices exist, and, therefore, the prices which others pay can be known, the negotiators should try to obtain a discount from the supplier when he is also the producer, in view of his other interests in the profitability and operations of the company. Similarly, when the management or technical consultant is the sole supplier of highly differentiated machinery or equipment, attempts should be made to clarify the basis of pricing. In neither case should purchasing fees be paid. The objective of the company buying the equipment or material should be to get the price as near as possible to the cost of production plus an agreed margin for profit and development expenses.

4. *Payment of salaries of foreign personnel*

In many agreements the managing company is obligated or empowered to provide senior managerial and technical personnel to serve the local company either on a continuing basis or when a special need arises. Sometimes such personnel are seconded from the parent company and remain on the establishment of the parent; sometimes they are supplied by the parent but not from its own permanent staff. Usually such personnel are either paid directly by the local company, or the foreign company is reimbursed for their salaries and associated expenses.

This type of arrangement has been criticised on the ground that when there is an agreement foreign personnel should be considered part of the services provided by the foreign partner and their cost paid by him. Alternatively, it is sometimes suggested that if foreign personnel, usually including the general manager, are competent to manage the company and are paid by the company then there is no need for a managing agency agreement.

In this connection it is necessary to distinguish between personnel who are seconded from the permanent staff of the foreign company and those who are simply recruited by it. In both cases the local company is assured of continuing managerial services, but in the former the foreign company loses the services of some of its own staff, while in the latter it only acts as a 'purchasing agent', so to speak, with the responsibility of ensuring the quality of the services supplied. In both cases if the foreign firm pays the salaries of the foreign personnel it bears an additional cost, indirectly for seconded personnel and directly for the personnel it recruits from outside.

Of course if the foreign firm pays for the salaries but, in estimating the fees it requests under a management contract, it considers any such extra costs and raises its total fee accordingly, which procedure is adopted may make little difference to the cost to the local company. On the other hand, salary scales of expatriate personnel may be much higher than those of equivalent local personnel. This creates a variety of well known problems and there is much to be said for aligning to local levels any salaries paid to expatriate personnel by the local firm and requiring the foreign partner to 'top up' such salaries as necessary, preferably abroad.

The second argument, that if a manager can manage competently, and his salary is paid by the local company, then there is no need for a management agreement, overlooks the 'package' of services provided under such agreements, including the assurance of continuity of management and the fact that other resources are put at the disposal of the local company. No matter how competent he may be personally there is little doubt that in many cases the ability of an individual manager to call at will on the skills and resources of an established company enables him to be more effective than he would otherwise be. When neither circumstance is relevant it follows that a managing agency agreement is not of great value to the local company, and it may then be preferable for the company to attempt to recruit its expatriate personnel on an individual basis.

It is often held that individual recruitment of managers would not only be cheaper, but would also ensure more effective local control of the company than is possible under management agreements. Whether or not it would be cheaper can only be evaluated with reference to the actual position of an individual company. Individually recruited managers have little long run security; work permits may be withdrawn, contracts cancelled or not renewed. For senior men this can be a serious problem, and a good man with alternative choices of employment will be reluctant to accept the risk unless the remuneration is high enough to offset it. The more senior and the more qualified the man, the higher will this risk premium be likely to be.

Moreover, if one of the purposes of management agreements is to provide for training of local people to replace foreigners, individually recruited managers may be less willing to speed this process than those who can return to an international company. It is sometimes objected that if the foreign managers of local companies are seconded from, and thus still consider themselves part of, the foreign parent company, they will be less committed to the interests of the local company. There may thus be a conflict of interest. This aspect of the question cannot be ignored, although clearly it is significant only when the interests of the local company and the foreign agent diverge. Such divergencies, if they exist at all, will for the most part relate to financial matters, transfer prices, sources and prices of purchases, investment policy, etc., all of which can be dealt with separately in the agreement as we have seen, or by government or central bank regulations.

It should be noted that although in the beginning a comprehensive management agreement may be required, under which almost the entire range of specialist services needed by the firm is provided for, in most countries the management element can be fairly quickly eliminated by the development of competent local personnel. It may then be necessary to continue limited agreements for the supply of other services, notably technology, and perhaps export marketing, but one measure of the success of a management agreement is, in fact, the speed with which it can become unnecessary.

Monopolistic elements

There are three types of monopolistic restrictions commonly found in management and technical agreements which we have briefly noted above and which call for comment. They relate to restrictions on exports, exclusive marketing rights, and restrictions on the source of purchases. The first may be connected with patent and trademark rights; the second is often related to the international business of the foreign firm; and the third to the desire of the management to supply, or control the supply of, certain products to the company, especially equipment.

Restrictions on exports. Restrictions of this type are found primarily in connection with the sale of technology, sometimes in patent licensing agreements and sometimes in technical agreements. The patent laws of all countries give the owner of a patent the right to control the conditions of sale (within certain stated limits) of the commodities produced under his patents. Thus in granting licenses the patentee is permitted to stipulate the geographical limits of the market that the licensee is permitted to supply.

A company may grant a patent license to another company in another country attaching the condition that sales can only be made within that country or within a specified group of other countries. Licenses may be granted to still other companies to produce for other markets. The purpose, of course, is to restrict competition among the licensees, for most of the value of the patent right lies in the control of competition that it provides. The licensee gains if there are others who would otherwise compete with him using the patented process or producing the patented product, but it often means also that exports that would otherwise have been possible are prevented.

Because of these and other restrictions on the use of technology, and the fact that fees must be paid to patentees when their patents are used, it is sometimes urged that the less developed countries should not recognise the international patent rights of foreigners. I have argued elsewhere (Penrose, 1951, 1973) that such countries gain little from doing so and that, although a case can be made for paying reasonable royalties, the monopoly aspects of patent grants should be eliminated. Even without patents, however, agreements for the use of foreign technology are often necessary if for no other reason than that the advice and assistance of foreign experts is required. Moreover, exports of patented products are not possible without a license to other countries which recognise the patent rights protecting the product. Hence even the abolition of the patent law might not go far towards solving the problems associated with the restrictions on exports of patent protected commodities, for technological agreements would often still be necessary and the problem of restrictions would remain.

It is also not uncommon for patentees to attempt to use their patents as the basis for imposing restrictions which go beyond those legally permitted under patent laws. There are a whole range of restrictive practices, including restrictions on exports to countries where exportation is *not* already limited by the existence of the patent, which are outside the rights normally granted in a patent law and which can, therefore, be attacked in the courts. Obviously it is important that a government ensure that such restrictions are not imposed and that 'legal' restrictions on exports be kept to a minimum.

Exclusive marketing rights. Some agreements will grant the foreign partner the exclusive right to purchase all or part of the output of the company for export. Sometimes the partner is granted sole rights, sometimes only if the company itself cannot sell on better terms. Such arrangements are common when the foreign company has facilities for further processing (and indeed may be interested in the local company only as a source of materials) or for handling the product in export markets.

Exclusive marketing rights may make possible greater exports than would otherwise be the case, but they also may reduce both the opportunities for, and the profitability of, independent sales by the local company. They should be very carefully examined to be sure that the local company benefits and is not receiving an unduly low return because of the monopsonistic position of the foreign firm.

Restrictions on source of purchases. I have already discussed the problems arising when the managing partner is also the supplier of equipment and materials to the firm and when it is difficult to find criteria against which to appraise the reasonableness of the prices he charges. Here I shall be concerned only with certain types of restrictions on the source of purchases which agreements with foreign companies commonly contain.

First, however, it should be noted that the source from which continuing requirements of equipment, machinery and technology can be obtained after a plant is established is often automatically restricted because of the nature of the technology and machinery, regardless of whether these come from capitalist forms or from state owned organisations in communist countries or elsewhere. Technology embodied in a particular plant is usually not interchangeable with 'similar' technology supplied by different producers for other plants. Spare parts, for example, must usually be obtained from the original supplier. It is often not easy to expand capacity or to replace existing equipment with machinery imported from a different source since it may not fit with existing machinery. In other words, the choice of a particular form of technology or a particular supplier may at times determine the source of supply for a large variety of items connected with the technology in use. This problem may be aggravated by the distribution of the ownership of technology through the operation of the patent system. In any case, a continuing 'dependence' on a particular supplier is created which is very difficult to avoid, especially if the industry in the country consists of only one factory.

To the extent that technology is the factor restricting the source from which the continuing requirements of the factory can be purchased, restrictive clauses in formal agreements are redundant; but to the extent that the technology leaves a choice of supplier, a foreign company may request restrictive clauses in the agreements under which it is to operate. Apart from those imposed by patent licenses, the most common type of restriction is found in what is known as 'tie-in' clauses, which require that specified other goods be bought from the company selling the machinery and undertaking the project, or from a source approved by it. Tie-in clauses which restrain competition, including such clauses attached to patent licenses which go beyond the scope of the patent, are illegal under the anti-trust laws of the United States, the Restrictive Practices Act of the United Kingdom, and in the European Community under the Treaty of Rome.

Tie-in clauses, unless they are redundant, clearly restrain competition among sources of supply; but from the point of view of the foreign supplier who is also charged with responsibility for the efficient establishment and operation of a factory, they serve another purpose as well which should not be entirely ignored. A foreign managing agent must have the right to satisfy himself that the quality and specifications of the equipment bought for the factory are of the standard required. If he supplies the equipment himself he presumably knows exactly what he is getting. If he is not to supply it himself he would like assurance as to the reliability of the supplier.

For a large number of industrial products the past performance and reputation of the supplier is one of the most effective guarantees of quality. (It is partly for this reason, of course, that trademarks are so jealously protected, since they permit the identification of past performance with the present and the future in an easily recognisable form. It is this, as well as advertising, that enables the owner of a trademark to differentiate his product and obtain thereby a degree of 'monopoly power'.) Alternatively, the foreign partner may feel more confidence in the quality of purchases if he can draw on his own past experience with various suppliers.

Thus a foreign company, in accepting responsibility for the efficient establishment and management of a company, may request clauses in the contract which provide that he must be allowed to supply, or at least approve, the purchase of certain kinds of commodities simply in order to ensure that he can protect the interests of the local company. The foreign manager may feel that if he does not have this control inappropriate purchases may be insisted upon through ignorance or because local officials of the company have personal or other profitable relationships with foreign suppliers which influence their judgement.

At the same time, however, this very situation provides an opportunity for the foreign company to gain at the expense of the local company because of its own links with foreign suppliers. In the business world it is not considered unethical to engage in price discrimination among different markets and between purchasers as is evident from the fact that many developed countries have felt it necessary to pass laws controlling such practices. The largest and most prestigious companies in the world have been prominent transgressors in this respect. Hence, to strike an appropriate balance between a desirable leeway in purchasing to be given to the manager and the controls necessary to ensure that prices are 'fair and reasonable' is a difficult task. No general rules can easily be laid down. It may be necessary or desirable to grant exclusive purchasing rights to a managing partner even if they contain clauses which would, in other circumstances, be completely unacceptable. The operation of such arrangements, however, needs to be carefully watched and prices justified.

De jure and de facto control

So much for the terms of management agreements. The board of directors has control and the government controls the board. But what determines the *de facto* role of the majority partner? This will depend largely on the competence of the government directors and the time they have to devote to the problems of the company. If these directors have enough knowledge and expertise at their disposal about the operations of the firm to enable them to understand the implications of the decisions taken by the board (most of which will be based upon the recommendations of management), and to evaluate decisions of management not referred to the board, then they will be able to exert effective control. This means, however, that they must have not only expert assistance, but also time at their disposal to study their briefs in order to appraise costs and form reasonable judgements about the effectiveness of management in this sphere; they must know enough about international markets for capital equipment, raw materials, consultancy services, etc. to judge quality, and whether or not the parent of the foreign partner is the most appropriate source of supply and whether the prices charged are reasonable; they must understand accounting and be able to check the sufficiency of the accounts as presented for the purpose of decision making and tax avoidance – and this often goes beyond the sphere of external auditors; they must understand the intricacies of license agreements; they must be able to appraise the economics of the firm's advertising; and so on. All of these require knowledge and expertise of a high order if effective control over management is to be achieved.

Such knowledge can, of course, be made available if the relevant government departments have adequate staff, trained and kept on the job long enough to acquire the requisite experience with the ways of the business. If, however, such people are in very short supply, or, which is just as likely, the organisation of government personnel is insufficiently stable and departments suffer a high turnover of staff, then 'control' will remain in, or by default drift into, the hands of the foreign partners. Government members of the board may take a special interest in certain types of decisions, for example, Treasury representatives in the distribution of profits, but even then, the effectiveness of their participation will be severely circumscribed by their own expertise or by that of their departmental advisers. It is not unusual for the same individuals, who themselves are often busy as high government officials or ministers, to be members of the boards of quite a number of companies.

It is very easy indeed to underestimate the amount of work that must be put into the task of 'controlling' the operations of a foreign enterprise, especially in the more complex industries, but even in some of the 'simpler' ones. None of the several aspects of the problem is, in itself, necessarily very difficult, but the time and effort of knowledgeable people must be available for diversion to the task. Very often this simply is not possible. Consequently it is not at all unusual for a government, after the expensive business of acquiring 51 per cent of the equity of an existing enterprise or insisting on 51 per cent of that of a new enterprise, to find that it has not the resources to provide the expertise required to assert the effective control a majority partner could be expected to exercise. This is particularly true when foreign management must be left in charge of the firm for lack of an adequate supply of local managerial capacity.

One of the greatest sources of the power of multinational corporations lies in their knowledge, which includes technological knowledge, and knowledge of markets and finance, as well as of managerial skills. It follows that the only really effective way of reducing this power lies in the development of similar knowledge in the host country. The question then arises of whether the acquisition of equity control of foreign enterprises accelerates the acquisition of the relevant knowledge or makes possible a more effective use of the knowledge already in hand.

Take the last question first. If the sources of divergence of interest between host countries and multinational firms are considered in relation to the provisions of the agreements between the parties which are designed to protect the interest of the former, one finds that all of them could easily be, and very often already are, the subject of financial or regulatory legislation; while for some of them the question of equity control of the company is not relevant. All sorts of payments abroad – dividend remittances, transfer pricing, technical and other fees – can be and usually are subject to foreign exchange control regulations; the government's tax share of profits is a matter for tax law; restrictive practices can be regulated by anti-monopoly legislation; all practicable localisation of personnel can be obtained through the control of work permits; investment policy can be controlled through investment licensing, etc. If the argument that was advanced earlier is accepted – that less developed countries often have even greater scope than do industrial countries to impose their will on multinational corporations and are often more willing to do so – then the primary question we have to consider in this connection is whether it is cheaper, and equally (or more), effective, to exercise control through legislation and government regulations than through the acquisition of a majority of the equity. If the same degree of control can be exercised without majority control of the board of directors of the firms, then it is clearly cheaper to avoid investing capital in order to obtain control. Investment to increase the government share of profits is a separate question, but in view of the cost of management agreements and the scope for taxation, there is no particular reason why the financial returns to the government should be greater as a result of such participation. However, can we expect that regulation of foreign companies without majority ownership will be equally effective?

Effective control by either method assumes that government officials have the technical capacity to exercise it, but for any given level of technical capacity there seems to be no reason to assume that the relevant operations of firms could not be as effectively controlled through government regulation as through control of boards of directors. Multinational firms in a less developed country are fully aware of the power of the government to make their life difficult or terminate it in the country, and a simple warning that government is concerned about any aspect of their activities is often sufficient to make them behave very cautiously indeed. The primary necessity, and one which is accomplished by representation on the board of directors, is access to information about what is going on within the enterprise – the decisions of the board and the practices of management. Directors have the right to demand information, to inspect internal memoranda and accounts, and to call for regular reports from management. But any director can have this power; majority control is not necessary, and special provision can always be made to ensure that any government director should have access to any information he wants whether the government holds 51 per cent or only 1 per cent of the shares.

If all that a government wants to do is to control those aspects of the operations of multinational firms which are likely adversely to affect the economic development of the country, it does not seem to me necessary that it acquire a majority of the equity. Something beween 5 per cent and 10 per cent can be an equally satisfactory means of obtaining access to information and an effective voice in the counsels of the board and management. Firms are always required to operate within the laws and regulations laid down by government, and the development of sufficient expertise within government, either through the training of local officials or through the temporary acquisition of knowledgeable expatriates, should, given the will to enforce the rules, provide as effective a means as any of controlling multinational corporations – and a much cheaper one.[3]

Objections to the activities of multinational corporations in less developed countries on the ground that they introduce inappropriate technology and products and create an undesirable dependence on industrial countries may be valid, but are not relevant for a discussion of means of controlling their local subsidiaries. The capital-intensive plants or less essential industries which are deemed 'inappropriate' are often introduced because the government itself wanted them. Sometimes a new industry may be so badly wanted by a government that it is willing to enter into highly unfavourable management/technological agreements in order to persuade some foreign company to establish it. In such circumstances it is, of course, unreasonable to charge the company with 'exploitation' because the terms of an agreement had to be extremely advantageous in order to make the investment worth its while. As noted above, the more a country insists on the need for a specific industry, the worse is its bargaining position unless there is considerable competition among international firms for the job. These issues are resolved in the initial bargaining over the terms of a firm's entry into the country. The expansion of existing companies can be controlled by investment licensing; and heavy excise taxes can be imposed on 'luxury' products.

The case for full ownership

I have argued above that a foreign partner can effectively control a local subsidiary even though it has a minority interest in the company. I think also that it is very likely that the foreign parent will be able to make as much money from a joint venture, under various kinds of agreements, as it did when the company was wholly owned, although, so far as I know, there is no systematic evidence to support this belief. It is clear, however, that multinational corporations are beginning to look very favourably on joint ventures in such circumstances. Nor is majority ownership a sufficient condition for effective control by a host country.

It is nevertheless argued by many that such ownership is necessary for the further development of genuine local control of the economy over time, partly because it gives the local people extensive experience in running industry, and partly because it helps to develop the spirit of independence which is necessary for the creation of a sense of economic cohesiveness and political identity. If my argument is correct, however, that majority ownership gives no greater opportunity for effective control and no greater opportunity for the advancement of local people than could be achieved with much smaller amounts of equity, combined with government insistence on as much effective regulation as its resources permit (including insistence on rapid localisation of management), then it follows that a simple takeover of companies may lead to expectations which will be disappointed and that popular disillusion with government policy will set in and spread.

There are, nevertheless, circumstances in which it is important, for all of the reasons advanced by the advocates of majority ownership, that a government does take over a foreign enterprise. This is especially likely to be the case with respect to foreign companies exploiting local raw material resources, or to foreign companies which loom very large in the economy in other fields. If it is possible for the local host country to organise effective management for such enterprises, perhaps with the help of some individually recruited expatriate technical assistance, then a strong case can be made, not for taking 51 per cent of the company, but for complete nationalisation. Selective ownership of this kind will avoid a needless dilution of indigenous but scarce management and technical resources over a large number of companies, and will also permit a concentration of the available investible capital in areas where it can be used really effectively and profitably under local control. If such companies are only half taken over the foreign partners will retain a great deal of influence over managerial decisions, and the indigenous managers will have fewer opportunities to chart a new course or lead the company in directions more appropriate to the developmental objectives of the economy. One hundred per cent ownership, with the capacity to exercise full control of certain basic industries, could well be a much more satisfying and successful method of asserting local capacity and economic independence than half nationalisation of a number of companies which remain effectively dominated by foreign expertise.

There is little question in my mind that, in the industrial field, multinational corporations have great advantages to offer a less developed country and have, in fact, been extremely important in the industrialisation of many of them.[4] But there are also disadvantages, and the activities of foreign firms must be subject to effective local control. The solution of many of the problems facing the countries of the Third World in the course of their development – stagnation of agriculture, high levels of unemployment (often nearly insoluble in the face of rapid rates of population increase), and grossly inequitable distribution of income – is more likely to be retarded than advanced by diverting attention and energies to the acquisition of majority ownership in foreign companies generally. A government may, of course, decide that only full socialism – public ownership of the means of production – is the basis on which it wants to organise its economy. Even in this case, however, 51 per cent control of foreign corporations may be largely an irrelevance, even as a beginning.

Notes

1 It is possible, of course, to construct 'models' of bargaining in which confrontations are part of the game, and hence part of the bargaining process. I would not necessarily quarrel with such models if they suit the problem in hand, but I do not find it useful here to attempt a more sophisticated discussion than the one presented.

2 It has been suggested that if compensation is less than the present value of the expected profits then the country is bound to gain through the element of confiscation represented by the gap. This is true if the net profits discounted are those of the firm *after* nationalisation (which may be less than the profits expected under foreign ownership if efficiency, however defined, declines), and if the opportunity cost of local resources absorbed is properly evaluated.

3 It has been argued that foreign firms take a very different attitude towards a government partner with majority control than to one that has only a minority interest and are much more willing to co-operate in the former case. A 'we and they' dichotomy may develop towards a minority partner and 'adversary' attitudes may be adopted on both sides. This point may well be important in some circumstances. On the other hand, very similar attitudes may arise in joint ventures where the government has an equal or majority share of the equity. See, for example, the management problems of joint ventures in the Egyptian oil industry (Stevens, 1974). Where such problems are important they add to the case for complete nationalisation, but are not necessarily decisive. I am indebted to R. H. Green for discussion of this type of issue.

4 In this respect I should like to call attention to a useful and important article by Bill Warren in the *New Left Review* (Warren, 1973), in which he concludes that a 'major upsurge' (p. 3) of capitalism is taking place in the Third World leading to extensive industrialisation and not to stagnation, and that the traditional left wing insistence that imperialism is retarding this kind of development misses the essential aspects of what is in fact happening in these countries.

References

Penrose, Edith, 1951. *The Economics of the International Patent System.* Baltimore: Johns Hopkins.
    1973. International patenting and the less developed countries. *Economic Journal,* **83**, 768–86.
Stevens, P. J., 1974. Joint Ventures in Middle East Oil, 1957–74. Ph.D. thesis, University of London, unpublished.
Warren, Bill, 1973. Imperialism and Capitalist Industrialisation. *New Left Review,* no. 81, 3–44.

PART III

Issues in International Finance and Monetary Policy

8. The post 1971 international financial system and the less developed countries

CARLOS F. DIAZ-ALEJANDRO[1]

Discussions regarding the stakes of less developed countries (LDCs) in international monetary reform have typically emphasised the benefits to LDCs of an international monetary system conducive to fast growth and freer trade and financial policies in the industrialised countries. Much has also been written regarding schemes to link expansions in world liquidity, either by issuing special drawing rights (SDRs) or by a once-and-for-a-while increase in the price of monetary gold, to an increased flow of financial resources to LDCs (Helleiner, 1974; Park, 1973; United Nations, 1972). Some attention will be given in this paper to these issues, but more will be said on two relatively neglected subjects: the position of LDCs in a world of greater exchange rate flexibility, and the interactions of LDCs with the emerging international capital markets.

The 1972–4 commodity boom, including the remarkable increases in oil prices on the one hand, and the plight of some African nations in the Sahel and of Bangladesh on the other, have dramatically underscored during recent years the old cliché about LDC heterogeneity. In this paper, two characteristics will receive special attention for the purpose of differentiating among LDCs: endowment of natural resources with high direct or indirect world demand, and degree of openness to international trade and finance. Inevitably, Saudi Arabia will seek from the international financial system services different in quality and quantity from those sought by Chad, while Brazilian attitudes toward greater exchange rate flexibility can be expected to differ from those of Upper Volta.

LDCs and exchange rate flexibility

The LDCs, speaking with notable unanimity via the 'Group of 24', have indicated a preference for fixed exchange rates for the currencies of industrialised countries, while reserving their option to adopt for themselves more flexible exchange rate arrangements. Such LDC preference for fixed rates (at least for the industrialised nations) has caused some bewilderment and criticism, even among observers most sympathetic to LDC positions.[2] Yet, as in the case of the general debate of fixed versus flexible rates, although with substantive differences in the arguments, something economically sensible can be said on both sides of the debate as to whether LDCs can be expected to benefit or suffer from the adoption by industrialised countries of more flexible exchange rates. While I end up preferring the greater flexibility which reality has imposed on the world, it seems necessary first to review the arguments on the other side, which the profession has tended to ignore very much as new converts fear showing any sign of sympathy for past abandoned beliefs.

Much of what follows relies on concepts developed in discussions regarding 'optimum currency areas' (McKinnon, 1963; Mundell, 1968, pp. 177–86). In these discussions a small, open economy is viewed as one with a high share of tradeable goods in its Gross National Product, with prices in foreign currency of those tradeable goods being given exogenously to the small country. Note that this definition can apply to Holland or Portugal as well as to Honduras; our concern here is with the latter type of country. Another key concept is that of a 'disturbance', which may be caused by policy or by nature, and which may originate inside or outside the country. These useful concepts, alas, are not easily quantifiable. The borderlines between tradeable and non-tradeable goods and between small and large countries are misty, and even the definition of a disturbance is not unambiguous. The analysis of exchange rate policy, including this one, is plagued by such difficulties which rule out a precise differentiation between small, open economies and others. But many LDCs can be characterised as small, open economies with a minimum of ambiguity. It may be useful first to consider why this type of LDC may prefer not only to fix its own exchange rate, but also to see all major exchange rates fixed in relation to one another.

Even the most ardent advocates of greater exchange rate flexibility have recognised that small, open economies would do well to fix their exchange rates in terms of a dominant currency. The basic argument is well presented by Harry G. Johnson, albeit with some departures from his usually high standards for scientific language:

One is accustomed to thinking of national monies in terms of the currencies of the major countries, which currencies derive their usefulness from the great diversity of goods, services, and assets available in the national economy, into which they can be directly converted. But in the contemporary world there are many small and relatively narrowly specialized countries, whose national currencies lack usefulness in this sense, but instead derive their usefulness from their rigid convertibility at a fixed price into the currency of some major country with which the small country trades extensively or on which it depends for capital for investment. For such countries, the advantage of rigid convertibility in giving the currency usefulness and facilitating international trade and investment outweigh the relatively small advantages that might be derived from exchange rate flexibility. (In a banana republic, for example, the currency will be more useful if it is stable in terms of command over foreign goods than if it is stable in terms of command over bananas; and exchange-rate flexibility would give little scope for autonomous domestic policy.)' (Johnson, 1970, pp. 97–8).[3]

The small, open economy will wish to peg to the currency of the country with which it has most of its trade and financial relations. Thus, Guatemala will peg to the dollar and Chad to the French franc. If the international trade and financial flows are exclusively with the country to whose currency the peg is determined, fluctuations between that key currency and other key world currencies will matter little to the small country. Its domestic price level will be unaffected by those fluctuations, while prudent managers of the external assets and liabilities of the small country will have little doubt as to the choice of foreign currency denomination for their financial instruments. Reserves held in hegemonic currencies will assure the citizens of the small country holding the national currency that domestic disturbances, such as the failure of an exportable crop, need not destroy the 'international moneyness' of their currency holding, and will allow the small country to draw on the real resources of the hegemonic power during the crisis. The balance of payments of the small country will be influenced by fluctuations among key currencies only in a very indirect fashion, of quantitatively negligible proportions.

Max Corden (1972, p. 3) has defined a 'pseudo-exchange-rate union' as one in which members agree to maintain fixed exchange rate relationships with one another, but without explicit integration of economic policy, and with neither a common pool of foreign exchange reserves nor a single central bank. Thus, Guatemala could be said to have a unilateral commitment to a pseudo-exchange-rate union with the United States, while Puerto Rico has a full exchange rate or monetary union. In the extreme case when the small country has all its trade and financial transactions with the hegemonic country, the practical invariance of its price level to fluctuations among key currencies establishes a 'pseudo-optimum currency area', needing only greater factor mobility, particularly of unskilled labour, to approach the complete requirements of an optimal (from the viewpoint of the small country) currency area. In this respect, one could also contrast the cases of Guatemala and Puerto Rico.

An extreme type of small, open economy practically eliminates the possibility of policy-induced domestic monetary disturbances by doing away with its own central bank, relying on the currency and monetary system of the hegemonic power to which it is attached, as in the case for many years of the Republic of Panama. Natural disturbances originating domestically, or disturbances of any kind originating abroad, trigger adjustment mechanisms similar to those described by text books for the gold standard, or by Ingram (1969) for the Puerto Rican case. Such an adjustment process requires, for the smooth achievement of both payments equilibrium and reasonably full employment, either flexibility in domestic money wages or freedom of factor movements between the small country and the hegemonic power. Since such small countries are likely to concentrate a very large share of their foreign trade and financial transactions with one large country, the relevant foreign disturbances will be those originating within that one economy, much as West Virginia is affected by what happens in the rest of the United States, and cares relatively little about disturbances originating in France. It is noteworthy that Milton Friedman has suggested (1973, pp.

114–18, 126–8) that the policies discussed above for an extreme type of small, open LDC (fixed exchange rates, no monetary autonomy) can be applied to most developing countries, whose alleged monetary concupiscence presumably cannot be restrained by any other means.[4]

So far the discussion has focused on the exchange rate between the small country and the large one with which it is associated. If, in fact, all the international trade and financial flows of the small country are with one large country, the exchange rate between that large country and the rest of the world will be largely a matter of indifference for the small country. But once some trade and financial flows are allowed between our small country and others (besides the large hegemonic power), matters change. Consider a world made up of two large countries and one small one whose exchange rate is pegged to one of the large countries. If a disturbance arising in one or another of the large countries, and affecting *only* their mutual trade, is handled by successful fiscal and monetary measures and reserve movements, leaving their exchange rates unchanged, the impact of such a disturbance on the small country will be negligible. If, however, the disturbance is allowed to modify the exchange rate between the large countries, the impact on the *effective* exchange rate of the small country, its terms of trade, and on the real value of its foreign debt and exchange reserves will be felt at once.[5]

Consider now a disturbance carrying more *general* effects, say a sudden expansion of public expenditures not covered by taxes in the large country to whose currency the small country's is pegged. If the large countries' currencies are pegged to each other, the excessive monetary expenditures will spill out toward the small country and the second large one, according to the relevant marginal propensities in the inflating large country. The small country, whether it follows a passive monetary policy, or actively wishes to keep in step with the hegemonic power, will inflate approximately in proportion to the hegemonic power. If the other large country, however, checks the imported inflationary pressures, it will maintain a tendency toward surplus in its balance of payments, including that *vis-à-vis* our small country, which will tend to switch its imports away from the hegemonic power, even as it tries to sell to it more of its exports. So long as this situation does not lead to a breakdown of relatively free trade and convertibility in the system, the adjustment burden for the small country will be relatively minor (and almost pleasant). Clearly, however, the situation described above will not have reached a new equilibrium until the second industrial country either inflates in proportion to the hegemonic power or revalues its currency.

Suppose now that the disturbance originates in the second large country, and that, again, it derives from a sudden inflationary expansion of its public expenditure. So long as the exchange rate between the two large countries remains pegged, and world trade and financial rules are unchanged, the impact of this disturbance on our small country will remain even more indirect and minor than in the previous example, given the assumptions regarding trade and financial links.[6]

Do most LDCs conduct all or nearly all of their trade and financial transactions with one major industrialised country? For many LDCs, a little noticed benefit of the 1944–71 world economic order, including relatively fixed rates among key currencies and their eventual convertibility, has been precisely the creation of a multilateral framework within which trade and financial diversification could occur, in contrast with the pre-1944 order characterised by inward-looking trading and financial blocs led by colonial and/or hegemonic industrialised powers. Of total Latin American exports, for example, 46 per cent went to the United States in 1950. By 1972, only one-third of these exports went to the United States. In 1960 almost half of all exports of African LDCs went to the United Kingdom, France and Belgium. By 1972 that share had declined to 31 per cent. Similar trends have characterised the import side; one should note, however, that convertibility has allowed substantial and persistent imbalances in the bilateral trade and payments of many LDCs *vis-à-vis* large industrial countries.[7]

Not all LDC regions have experienced the diversification noted for Latin America and Africa, and it could be argued that gains in trade diversification with respect to the industrialised countries of Western Europe are partly illusory, as that area has itself become more of a single decision making unit. Moreover, intra-LDC trade, and that between LDCs and socialist countries, have remained relatively modest. But diversification has advanced sufficiently far, in most LDCs, to render untenable the view that for all practical purposes the optimum currency area for the typical LDC is that between itself and its hegemonic trading partner. Once actual and expected (or desired) trade and financial diversification is introduced, decisions on exchange rate policy and financial management for LDCs, particularly the smaller ones, become more difficult.

These difficulties may be illustrated as follows. Consider a hypothetical example of an LDC whose exports (or imports) amount to 30 per cent of its Gross National Product. Say half of its exports go to France and half to the United States, while 40 per cent of its imports come from France and 60 per cent from the United States. Assume its capital account transactions are divided equally among three countries – France, the United States and Japan. Question one: would this LDC rationally prefer fixed or floating rates among the dollar, the franc and the yen? Question two: is this hypothetical example, with its trade and financial diversification, more likely to be sustainable under regimes of fixed or of floating rates among the dollar, the franc and yen?

For the small country having or aspiring to have the indicated international diversification, a world in which balance of payments adjustment among France, the United States and Japan occurred *somehow* without changes in their exchange rates, and without limiting their freedom of trade and financial transactions, would clearly be preferable to one with floating rates among these three key currencies. The difficult decisions presented by floating rates are several.

A first obvious decision has to do with the peg: should it be with respect to the dollar, the franc, the yen, or to some kind of a weighted average of the three (or to SDRs)? In the simple case discussed earlier, pegging to the hegemonic key currency tied the small country price level to that of the major country, while keeping it invariant to changes among key currency values, and price levels in the rest of the world. With our new, more complex example, no peg to any single currency will achieve the objective of isolating the domestic price level from fluctuations among key currencies. Put another way, under conditions of diversification, pegging to a single key currency will result in variations in the *effective* exchange rate of the small country. Those variations will result from fluctuations among key currencies, and will have nothing to do with the balance of payments position of the small country. The variations among key currencies may result from fundamental disturbances, such as those discussed above, or from the erratic performance of exchange markets. Post 1971 experience has served to allay the worst fears of those opposing exchange rate flexibility, but it also casts doubts on the hope that stabilising speculation would keep exchange rate movements small and gradual, and responsive only to fundamental disturbances.[8]

To reduce its loss of control over its effective exchange rate, the small country will have to peg to a weighted average of key currencies. If the goal is to keep domestic prices in line with the 'world' price level, the weights will have to correspond to those of each major country in that price level. If the explicit goal is to maintain balance of payments equilibrium by manipulating the effective exchange rate, more complicated calculations involving price elasticities by regions will be required. In practice, crude (and changing) weighting rules are likely to be followed, as the ideal weighting system is difficult to define even in theory. For example, how should *financial* flows with different countries be weighted as compared to *trade* flows? In short, the simplicity and neatness of pegging to a single key currency in a fixed rate system will inevitably be lost.

Secondly, the small, diversified LDC hypothesised above enjoyed a trade surplus with France, matched by a trade deficit with the United States. Historically, this kind of triangularity has created headaches for countries such as Canada and Argentina at times of stress in the international economy, as during the 1930s. Many LDCs are in similar positions today. Current account surpluses, for example, are earned by many Caribbean islands in their dealings with the United States, while they register deficits with Western Europe. Fluctuations among key currencies introduce one more source of uncertainty about the terms of trade, the cost of servicing the foreign debt, and the balance of payments in small countries which previously benefited from convertibility at fixed exchange rates. Even if it is assumed that the fluctuations take place around a known long run average dollar–franc rate (using our hypothetical example) at which the franc surplus and the dollar deficit match, franc–dollar rate fluctuations will, in all likelihood, lead to higher reserve holdings by the small country, as the balance of payments position of any such LDC, defined in either currency (or in domestic currency) for a given month or year, will be subject to a further element of uncertainty. The increased reserve holdings, of course, carry a significant cost.

Thirdly, when our small country carried all of its trade and financial transactions with one hegemonic power, with which it kept a permanently fixed exchange rate, the decision as to the currency in which external assets and liabilities (public or private) should be held was straightforward. If, somehow, the small country could be assured of permanently fixed rates, with convertibility among key currencies, that decision would remain easy. With floating key currencies, however, portfolio management becomes more difficult. Crude rules of thumb similar to those guiding the multi-currency pegging can be devised. For example, the central bank holdings of different foreign currencies can be made a function of possible deficits with the different key currency zones, as well as the expected fluctuations among key currencies and interest rates. Foreign public liabilities in a given key currency could be made a function of expected payments surpluses with that currency area, again adjusted by expected fluctuations among key currencies and interest rates. Such general rules, however, are easier to enunciate in general than to make specific in practice, particularly when substantial capital flows are involved in the payments and surpluses with different currency areas. Furthermore, the search by monetary authorities for avoidance of exchange risks will not be a costless operation, although such costs may eventually be partially offset by learning effects and gains in self-confidence.

Attempts to minimise risks in a world of floating key currencies could lead to other costs for LDCs, going well beyond those involved in expanding and upgrading central bank (and private sector) staffs of financial analysts. If the small, open LDC pegs its currency to just one of the key currencies, trade and financial transactions could be diverted toward the area using this hegemonic currency, even when real costs would suggest a more diversified pattern. The anti-trade bias of greater exchange rate flexibility perceived by some analysts becomes a trade diverting bias for the small LDC pegged to one key currency. Similar considerations would apply, perhaps with greater force, to its international transactions on capital account; the small country may perceive that its exchange risks will be reduced by denominating its foreign debt in the intervention currency. To avoid such departures from effective multilateralism, the small LDC will have to peg to a bundle of key currencies, a decision which, as already discussed, presents its own problems.

The political implications of this analysis are fairly clear. But it is well to emphasise that it is not just an 'irrational' dislike of the neo-colonial flavour of pegging to just one key currency in a world of generalised floating which

7

leads several LDCs to prefer fixed exchange rates across the board. The likely retreat from effective multilateralism, and the reversal of trends toward trade and financial diversification involved in pegging to just one key currency would involve real economic costs, and so would pegging to a bundle of them.

As already noted, in spite of the arguments presented in the previous pages, I end up believing that generalised floating among key currencies, although presenting LDCs with new problems, is a better system from their viewpoint than any *feasible* alternative. When discussing disturbances originating within large industrialised countries, it was pointed out above that those countries could generally avoid exchange rate changes by wise fiscal and monetary management offsetting them. But it is precisely departures from such wisdom which have created most of the disturbances in the first place, so that hopes for offsetting wisdom seem utopian. While the relatively fixed rates for key currencies during 1944–71 were compatible, on the whole, with trade and financial liberalisation in the industrialised countries, the late 1960s offered clear indications that, with the degree of interdependence achieved and with a realistic assessment of the macroeconomic policy performance of the rich countries, fixed rates required for their survival growing trade and financial controls, which stimulated protectionist sentiments. Given the post 1966 failure of hegemonic powers to carry out sensible macroeconomic policies, and given the degree of trade and financial interdependence achieved, asking industrialised countries to maintain fixed exchange rates *and* liberal trade and financial regimes *and* expansionary policies is 'asking for the moon', and supposes a degree of competence among rich country policy makers (and/or social cohesion in those societies) which simply is not there. The misuse by the US of the 'exorbitant privilege' of the dollar, in particular, doomed the Bretton Woods system.

There are also some positive aspects of generalised key currency floating for LDCs. Some large and not so large LDCs, such as Brazil and Colombia, have already experimented successfully with crawling or trotting pegs. While in these countries exchange rate policy has been used primarily to offset domestic inflationary trends, yielding only modest fluctuations in the real effective exchange rates, their example coupled with that of key currencies may induce other LDCs to rely more on exchange rate policy and less on quantitative restrictions for balancing their international accounts, with likely gains in efficiency and growth. Besides LDCs with secular inflationary problems, or inefficient trade and payments policies, and those in peculiar entrepôt circumstances, such as Lebanon and Singapore, it will be the LDCs with the larger and more diversified domestic markets which will find it easiest to experiment with greater exchange rate flexibility. Those countries may thereby be able to follow more independent monetary policies, complementing their political independence.

The dilemma imposed on the small, open LDCs by generalised floating is, in fact, just one more manifestation of the 'small country problem' in a contemporary international scene in which political power accumulates in large countries, or coalitions of them, and is used to further economic goals. The small country also occupies a paradoxical position in the theory of trade and finance: it is supposed to face a perfectly elastic demand for its exports (so it need not worry about meeting the Marshall–Lerner condition), yet its smallness presumably deprives it of policy tools available to larger countries. When trade theorists discuss interactions between tariffs, subsidies and the exchange rate (or multiple exchange rates), showing how alternative mixes of those policy instruments can yield equivalent relative price structures, little or no attention is given to how different decisions on exchange rate policy influence the capital account of the balance of payments or the 'moneyness' of domestic currency. All of this, of course, is one more example of the lack of integration between the real and financial elements of international trade theory. On balance, the emphasis of trade theorists may be correct and it may well be that the monetary impotence of small open LDCs has been exaggerated by focusing on the limits set by the tradeable/non-tradeable goods dichotomy. Although, by definition, small open economies have a high share of imports and exports in GNP, it is now obvious that their share of *importables* and *exportables* in GNP will also be higher than in larger economies. To start with, the share of services in GNP does not seem to be very strongly related to size (whether geographic or economic) or to *per capita* income. In some economies, tourism or temporary emigration may transform some services into 'exportables', but these phenomena do not appear to be systematically related to size. Local tastes or the relative size of the subsistence sector can also influence the degree of substitutability between locally produced and consumed agricultural and manufactured goods, and similar ones traded internationally

A way out of these ambiguities may be sketched as follows. The universalisation of markets for clearly tradeable goods has been accompanied by a similar universalisation of capital markets; it would be difficult to settle whether in recent years the mobility of tradeable goods has been greater or less than that for financial capital. Thus, it is not only the prices of tradeables, but also the rate of return on capital which have tended to equality within the Atlantic and Pacific trading communities and those LDCs attached to them. Unskilled labour remains the factor (after 'land') least mobile internationally, as the postwar period has also witnessed growing universalisation in the market for skilled labour. Under these circumstances, a change in the exchange rate by a given country may be viewed as an attempt to change the wages of its domestic unskilled labour expressed in truly tradeable goods. The key policy variable becomes, *ceteris paribus*, the ratio of unskilled wage rates expressed in domestic money to the exchange rate. As a single unemployed or partly employed individual attempts to improve his lot by cutting down the wage at which he will supply his labour, a country with payments problems is faced with the need to shade the real rewards in terms of tradeable goods of its major immobile factor of production. Such a change, of course, can be accomplished either by changes in the exchange rate or in money wage rates. Either change can be said to be caused by the international immobility of unskilled labour in the face of payments imbalances. As a result, larger net exports of goods and services, as well as larger net inflows of capital can be expected. It could also be assumed, not implausibly, that non-traded goods use unskilled labour more intensively than traded goods, which rely more on skilled labour, capital and rare natural resources.

Modern devaluation theory emphasises that an exchange rate alteration, starting from an equilibrium situation, will not change any relative prices or any other real variable over the long run. Devaluation is then best viewed as a way of getting around some market imperfection, such as wages and prices which are sticky downward, which blocks a speedy and smooth return to equilibrium after some disturbance has shocked the system. When viewed from this perspective, it becomes less obvious why a small open LDC cannot use exchange rate changes, just as larger countries do, to achieve desired reductions in real wages or in real money supplied. 'Money illusion' among wage earners in the modern sector of small countries is less likely, *a priori*, than among those in larger countries, but their social cohesion (or 'discipline') may be higher.

It may be noted that in some LDCs convertibility at a rate firmly pegged to a hegemonic currency is not only a policy designed by conservative central bankers to assure holders of domestic currency of its 'moneyness', but also (or even primarily) a policy aimed to assure elites that, if political trouble threatens domestically, they can speedily transfer their locally held wealth to New York, Paris or London. Such wealth, of course, will include many assets besides domestic money. Large reserves and a pegged rate under such circumstances may be convenient insurance for the elites, but not necessarily desirable policies from the viewpoint of, say, unemployed unskilled workers. While in some countries the elites may derive most of their earnings from exports, making them willing to contemplate frequent devaluations, in other countries elite expenditure patterns may be so oriented toward truly tradeable goods and services (e.g. tourism abroad) as to induce them to support firmly pegged and convertible exchange rates.

During the 1950s and early 1960s even small countries with fixed parities maintained a modest degree of autonomy over monetary policy, thanks to imperfections in international capital mobility. As such mobility improved dramatically during the late 1960s and early 1970s, small countries (and not so small ones, like Mexico) were faced with new choices, familiar to small industrialised economies: letting their remaining monetary autonomy evaporate, imposing or tightening exchange controls, or abandoning fixed rates.

It remains true that the socially optimal degree of exchange rate flexibility in a small open LDC is likely to be, *ceteris paribus*, somewhat smaller than that in large industrialised countries. Very frequent devaluations of the effective exchange rate or low levels of international reserves will raise doubts among holders of domestic currency as to the 'moneyness' of this asset. Ultimately, however, one returns to key assumptions regarding central bank behaviour in different countries. A small open economy following a prudent monetary policy and producing a staple with good export prospects (oil instead of bananas), and surrounded by large industrialised countries undergoing rampant inflation coupled with generalised key currency floating, could certainly *revalue* its exchange rate fairly frequently without jeopardising the 'moneyness' of its domestic currency or upsetting its (non-exporting) wealthy elites. If one were to explain why Canada has followed a more flexible exchange rate policy than Mexico it is unlikely that a plausible answer can be built around differences in the share of tradeables in GNP between those two countries; different degrees of confidence in monetary and political authorities, allowing tolerance for flexibility in one case while imposing the discipline of fixed rates plus convertibility in the other, appears to offer a more likely (if unquantifiable) explanation.

Those arguing that LDCs should, for their own good, lock up their monetary tools and throw away the key, prefer to assume a relatively tranquil world environment providing an anchor of price level stability. Such a view was valid for the late 1950s and early 1960s, but certainly not during the 1930s and early 1940s; it is quite debatable for the 1970s. LDCs which followed autonomous monetary policies during the 1930s, including exchange rate changes, such as Argentina, Brazil and Colombia, weathered the great depression far better than those adhering to Friedman–Johnson policies of passive adjustment to the actions of hegemonic powers.[9]

To summarise: the failure of industrialised countries to discipline their macroeconomic policies led to the collapse of the Bretton Woods system and it is unlikely that those countries will be able to provide an international framework characterised by relatively free trade, convertibility, steady growth *and* fixed parities in the foreseeable future. Such a turn of events need not, however, be an unmixed curse for LDCs. Some LDCs may take up the opportunity to revamp their own trade and payments systems, improving their economic efficiency. Others may move in the direction of greater autonomy in monetary policy, a step which is consistent with the often voiced desire of these countries to eliminate neo-colonial dependency inherited from the past. (In many sovereign LDCs, in fact, monetary arrangements have changed little since the days of colonial 'currency boards', and those monetary arrangements are not fundamentally different from that of Puerto Rico.)

For the sake of maintaining an effectively multilateral and diversified framework in their international trade and financial links, small LDCs may wish to peg their currencies to a bundle of key currencies, or to the new SDRs. In a world of convertibility, pegging to SDRs need not imply using more than one key currency for market intervention, or having more than a small share of international reserves held in such currency. Over the longer run, the new international financial system may give an additional push to integration efforts, particularly among the smaller LDCs, by emphasising the connection between economic size and effective monetary sovereignty.

Inevitably, LDCs will have to face several types of burdens in adjusting to a new international environment characterised by floating key currencies. Such an environment will impose additional maturation requirements on LDC 'infant entrepreneurs', whether of the public or private sectors, particularly those engaged in export drives. Competition with multinational corporations, each having their own specialised group of foreign exchange experts, will not be made easier in the foreign trade arena, even assuming LDC use of forward exchange markets located in hegemonic financial centres. Insofar as floating key currencies hamper the workings of international capital markets, extra costs may also be incurred by LDCs in tapping that source of finance.

Before turning to the changing relationship between many LDCs and international capital markets, it may be noted that if, on balance, LDCs rely less on exchange rate flexibility than the industrialised countries, the case for a larger LDC share in world reserves created by international agreement (the SDRs) is strengthened. While the float of the currencies of industrialised countries should presumably reduce their demand for reserves (eventually, at least),[10] for reasons given above many LDCs will continue to face limitations on their exchange rate flexibility due to their smallness, and will keep their currency pegged to one or more key currencies. Their demand for reserves (to hold) will therefore be no smaller, and is likely to be higher, *ceteris paribus*, than under the previous system.

LDCs and evolving world capital markets

If the greater mobility of financial capital observed in recent years accentuates LDC policy dilemmas, it also presents them with new opportunities. Some years ago Charles P. Kindleberger (1970) proposed a greater use by developing countries of world capital markets, at purely commercial terms, particularly in view of LDC misgivings about direct foreign investment and their dissatisfaction with concessional international finance.[11] Since then, even though LDC borrowing in the national markets of industrialised countries in the form of long term bonds has remained relatively thin, their gross borrowing in the Eurocurrency market in the form of medium term bank credits has boomed. Up through the first half of 1974, neither generalised floating among key currencies nor the stresses placed on the Eurocurrency market by the turbulent world economic scene of 1973–4 had checked the upsurge in LDC borrowing. Although data in this area are notoriously imperfect and incomplete, reliable estimates place publicly announced LDC borrowing in Eurocurrency markets at $1.4 billion in 1971; $3.6 billion in 1972; $9.1 billion in 1973; and $6.0 billion during the first half of 1974. Additional borrowing not recorded in published 'tombstones' is said to be substantial.[12] The borrowing entities include governments, state enterprises and, to a lesser extent, private businesses.

These amounts are quite spectacular and one is tempted to contrast them with the stagnant figures for concessional finance. But several warnings are in order. The amounts shown are gross magnitudes and little is known as to the extent that Eurocurrency borrowing is replacing more traditional forms of LDC borrowing, particularly suppliers' credits; or the exact degree to which the borrowing is offset by LDC lending in the form of short term deposits with Eurobanks, which are said to make up a good part of recent sharp increases in the international liquidity of some LDC central banks. LDC borrowing in the Eurocurrency market can reduce their borrowing opportunities elsewhere, either by making them less creditworthy in the eyes of other potential lenders, or simply by revealing that their need for, say, tapping the new oil facility of the IMF is not as pressing as that of other countries. In short, neither the degree to which gross LDC borrowing in Eurocurrency markets has led to decreased borrowing elsewhere, nor the extent to which such borrowing has led to a real resource transfer toward these countries are known with accuracy.

The figures shown above also hide considerable concentration among borrowers. The eleven largest LDC borrowers in the Eurocurrency market during 1973, each accounting for more than $200 million, represented 84 per cent of the total borrowing. They were, in descending order of importance: Mexico, Algeria, Peru, Brazil, Iran, Greece, Indonesia, Spain, Zaire, Yugoslavia and Panama. While this short list shows a heavy concentration of semi-industrialised or natural resource rich countries, it also accounts for a non-trivial share of Third World population. A similar concentration exists among LDCs issuing long term bonds in world capital markets. In 1972, for example, the top ten borrowers were, again in descending order of importance: Israel, Mexico, Spain, Brazil, Singapore, Philippines, Hungary, Greece, Panama and Venezuela, each borrowing at least $40 million, and together accounting for 90 per cent of all LDC bond issues reported by the World Bank.

Several interrelated issues are raised by the observed trends. A first one has to do with the stability and permanence of the Eurocurrency capital market. A second one concerns the desirability of LDC borrowing in such a market, either to obtain real resources or greater liquidity. A third issue relates to the possibility of generalising the experience of a few LDCs and semi-industrialised countries to a larger group. Finally, one may wonder what the upsurge in the role of the world capital market implies for the future of those international institutions which, during most of the post Second World War period, replaced it, from the LDC viewpoint.

Even before the oil price increase of late 1973, and the 1974 'slumpflation' in major industrialised countries, the unregulated Eurocurrency market had generated much nervousness, as it tended to lend on longer and longer terms, even to newcomers, while continuing to rely on deposits of short term funds (often *very* short term deposits, such as overnight). While few doubt that central banks of industrialised countries would step in with generous rediscounting facilities if major Eurocurrency banks got into trouble, the uneasiness has persisted, apparently reaching a peak with the 'Eurowillies' of the European summer of 1974. It is noteworthy that such nervousness originated mainly from worries about the British and Italian economies, plus the incompetence or venality of some developed country banks in their foreign exchange transactions, rather than from fears of LDC defaults.

From the viewpoint of this paper, the principal lesson from the expansion of the Eurocurrency market is straightforward. When unshackled from restrictive regulations, often inherited from the special conditions of the 1930s, private capital markets can mobilise gross sums dwarfing those available from bilateral and multilateral concessional finance, at least for one important type of LDC. Furthermore, such transactions are carried out in a cold standoffish commercial spirit which contrasts sharply with the tangled, emotional relations surrounding concessional finance. Without dramatics, countries as diverse in their domestic policies as Algeria, Bulgaria, Cuba, Peru, Colombia, Ivory Coast, the Philippines and South Korea have been making quiet deals with the money lenders, and obtaining funds which may be spent, largely, on any country and for anything. It appears self-evident that the LDCs as a group have an important stake in the continuation of a Eurocurrency market which, even if it becomes somewhat more regulated than it is at present, retains its characteristics of free access, competitiveness and depoliticisation. Indeed, the LDCs may benefit from an extension of these characteristics of the Eurocurrency market to the national capital markets of the industrialised countries, although it is not clear that any contemporary national capital market can attain the flexibility and depoliticisation reached by the Eurocurrency market. But a broadening of capital markets available to LDCs could help correct what are, from the LDC viewpoint, the most disturbing features of Eurocurrency operations. More on this below.

Eurocurrency operations remain medium term banking revolving credits, typically for a period of three to eight years, with floating interest rates.[13] While the commitment period is as indicated, the loans are renewable at the end of each six month period, at which time not only the interest rate, but other conditions of the loan, such as the currency which is to be used, can be modified. In contrast with long term bonds issued by LDCs at given interest rates, or borrowing from the World Bank, the LDCs undertake a considerable share of risks and potential adjustment burdens. Until the first half of 1974, the Euromarket trend was toward a lengthening of maturities and a narrowing by lenders of the spread between their borrowing and lending rates. These trends in Eurocredits seem to have been checked or reversed during 1974, but for *all* borrowers, not just LDCs. It is also noteworthy that the Eurobond market, little used by LDCs so far, witnessed a sharp decline in transactions during the first half of 1974.

Influential voices in the development finance field have been raised, warning LDCs of the dangers of Eurocurrency transactions. It is worth quoting them at length. The President of the Inter-American Development Bank, Mr Antonio Ortiz Mena, stated in April 1974:

The euro-currency market has provided a large volume of financing for the region [Latin America] in the last two years, but...this financing is being obtained on conditions that, without careful planning, can frustrate orderly management of the external debt and even weaken the internal savings efforts of our countries.

As you know, the usual form of loans in the euro-currency market is the revolving credit with a fluctuating interest rate. Although the credit is extended for periods that have been lengthening gradually to 10 and 12 years – and 14 and 15 years in some cases – in practice the credit is renewed every six months, each time at the interest rate prevailing in the London market (interbank offer rate, IBOR). Since 1969 there have been sharp fluctuations from a low of slightly over 5 per cent to a high of 11 per cent... It should be noted that the loans usually are amortized in full at the end of the agreed period and that the resources are completely untied.

These operations are transacted with scant knowledge of the feasibility of the projects, since brokers are commonly used to promote lending operations, especially in the developing countries. Obviously, such practices can lead to the excessive use of credit and to an improper allocation of financial resources... This observation is even more to the point if it is kept in mind that the countries sometimes resort to the euro-currency market to finance the total cost of an investment...

In actual figures the euro-currency market supplied resources to those countries [eight major Latin American countries, in 1973] for more than double the financing authorized by the international agencies [the Inter-American and World Banks].

Finally, we note that the oil crisis is forcing the industrialized countries into the euro-currency market in order to finance their balance-of-payments deficits, which could displace the developing countries...

The foregoing considerations suggest the advisability of broadening the Bank's activities so as to increase its advisory services.

Similar concepts were expressed by Mr William S. Gaud, then head of the International Finance Corporation, on 7 November 1973:

There are those who have welcomed this growing recourse to the private capital market by the developing countries as a desirable trend. It is said to represent a return to the traditional method of financing economic expansion, leaving the borrowing country free to make its own decisions on how the funds should be used.

I recognize that the Euro-currency market has played an important part in giving the developing countries access to the international capital market to an extent previously impossible since the end of World War II. I also recognize that it has permitted a transfer of resources to those countries that would not have been possible without it.

Nevertheless, I see very real risks for the developing countries in borrowing so heavily in a market with no established lending standards and no overall surveillance to prevent unsound practices...

There is also the fact that the Euro-currency market is, by its nature, delicately poised and very sensitive both to speculative monetary investments and to changes in the economic and financial policies of the capital-exporting countries...

Another basic uncertainty inherent in Euro-currency funds stems from floating interest rates on which those funds are generally made available to the developing countries. These constitute too volatile a base on which to finance long-term industrial and infrastructure projects.

There is another feature of these Euro-currency loans which should not be overlooked. Foreign private investment is important to the developing countries not only because it contributes capital for their development, but because it brings with it technology, management, training and access to foreign markets – items which are all in short supply in the Third World. Euro-currency loans bring with them none of these. Indeed, they are often made even without any appraisal of the soundness of the projects they are intended to finance.

Speaking to the U.N. General Assembly the other day Sir Alec Douglas-Home said: 'the key word for the future of economic development is partnership.' But there is no partnership between lenders and borrowers in the Euro-currency market – not only because lenders and borrowers are inevitably remote from each other, but also because the lenders have no direct involvement in the enterprise in which their funds are ultimately invested.

I believe a greater effort needs to be made to supplement Euro-currency funds for the developing countries with other, long-term funds. That brings me to private foreign investment...

Europe can play an important role in creating new forms of mutually beneficial relationships between foreign investors and the Third World, and we in IFC are eager to support any initiatives to that end.

Other, less diplomatic, criticisms of LDC borrowing in the Eurocurrency market are also heard. In some cases, the borrowing is said to go to purchasing weapons, or to finance current expenditures. Corruption is alleged to exist in many deals, and 1920s-type stories of unholy alliances between unscrupulous and pushy brokers and venal LDC politicians abound.

Differing grounds for criticising LDC Eurocurrency borrowing should be kept distinct. One strand deals with excesses, dangers, and misallocations which may exist in *any* type of foreign borrowing by sovereign but imperfect governments, from rich but sometimes greedy bankers or institutions. (The greed may be for money or power.) Another strand refers to relative benefits and costs of different forms and combinations of foreign borrowing. The general issue of the developmental impact of foreign borrowing has been discussed amply; here it should be enough to remark that growing indebtedness, either in absolute amounts or relative to other variables, may be a sign of trouble, or a sign of economic health and high expectations. Compare, for example, a Mexican debt service to exports ratio of 24 per cent in 1972, with the 1 per cent of Mali, or the 3 per cent of Honduras. One may observe, incidentally, that for many LDCs which borrowed in the Eurocurrency market during 1970–3, the real burden of servicing that debt has been lower than calculated at the time the loans were made, as the magnitude of world inflation actually recorded was not expected by most lenders.[14] But inflationary expectations, perhaps excessive, are now being built into new loan agreements, so that such an unexpected break for LDC debtors is unlikely to be repeated in the case of fresh debt.

The remarks by the heads of the IADB and the IFC can be, perhaps somewhat unfairly, summarised as: 'LDC foreign borrowing is fine, but only if kept under our tutelage'. Distrust both of LDC ability to manage sensibly their own financial affairs and of competitive international financial markets is not far from the surface. These are judgements which cannot be proven or disproven *a priori*; clearly, however, they represent a view of development and self-determination not universally shared. The point is *not* that one should assume that all LDC borrowing in private international markets is sound and healthy, nor that Eurocurrency bankers are the new heroes of development; the point is to ask whether in the long run there is any other way to achieve both international interdependence and national self-determination than to deal through more or less competitive, standoffish *and* remote international markets, fully aware of their risks and dangers.

Access to Eurocredits has expanded the financial options facing many LDCs, and perhaps little more needs to be said to show the positive impact of the Eurocurrency market on those countries. It should be emphasised, however, that different LDCs are likely to use borrowing in that market for different purposes. To some, Eurocredits appear to be mainly a readily available source of international liquidity, at a cost equivalent to the difference between interest charges on the loans and the interest they receive on their Eurocurrency deposits. In these countries, Eurocredits and the large gross foreign exchange reserves accompanying them seem designed to increase confidence among local and foreign investors. In other words, in such cases inflows of portfolio capital are complementary to inflows of other types of foreign capital, particularly direct foreign investment. That complementarity can be quite specific as when an LDC heavily engaged in the use of Eurocredits allows the local establishment of branches of foreign banks and financial institutions active in the Eurocurrency market.

Other LDCs tap the Eurocurrency market mainly to finance medium or long term projects involving real resource transfers, which could have been financed by direct foreign investments or concessional capital flows (or even domestic savings). While Algeria and Peru appear to use Eurocredits primarily for this purpose, Brazil and the Phillipines seem to use such credits mainly for the former.

Eurocredits, then, can either complement or substitute for other capital inflows, in the same way that foreign borrowing in general can either substitute for or complement domestic savings, depending on policy and circumstances. A corollary is that links with world capital markets could also be used by LDCs either as complements or substitutes for the expansion of their own domestic capital markets, depending on their dominant socio-economic philosophy, policies and domestic economic conditions. It could be that, whether by policy design or as a result of market pressures, links with foreign capital markets tend to hamper rather than promote local long term capital markets.[15]

In a world characterised by substantial and erratic rates of inflation, Eurocredits have one little noticed advantage over traditional loans from aid agencies. The loan commitments from the latter, expressed in nominal terms, are typically disbursed slowly over a number of years; their real value will depend on the disbursement speed (much influenced by the lender) and rates of inflation. Eurocredit disbursements are faster and more under the influence of the borrower, who can protect himself against erosion of the real value of the loan either by rapid purchases or by placing unspent amounts to earn market rates of interest.

As noted earlier, most LDCs have not been directly involved with the Eurocurrency market or with other international capital markets. Some are too small or too poor to be creditworthy to private bankers. As in the case of generalised floating by key currencies, the expansion of world capital markets may nudge the smallest LDCs into forms of integration involving greater financial co-operation, including joint development banks which could act as intermediaries with international capital markets. In other cases, small and poor countries may choose to search for an LDC 'big brother' to guarantee their borrowing, as in a recent Sudanese loan from the Eurocurrency market guaranteed by Saudi Arabia. 'Smallness' is likely to prove less of a barrier to market access than poverty, particularly poverty in natural resources. Bolivia and Nicaragua, for example, have been able to tap the Eurocurrency market on their own; but it is unlikely that Bangladesh or India will be able to do so in large amounts during the foreseeable future. The solidarity needed to obtain intra-LDC guarantees or joint borrowing, however, may not exist outside the Arab and Latin American countries. Still, even LDCs excluded from the Eurocurrency market will benefit indirectly from the borrowing by luckier LDCs in that market, in so far as the latter LDCs absorb less concessional finance, freeing it for the neediest cases.

During most of the post Second World War period, international institutions, such as the World Bank group and the regional development banks, have been playing a key financial intermediation role (in addition to multinational corporations, one may add). As the biggest and richest LDCs obtain direct access to external funds, and other LDCs choose to encourage other financial intermediaries over which they feel they have greater control, one may wonder about the pressures on the World Bank group and the Asian and Inter-American development banks. Clearly, the bargaining balance between these institutions and the more prosperous LDCs have been changed by the proliferation of alternative sources of funds. Indeed, the rationale justifying Brazilian, Nigerian and Philippine borrowing from the IBRD (*excluding* IDA credits) at terms similar to those of Haiti, Ethiopia and Bangladesh is far from self-evident and persuasive. As LDC heterogeneity becomes more marked the traditional multilateral intermediaries would do well to concentrate their attention on the least developed countries, raising the price at which their services, including technical help, are made available to the more fortunate LDCs.

The most significant accomplishment of the recent expansion of LDC borrowing in the Eurocurrency market has been to show that the debacle of the 1930s did not kill LDC access to world capital markets for all time. It is natural to ask why such a renaissance did not take place in the national capital markets of the industrialised countries, and whether it can be extended to them. It may seem foolhardy to raise such issues during 1974–5, at a time when world financial markets quake under the pressure of recession, unusual inflation, dramatic increases in oil prices, enormous balance of payments deficits in important industrial countries, as well as in several LDCs, and an international monetary order groping its way toward a system. But the long run must be given its due and, barring disaster in the world economy, the dominant trend is still toward complementing the trade liberalisation achieved during 1944–71, with liberalisation and widening of long term financial flows, in spite (or because?) of floating exchange rates.

Merchandise and service exports from LDCs to industrialised countries, while still hampered by protectionist obstacles, have expanded markedly during the 1960s and early 1970s; but their exports of IOU's have, for the most part, been blocked by formal and informal barriers first imposed by many of the industrialised countries during the 1930s. A recent study, for example, concludes that the United States securities market has a regulating apparatus too complex and costly for the purposes of most Latin American foreign issues (OAS, 1973). Such regulations, including those of the US Securities and Exchange Commission and those of individual states, have the effect of substantially, if not entirely, closing the United States' markets to LDC securities, whether debt or equity, as effectively as have the more stringent legal limitations imposed on entry into the national capital markets of the European countries. As in the case of certain non-tariff barriers to merchandise trade, such as health regulations, it is not always clear whether such regulations do much for the welfare of the consumer or security buyer in the industrialised country.

The barriers in industrialised countries to the importation of LDC IOU's (and those of others) can be summarised as follows (Treadway, n.d.).

(1) Regulations related to balance of payments problems. These have tended to be relaxed by countries trying to avoid revaluation, and tightened by those warding off devaluation, of their currencies. Some LDCs have thus been led to place debt where they were likely to suffer when revaluations subsequently became inevitable, while losing out on any possible gains arising from creditor country devaluations.

(2) Requirements for permission from national authorities. These are important mainly in Europe and Japan, where ex-colonies and particular LDCs obtain favoured treatment.

(3) Information disclosure requirements, including numerous and cumbersome regulations which increase the cost of public bond flotations. Many observers consider them unnecessary for the protection of purchasers of securities and/or discriminatory against LDC issuers.

(4) Restrictions on financial institutions. In many states in the United States and in virtually all European countries, banks, insurance companies and pension funds are either prohibited from investing in LDC and other foreign issues, or are severely circumscribed as to the amounts that can be held in their portfolios.

Not all plans for greater LDC access to capital markets will be equally desirable. It has sometimes been proposed, for example, that industrialised countries guarantee LDC public securities issued in their capital markets, at least with respect to political risks. Other suggestions include the establishment in industrialised countries of open-end mutual funds to develop portfolios of diversified corporate LDC securities, or of investment companies guaranteed by industrialised countries. To a greater or smaller degree, these proposals would retain the initiative and control over the financial flows within the industrialised countries, with centralised agencies deciding which countries should receive how much. The LDCs have long resented having their commodity exports, even when produced by local entrepreneurs, transported and sold by foreign commercial firms; such proposals would again bring a rich country intermediary between the exporters of IOU's and their final buyers.

For a number of LDCs, such guarantees may, in any case, be unnecessary to generate an important flow of portfolio investment, once the most cumbersome and arbitrary restrictions to entry, discussed above, are removed from the national capital markets of industrialised countries. After such restrictions are lifted, further encouragement of those flows could take the form of generalised tax exemption for interest earned on LDC securities by industrialised country buyers, such as those enjoyed by US buyers of US municipal bonds. It should be noted that, at present, direct investments in LDCs from industrialised countries benefit from a number of advantages, such as tax deferral, insurance facilities and other public sector encouragement, all of which discriminate in favour of those flows over portfolio investments (and in favour of large over small investors, one may add).

Even under present circumstances, some LDCs could do more to test the limits of existing regulations in the capital markets of industrialised countries, as a prelude to seeking changes in those restrictions. For example, while in the United States many states limit purchases of foreign securities by insurance companies to a small percentage of the total portfolio of those companies, it appears that in most cases such ceilings have not yet been reached. Only Mexico, it is said, has taken advantage of existing margins. Another example is the increased use of private placements of long term bonds, instead of public offerings, which at least in the United States market involves a significant difference in costs, in favour of the former.[16]

Even if it means 'helping the competition', multilateral and bilateral development financial institutions could supply LDCs with a much greater flow of information and technical assistance regarding direct access to world capital markets than is offered at present. For those LDCs unable to go to those markets on their own or in groups, even if rules of access become liberalised, guarantees of their securities by the World Bank or regional banks could provide a practical and acceptable formula, with or without interest rate subsidies. The application of such guarantee schemes for particular purposes, such as export financing, also deserves study and could be justified on 'infant market' grounds (Weinberg, 1973).

Liberalisation of access to the national capital markets of industrialised countries and politically acceptable guarantee schemes are unlikely to be of much help to the poorest LDCs, particularly those with import bills heavily loaded with food and oil. For these countries concessional finance, of old and new types, seems necessary to achieve even modest *per capita* income growth. Imaginative new types of concessional flows, including schemes to facilitate repayments in the form of new exports, as in recent agreements between Iran and India, could ease both adjustment costs and political frictions.

To summarise: possibilities appear to exist for tactical alliances between at least some capital importing LDCs and some financial institutions from industrialised countries. While the LDCs wish to expand their options in international finance, the developed country institutions desire to remain free from severe controls (as in the Eurocurrency market) or wish to be unshackled from anachronistic regulations, benefiting mainly specialised lawyers and bureaucrats in regulatory agencies. The desirability of a more flexible and expanded world capital market has been reinforced by the expected accumulation of financial assets by some oil exporting LDCs, which have their own reasons to cement links with industrialised country financial institutions. Both types of LDCs have a clear and direct interest in the evolution of the rapidly changing system of international financial inter-mediation. For example, the effect of the recent lifting of some United States restrictions on its national capital market upon the evolution of the Euro-currency market, and the quantity and quality of financial assets and liabilities available to LDCs, are matters of concern to many such countries. In particular, concentration trends among Eurobanks (reported during 1974) and joint moves by OECD countries to 'rationalise' Eurocurrency lending and control world capital markets could threaten the relative openness and competition which characterised those markets during 1970–4. In the on-going discussions on international monetary and financial reform, these are matters the LDCs would do well to emphasise and monitor.

The LDCs and the new SDRs

By 31 December 1973 the LDCs had used about one-third of the SDRs allocated to them, a smaller proportional net use than that of the United Kingdom, but higher than those of most industrialised countries. In absolute amounts, however, the net use of SDRs by the United States and the United Kingdom, as of the indicated date, was larger than that of all LDCs put together (Gupta, 1974, p. 9). As it can be expected that LDCs will remain net users of SDRs, one may wonder whether the 'hardening' of SDRs agreed upon in June 1974 by the Committee of 20 will benefit those countries.

The LDCs have supported the thesis that the SDR should become the basis of a reformed monetary system, in which gold and reserve currencies would play a declining role. As emphasised by Gerald K. Helleiner (1974), even without a link the LDCs benefit substantially from SDRs relative to alternative realistic means of expanding international liquidity. The new SDR definition as a large basket of currencies and its higher interest rate serve to further the goal of making SDRs the principal reserve asset and the *numéraire* in the international system. Note that the new SDR provides an attractive asset to hold, particularly for those LDCs wishing to avoid complications in their reserve management. It could also provide a natural unit of account for international arrangements, such as commodity agreements, in which LDCs are interested. Such practices would meet one of the arguments used against the generalised floating of key currencies.

The 'grant element' in the net use of SDRs is, of course, reduced by the higher interest rate. But, while for Brazil and Nigeria the credit line conditions implicit in the net use of new SDRs may not be *that* different from those available to them in private markets, they still represent a bargain for less fortunate LDCs whose access to international liquidity involves heavier costs. To this extent, the SDRs carry their own built-in but modest progressivity.

Another price may eventually have to be paid by LDCs for the consolidation and expansion of an SDR system. Over the long run, collective control over international reserves will require rules limiting holdings of currencies. The LDCs, as well as other countries, are reluctant to accept international rules limiting their freedom regarding reserve composition. With the old SDR, there was a large gap between returns in that instrument and those available in the Eurocurrency market; this gap has now been narrowed. Nevertheless the issue remains. It illustrates the broader question as to whether or not LDCs should seek exemptions from general rules governing the international monetary system. It appears that those LDCs most interested in retaining flexibility over reserve compositions are also those least likely to benefit from an SDR standard, i.e. relatively fortunate countries with considerable access to Eurocurrency and other capital markets. It is precisely because of these contacts and their financial sophistication, and the close link between reserve and debt management, that such semi-industrialised countries oppose both limitations on reserve composition freedom, and the application to them of objective indicators based on reserve levels for policy changes. It may be added that these are also countries whose public support for the link is not always backed up by private comments of some of their financial officials.

Besides reducing the grant elements of net SDR use, the 'heavy' SDR presents some technical complications for link schemes, which, however, could be handled if there is the political will to go ahead with such proposals. There is little to add to John Williamson's brilliant review (1973) of the mostly secondary and unpersuasive arguments for and against the link.

The simple and fundamental argument in this debate is well stated by Williamson:

The international community has few instruments to improve the world distribution of income, and therefore it should utilise such opportunities as arise. One of these is the seigniorage resulting from the production of fiduciary reserve assets. There is a long and unfortunate tradition in economics of dismissing this type of argument just because it involves a value judgment additional to that embodied in the Pareto criterion. The degree of egalitarianism needed to justify preference for the link rather than neutrality is minimal, given the existing facts on world income distribution (p. 728).[17]

In view of the difficulties being experienced by the least developed countries, the case for distributing the linked share of SDRs according to a formula taking into account *per capita* income as well as population, so it contains an explicit and substantial progressivity, appears particularly strong; and allocation of such SDRs directly to the countries concerned continues to be the best way to promote responsible local leadership; the institutions most in need of build-up are in the LDCs, not elsewhere.

If most or all of the new SDRs go in their first round to developing countries, particularly to the poorest ones, who will pay interest to those countries becoming net receivers? Is it credible to expect the poorest LDCs to continue to pay interest on their net use of SDRs, particularly once the value to LDCs of new issues falls below interest payments? Because of these queries, as well as to enhance the grant element of linked SDRs, an *ex ante* scheme to subsidise LDC interest payments clearly appears desirable, and less complicated than issuing different types of SDRs.[18]

Whatever the fate of the link, the case for increasing the LDC share in IMF quotas has been strengthened by the generalised floating of key currencies, as discussed earlier in this essay, so that allocation to LDCs of SDRs 'to hold' should be correspondingly increased.

Increases in the private market price of gold have raised hopes for an 'instant link'. One scheme would involve a sharp rise in the official gold price, with a share of the resulting paper or realised profits on the gold stocks of industrialised countries going to the LDCs. Such a return to a gold exchange standard would, of course, mean a weakening or disappearance of SDRs, so the LDCs would be trading an immediate gain for a steadier, longer run advantage. Their hard-won new positions of influence within the IMF would become less meaningful, as that institution would also be weakened by a remonetisation of basically South African gold. This siren song of instant profit, one hopes, will not lure LDCs to support such a retrogressive scheme. Others have put forth another proposal, much more attractive to LDCs, which implies the demonetisation of gold by gradual sales to private markets of the gold hoards of the IMF and central banks. Profits from such transactions, at least those realised by the IMF, could go to help (via one mechanism or another) primarily the least developed countries. Using resources provided by wealthy individuals, who for whatever reason are willing to pay extravagant sums for a yellow metal, to feed starving children is a bargain the world should not pass up.

A final word

While short and long term pessimism about the non-socialist part of the world economy has been rampant during 1974, the most plausible forecasts still call for an eventual resumption of growth in major industrialised countries and a continuation (at a slower pace) of the expansionary trends in international trade and finance enjoyed since World War II. Changes in world economic circumstances, particularly those involving increases in the relative prices of food, fuel and other primary goods, will affect LDCs in sharply different ways; a possible decline in the growth of industrialised countries will also have a variety of repercussions in different LDCs. The pull of forces originating in the world economy on LDCs will remain potent, presenting opportunities as well as problems. During recent years the opportunities have been reflected in export performance and sources of finance which only fifteen years ago would have seemed out of reach. For many LDCs even a less prosperous but still multi-polar world economy, tensions and all, will continue providing a non-trivial amount of room for some (but not all) kinds of political and economic flexibility. My fundamental assumption here is that the industrialised countries will not let the essentially transitory and manage-able problems faced by the world economy during 1974 degenerate into a serious depression accompanied by a backsliding into protectionism in trade and finance. But if the worst comes, middle income countries could react by stimulating import substitution within LDC common markets.

Even under optimistic assumptions regarding growth in the industrialised world, the least developed LDCs, it bears repeating, face problems more fundamental and less subtle than, say, co-ordinating monetary with exchange rate policy. These problems are likely to require either dramatic domestic reforms in the indicated countries, or increased concessional capital flows from the rest of the world, or both. This group of countries, located mainly in South Asia and tropical Africa, has been growing at lower *per capita* rates than other LDCs for many years. During 1972–4 natural calamities, an inflation-induced decline in the real value of aid disbursements, and price increases in their imports of food, fuels and fertilisers have sharply worsened the outlook for the almost one billion persons in those countries.

For the more fortunate and market-oriented LDCs, the expansion and integration of world commodity and money markets have raised the price of domestic policy mistakes and reduced some kinds of policy flexibility. Experimentation with controls and other policies which buck pressures emanating from world markets now requires more sophistication than, say, during the 1950s. Undoubtedly, LDC planning offices and policy making machinery improved at a dramatic pace during the 1960s. Every ounce of such gains, and more, will be needed during the 1970s to take advantage of world market conditions without sacrificing domestic goals. One example should illustrate the problem: with increasingly mobile capital and skilled labour, it will be more difficult for an LDC with extensive links with advanced market economies to influence its income distribution by manipulating by itself the rates of return of those factors.[19]

The international financial system which will eventually evolve out of the troubled post 1971 circumstances will remain a source of concern to all types of LDCs, even though one must admit that a good share of the time devoted by LDC finance ministers and their staff to attending international monetary conferences since 1971 might have been more productively devoted to tackling domestic economic problems in those countries. Be that as it may, substantial LDC participation in decision making on international monetary issues is an accomplishment now unlikely to be reversed, particularly in view of the importance of OPEC. The 'disappointment' of some observers in industrialised countries regarding allegedly 'selfish' LDC behaviour during debates on international monetary reform seems to be simply one more symptom of the difficulty everyone has adjusting to more complex realities. LDCs, lacking many weapons in international power games and with dismal poverty at home, should not be asked to set an example of statesmanship and generosity in international forums in which such virtues have hardly been characteristic.

Notes

1   Helpful comments from Benjamin I. Cohen, Richard N. Cooper, Gerald K. Helleiner, Harry G. Johnson, Peter B. Kenen, Charles P. Kindleberger, Edwin M. Truman, Delbert Snider, Ernest Stern and John Williamson are gratefully acknowledged. Participants at the Uppsala seminar in August 1974 also provided useful advice. Responsibility for remaining errors and eccentricities is all mine.
2   Thus, Jagdish N. Bhagwati has remarked: '*Any* reform of the Bretton Woods system which builds into itself, *via* widened bands...or gliding parities...would be of enormous value in getting several LDC's off their fixed-rate fixation and prompting them to use their exchange rate regimes more freely and efficiently to balance their international accounts. Their objections to more flexibility need therefore to be resolutely ignored – in their own interest!' (1972, pp. 322–3).
3   The so-called banana republics will thus tend to have inflationary trends no larger than those of the hegemonic industrialised countries. In the Western Hemisphere, for example, countries such as the Dominican Republic, Guatemala, Honduras, Haiti and Mexico registered rates of inflation during 1959–73 very similar to that in the United States. Contrast this with Paul A. Samuelson's column in *Newsweek* (17 June 1974, p. 91), in which he uses 1923 Germany and 'banana republics' as examples of wild inflation. Clearly, at least some scientific economists do not know their bananas!
4   The statements by Allan H. Meltzer and Ricardo H. Arriazu in the same congressional source (see Friedman, 1973) are also relevant to our discussion. Harry G. Johnson elsewhere advises Panama against having its own central bank (1972, p. 274).

5   For an elaboration of this and related points see UNCTAD, 1969, pp. 22–4.
6   If the disturbance in either of the two large countries is in a deflationary direction, the small country will still be least affected if such disturbance is handled by compensatory fiscal and monetary policies in the large countries, without resorting to exchange rate changes between them. Parenthetically, when the disturbance originating abroad involves only one international commodity market (which may be of particular importance to the small country, e.g. that for its major export, such as the banana market, or for its major import, such as the oil market), the small country will typically prefer to handle it by taxes or subsidies specific to the relevant commodity rather than by changing its exchange rate, a measure which would affect all domestic prices for importables and exportables.
7   Basic data on trade flows were obtained from International Monetary Fund, *Direction of Trade.*
8   Fred Hirsch and David Higham, after reviewing recent experience of key currencies (through early 1974) conclude: 'Fluctuations and swings in rates have been substantial. Private operators have not given an impressive performance of their superior capacity to stabilise the exchanges. Markets in forward exchange remain limited to short maturities, and margins have widened except by comparison with the more speculative episodes under the par value regime' (1974, p. 32).
9   As noted by Kindleberger, the Friedman–Johnson view omits mention of the disadvantages for a small country of financial integration with a hegemonic power. He puts the general point as follows: 'Financial integration is helpful when mistakes of policy or other disturbances are likely to originate at home. In a liquidity crisis, the smaller entity is assisted by financial intermediation, i.e. discounting, at a higher level in the financial structure. But where the trouble originates abroad, financial integration communicates it to the local level. The fear of the locality without independence of monetary policy is that its interests will be neglected in time of stress. The counterpart of lack of knowledge of local conditions at the center is lack of interest in them' (1974, pp. 13–14).
10 After reviewing 1970–4 experience regarding exchange rate flexibility and reserve use, John Williamson concludes (in an unpublished paper) that there is no evidence that floating has led so far to the expected economies in the use of reserves. Although the evidence is still sketchy, he argues that a system of managed floating during an unsettled period results in at least as much reserve use as does a reasonably well functioning par value system with credible parities. He also argues (as we did earlier) that a country pegging to a given intervention currency seems likely to have its reserve use increased by the advent of generalised floating and that a country pegging to a composite of currencies might experience some similar, but mitigated, effect.
11 See also Cooper and Truman, 1971.
12 The major data source on Eurocurrency borrowing has become the World Bank's International Finance Division, which prepares a quarterly report entitled *Borrowing in International Capital Markets*. Summaries of such reports are carried regularly in the *IMF Survey* (published twice a month). Our data come from these sources. Preliminary information indicates that Euromarket lending to LDCs has declined during the second half of 1974.
13 For these and other technical features of Eurocredits, see Mohammed and Saccomanni, 1973, especially pp. 618–24.

14   Arghiri Emmanuel has also noted that one should not equate 'debt with a debt problem', and has added (somewhat impetuously): 'in a period when all currencies are losing between 5 and 10% of their value each year, I would strongly recommend any individual or any state to run into debt up to the extreme limit of their lenders' readiness to oblige, notwithstanding any apprehension about future servicing' (1974, p. 63).

15   In spite of government promotion an active long term capital market has not materialised in Brazil; rather, Eurocurrency borrowing has flourished (Fishlow, 1974, pp. 274–6).

16   A reliable New York investment banker estimates the following costs for a first time issue by an LDC of 15 year bonds, for $15 million, around the middle of 1974.

	U.S. registered public issue	U.S. private placement	Eurodollar public issue
Coupon	8.25%	8.25%	9.00%
Legal fees and other expenses	$149,000	$75,000	$150,000
Selling spread	$300,000	$162,500	$375,000
Net interest cost	8.53%	8.40%	9.33%

Public issues in the United States require, *inter alia*, a hefty prospectus some have compared, for its length and detail, with IMF country reports. The prospectus must include a section on the debt record of the issuing country.

17   See also my comment in International Monetary Fund, 1970, pp. 34–5.

18   John Williamson (1972) first raised the concern that a competitive interest rate would increase the danger that recipients of linked SDRs would default on interest payments. He proposed paying directly out of new SDR link allocations the interest due to net accumulators of previously issued SDRs. Isard and Truman (1974) convincingly argue that interest payments by LDCs on their use of SDRs allocated under an aid link could be subsidised to increase the development assistance content of the link without impairing the relative attractiveness of the SDR as a reserve asset, a point also stressed by Helleiner (1974).

19   This reflects, of course, the general problem of growing world interdependence, emphasised by Richard N. Cooper, most recently in his 1973 Wicksell Lectures (1974).

References

Bhagwati, Jagdish N., 1972. The international monetary system: issues in the symposium. *Journal of International Economics*, 2, 315–23.

Cooper, Richard N., 1974. *Economic Mobility and National Economic Policy* (Wicksell Lectures 1973). Stockholm: Almqvist and Wiksell.

Cooper, Richard N. and Truman, Edwin M., 1971. An analysis of the role of international capital markets in providing funds to developing countries. *Weltwirtschaftliches Archiv*, **106**, 153–82.

Corden, Max, 1972. Monetary integration. *Princeton Essays in International Finance*, no. 93.

Emmanuel, Arghiri, 1974. Myths of development versus myths of underdevelopment. *New Left Review*, no. 85, 61–82.

Fishlow, Albert, 1974. Indexing Brazilian style: inflation without tears? *Brookings Papers on Economic Activity*, **1**, 261–82.

Friedman, Milton, 1973. Statement by Milton Friedman. In *Hearings before the Subcommittee on International Economics of the Joint Economic Committee, Congress of the United States, June 21, 1973*. Washington: U.S. Government Printing Office.

Gaud, William S., 1973. Speech to the Financial Times Conference on the European Community and the Third World. London: distributed by the International Finance Corporation.

Gupta, Dhruba, 1974. The first four years of SDRs. *Finance and Development*, **11**, 6–9, 31.

Helleiner, G. K., 1974. The less developed countries and the international monetary system. *Journal of Development Studies*, **10**, 347–73.

Hirsch, Fred and Higham, David, 1974. Floating rates – expectations and experience. *The Three Banks Review*, no. 102, 3–34.

Ingram, J. C., 1969. Some implications of Puerto Rican experience. In *International Finance*, (ed.) R. N. Cooper, pp. 87–104. Harmondsworth: Penguin.

International Monetary Fund, 1970. *International Reserves: Needs and Availability*. Washington.

Isard, Peter and Truman, Edwin S., 1974. SDRs, interest and the aid link: further analysis. *Banca Nazionale del Lavoro Quarterly Review*, 3–8.

Johnson, Harry G., 1970. The case for flexible exchange rates, 1969. In *Approaches to Greater Flexibility of Exchange Rates: The Bürgenstock Papers*, (ed.) George N. Halm, pp. 91–111. Princeton: Princeton University Press.

1972. Commercial policy and industrialisation. *Economica*, **39**, 264–75.

Kindleberger, Charles P., 1970. Less developed countries and the international capital market. In *Industrial Organisation and Economic Development, In Honor of E. S. Mason*, (ed.) Jesse W. Markham and Gustav P. Papanek, pp. 337–49. Boston: Houghton Miflin.

1974. International financial mediation for developing countries, mimeographed.

McKinnon, Ronald I., 1963. Optimum currency areas. *American Economic Review*, **53**, 717–24.

Mohammed, Azizal F. and Saccomanni, Fabrizio, 1973. Short-term banking and Euro-currency credits to developing countries. *International Monetary Fund Staff Papers*, xx, 612–38.

Mundell, Robert A., 1968. *International Economics*. New York: Macmillan.

OAS (Organisation of American States), 1973. *The Capital Market of the United States in Relation to the Financing of Latin American Industry*. Washington.

Ortiz Mena, Antonio, 1974. Address at the Inaugural Session of the fifteenth meeting of the Board of Governors, Santiago, Chile, Inter-American Development Bank.

Park, Y. S., 1973. The link between special drawing rights and development finance. *Princeton Essays in International Finance*, no. 100.

Treadway, Peter (Organisation of American States) n.d. Measures affecting Latin American access to developed countries' capital markets and proposals for reform, mimeographed.

United Nations, 1972. The present international monetary situation and the reform of the international monetary system. *Economic Bulletin for Latin America*, **17**, 124–9.

UNCTAD (United Nations Conference on Trade and Development), 1969. *Inter-*

national Monetary Reform and Co-operation for Development (*Report of the Expert Group on International Monetary Issues*). New York; United Nations.

Weinberg, Channa, 1973. Sanbar proposal: plan for increasing trade between developing countries. *Kidma*, no. 2, 3–6.

Williamson, John, 1972. SDRs, interest and the aid link. *Banca Nazionale del Lavoro Quarterly Review*, no. 101, 199–205.

  1973. International liquidity: a survey. *Economic Journal*, **83**, 685–746.

9. Debts, development and default

GÖRAN OHLIN

The debts accumulated by developing countries began to attract attention more than a decade ago. Many of the pertinent questions were raised at that time by Dragoslav Avramovic and his World Bank collaborators (1964). Thereafter, however, most of the studies emanating from international organisations have reiterated a primitive concern about the sheer size of the debts and, above all, about the growth of the debt service.

The debts result from capital movements in the form of foreign aid and other credits from rich to poor countries. The general assumption is that these should be increased. But as long as these capital movements take the form of credits they are bound to increase debt and future debt service. The question raised by the alarm about the debts is, therefore, whether development can really be financed on credit, or whether there are reasons to think that this is impossible or inadvisable.

There is, of course, nothing new about credit finance. It is inseparably associated with the development of the industrialised countries and their economic institutions. It is often forgotten, however, that the emergence of credit markets raised a great many problems relating to the confidence or lack of it between creditors and debtors. The evolution of legal and commercial practices with regard, for example, to collateral and bankruptcy, illustrates the intricacies that were and remain involved in any trade in promises to pay in an uncertain future.

International finance has been marked by even greater precariousness than domestic, and institutions to reduce risk have, for obvious reasons, remained more rudimentary. International diplomacy has always been a weighty factor in foreign finance, and this obviously remains true of development credit where official loans loom large and the private credits normally carry a guarantee from one or both governments involved.

In the last two decades, the international debt reported for developing countries by the World Bank, i.e. the public or publicly guaranteed debt, has grown at almost 15 per cent per annum. It was negligible at the beginning of the 1950s, but by the early 1970s it was about $100 billion. This total does not include direct private investment which, in many countries, started much earlier. Nobody knows precisely what the total of such assets amounts to, but it is probably of about the same magnitude as the debt. In most discussions of the debt problems, these direct investments are left out of account. How serious this is depends on the question at hand, but it is clear

[207]

that in many contexts direct investments are a fairly close substitute for other capital movements and that profit remittances affect balances of payments in much the same way as other investment income. There are a number of important distinctions between fixed debt and equity but both belong in the spectrum of international finance. This means that the extensive statistics about the indebtedness of developing countries do not give a complete picture of their capital imports and should not be pressed too hard.[1]

Such as they are, the World Bank figures show that about half the debts of developing countries is borne by only eight countries, but these are large countries which account for something like half the population of the developing world outside of China. Another eight account for half the remaining debt, so the very big debts are not very many. The history of the debt is also very different in different parts of the world. The Latin American countries already carried a good deal of foreign debt in the 1950s, and their indebtedness has grown at less than the average rate since then. African countries were relatively free from debt, and, with some spectacular exceptions, their debts have grown rather slowly as their foreign aid has largely consisted of grants. In Asia, on the other hand, the debt was low two decades ago but grew at a dizzy pace as India and Pakistan borrowed to the hilt. In the second half of the 1950s, the debt of the South Asian region grew at 33 per cent per annum and it continued at an average rate of 17 per cent throughout the 1960s.

About two-thirds of the debts reported by the World Bank are official debts, and one-third stems from private credits, most of them suppliers' credits. Some private credits go unreported, but private debt also represents a smaller part of the debt than of new lending because it is repaid rather fast, leaving the longer term official credits to make up the bulk of the unpaid debt. Of course, the mixture varies a great deal between countries and continents. Private debt is about half of the Latin American debt, whereas it plays practically no part at all in Asia.

The bogy of shrinking net transfer

The discussion of the debts of developing countries has been unduly focused on the mechanics of the so-called net transfer, i.e. the new lending less the debt service. In 1970, for instance, when new lending amounted to $9.3 billion, some $4.1 billion were repaid and interest payments were $1.8 billion. For developing countries as a group, debt service thus amounted to almost two-thirds of the new lending, and for some individual countries net transfer was negative. The high level of debt service may be cause for concern for a variety of reasons, but the suggestion that the purpose of credit should be to maintain a positive transfer is grossly misleading. The usefulness of credit does not depend on the net transfer at all.

The net transfer can be expressed as the net increase of debt minus the interest. Therefore, as long as the rate of growth of the debt exceeds the average rate of interest paid on it, there will be a positive net transfer. With a debt growing at 10–15 per cent, and an average rate of interest of only 4, it is obvious that there is a substantial net transfer to developing countries as a whole, amounting to about 10 per cent of the debt, and that it grows *pari passu* with the debt. That is what has happened – debt service has for some time been a fairly stable proportion of new lending and there has been no general attrition due to rising debt service.

When aid agencies, nevertheless, speak of an alarming shrinkage of the net transfer, it is for an entirely different reason. They add grant aid to the net transfer from lending, and grant aid to developing countries has been declining rapidly. In the second half of the sixties it shrank by one-third. This is why the combined net transfer stagnated in the 1960s and turned down towards the end of the decade. The two least developed continents were most exposed to this as they had received more grants earlier – in Africa the net transfer in this broad sense levelled out, and in South Asia it dropped sharply.

There has been much irrelevant talk about the terms of lending in connection with the net transfer, which is why it is important to underline that the squeeze has come from the grant side. As for the terms, there is a tendency in discussing 'hard' and 'soft' terms of aid to lump amortisation and interest together. But there is a difference between payments that reduce the debt and payments that do not. The terms of repayment are the most important factor determining the leverage between the net transfer and the volume of new lending. With shorter maturities the debt is turned over faster. This can be a problem to any debtor, and in the case of the developing countries it is easy to see that it can be particularly difficult as new loans are almost always linked to a project or to some specific imports.

The rate of interest on the debts of developing countries is on the average fairly low, thanks to the large share of concessional aid loans, and interest has not, even in a mechanical sense, mattered as much to debt service as amortisation. It may be worthwhile to point out that the size of the debt at any given moment is nothing but the present value of all past net transfers, compounded at their respective rates of interest. In the case of the development debts the net transfers have been growing so fast, and the rates of interest have been so moderate, that it is the growth rather than compound interest that accounts for most of the present debt. When the rate of inflation is taken into account it is obvious that real rates of interest are often negative, in the case of development loans sharply so.

Economists have reason to object to the very concept of net transfer. Why subtract interest payments on old debts? Interest belongs in the current account, not in the capital account. But the origin of the net transfer concept is the 'resource gap', which planners assess, between import requirements and export earnings, or between domestic savings and investment needs. It expresses a macroeconomic and aggregative view of the use of foreign resources. As long as growth targets indicate that there is a resource gap, it should be filled by a positive net transfer. This will, of course, create a very large debt. How long should it continue? Growth targets being fairly arbitrary, it may continue as long as willing lenders can be found.

There is something missing from this approach. Talking only of the net transfer or the net lending is like discussing only one side of a balance sheet. The missing element is what is done with the borrowed resources. In development finance, a rather crude planning approach often clashes with a more traditional banking view of lending which focuses on the uses of borrowed funds.

Debt crises

There have been a number of so-called debt crises in developing countries, involving the rescheduling or refinancing of the debt by the creditors. Many have seen the increasing frequency of such exercises as an ominous sign of the intrinsic impossibility of continuing development lending at high and growing levels. But what is a debt crisis?

If a debtor finds it difficult to meet his service obligations it is natural that he should ask his creditors for relief. In an extreme situation he may unilaterally decide on a moratorium but neither the word nor the institution of national bankruptcy have actually been used in postwar international finance. Things are very different from the days when Cromer took over Egypt, or the Anglo-French Debt Commission installed itself in Constantinople and the US marines collected debts in Central America.

This is not to say that creditor countries respond enthusiastically to requests for debt relief. They do so with extreme distaste and a great deal of sanctimonious talk about the breakdown of financial discipline, the risk of contagion, and 'Kontrakt ist Kontrakt'. The result is usually some grudging stretching of debt service for a few years. There is much to be said about these curious episodes, but here the diagnosis of the difficulties of the debtors is more important. What is the root of the trouble?

In order to suffer a debt crisis one must obviously first have a debt, but this is not to say that the debt itself has to be the source of the difficulties. Developing countries, and others too, get into balance of payments crises for a variety of reasons. In such situations there are a number of policy options open – drawing down reserves, borrowing from the IMF or other available helpers, compressing imports, etc. If debt service is an important item in the balance of payments, asking for debt relief is one such option. The debt in fact provides the opportunity for debt relief without having to be the cause of any crisis.

The countries which have so far asked for debt relief have been big absolute debtors and the debt has been big in their balances of payments and in their foreign trade sector. Many have been large countries where foreign trade tends to be small in relation to GNP. The debt service may then be small in terms of the economy as a whole, but large in terms of foreign exchange.

The crude index used to measure the incidence of debt service is its ratio to exports of goods and services. This debt service ratio is used to measure the liquidity problem that may arise from fixed debt service obligations. It is obviously a poor measure. What one would like to have is an index summarising at least three things: (i) the risk of sharp declines in any kind of foreign exchange inflows, including credit; (ii) the risk of sudden increases in import needs due to such things as inflation, harvest failure, etc.; and (iii) the offsetting possibility of meeting such disruptions by compressing import rapidly, by compensatory finance, or by drawing down reserves. The debt service ratio says nothing about any of these things, although it obviously tells us something about the general magnitude of the charges; and it is undeniable that the countries which have sought debt relief have also had rather high debt service ratios, invariably over 15 per cent. In fact, the only countries with high debt service ratios that have not asked for debt relief have been Israel and Mexico.

But looking at the countries which have asked for debt relief one can only be struck by the variety of the underlying situations. Tentatively one may distinguish between three different types.

Three Latin American countries – Argentina, Brazil, and Chile – got into trouble very early and illustrate a first type of debt crisis. In Argentina, the first rescheduling occurred as early as 1957 when there were rampant inflation, huge budgetary deficits, export stagnation, and a huge accumulation of suppliers' credits to public enterprises. In Brazil, coffee prices and export earnings dropped sharply in the late 1950s and a large budget deficit gave rise to heavy short term borrowing abroad, commercial arrears, and a rescheduling of the commercial debt in 1961. In the pre-Allende Chile of the late fifties, declining copper prices, domestic inflation and an overvalued currency produced a difficult balance of payments situation, which was financed both by long term foreign borrowing and suppliers' credits.

In these cases, conventional balance of payments crises were temporarily stayed (and aggravated) by short term borrowing which constituted a 'soft option' to astringent domestic measures such as tax reform. It would certainly be wrong to speak of debt crises when the background was one of unstable export earnings combined with only too familiar failures of short term economic management. These problems would have been acute with or without the debt, the principal role of which was to provide the opportunity for one kind of relief.

A different type of problem was encountered in Ghana and Indonesia. Nkrumah's second five year plan was very ambitious and the 'resource gap' of Ghana grew steadily in the first half of the sixties. It was met almost entirely by short and medium term suppliers' credits, contracted without any central control machinery. Mismanagement and waste made for a slowdown of GDP rather than growth. In addition, cocoa prices dropped and export earnings stagnated. The debt service ratio shot up and by 1965 the country was in a state of economic emergency. The total debt service due in 1966, including arrears, was equivalent to 49 per cent of exports in 1965 (Krassowski, 1974, p. 92). After the overthrow of Nkrumah in February 1966, long and tedious negotiations began in which Britain, as the biggest creditor, was very reluctant to renounce any of its claims.

Simultaneously, Indonesia got into very similar troubles although Sukarno's nationalisation of foreign enterprise, his costly military adventures, and his withdrawal from international organisations added to the difficulties caused by the calamitous inefficiency of the public sector. Prices in Djakarta rose by a factor of 100 between 1961 and 1965. Significantly, however, even the financial chaos did not deter some industrialised countries from extending guarantees for export credits in large amounts. After the fall of Sukarno, the new government asked for a rearrangement of the huge debts contracted in only a few years. Perhaps the most interesting thing about the Indonesian case is how unusually generous the settlement eventually was. While most other debt relief operations have been so-called short leash extensions of credit on rather hard terms, the Indonesian settlement virtually wiped the slate clean.

Why was Indonesia treated so generously while Ghana was given such a hard time? Diplomacy obviously counted, but probably it was not without importance that in the case of Indonesia no single creditor was as dominant as the British were in Ghana and that the creditors, therefore, asked a prominent banker, Hermann Abs from Deutsche Bank, to draft a proposal for a settlement. Unlike government officials from finance ministries and export credit guarantee agencies, whose task is to protect the taxpayers' money, Mr Abs was used to bad debts and his principal concern was to restore creditworthiness and to enable growth to be resumed along sensible lines.

One may obviously call these two debacles debt crises, but the term seems too weak. It would be more appropriate to speak of development crises. Overambitious long range projects were financed by short term credits without supervision, and executed with monumental inefficiency and corruption. Export credit guarantees made it possible for suppliers in rich countries to set aside the prudence which such evident mismanagement should otherwise have prompted. On the Ghanaian side, the easy access to credit is even said to have pushed up investment beyond the levels set by the planners (Krassowski, p. 72). In the end, a convulsive political crisis put an end to the adventure, leaving the country saddled with a huge and barren debt. There are lessons to be drawn from these sorry tales, but not the one that development cannot be financed by debt.

Many other countries which have asked for debt rescheduling fall somewhere between the two types so far outlined. But the reasons for the renegotiations about the Indian debt are quite different and illustrate a third type of situation. India asked for debt relief in 1967 but had not relied on short term export credits and had not been subject to any abrupt balance of payments crisis. Exports, on the other hand, had been disappointing, and although the terms of the debt were very soft the debt service ratio had reached 18 per cent by 1966. The harvest failures of that year raised import requirements, and the devaluation was not followed by the expected aid. Instead, there was a sharp drop in capital inflow, chiefly due to a cut in US aid and a hardening of her terms of food aid.

This sudden reduction of gross inflows was the dominant element in the Indian squeeze. The crisis, if there was one, was an aid crisis brought on by the drought of soft money for India, not a debt crisis. This is a reminder, if one is necessary, that creditors have a lot to do with whether debt finance works smoothly or not. A large debtor is vulnerable to many things, but most of all he is vulnerable to the loss of his credit.

Neither of these types of debt problem was thus brought about by the automatic attrition of net transfer or by the mounting debt burden as such. They illustrate certain types of risk faced by creditors and the wisdom of the proverbial warnings against borrowing short for long investments. But they tell us nothing about the contribution of debt finance to development.

Costs and benefits

Whether it is a good idea to borrow or not obviously depends on whether the funds can be used to such an advantage as to warrant the cost of borrowing. If foreign loans are wasted, the obligation to service the debt will leave a country worse off than if it had never sought or accepted foreign loans at all.

It is tempting to draw the conclusion that the only thing that matters is, therefore, that the loan is used for a good project. A project with a return that is higher than the interest should not create any problems. It will generate its own repayment capacity and then some. This simple and straightforward view of the matter has dominated development financing practices and it has some merit. But it is obviously incomplete. It would be foolish to lend money to a company for, say, an eminently promising extension, if the rest of the enterprise is in disastrous shape. A loan for an excellent development project may give rise to debt service problems if other resources are used inefficiently. Most of the credits to developing countries are taken up by the state or guaranteed by it. Unlike direct investments they represent a charge on the economy as a whole. If a project fails, the loan is nevertheless to be paid back; even if it is successful, repayment may be rendered difficult by general stagnation of production or exports.

The 'efficiency criterion' for deciding whether it is economically warranted to take up a foreign loan is, therefore, not whether the project which it is ostensibly intended to finance will be able to carry the cost of the loan. Instead, as economists have, from time to time, pointed out, it is the marginal project, or rather the ultimate effect on the use of resources, that matters. But looking at such a marginal project is easier said than done.

In practice, it is difficult enough to ascertain the returns of any project at all. Besides the intrinsic uncertainties of the future, there are all the problems emanating from a distorted price system to which economists have applied themselves zealously. In particular, balance of payments disequilibria with import restrictions and overvalued exchange rates will have to be corrected for, as well as taxes and tariffs. To assess the returns across the exchanges one needs some method of shadow pricing to express scarcities and benefits more adequately than nominal prices.

Then there is the marginal project. It cannot be identified. Instead the appropriate planning technique is to decide on an 'accounting rate of interest' to be applied to all major projects. To determine such an accounting rate of interest is no easy matter, as anyone will know who has studied Little and Mirrlees (1969) and the literature which has grown up in their wake. But there is no other way of formulating a consistent criterion of efficiency. The accounting rate of interest should serve as a lower cut-off point for projects to be undertaken and as a higher limit for foreign borrowing on different nominal terms. Normally, the effective rate of interest should be below the accounting rate of interest for a loan to be a good idea. The accounting rate of interest is nothing but the social return to capital, so this makes good sense.

Although aid-tying and other practices raise the effective rate of interest on development loans above the nominal ones, inflation and terms of trade improvements for primary producers will pull in the opposite direction. The cost, at least of concessional loans, cannot be called high and is usually negative. Whether development is feasible on such a financial basis is to ask whether development is feasible at all, whether there are any projects that will make the country better off instead of impoverishing it. The conclusion must be that it is not cost that constitutes a possible obstacle to development finance.

Growth and savings

But there are other issues involved. One is whether a foreign loan which may be entirely warranted in terms of its cost will also make a contribution to growth. This is not self-evident. If an aid project is so attractive that it would have been undertaken even without an aid loan, one must conclude that the effect of the loan will be to enable some entirely different expenditure at the margin, which need not be an investment expenditure at all. It may raise consumption or military spending. In such cases, foreign capital will not supplement domestic savings but substitute for them. Some such substitution should be expected. It would be odd, particularly in the light of economic theory, if an increase in available current resources were not used for some increase of present consumption as well as to provide for future consumption. Foreign borrowing should thus lead to some curtailment of domestic saving.

This does not vitiate the proposition that such borrowing is advantageous so long as the effective interest rate is below the accounting rate of interest.

It does mean, however, that the contribution to growth will be smaller than if external savings were all additional to domestic ones. The amount of foreign capital required to achieve a specified increase in growth will be increased. Indeed, if the substitution of foreign borrowing for domestic savings is complete, no amount of foreign borrowing will have any effect on growth.

But the objective of development finance is usually taken to be growth. It is one of the cherished tenets of foreign aid that it should raise investment and not consumption. International lending agencies do not even like to consider the possibility that the resources they make available might raise present welfare. They therefore attach very great importance to what they call 'savings performance'. Their preferred conception of how aid works is that it should raise domestic savings, not reduce them. Rising incomes and high marginal savings rates should close the resource gap and eventually eliminate the need for foreign resources, as the debt cycle is consummated.

The debt cycle

Discussions of project finance usually assume that an initial gestation period is followed, sooner or later, by a time of fruition and repayment. In developing countries, as in others, individual undertakings can be financed by foreign creditors, whether or not the overall foreign debt is increasing or decreasing. While some projects are in their gestation phase, others will, one hopes, be paying off. But applied to national economies, the same conception suggests a longer period of borrowing, followed by a period of capital exports to repay and liquidate the foreign debt, possibly followed by a creditor phase.

Avramovic, *et al.* derived a debt cycle from a model in which the need for foreign resources was simply the gap between domestic savings and the investments required to attain a target growth rate. The debt would begin to be drawn down when the capacity to save had increased enough. What this model brought out was that unless the economy grew fairly fast, the debt would grow faster under the impact of compound interest. If the borrowing continued for very long, the debt could never be repaid, and, in any case, prolonged borrowing produced a very large debt which would take unreasonably long to settle.

While the underlying ICOR model[2] may not inspire much confidence, the debt cycle concept is obviously pertinent. It raises the question of how long development lending makes sense. As in many other situations of long term finance, the answer will not be derived from considerations of profitability and efficiency. The debt may rise to such proportions that liquidity problems make further borrowing difficult or impossible.

Liquidity

There are limits to the amount of debt service either creditors or borrowers want to see in the balance of payments. These limits may depend on their mutual confidence, the available credit facilities and the ease of rolling over the debt, and so forth. But they do exist.

'Liquidity' is anything but a simple concept. As already suggested in the discussion of debt crises, the risk is not, in this context, primarily that of project failures but that of balance of payments crisis. This provides some rationale for the assumption that debt service cannot indefinitely grow faster than the foreign trade sector of the economy.

It also suggests something like a take-off situation, in which a country starting out without much foreign debt has a certain breathing space – a one shot chance of borrowing fairly large amounts of foreign resources. This opportunity is cumulatively enlarged to the extent that advantage is successfully taken of it. Rapid export growth will make it possible to continue large borrowing in spite of growing debt service. But sooner or later, there is a ceiling beyond which further net borrowing must not be greater than warranted by export performance, if that is what determines debt servicing capacity or can be taken as a proxy for the more complex variables that determine the country's credit standing.

What many worry about is that the developing countries might already have used up their borrowing capacity and will, therefore, have to curtail borrowing sharply – perhaps so sharply that they cannot even borrow enough to meet the interest on past debt. This will send their thoughts in the direction of repudiation and withdrawal from the whole system of international finance that apparently can offer them nothing but onerous burdens. To see if this worry is justified one may first look at the global situation for some orders of magnitude.

World inflation and export revenues

In the sixties the debt increased at an average annual rate of 14 per cent, a little faster in the beginning and a little more slowly towards the end. Debt service increased at much the same rate, with slight deviations due to changes in terms such as the introduction of grace periods, which held back debt service until the first grace periods had expired after which debt service jumped back to the trend line.

How fast has the foreign trade sector of developing countries grown? Overall exports of developing countries only grew at something like 6 per cent. The comparison between 14 and 6 per cent looks bad. But the 6 per cent figure was in real terms. In the first half of the sixties, export and import prices actually rose only slightly, and export earnings certainly did increase more slowly than debt service. But in the late sixties, the exports of developing countries in US dollars rose almost 11 per cent per annum. The debt and debt service in those years rose at almost exactly the same rate. In such conditions, lending can go on increasing without any deterioration of the liquidity position.

Certainly there are no grounds for complacency. There are wide deviations among individual countries, many of which are heavily exposed. At the present time, the increase in oil prices has wrecked the balances of payments of many developing countries and in one stroke increased the potential demand for debt relief.

It nevertheless remains true that the consequences of world inflation for the debt problem have been neglected. There have been references to its impact on effective interest rates but it is rarely appreciated that, unlike a reduction of interest rates, which only affects the debt structure very slowly, inflation reduces the whole debt burden immediately.

Nobody expects the low rates of inflation of the early sixties to return in the near future. This must presumably be welcomed by debtors who, like the developing countries, have very long term contracts. On the other hand, high rates of international inflation expose developing countries to a long list of serious difficulties in other ways if they are not able to pursue policies to protect their domestic economies from imported inflation. The need for new borrowing is also inflated, and in the end, an adjustment of interest rates to an expected rate of inflation at a high level would nullify the gains. It is also true that the terms of trade, which for a while improved for many developing countries, are now turning against them. Nonetheless the fact remains that the stepping up of inflation has so far brought unexpected relief to indebted countries.

Even with regard to liquidity, the global trends of the development debts do not seem quite so alarming as often thought, largely because the present contribution of outside borrowing to total capital formation in developing countries is not all that great. One can make a rapid estimate of what the liquidity constraints allow in this regard. If debt service is not to exceed the range of 15 to 25 per cent of exports and represents, as it has done, an average of 13 per cent of the debt, it would not be advisable to carry a total debt of more than 1 to 2 times exports. The debt can grow as fast as export earnings – say at a conservative rate of 10 per cent in money terms, so each year one can borrow an amount that equals 10 to 20 per cent of exports. If exports are as high as 20 per cent of GNP, this is 2 to 4 per cent of GNP. If total capital formation is also 20 per cent of GNP, net foreign borrowing will be 10 to 15 per cent of total capital formation. That is pretty much what we have had in many developing countries. As long as that is what is meant by financing development on credit, it would seem feasible as long as the terms stay relatively soft.

In a large country, the situation is different. For India, which is in a class of its own, the picture is particularly bleak. Indian exports are only about 4 per cent of GNP, so the earlier calculation suggests that it should not prudently borrow more than 0.5 to 1 per cent of GNP or, at most, something like 5 per cent of capital formation. That is also what India has done, although India's terms have been better than average as it has studiously refrained from hard short term credits, and it can, therefore, carry a debt which is not 1 to 2 but 3 times as large as export earnings. If one wants to make a more substantial contribution to Indian development by external finance, one must either make the terms even softer or simply make it possible for India to operate at a higher debt service ratio, which would require both India and her creditors to demand much less of her in the way of liquidity.

Debt management and risk taking

The problems associated with development debts turn out on inspection to have less to do with repayment difficulties than with the carrying of a large debt. The bigger the debt the greater the risks involved, both for creditors and debtors. Some of these risks are genuine and originate in the uncertainties about future 'states of nature' and human actions. But the history of financial institutions also suggests that some risks can be reduced by improvements of the institutional arrangements involved.

One of the obstacles to rational debt management by developing countries is the fragmentary character of the market for credit and capital to which they have access. As the structure of their debt shows, at the long end of the spectrum there are bilateral aid loans and IDA loans, at the short end export credits. Although the role of programme lending is growing, these latter types of finance still dominate, and they are fairly inflexible and typically linked to the financing of imports of one specific kind or another. Even when there has been no excessive use of short term credits for long term purposes, there is no particular reason to think that the conventional time profiles of such loans will match those of project maturation, let alone of balance of payments developments. But apart from IMF facilities for very short term balance of payments support, the system does not provide the range of untied medium and short term credits that would be necessary for a flexible adjustment and management of the debt. The only recourse for most developing countries has been debt rescheduling, and it is in this light that many 'debt crises' must be seen. In all their clumsiness, they are an integral part of the very imperfect international credit market rather than a sign of the breakdown of that market.

Risk is prominent in all finance but it dominates that of development finance. Public aid and the creation of international institutions have been prompted by the fact that the risks are too great and the creditworthiness of developing countries too low to give them much of a chance in regular capital markets.

It is often argued that hard term lending to developing countries by governments or the World Bank cannot be termed aid since it does not involve any cost. But lending to developing countries at the rates one can get for oneself in the market means renouncing a risk premium. The risks of development finance are real. They are not figments of the imagination in Wall Street or Frankfurt. It is true that institutions like the World Bank can reduce the risks by pooling them and by acquiring special expertise. That is the *raison d'être* of investment banking generally. But there will still be a real risk, and one big question in development finance is how it should be allocated.

In many debt rescheduling exercises, official creditors simply refuse to assume any part of that risk. Not having charged any risk premium, they may see no earthly reason why they should be exposed to any risk at all. Unlike private creditors, they can use a great deal of political and financial strength to throw the whole risk on the debtor. Although a large part of the advantage to the recipient at the time when the loan was contracted stemmed from the fact that he was relieved of a heavy risk premium and often benefited from a large additional interest concession, he may later find himself paying dearly for this if he does not have the option of default.

A particularly pernicious variant of this situation arises from the encouragement of export credits by cheap guarantees. Suppliers are relieved of risk – the advertisements of the British export credit guarantee agency in *The Financial Times* used to carry the slogan, 'Export with an easy mind'. To be sure, there are legitimate risks to insure against, but the theory of insurance also recognises so-called 'moral hazard' in situations where the offer of insurance might have undesirable consequences. In the case at hand, it only too often happens that guarantees encourage unscrupulous salesmanship which takes advantage of the lack of experience or the understaffing of government agencies in developing countries.

If and when things then go badly wrong, the guaranteeing agencies take over the claims and press to collect their pound of flesh. They have collected a fee for the guarantee and generally also manage to collect the debt. It is an anomalous aspect of the relationship between rich and poor when they actually report a profit.

The World Bank, which actually administers debt relief exercises and has a very large and growing stake in most debts of developing countries, finds it impossible to participate in any adjustments of its own claims, believing as it does that its high rating in capital markets depends on the fact that its clients honour their obligations to the Bank punctiliously, whatever happens to other creditors.

What one would like to see is some recognition of the fact that it is one of the essential functions of development assistance to assume part of the risk of development. This argument is, of course, also a case for equity participation and the risk sharing it implies. In the case of government aid it can be arranged through public or semi-public development corporations, and this type of arrangement has been gaining favour. The possibilities of equity financing in developing countries are often limited by nationalistic and ideological objections, but even in the case of government to government loans, the same effect could be achieved if the riskiness of development was faced up to.

Development finance needs something like the institution of 'honourable bankruptcy'. This inspired innovation was not introduced in industrialised countries until well into the nineteenth century, although limited liability companies met some of the same needs slightly earlier. It is not always recognised how important the institution of bankruptcy is to enable the credit system to work without too much risk aversion and to recover quickly from failures. The option of bankruptcy would prevent the machinery from getting clogged up by a lot of dead debt. Nobody can argue for undisciplined irresponsibility, which is the perpetual worry of the financial community. But irresponsibility is precisely what is being fostered by indiscriminate guarantees of export credits to any and all countries regardless of their financial position.

A capital market for developing countries

A major increase in aid is most unlikely in coming decades. The external sources of development finance will include some soft aid and IDA loans, but a large and growing share of the capital flows to developing countries will presumably be on hard terms, partly from the World Bank and the regional development banks, partly from commercial sources. It is still too early to say what the character of OPEC aid will be, but there is no reason to expect its terms to fall outside the range already prevailing.

There are those who claim that the growth of debt in developing countries is somehow intrinsically untenable. Presumably the creditors do not share this view. If they came to hold it, the flow of credit would dry up fast, so it is not just an academic matter to ask whether it is possible or sensible to finance development on a credit basis.

The conclusion of the previous discussion is in line with common sense. When development is likely to succeed at all, there is a case for credit which is all the stronger when aid is in short supply. Long term capital, even on commercial terms, is certainly not free from political constraints but it is likely to be more readily available than concessional aid.

The cost of credit is not likely to be the basic obstacle. In recent years, the real rate of interest paid by developing countries has probably been negative. If capital borrowed on such terms cannot be used to good advantage, development would be a losing proposition with or without foreign borrowing. Even at higher rates, there is no reason to believe that there is a long run shortage of worthwhile uses for finance in the developing world.

As in all financial contexts, the basic issue is, rather, how to maintain mutual confidence in spite of inevitable failures and frictions. Financial institutions reduce the risk premium through a variety of devices. In the case of development finance this is the function of such intermediaries as the

World Bank and the regional development banks. It is also the purpose of export credit insurance schemes. Such devices shift the risk away from the investor but leave it squarely with the borrower.

It would not be wise to relieve borrowers of all risk. The case against it is both theoretical and empirical. The theory of moral hazard simply suggests that incentives to avoid waste and losses would be impaired. This would seem to be confirmed by a wealth of experience, and it would be strange if developing countries were immune to such a general tendency. 'Borrowing dulls the edge of husbandry' according to Polonius's advice in *Hamlet*, and if the need to repay is known to be waiveable it must be doubly true. Kenneth Arrow has observed that 'if a complete absence of risk-shifting is bad because it inhibits the undertaking of risky enterprises and if total risk-shifting is bad because it reduces the incentives for their success, then it is reasonable to suggest that partial risk-shifting might be best' (Arrow, 1971, p. 143).

How the balance should be struck in the case of creditors and debtors respectively is a delicate question, and in the context of development finance it has not received much attention. But it is clear that shifting most risks to the governments of developing countries may deadlock the market. Unlike private borrowers, they cannot be liquidated in case of failure. It would be a reasonable task for foreign aid to break such deadlocks when there is a case for 'honourable bankruptcy' so that bygones can become bygones.

Many other things ought to be done to make development finance work more smoothly and reduce the risk of snags that do not originate in investment failure but in such things as international trade disruption, monetary disturbances, etc. The debt crises and debt renegotiations of recent years have earlier been described as integral parts of the capital market for developing countries, such as it is. There should be less awkward ways of dealing with such situations.

Many proposals have been made for international conventions to restrain export credit guarantees to countries which already are in bad shape. The worst offenders might, for instance, be forced to the end of the queue and take a loss in the rescheduling. Experience so far has shown that voluntary restraint is hardly to be expected from government agencies which have as their task the promotion of exports. It is nevertheless disgraceful that governments in rich countries are not able to co-ordinate this activity better with their aid policies.

The instability of commodity prices has been a major source of liquidity crises in developing countries in the past and promises again to work havoc now that oil prices remain up while those of other primary commodities are coming down. In the absence of successful stabilisation of commodity prices, compensatory finance of the kind so long discussed remains a possible way of facilitating debt management.

However, a more basic attack on the problem would be to enlarge the general capacity for debt management. A basic requirement for this is that developing countries are accorded credits for general financial purposes. One of the functions of the IMF and the IBRD should be to ease developing countries into a working relationship with the international capital markets which would enable them to carry their debts with some flexibility. The scope of the operations of these institutions has remained fairly narrow, with the Bank restricting itself to project finance in spite of a more liberal view of what constitutes a project, and the Fund confined to very short term balance of payments support. An increasing number of developing countries have managed to float their own issues in rich countries, and during the glut on the Eurodollar market a surprising number of less creditworthy countries raised substantial amounts there. When this was done at considerable cost, it suggests that the value of free foreign exchange was deemed to be very high. An obvious direction for development finance in the future would be a wider use of guarantees, by aid giving governments or international institutions, of long term credits of a purely financial character, i.e. ones not linked to projects or imports.

Finally, there is the classical transfer problem. If creditor countries raise barriers to developing country exports, they will themselves knock out the only assumption on which development credits make sense. It is not just a matter of the ultimate repayment – as we have seen, increasing export earnings are necessary to meet the liquidity constraint and make it possible to continue borrowing without running up excessive debt service ratios. In this, as in many other respects, the feasibility of the huge credit operation which is under way to finance development depends on the wisdom of the creditors as much as on the performance of the debtors.

The biggest risk of a large debt owed by poor countries to rich ones is that, in a climate of increasingly strained relations, it may become politically provocative and hang as a dark cloud over the international scene. In that case, the financing of development by debt will not work well. Nor will any other way. Conversely, the case for trying to make the machinery of international credit work smoothly lies not only in the benefits it is capable of providing, but also in the hope that these give rise to a joint interest in the preservation of international co-operation.

Notes

1 For other statistics, including an estimate of the book value of direct investments see Nurul Islam's discussion below (pp. 225–7).
2 Models based upon the assumption of a constant aggregate incremental capital–output ratio (ICOR) are much too crude to be very useful.

References

Arrow, Kenneth, 1971. *Essays in the Theory of Risk-Bearing.* Chicago: Markham.

Avramovic, Dragoslav *et al.* 1964. *Economic Growth and External Debt.* Baltimore: Johns Hopkins.

Krassowski, Andrzej, 1974. *Development and the Debt Trap: Economic Planning and External Borrowing in Ghana.* London: Overseas Development Institute.

Little, Ian M. D. and Mirrlees, James A., 1969. *Manual of Industrial Project Analysis in Developing Countries, Volume II, Social Cost Benefit Analysis.* Paris: Development Centre of the OECD.

10. The external debt problem of the developing countries with special reference to the least developed

NURUL ISLAM

The international context

The external debt problem of the developing countries, individually or as a group, has to be viewed in the context of their growth prospects and, in particular, prospects for their exports, terms of trade and resource inflows. The United Nations' strategy for the Second Development Decade postulated a rate of growth of GDP of 6 per cent for the developing countries. Many poor countries, especially those with annual incomes *per capita* below $200, did not attain this growth rate in the early 1970s. In fact, there was a decline in the developing countries' growth rates in the late 1960s and early 1970s, particularly in the poorest countries; between 1965 and 1973 the average rate of growth of *per capita* income in developing countries with *per capita* incomes under $200 per year amounted to only 1.1 per cent (McNamara, 1974, p. 13). The UN's strategy also called for an increase in the annual net flow of resources from the rich to the poor nations, reaching a level of about 1 per cent of the rich countries' GNP by 1975. The actual such flow fell considerably short of this target and official development assistance amounted only to 0.30 per cent of the GNP of the rich countries in 1973. In consequence there was a decline in the ratio of net annual inflow of external resources to GNP in the developing countries between 1968 and 1972.

During 1973–4 the developing countries were affected by a combination of unfavourable circumstances which have serious and adverse consequences for their future growth. Those factors are: (*a*) a substantial increase in the price of energy; (*b*) high prices of raw materials; (*c*) increasing costs of manufactured goods imports; (*d*) absolute shortages of strategic inputs like fertilisers and food; (*e*) world-wide inflation; (*f*) a slowing down of growth in the industrialised countries.

As a consequence, the terms of trade of the developing countries, excepting oil and some mineral exporting countries, are expected to decline between 1973 and 1980; for the poorest developing countries the decline is expected to be as large as 25 per cent. The rates of growth of the OECD countries are expected to decline from an average of 5 per cent during the 1960s to somewhere between 3 and 4 per cent, if that, during 1974–80 (McNamara, 1974, pp. 10–13). Between 1968 and 1973 the annual total net flow to the developing countries of external resources, including private capital as well as official development assistance, increased, in money terms, by about 70 per cent. If it is assumed that between 1973 and 1980 the total annual net flow of external resources to the developing countries will increase by about another 70 per cent, i.e. at a slower annual rate than in the past – an assumption judged not unreasonable in the light of recent trends – the rate of growth of *per capita* income of the developing countries, excluding oil and mineral exporters, will fall to about 3.4 per cent for those countries with *per capita* incomes above $200 and to minus 0.4 per cent for those below (McNamara, 1974, p. 13; World Bank, 1974, p. 82).

A negative rate of growth for the poorest developing countries is socially and politically unacceptable. Yet it has been estimated that even if the target were only the attainment of a rate of growth of *per capita* income of about 4 per cent for those countries with *per capita* income above $200 and of about 2 per cent for those below, the required rate of annual capital inflow would be substantially higher than that projected above, roughly by an additional 60 per cent by 1980 (McNamara, 1974, p. 18). Moreover, 60 per cent of the total inflow of resources would, under these assumptions, need to be in terms of concessional development assistance, mainly for poorer developing countries with *per capita* incomes of less than $200.

It is expected that there will be a considerable increase in the availability of credits on commercial terms but only the middle-income poorer countries will be sufficiently creditworthy to borrow on such terms. During 1973 about $8.8 billion were lent by the Eurocredit markets to the developing countries; 40 per cent was used by three countries, Mexico, Brazil and Peru, and another 20 per cent went to the mineral exporting countries. Even middle-income countries like Turkey, Korea, the Philippines and Thailand, which need large amounts but borrowed little in the past, will probably be able to borrow larger amounts in the future.

The focus of subsequent discussion in this paper, unlike that of Diaz-Alejandro and Ohlin above, is therefore on the poorer developing countries with limited natural resources, few or no dynamic exports, and heavy import dependence. For the middle-income developing countries with high credit-worthiness and the ability to use capital productively by borrowing at commercial rates, the nature and magnitude of the debt problem is very different from that of the poorer developing countries. Furthermore, the discussion will centre more on the long term availability of resources for development rather than on the problem of short term liquidity, i.e. inability to service debt payments in the face of short term fluctuations in the balance of payments.

It is in the light of this overall perspective that the problem of the outstanding as well as the new debt for the developing countries has to be reviewed. One important aspect of the flow of resources is how to reduce the burden of outstanding debt. Even prior to the recent economic crisis, which contributed to the urgent need for a substantial increase in the net inflow of external resources for the non-oil producing developing countries, the depressing effects of the debt service burden on the net availability of resources, future growth and prospects of the developing world have been a matter of increasing concern.

The size and burden of the debt

The total outstanding official or publicly guaranteed debt of developing countries at the end of 1971 amounted to about $80 billion (disbursed), but the total debt including committed but undisbursed loans already amounted to $100 billion. Of the total outstanding and disbursed debt, official development assistance from bilateral and multilateral sources accounted for 43 per cent, i.e. $34.5 billion; export credits and other commercial borrowings amounted to 48 per cent, i.e. $38.3 billion; and borrowings from the communist countries and from other countries amounted to 7 per cent and 2 per cent respectively. In 1972 the total debt service burden, including amortisation and interest payments, amounted to $12.2 billion, which is about 15 per cent of the total outstanding debt at the end of 1971, of which interest payments were about 4 per cent (OECD, 1973, p. 68). In addition, the estimated book value of private overseas direct investment at this time amounted to about $47.9 billion (OECD, 1973, p. 72). These totals have since continued rapidly to rise.

Table 1. *Debt and debt service payments of eighty-six developing countries, by geographic area and type of lender, 1973–82*

	Debt outstanding, end of 1972 ($ billion)	Service payments, 1973–82 ($ billion)	Ratio of debt service payments to debt (%)
Geographic areas			
Africa	16.2	13.7	85
East Asia	13.8	10.6	77
Middle East	11.0	11.4	104
South Asia	18.4	10.8	59
Southern Europe	10.3	9.9	96
Western Hemisphere	29.6	29.8	101
Total	99.4	86.1	87
Types of lender			
Bilateral official	49.1	35.8	73
Multilateral	19.8	14.3	72
Private			
Suppliers' credits	12.2	14.6	120
Banks	11.0	13.4	122
Others	7.4	8.0	108
Total	99.4	86.1	87

SOURCE: World Bank, 1974, pp. 88–9.

The proportion of commercial credit in the net flow of financial resources has been on the increase during the sixties. Moreover, the grant element in official loan commitments declined from 40 per cent to 31 per cent between 1965 and 1972 (World Bank, 1974, p. 93). The resulting rising trend in debt service payments in relation to the outstanding debt is likely to persist and even to be accentuated in the coming years, as, on the one hand, the role of commercial credits continues to grow, and on the other, grace periods in many of the existing development loans come to a close. Table 1 shows debt service payments expected to be made during the period 1973–82 as a percentage of debt outstanding at the end of 1972. The differences in the burden of future debt service payments as between different regions, are partly due to the differences in the relative importance of commercial credit and partly due to those in the time profile of the debt. The highest ratio of payments to outstanding debt, resulting in net outflow from the developing countries, relates to the credits from banks and suppliers' credits, representing short maturity and grace period, as well as high interest rates; whereas the lowest ratio is in the case of multilateral assistance, representing a large grant element.

The burden of debt service payments is inflexible and involves serious strain on the balance of payments at times of shortfalls in foreign exchange earnings caused by factors outside the control of the debtor country. Moreover, the implications of debt service payments for the balance of payments have to be considered in combination with the burden of income remittances on account of private foreign investment. The ratio of debt service payments, *including* investment income payments, to exchange earnings is shown in Table 2.

Table 2. *Exports, debt service and investment income payments ($ billion)*

	All developing countries			Developing countries excluding oil exporters		
	1960	1970	1972	1960	1970	1972
Total exports	29.6	63.0	79.9	23.0	45.4	53.6
Debt service						
payments	2.0	5.4	7.3	1.9	4.6	6.1
As % of exports	6.8	8.6	9.1	8.3	10.1	11.4
Investment income						
payments (net)	3.0	7.6	10.0	1.1	3.2	3.0
As % of exports	10.0	12.1	12.6	4.8	7.1	5.4
Total debt						
service payments	5.0	13.0	17.3	3.0	7.8	9.1
As % of exports	16.8	20.7	21.7	13.1	17.2	16.8

SOURCE: Howe, 1974, pp. 156–7.

At the end of 1972 nearly half (49 per cent) of the total outstanding debt was held by countries with *per capita* income of less than $375 which experienced *per capita* growth rates of between 1.7 and 2.4 per cent in the late 1960s and early 1970s. Twenty-eight per cent was held by countries with *per capita* incomes of less than $200 which grew more slowly still (World

Bank, 1974, p. 90). Thus a large part of the outstanding debt is held by countries, with low *per capita* income and low rates of export (and total) growth, which in turn require a large inflow of resources for development. The lower the level of income of the debtor countries, the lower is the rate of growth, the higher is the ratio of debt service payments to exports and the lower is the rate of growth of exports, as is seen in Table 3.

Table 3. *Debt service ratios and export growth rates, by income category,*[a] *eighty-six less developed countries*

	Debt service ratio, 1972[b] (%)	Export growth rate, 1965–72 (%)
Higher-income	9.2	11.4
Middle-income	9.2	9.5
Lower-income	18.4	−0.9

[a] Membership in these categories may be found on p. 84 of the source document.
[b] Debt service for 1972 divided by 1972 exports.
SOURCE: Calculated from data in World Bank, 1974, pp. 92, 101.

The 'debt service ratio', relating current debt service payments to current exports, does not fully convey the implications of debt burden for the balance of payments of a country over the longer run future. The higher the level of outstanding debt, the higher the debt service payments will be in the future. Depending on the rate of growth of exports, they can pose a heavy drain on future foreign exchange earnings.

The OECD Development Assistance Committee uses two additional measures of debt service burden. The first is the ratio to the GNP of the sum of the total stock of private foreign investment and the discounted present value of the next fifteen years' debt service payments, less current foreign exchange reserves. This expresses the domestic resource equivalent of debt service payments which must be extracted from domestic output for transfer to the foreign creditors. For forty out of ninety developing countries, this ratio was higher than 25 per cent and for eighteen countries it was higher than 40 per cent in 1969. The second measure of debt service burden focuses on the balance of payments implications of the debt service payments on outstanding official debt (excluding private foreign investment). It takes the total debt service payments over the next fifteen years, deducts the excess of foreign exchange reserves over two months' import requirements, and divides the residual into equal annual payments which are expressed as a percentage of annual average export earnings during the most recent 'normal' three year period. In 1969, twenty-six out of ninety developing countries had a debt service ratio, defined in this way, of 10 per cent and higher; and four of them had a ratio higher than 50 per cent (OECD, 1972, pp. 80–4).

Large debt service payments reduce the net inflow of external resources; with a given gross flow, and increasing debt service payments, the net receipts decline or increase at a declining rate. This is particularly disturbing if the gross disbursement of foreign assistance also grows slowly. Moreover, there is an important aspect of foreign credit, i.e. tying of credit to purchases in the donor country, which reduces the real value of credit by no less than 20 per cent (Bhagwati, 1970, pp. 16–17), while debt service payments must still be made at full money value in free foreign exchange. The cost of tying, in the case of food aid and project aid including technical assistance, is higher than that of general commodity assistance by another 10 to 20 per cent (Pinstrup-Anderson and Tweetin, 1971).[1]

The increasing burden of debt service payments thus causes concern for several long run reasons: it requires the debtor countries to divert a part of their growth in output for debt service payments; it reduces the amount of domestic savings available for reinvestment and, therefore, for increasing their rate of investment; and it preempts a part of their foreign exchange earnings for debt service payments and reduces the amount available for essential consumer goods or development imports.

Increasing resource flows through adjustment of the outstanding debt

To use an increasing rate of gross lending to ensure a given increase in net inflow is not without problems, for it increases very rapidly the outstanding debt. The greater the proportion of debt to domestic assets, the greater is the risk of alien influence on the domestic economy. With an increase in gross inflow, especially where the loans are tied, both the creditor and debtor countries have to expand the administrative apparatus both at home and abroad; and the creditors have to increase the visibility of their presence through large overseas aid missions. Moreover, any interruption in the rate of new lending is likely to jeopardise the ability of the debtor country to meet its obligations. While an increase in the rate of gross inflow requires annual approval, political or parliamentary, soft terms, once agreed upon, can achieve the same net flow without the need for repeated approval of increases.

The net resource inflow can be increased, *given* a gross inflow, by (*a*) softening the terms of new loans, and (*b*) cancellation or renegotiation of the outstanding debt. The rescheduling of outstanding debt increases the net inflow by reducing the current outflow on account of debt service payments. In the past, a number of countries have undertaken renegotiation or rescheduling of outstanding debt. The circumstances which led to such rescheduling arrangements for individual countries were varied; they did not fall into a specific pattern. Most of the developing countries habitually have lived in a state of perpetual balance of payments crisis; whenever this deepened into an acute balance of payments crisis, some countries attempted to reschedule debt. The crisis was sometimes caused by an unexpected decline in export earnings or sudden rise in import prices (a deterioration in the terms of trade); fixed debt service obligations in these circumstances produced severe strains on the balance of payments which could not always be relieved by drawing down existing foreign exchange reserves or by using drawing rights on the IMF or borrowing in world capital markets. In such situations, if imports have to be maintained above some critical level so as not seriously to jeopardise the maintenance of current consumption levels and a minimum rate of development activity, a developing country has no choice but to press for some kind of debt relief.

Basically, if a country's borrowing from abroad yields a return (net of amortisation) higher than the rate of interest and if increases in foreign exchange earnings are also greater than the required interest payments, it should face no difficulty in servicing external debt in the long run; a country may nevertheless face a short run liquidity problem, when interest and amortisation payments exceed increases in foreign exchange resources because loans are inappropriately 'bunched', and there is a 'bulge' in debt service payments. Countries like Singapore, Malaysia, Mexico or Israel may have high ratios of debt service payments to exports, but face no debt servicing problems because both income and exports grow at a high rate and they are always able, precisely because of their high rates of growth of GNP and exports, to maintain sufficient creditworthiness to borrow in international capital markets.

Balance of payments crises have also been caused by deficit financing and rapid domestic inflation, compounded by delays in the adjustment of exchange rates and accumulations of short term foreign credits. In a few cases, domestic inflation was aggravated by unproductive investment projects which were inefficiently executed with little or no impact on economic growth and productivity in the short run. In other cases, it was the product not so much of economic mismanagement as of the long run structural problem of slow growth of income and exports, coupled with inability to mobilise adequate domestic savings in view of acute poverty and high population growth, and a high proportion of investment in projects of long gestation, such as physical or social infrastructure. The basic problem in countries such as India, Pakistan and Sri Lanka is the acute scarcity of resources in relation to investment requirements, and slow growth of exports in relation to the need for imports. These countries suffer from inadequate social and physical infrastructure and limited ability to formulate and execute development projects. Since the necessary transformation of their domestic economies and structures of foreign trade takes time, they will need a net inflow on a continuing basis for a long time to come.

Past rescheduling exercises were designed to reduce debt service payments in the early years with an eventual increase in payments in the longer run; they deferred existing amortisation payments which, in turn, increased the amount of interest payments over a longer period. Total debt payments were, therefore, higher in the majority of the cases over the period as a whole, than would have been the case in the absence of rescheduling. Argentina, for example, had to pay $1,956 million in place of $1,857.8 million; Brazil had to pay $2,094 million instead of $1,956 million and Chile had to pay $1,245 million in place of $1,219 million. The corresponding figures for Ghana were $425.8 million in place of $329.3 million; for Indonesia, $784 million in place of $667 million; and for Peru, $966.1 million in place of $934 million (IBRD, 1971, pp. 26–30).

The debt rescheduling exercises, so far undertaken, both bilaterally and on a multilateral basis, may be summarised as follows. Debt relief was mainly related to service payments due in the immediate future. In some cases, it related only to a part of the total debt burden, excluding the part which was not insured or guaranteed by the creditor government. Most of the creditor countries preferred a 'short leash' approach, and kept their options open to review debt service problems after a relatively few years. In some cases, the debt rescheduling exercises were undertaken more than once. A very long term rescheduling, it was feared, might not ensure sufficiently strict economic discipline and sound debt management policies. In many cases, the interest rate applied to the rescheduled debt was the commercial rate of interest and only in a few cases was it the concessional rate at which official development assistance was extended. The use of the commercial rate of interest further added to the future debt service obligations. In almost all cases some understanding was reached about future debt management. The debtor countries were often expected to keep the debt service ratio within a prescribed limit; in a few cases they were expected to maintain foreign exchange reserves above a certain minimum level. In Ghana and Indonesia, the debt rescheduling programmes were conditional upon overall stabilisation programmes implemented through drastic changes in monetary, credit and exchange rate policies, supported by stand-by agreements with the IMF (Adler, 1973, pp. 111–12; IBRD, 1971).

Debt rescheduling is an important method of ensuring a *long term* net inflow of resources only in countries which are very poor, and need large investment in long gestation projects; and where the level of poverty imposes a severe strain on the mobilisation of domestic savings and exports are dominated by primary commodities with stagnant demand and sagging prices. In these cases, as has been argued above, economic growth is a slow, time-consuming process and requires a net inflow of resources on a continuing basis for a long period. That is why the method and terms of debt rescheduling for the poorer countries needs to be determined in the context of their long term requirements for net resource inflows. As indicated above, with recent events, their need for net inflows has risen considerably. In a large number of poor countries, debt rescheduling now needs to be recognised as an essential component of a wider exercise to determine net inflow requirements to ensure socially and politically tolerable minimum rates (and patterns) of development. The terms of debt rescheduling, combined with the terms and amounts of new gross inflows, should be such that the combined debt service burden, on old and new debt, ensures availability of free resources, external and internal, sufficient for the minimum needs of development. It should be clear from the above that the long run developmental aspect of the debt burden is very different from the issues surrounding debt service crises which arise from overdependence on short term credits, inappropriate exchange rates and commercial policies.

Repudiation of the existing debt burden may be one way of augmenting resources at the disposal of the poor nations. The resources which would be made available to the debtor countries in this manner are the amounts of debt service payments which otherwise would have flowed to the creditor countries. Repudiation of debt has to be considered in the light of the possible reactions of the creditor countries to the act of repudiation. The legal framework for foreign lending in many creditor countries is such that unilateral default by the debtor countries would deprive them of future loans. If the creditor countries react by stopping future loans, what is the net effect on the debtor countries? In the last decade, even though the rate of increase in the net flow has slowed down, especially in the case of official development assistance, the net inflow has nevertheless been positive and increasing. The net inflow from the DAC countries was about $24 billion in 1973. This includes an annual net flow of direct investment to the tune of about $5.9 billion (but excludes most Eurocurrency borrowing). Therefore, the net inflow, exclusive of direct investment, was about $18 billion. From this must be deducted the annual interest payments on foreign debt of over $2 billion, leaving a net transfer of $15–16 billion. Assuming that direct investment would not be affected, the debtor countries could, therefore, lose access to about $15–16 billion as a result of the repudiation of the existing debt (of about $80 billion in 1971). Allowing for the continuing increase in the debt since 1971, the net transfer is about 15 per cent of the outstanding debt. The ratio of new inflow of resources (not net transfer) to the outstanding debt for different regions of the world is highest in the case of Africa and East Asia (16 to 18 per cent) and lowest in the Middle East and South Asia (9 to 10 per cent).

Until the time when the net inflow becomes negative or very small, the repudiation of debt would not be worthwhile on the part of the debtor countries as a group, since this would be likely to involve a net loss. Projections of the net inflow in future years, spreading over a long period, are obviously relevant for a decision as to the worthwhileness of repudiation by the debtor countries. Such projections are extremely uncertain, since these resource flows depend upon the changing developments in the international political and economic scene.

The foregoing discussion does not distinguish between different types of outstanding debt. Are the implications of default on public debt or publicly guaranteed private debt different from those of default on private debt? Any repudiation of bilateral official debt is likely to evoke the same reaction as that of the multilateral debt, since the multilateral organisations derive their finances from the major bilateral donor governments. Repudiation of private debt would also probably have adverse effects on official lenders whether or not private credit was formally guaranteed by the governments; private creditors are usually powerful enough, where it was not, to persuade their respective governments to adopt countervailing measures. Similarly, if private credit is repudiated, borrowings from multilateral agencies like the IBRD, which rely on private capital markets for their funds, would also be affected adversely. The recent behaviour of the IBRD with respect to countries which nationalised private foreign investment without what was considered by multinational corporations to be adequate, fair, prompt and effective compensation, is referred to by many as a case in point. Repudiation of private debt, apart from its effects on the flow of official assistance, may have adverse effects on the foreign trade of the debtor countries. International commercial and banking circles are closely knit. The debtor country may find it difficult to find short term accommodation for the normal financing of its exports and imports, e.g. the discounting of export bills or opening of letters of credit for imports. Any unilateral repudiation by the countries of the developing world, either of the entire amount or only a part of the outstanding debt, would have serious consequences on the future flow of resources. Any such repudiation or cancellation of debt, therefore, has perforce to be a matter of either bilaterally or multilaterally negotiated arrangement.

The impact of repudiation of the outstanding debt would be different for different individual countries, depending on the amount of outstanding debt, debt service payments, and present and prospective net inflows. The countries which have large outstanding debt and receive comparatively small net inflows are more likely to gain from defaulting on debt, especially if they expect future gross inflows to decline and net inflows to be negative. The countries which receive grants will be the worst losers, if grants cease to flow as a consequence of their repudiation of the outstanding debt. The countries which already have attained high levels of income, have borrowed mainly on commercial terms and have large debt service payments in relation to outstanding debt, but can do without inflows of external resources in the future (examples of which can be found mainly in Latin America and the Middle East), might gain by defaulting on existing debt. If they did so, they would need to introduce appropriate policies and institutional changes to mobilise domestic resources, and to try to ensure that the act of default or repudiation did not adversely affect their trade relationships with the creditor countries.

There are various ways of reducing the burden of outstanding debt, short of outright repudiation or cancellation of all outstanding debt. There are possibilities of writing off or scaling down components of the outstanding debt. For example, to the extent that the outstanding debt is the result of tied aid flows in the past, about 20 per cent could justifiably be written down on the basis of what is by now a universal understanding that tied aid implies excess valuation of aid. Similarly, food aid which, in many instances, was also valued considerably in excess of the competitive world price could be written down or off. Food-associated debt should, at a minimum, be revalued to the level of its true worth in terms of the competitive world price prevailing at the time the food aid was received. The humanitarian rationale for writing food aid right off is strong, if one considers that such aid was offered for the purpose of the relief of suffering from hunger, starvation and malnutrition (either because food supply could not keep pace with increasing population, or because countries were hit by natural calamities – droughts or floods – reducing domestic food supply). In countries like the USA the real burden of food aid was, in any case, very small, in terms of its alternative uses or in terms of the opportunity cost of reducing its food surplus. The writing down of the food aid which was repayable in domestic currency, in the form of counterpart funds, is even more justifiable because the use of domestic counterpart funds for financing of development projects in the future is tantamount to inflationary financing. The recent agreement between the USA and India, under which 70 per cent of the accumulated counterpart funds were written off by formally 'attributing' them to development projects already underway or financed otherwise, from domestic resources, is an example of what can be accomplished, once the political will exists and a solution is seriously sought.

There are two other components of past debt for which there exists a rationale for scaling down or writing off. First, there are unproductive projects financed by foreign capital in the past. History is replete with examples of projects, in the developed countries, which have failed to yield any return and ended in failures and bankruptcies, owing to miscalculation of demand or of costs or of both. Such projects, when financed by private investors, were written off, if not formally then in fact, in so far as the investors, including foreigners, went bankrupt. In modern times, the creditor governments refuse to accept the phenomenon of bad debts or bankruptcies. Although the planning and preparation of projects is always done under conditions of great uncertainty,[2] and despite the fact that the choice of aided projects or programmes was typically the result of joint decisions of the debtor and creditor countries, the creditors require the debtor countries to bear the full consequences of mistakes. Particularly in the case of projects financed by export credits, proper evaluations were frequently not conducted (Pearson *et al.* 1969, p. 120); for this, creditors and debtors were equally responsible. There were many instances where wrong specification of equipment, lack of proper balance in plant and equipment, and inappropriate choice of technique led to overcapitalisation. There are many cases where the initial cost estimates of a project underwent, in the course of its implementation, substantial increases, either because there was underestimation to start with or because there was a subsequent rise in the price of equipment, aggravated by long delays in execution in a world of rising prices (Frank, 1970, p. 19). Sometimes mistakes were the result not only of wrong analysis but also of careless and high pressure salesmanship on the part of foreign aid agencies and supplying firms, which are often interlinked. Unproductive projects could, therefore, legitimately be written off in the same way that wrongly chosen domestic projects undergo bankruptcies. Debtor and creditor countries could jointly examine individual projects to identify such unproductive, wrongly chosen projects and agree to scale down or write off debt relating to them.

In many poor countries the results of other past investments financed by foreign credit were nullified by natural calamities like floods, cyclones or earthquakes, or by wars. There is an obvious rationale for writing off debts which financed investments, results of which are no longer available. Similarly, there are projects which have been rendered unproductive by adverse movements in international markets, the product of competition from rich countries or stagnation in demand, caused by restrictive trade policies or changes in consumption habits or technological change in developed countries. These projects should also qualify for writing off or for a substantial scaling down of related debt.

Secondly, in that commodity assistance in the form of raw materials and intermediate inputs helps in the utilisation of existing capacity and increases current income, but does not directly create a permanent physical asset so as to yield a flow of income over a period of years, it may also be a candidate for writing down. To the extent that commodity assistance enables an increase in current consumption rather than investment, this could be treated as a direct contribution by the rich to raise the levels of living of the poor countries and be written off as a net gift.

It is quite clear, however, that not all the outstanding debt of a poor country can be treated on the basis of the above considerations. For the rest of the outstanding debts, a reasonable approach would be to project the long run prospects of a particular borrowing country, in terms of its minimum growth targets and its maximum rates of domestic resource mobilisation and export expansion, and then to estimate the maximum debt service payments which it can be expected to bear. On the basis of such maximum feasible debt service payments, a debt rescheduling exercise can be undertaken for each country. This exercise is particularly relevant, as has been seen, for the poorest part of the underdeveloped world, i.e. those countries with *per capita* incomes of less than $200 per year, and should be combined with a programme for the future level and terms of assistance which the rich countries should provide to them.

For the poorest countries, it is essential that outstanding debt be rescheduled on a very long term basis. The DAC has already recognised that the 'least developed' countries should get credit with no less than an 84 to 86 per cent grant element. With the impact of the new economic crisis and prospects of very low rates of growth in the future, in so far as debt rescheduling loans are concerned, all the countries with less than $200 *per capita* income should receive the benefit of an 84 per cent grant element.

(Countries with less than $100 *per capita* income, should receive a still higher grant element in their debt rescheduling.) There are some creditor countries, which can, within the terms of their present law, completely cancel debt. Other creditors, although they face legal and constitutional obstacles in the way of outright cancellation of debt, can nevertheless extend the grant element up to 95 to 99 per cent; in other words, within the limits of their laws, they can extend the grant element to the fullest.

The outstanding debt of the countries with *per capita* incomes of less than $200 was $23.1 billion in 1972. If it were rescheduled with an 84 per cent grant element, the discounted (at 10 per cent per year) present value of the future debt service payments would be no more than $3.7 billion, even though the actual payments could be much larger, depending on the repayment period. If any debtor country were able and willing to deduct the grant element from the outstanding debt and pay off the remainder, the creditor countries should be prepared to accept repayment in this manner. (If the rate of time discount is very much lower in the creditor countries than in the debtor countries, such a settlement may not be acceptable, unless the rate of discount which is used in estimating the grant element is first negotiated to the mutual satisfaction of both debtor and creditor countries.)

Debt rescheduling exercises should also include changes in the *methods* of repayment so as to relieve the burden on the debtor's balance of payments. The burden on the debtor country is increased by the fact that while inflows take place in the form of tied loans, debt service payments are to be met in the form of free foreign exchange. The real burden of debt servicing on tied aid can be reduced to some extent if debt service payments are also tied to the exports from the borrowing country. Repayment of debt to most socialist countries of Eastern Europe is either wholly or partly tied to the exports of the debtor countries. The tying of debt service payments to the exports from the debtor country does not, of course, compensate for the high cost of tied aid unless exports from the borrowing country are also sold at higher than the world price. Repayment should, therefore, where possible, be tied to a specific list of commodities which the debtor countries cannot otherwise readily sell in the world market at a competitive price. This would imply that such exports should be newer exports rather than traditional exports with ready markets. (These are likely to be manufactured exports or semi-processed primary exports which do not face expanding markets in the rich countries.) Exports tied to debt service payments must be additional to what otherwise would have taken place under normal commercial channels. The 'normal' rate of expansion of exports, therefore, needs to be evaluated and agreed to by the borrowing and lending countries. Furthermore, re-exports of such tied exports by the creditor country must be prohibited. It is obvious that successful implementation of export expansion schemes tied to debt service payments involve complex administrative and analytical problems.

Debt service payments could also be used to promote exports of the debtor countries if the creditor countries agree to lend the debt service payments that are due to them from one debtor country to another developing country, with these loans tied to the exports of the original debtor. This would promote expansion of trade between the developing countries. Since the developing countries can only service their debts by generating a net export surplus, the creditor countries must, in any case, follow trade policies which promote exports from the debtor countries.

An alternative way of dealing with the debt service burden is to permit debtors to use new loans directly to repay the old loans, so that the debtor countries only receive the 'net transfer' after settlement of claims of the creditor countries. This would obviate the need for meeting debt service payments in free foreign exchange while accepting gross inflow entirely in tied form. In the IMF, the system of repaying old loans by drawing upon new loans is already standard practice. This principle could be extended to other international and bilateral agencies. Moreover, from the point of view of the donor countries and agencies, this system is simpler in so far as the amount of net transfer which a debtor country receives would be more obvious.

The above analysis indicates that it is possible to establish *general* criteria and considerations, irrespective of the individual characteristics of a particular debtor country, which provide the basis of and justification for a partial or complete writing off of external debt. These considerations include excess costs from tied aid, unproductive projects, commodity and food aid meant for consumption at times of domestic shortage, unforeseen deterioration in the terms of trade, and loss of assets through man-made or natural disasters.

Moreover, the recent economic crisis, caused by world-wide inflation and a collapse in the terms of trade, has added substantially to the burden of debt service payments for the countries with *per capita* income less than $200. Most of the countries in this group have been categorised by the UN Emergency Fund as the most severely affected by the recent crisis; they qualify for unconditional debt relief. The intercountry distribution of debt relief can be based on the same set of criteria by which their additional requirements of capital have been estimated and by which their entitlement to special emergency assistance has been assessed (i.e. the need to preserve a minimum rate of growth as well as a minimum import bill, especially of food, fertiliser, and fuel, keeping in view the normal assistance expected to flow from commitments or pledges obtained prior to 1974).

Increasing the amount and efficiency of new external resource flows

The reduction of the burden of the debt service payments is only one of the ways of increasing the net inflow of external resources to the developing countries. An increase in the gross inflow on soft terms is another. The solution of the external debt problems of the developing countries is a matter not only of the quantum but also of the forms in which the flow of external resources takes place. Grants do not create debt servicing problems; but the donors are not enthusiastic about grants. The majority of the donor countries and agencies continue to prefer loans, even with a high grant element to outright grants.[3] The presumption that loans ensure a more productive use of external resource inflow is corroborated, however, by neither logic nor experience. A distinction must be made between grants to a country, and grants to a project or a programme within a recipient country. Grants to a developing country are consistent with the actual users of funds receiving them as loans at an appropriate rate of interest; this frequently happens in practice. If loans could, by themselves, ensure the most productive use of foreign resources, then one would not expect to witness the phenomenon of export or suppliers' credits on hard terms financing some of the most unproductive projects. Whether a country 'deserves' a grant or a loan should be decided on the basis of its requirements for net inflows of resources and the best estimates of the period over which such net inflows must continue.

The misplaced creditor bias towards (or preference for) project loans as against programme loans, purportedly to ensure their productive use, has also been discussed for years. If a country does not follow appropriate economic policies, and formulate and execute sound and productive development projects over the economy as a whole, project tied loans, which in any case finance only a fraction of the total development programme, can ensure neither productive use of resources nor the viability or progress of an economy. The important long run impact of project loans is basically on the inducement or incentive they provide for the preparation of economically sound projects. They stimulate the development of capability for the pre paration and appraisal of projects and for their careful supervision. The rationale for local-cost financing of projects as against outright programme loans is the same, even though both provide foreign exchange for financing the general import programme.

There has been progress over the years, both among bilateral and multi-lateral donors, towards programme loans as well as local cost financing of projects. The case for programme loans has been strengthened by widespread emergence of underutilised capacity because of foreign exchange shortage in the developing world. Programme loans can provide a compensating flow of foreign exchange when debt service payments make heavy demands on stagnant export earnings. To assume that project loans provide scope for leverage over domestic policies while programme loans do not, is politically naive. The contrary may be the case, since project loans with a long time horizon are dependent for their success on future governments, whereas programme loans are disbursed during the lifetime of the very government which negotiates the loan. Local cost financing, like programme loans, expands the possibilities for effective use of external resources. The tying of assistance to the foreign exchange component of a project leaves the indirect foreign exchange liability of a project uncovered; moreover, in a situation of acute scarcity of resources in general and not just foreign exchange, it limits the possibility of use of external capital. Investments in social and physical infrastructure, like road construction, public works programmes, health, education and family planning, all with very high local cost components, suffer particularly; and these are usually the very types of investments most necessary in the poorest countries. Local cost financing also creates demand for the services of local construction firms and industries and thus helps in the growth of self-reliance.

One important and immediate method of increasing the net flow of high quality resources to the poorest countries is to establish the much discussed 'link' between the creation of additional international liquidity through SDRs and the provision of concessional assistance for development. The great virtue of the link is that it imparts a certain degree of automaticity and regularity to the flow of concessional assistance over time. The acceptance of the 'link' proposal would obviate the need for annual budgetary appropriations. The resistance to the 'link' is really indicative of the opposition to the concept of regular and automatic flows of concessional development assistance. It would detract from the exercise of power and influence by the rich countries over the volume of assistance; every time the rich countries want additional liquidity for meeting their requirements of expanding trade and payments, they would have to pay a price in terms of additional assistance to the poor countries. If SDRs were distributed to the poorest countries and on terms which involved a significant grant element, the 'link' could be among the most important instruments of an improved net resource flow to the developing countries.

The emergence of non-traditional donors

The emergence of oil exporting countries as sources of development finance has introduced a new dimension into the external debt problems of the developing countries. The oil revenues of the eleven member governments of the OPEC are expected to be about $85 billion in 1974 as compared with $14.5 billion in 1972. The total balance of payments surplus of the oil exporting countries is expected to increase from $1.6 billion in 1972 to $66 billion in 1974 (Howe *et al.* 1974, pp. 32–5).

The net result of a rise in oil prices is a transfer of income from the advanced industrial countries to the oil producing countries. The combined GNP of the OPEC countries as a proportion of the combined GNP of the OECD countries is expected to increase from 2.5 per cent in 1973 to about 5 per cent in 1980; the average *per capita* income of the OECD countries, which was 5 times that of the average of the OPEC countries in 1973, is expected to be only about 2.5 times the latter by 1980. One of the ways, frequently discussed in the past, of augmenting the flow of resources to the poor nations is for the industrial countries to pay a higher price for the exports from the former. The rise in oil prices, which has taken place in response to a multiplicity of factors, demonstrates a special case of this general proposition.

What the developing countries have been advocating, persistently since the end of the Second World War, is a net transfer of income from the advanced industrial countries. But the voluntary flow of external resources from the industrialised countries as a proportion of their GNP has been stagnating; on the other hand, the claimants on, and absorptive capacity for, external resources in the developing world have substantially increased. The pool of investible resources, now at the disposal of the oil producing countries, through a process of compulsory transfer from the industrialised world, opens up new opportunities and poses new challenges for world development.

Some of the oil exporting countries will not be able to absorb fully their substantial resources in domestic investment in the foreseeable future. In the short run, none of them can do so. In the past, they have been used to investing their surpluses in real estate or in the money and capital markets of the advanced countries. These investments are safe and bring in high returns from familiar lines of activity in the industrialised countries. If direct investment in equity or property in the rich countries is extended beyond a certain limit, however, the oil surplus countries may perceive risks of expropriation or excessive and discriminatory taxes, especially since the rise in oil price has been forced by the oil producing countries in the face of considerable opposition by the industrialised nations, who are overtly discussing countervailing action and a consumers' cartel to offset the oil producers' cartel.

During 1974, the revenue surpluses of the oil producing countries have been mainly invested either in short term deposits or securities in the advanced industrial countries. The financial markets of the USA tended to attract a larger share of the flow of oil resources than their Western European counterparts. The financing institutions in the industrialised nations have used these short term funds for meeting balance of payments deficits of the oil importing, developed countries. But short term deposits by the oil producers cannot be used on a continuous basis to meet the persistent balance of payments gap of the oil importers. The financial institutions are unable to find profitable outlets for short term funds on such a massive scale, and the short term deposits by oil producers may soon, especially if they increase at the anticipated rate, exceed the capacity of the existing financial system to absorb and productively utilise such funds. Moreover, these funds which have flowed to the financial markets of the industrialised nations are not readily available for the poor, oil importing countries. According to the conventional criteria of the financial markets, the worst affected countries are not creditworthy; for they are unable to service short term loans. It will, therefore, be necessary to evolve a longer term mechanism for recycling resources from the oil producers to the oil-deficit countries in order for them to meet their balance of payments deficits.

The longer term solution, for the transfer of income to the oil producers to be effective, has to be conceived in the context of a slower rate of growth and a different pattern of consumption and investment in the industrialised world, both of which would have to be consistent with the stability of the international monetary system and to avoid depression and unemployment in the rich countries. The flow of funds to the rich countries has to be closely linked with the need for a substantial increase in the flow of resources to the poor countries. Already, in the past year, long term investment and trade agreements between a number of oil producing countries and industrialised nations have been concluded, involving long term loans by the oil countries to the governments of the industrialised nations. Similarly, the oil countries in the meanwhile have lent to the IMF and invested in IBRD bonds. The flow of resources, however, has been inadequate to date. Some poor countries, especially those in the Arab world, have secured access to surplus oil funds. The UN Emergency Fund and the newly established oil facility of the IMF have also been available to a few worst affected countries.

In the long run, however, there is a need for a triangular arrangement among the industrialised nations, the developing countries, and the oil producers. The oil producers have financial resources, but they do not have technology or physical capital, i.e. machinery, equipment, and intermediate inputs, which the industrialised countries are capable of producing and selling to the poor countries. The poor countries need both; therefore, to the extent that they are able to borrow financial resources from the oil producers they may import machinery and equipment, inputs and technology from the industrialised nations. On the one hand, this would provide the oil producers with profitable investment opportunities in the developing world and, on the other hand, the industrialised countries would be able to expand exports to pay for their rising import bill. The flow of resources from the oil producers to the poor countries should take the form not only of project loans but also of programme loans, if the gap in their balance of payments is to be met and if the disbursement of the oil surplus is to be fast enough to meet the rising cost of imports in the rest of the world.

How best can a flow of resources from the oil producers to the poor countries be induced? What is the best institutional arrangement? There is no unique answer, and there is likely to be an evolution of institutions and attitudes over time; the oil producing nations will take time to learn the implications of having a large accumulation of reserves, and the limitations of short term deposits, or of the excessive acquisition of physical assets in the industrialised countries. One possible arrangement is to recycle the resources of the oil producing nations to the developing world via the existing international financial organisations. In this case, one needs to distinguish between soft loan institutions like the IDA and the UN Special Emergency Fund for the worst affected poor countries, on the one hand, and the financial institutions like the IBRD, the IMF and others providing loans either fully or partly at commercial rates of interest to the middle-income developing countries, on the other. Is it realistic to assume that the oil producing countries would provide substantial amounts of loans on very concessional terms in the near future through the established international institutions? The answer is probably no. The structure, organisation, practices and policies of the existing international institutions would need to undergo major changes and adjustments if they were to serve as the most important medium for attracting oil resources and investing them in the poor nations.

It would require a drastic departure from past practice and experience for the oil countries now to become the principal source of concessional assistance for the development of the poor countries, either by means of programme or project loans. In view of the urgency of the needs of the poor nations and in the interest of the stability of the international financial system, it is necessary to initiate international action to expedite the process so that the oil producers can become important partners in the development of the poor nations. The industrialised countries took decades before they were able to play an active role in providing development assistance, in spite of their long experience in international banking and in private overseas investment. Even then, there have been considerable differences among the developed countries in their response to the needs of the developing world. There have been conservative as well as progressive donors. The long drawn and painstaking negotiations by the DAC for softening the terms of loans of the OECD countries demonstrate this more than adequately. Since the oil exporting countries, in the short run, are more likely than not to invest their surplus funds in the advanced countries, it is necessary in the first instance to devise ways and means for recycling or redirecting these funds to the poor countries. The most practical way is for the oil countries to be provided with opportunities for long or medium term investment at attractive rates of return in the rich countries, who then would lend to the poor, developing countries at lower rates, with the difference between the rates of lending and borrowing to be subsidised by (grants from) the rich countries. Such a scheme for recycling oil funds to the poor countries at subsidised rates of interest would involve considerable costs, if subsidised lending were continued for a long time. For a limited period, however, the burden of subsidies is manageable.[4] This could, at best, be an interim measure for channelling surplus funds to the poor countries until the oil exporting countries develop their own capability and institutions to disburse investment funds directly to the poor countries.

It is desirable (and likely) that in the medium run, part of the recycling of funds would take place through international organisations like the IMF/IBRD/IDA. The Eurodollar market cannot absorb such a large increase in surplus funds without adversely affecting the security of and rates of return on such funds or without involving large scale switching of funds between borrowers. The borrowings by international agencies can provide greater security, both economic and political. Moreover, this means of recycling should provide a solution to the dilemma of borrowing at high commercial rates from the oil exporters and lending at concessional rates to the developing countries. The international institutions could lend at higher rates – higher than the borrowing rates – to the developed countries, the difference between the two financing the subsidy involved in lending at concessional rates to the developing countries. The oil facility which has been recently established by the IMF (offering medium term loans) is inadequate from the point of view of the developing countries, not only because it is small in relation to requirements, but also because it carries high interest rates and involves short maturity periods.

However, the international institutions will not be the only source of recycling of funds to the poorer nations. Nor will subsidised relending be easy or substantial, especially if it is expected to continue for a long time. The oil producing countries have already established their own bilateral agencies such as the Abu Dhabi, Saudi Arabian, and Kuwait Development Funds, and regional institutions such as the Islamic Bank to provide development assistance on their own. It is expected that, as in the case of the bilateral lending programmes of the industrialised nations, these credit institutions will have their own criteria for intercountry allocation of loans. The Arab oil producing countries' criteria for selection of potential borrowers appear, in order of priority, to be as follows: (1) poorer, Arab countries; (2) Muslim countries outside the Arab world; (3) other developing countries; and (4) other countries in the capitalist world.

Up to August 1974 about 74 per cent of the bilateral aid from the Arab oil producing countries went to the Arab countries, of which Egypt and Syria alone received 66.3 per cent of the total (EEC, 1974, p. 1). To the extent that the oil resources are lent by these countries to only a selected group of poor countries, the industrialised nations will need to direct their concessional lending to the countries which are not so favoured. Moreover, in so far as the oil producers are persuaded to lend in the first instance to 'middle income' countries, which are more creditworthy in the short run, and can absorb funds offered at commercial rates, the industrial nations will need to concentrate still further on the poorest countries. Therefore, the emergence of the oil producers as potential lenders warrants and, in fact, urgently requires a re-examination of the existing pattern of allocation of external resources by the industrialised nations among the developing countries.

The establishment of new institutions, regional or otherwise, by the oil producing countries certainly adds to the multiplicity of lending institutions. This is not an undesirable development, so long as they augment the total flow of resources to the poor nations. They may even increase the freedom of choice and manoeuvrability for recipient countries. The international institutions and bilateral donors in the industrialised world do not allocate funds among countries purely on the basis of objective assessments of needs and capacity to absorb. The preferences of individual donors vary widely in terms of countries to be aided as well as sectors and projects to which priority is attached in their aid programmes. The relationship between individual donors and recipients is basically unequal, and is seldom un-affected by donor value judgements regarding recipients' economic and political systems and policies. The wider the number of lenders, the greater is the freedom of choice on the part of the recipients.

It is necessary at the same time to restructure the international financial institutions to allow greater participation by the oil exporting countries, not only in terms of their financial contributions, but also in terms of control over management and policy. Whether the advanced, industrialised countries and the oil exporting countries will co-operate in a joint endeavour such as has been recommended here depends on their recognition of a joint responsibility towards the poorer countries. The relative burden of development assistance to be shared between the new and the old rich, depends upon (a) how they visualise their bilateral relationships with the developing countries evolving in the future; and (b) how the two groups can share power and influence in the new economic order. These two factors are interrelated; the relative influence of the oil rich countries in the international economic system is partly dependent on their relationship with the poor, developing countries. Moreover, it needs to be remembered that the way the world manages its political and security affairs, is closely linked up with the way it manages the international economic order (Gardner, 1974, pp. 1–9).[5] The crisis in the world today is the product not only of scarce raw materials, high prices and inadequate resources for the development of poor nations, but also of scarcity of political leadership and statesmanship to deal with the changing economic and political reality of the 1970s.

Notes

1 For capital equipment supplied under tied project aid there is no such thing as a world price and there is no convenient point of reference for such prices to be compared. The salaries which technical assistance personnel are paid are not internationally competitive and are considerably higher than home salaries.

2 'Because of the large element, in economic and social development, of chance, political wisdom or stupidity in aid giving and aid receiving governments, wars and rumours of wars, the calculation of credit worthiness for most ordinary Bank loans is a heroic exercise in creative imagination' (Reid, 1973, p. 64).

3 To maintain a given net inflow by means of loans rather than grants requires periodic debt rescheduling or an increasing amount of gross flows. 'In many donor countries the political pain associated with aid giving is a function, not mainly of the donor's volume of net aid, but of the size and frequency of its fresh or "gross" aid provisions. Thus, the loan's mode of transfer over time maximizes the political difficulties of maintaining adequate net flows' (Lewis and Kapur, 1973, p. 78).

4 A programme loan of $1 billion per year for five years carrying an interest charge of 2¼ per cent (i.e. 5 per cent below the current IBRD lending rate), with thirty years' maturity, including ten years' grace period, would require a peak annual subsidy of $250 million from the sixth to tenth year, the amounts of subsidy being $25 million in the first, $75 million in the second year and $125

million in the third year. The subsidy would decline from the eleventh year onwards as repayments begin. The same objective could be attained on an assured basis through the establishment of a capital fund for the generation of necessary income. A capital fund of $2.4 billion would allow disbursement of programme loans of $1 billion a year over five years at a subsidy of 5 per cent below the current IBRD lending rate, with thirty years' maturity including ten years' grace period. This would require once-for-all action by the developed countries (IMF, 1974, pp. 14–16).

In this context it is relevant to inquire whether the large profits which the international oil companies have made from the recent energy crisis do not provide a potential revenue source for financing the rich countries' channelling of funds to the poor countries. One other important potential source of revenues for the subsidisation of the cost of borrowing by the poor countries is provided by IMF official gold holdings. The IMF could be authorised by the member countries to sell official gold holdings in the open market; the considerable profits which would thus be made could be used to subsidise its rates of interest on lending to the poorer developing countries.

5   Expenditure on armaments in the world today, the largest part undertaken in the rich countries, totals about $220 billion a year. Even a 10 per cent reduction in expenditure on armaments and their diversion to development would meet the poor countries' immediate requirements for additional assistance.

References

Adler, John, 1973. The external debt problem. In *The World Bank Group, Multilateral Aid and the 1970s*, (eds.) J. P. Lewis and I. Kapur, pp. 111–22. Toronto and London: Lexington Books.

Bhagwati, Jagdish N., 1970. *Amount and Sharing of Aid*. Overseas Development Council.

EEC, September, 1974. Community's participation in UN emergency operation for countries most seriously hit by recent international price movement, Annex II. Brussels.

Frank, Charles R., Jr., 1970. *Debt and Terms of Aid*. Overseas Development Council.

Gardner, R. N., 1974. Statement of Conclusions. *Conference on the World Food and Energy Crisis, The Role of International Organisations*. New York: Columbia University.

Howe, James W., *et al.* 1974. *The U.S. and the Developing World, Agenda for Action 1974*. New York, Washington and London: Praeger.

IBRD, 1971. The external debt of developing countries. Washington: unpublished.

IMF, 1974. Committee of Twenty. Report by the Technical Group on the Transfer of Real Resources (April).

Lewis, J. P. and Kapur, I. (eds.), 1973. *The World Bank Group, Multilateral Aid and the 1970s*. Toronto and London: Lexington Books.

McNamara, Robert S., 1974. Address to the Board of Governors. Washington.

OECD, 1972. *Development Co-operation, Efforts and Policies of the Members of the Development Assistance Committee, 1972, Review*. Paris.

OECD, 1973. *Development Co-operation, Efforts and Policies of the Members of the Development Assistance Committee, 1973, Review*. Paris.

Pearson, L. B. *et al.* 1969. *Partners in Development*. New York: Praeger.

Pinstrup-Anderson, P. and Tweetin, 1971. The value, cost and efficiency of American food aid. *American Journal of Agricultural Economics*, **53**, 431–40.

Reid, Escott, 1973. *Strengthening the World Bank.* Toronto: University of Toronto.

World Bank, 1973. *Annual Report.* Washington.

World Bank, 1974. *Annual Report.* Washington.

HWD

PART IV

Planning for a World in Disorder

11. Aspects of the world monetary and resource transfer system in 1974: a view from the extreme periphery

REGINALD H. GREEN[1]

Things fall apart; the centre cannot hold;
Mere anarchy is loosed upon the world...

The Second Coming, W. B. Yeats

In my beginning is my end
. . .
Time present and time past
Are both perhaps present in time future,
And time future contained in time past.

Four Quartets, T. S. Eliot

The choice is clear, either we really become one world, with the problem of poverty in certain areas being attacked scientifically on a world scale; or, alternatively, we recognize that there are two worlds, the rich world and the poor world and the latter gets down to the problem of protecting itself against the dominance of the former.   Julius K. Nyerere (1966, p. 248)

It is not enough to set tasks, we must also solve the problem of method, for carrying them out. If our task is to cross a river, we cannot cross it without a bridge or a boat...Unless the problem of method is solved, talk about the task is useless.
                                      Mao Tse-tung (1965, p. 150)

On the face of it, 1974 is a rather poor time and Dar es Salaam a rather poor place for analysing international monetary and resource transfer systems and situations. Today it does look as if the world economic system as it existed over 1945–74 has come to an end; and a major credit card recently advertised world-wide that it was accepted even at the 'end of the world', that is Tananarive and Dar es Salaam! In practice, no apology is needed for: the existence of crisis increases the need for an applied analytical basis for policy; a crisis may lay bare some of the aspects of the system which in less hectic times are more easily denied or concealed; the place from which to evaluate the impact of a centre-based system on the periphery *is* at the periphery, *not* at the centre.

The evaluation from the point of view of a political economic unit – Tanzania – which certainly qualifies as a member of the extreme periphery in any normal global economic typology, thus placing it at the analytical centre, is not a matter of geographic location. Plenty of analysis in the periphery is industrial-economy-centric to the point of caricature. Nor is it a matter of standard ideological classifications – the doctrines of unequal

[251]

exchange and world economic hierarchy have not always led to real emphasis on analysing what is accurately (but also arrogantly) described as the periphery in its own terms and on the basis of its own needs and potentials. The line from Hobson through Lenin and Trotsky to Barratt-Brown or Theresa Hayter calls for revolution at the centre first, with the new revolutionary centre to impose (or 'allow', in its most condescending sense) change at the periphery. However unconsciously, this line of analysis and prescription is no less arrogant, no less Eurocentric, and no less neo-colonialist than its bourgeois parallel.[2]

The premises underlying this paper are:

(a) 'fourth world' economies[3] are particularly vulnerable to motion in the international monetary and resource transfer system;

(b) these economies need to use what leverage they have to secure both palliative and structural changes in these systems;

(c) in addition, they need to take domestic action as to production structures (especially in respect of basic foods), reserve levels, and standby planning for response to externally imposed dislocation, to reduce their vulnerability;

(d) analysis of the existing international systems and trends *as they impinge on 'fourth world' economies* is necessary to identify what international or domestic measures are appropriate, attainable, and cost-efficient.[4]

A brief overview of the trends in the global situation confronting small, very poor polities over 1970–4 will be followed by an examination of the Tanzanian case. A résumé of its 1967–73 settings and policies will be followed by an examination of the period from October 1973 to June 1974, and an evaluation of a possible strategy of response. The Tanzanian case is *not* generalisable to all developing countries, but it does have major areas of similarity, particularly so far as the objective external setting is concerned, with at least a dozen other African and perhaps about as many Asian, Latin American, and Caribbean states.

Global trends and the extreme periphery

The international monetary and resource transfer system has changed radically since 1970. It has become both more flexible and more unstable. Floating exchange rates and the growth of the Eurocurrency market typify both of these trends. As far as resource transfers are concerned, there has been an overall increase in availability (even in constant prices) but within that increase is hidden a decrease in finance offered on concessional terms. The explosive rise of Eurodollar borrowing by developing economies in 1972 and 1973 and the parallel fall in real terms of concessional aid, as measured by OECD, exemplify these shifts. The terms of trade of most primary exporters improved through early 1974, but only because commodity prices spurted ahead more rapidly than industrial economy inflation. Unfortunately, inflation in the industrial economies is already proving more durable than the commodity boom.

The oil price increase, first seen as ensuring continued commodity price increases and as the herald of a new era of poor exporter trade unions, now looks rather different. It has greatly increased monetary instability and led to deflationary and trade policy measures in the capitalist industrial economies which are pushing them toward general recession and generating collapse in many primary commodity prices. Exporters of oil may hold or expand their gains, and exporters of temperate-zone foods (largely industrial, high-income economies) most of theirs, but these exceptions only worsen matters for the really poor.

The failure of the concessional resource transfer mechanism is amply illustrated by the response given to four years of spreading drought now affecting at least a score of developing countries. The price of grain has (since 1970) risen almost as much as that of oil. However, as President Boumedienne fairly, if acidly, pointed out at the United Nations Special General Assembly Session (1974), no great international concern was expressed at the economic impact on importers. He suggested the reason was that the central industrial economies, on balance, exported grain to the poor on the periphery whereas, on balance, the periphery exported oil to the centre. Nobody called a world conference to force down grain prices or (prior to the 1974 Special Session) to mount a global food transfer programme. Rather, several industrial economies (notably the USA) could scarcely conceal their glee that food aid could now be cut because the stocks could be sold commercially! (The USA was, until 1974, by far the largest single gainer from the commodity price boom.) The 1974 World Food Conference, despite its rhetoric, offered little reason for believing that major resource transfers or re-allocations would follow from it.

The foregoing does illustrate one fact that has *not* changed. Anything which concerns the welfare of the central industrial economies is of central concern to the international economic system and its institutions; anything which affects only the periphery is peripheral, no matter how seriously the periphery is affected. The IBRD and the UNCTAD are, of course, honourable exceptions, but neither really lies at the centre of the system. The Group of Twenty was no exception. The peripheral economies were brought in at US insistence to balance the Europeans. The progress on the role of the SDR was based on this alliance between the USA and the less developed countries. Failure to adopt the link (which was opposed by some central economies and of peripheral interest to the rest) demonstrates how asymmetrical the alliance was. The Group of Twenty probably did advance the trend toward a global international reserve asset (which benefits the less developed countries but is even more critical for the metropolitan economies), but otherwise ended with a whimper as the oil crisis swept over currency and capital markets.[5]

In principle, the greater flexibility of the monetary and resource transfer systems since 1970 has created opportunities as well as risks for peripheral economies. The floating exchange rates, and particularly the decline of sterling, created an occasion for establishing an independent exchange rate policy. The fact that over the 1970–4 period a majority of LDCs were *importing* inflation, not generating it at home,[6] should have enhanced the appeal of such an approach.

Similarly, the Eurocurrency markets have for the first time since the 1920s provided a large commercial, international capital market open to developing economies. While costs have been high, it has been possible to raise resources additional to those available on concessional terms. Further, the commercial nature of the market allows greater independence of decision taking – witness Gabon's resort to Eurocurrency borrowing for its railway project when the IBRD disagreed as to its viability.[7] However, this opportunity may be more apparent than real for the least developed. First, like the supplier credit-export insurance 'boom' of the first half of the 1960s, it may prove ephemeral for all but the most solvent of the peripheral economies. Second, it is fairly clear that at least the twenty-five 'least developed' cannot afford much commercial debt. The higher the servicing cost, the lower the total debt consistent with any given level of servicing burden. High Eurocurrency borrowing in the short term might force larger amounts of bilateral concessional and IBRD (bank term) loans to be rejected in the medium term because of then existing external debt servicing burdens.

The counterpart of the opportunities from flexibility are its risks. For the vast majority of the peripheral economies neither adequate data, nor numerous enough transactions, nor any 'insurance' mechanisms exist to allow the true risks to be calculated or 'evened out'. They become uncertainties and – unless a desperate Monte Carlo preference is assumed – are probably best accepted only to a marginal extent.

For high priority, high payoff, high foreign exchange earning or saving projects with a short gestation period, Eurocurrency loans are a welcome addition to funding sources for many developing countries.[8] As a more basic element in development finance, they are probably suitable only for those countries which are already half way to being industrialised, middle-income exporters of manufactured goods.[9]

The poorest economies are singularly ill-situated to benefit from the foregoing package of opportunities and risks. The first problem, as noted earlier, is that of securing and evaluating data. Commodity markets – which they must learn to analyse to avoid losses on exports and imports – baffle a majority.[10] With floating rates, foreign exchange and capital markets are even more difficult to master. The data flow, timing, and cost problems are very real, but the greatest barrier is manpower. Even assuming expertise could be developed rapidly, that would mean diverting a high proportion of scarce first-rate decision takers away from the directly productive and public planning sectors. Would that really be a sensible allocation for Tanzania or Nepal or Haiti or even Sri Lanka?

The second problem is the narrowness of margins for error. Hill Samuel can view a £9 million uncovered transaction with a bankrupt bank with alarm but not horror. For many developing economies and for almost any financial institution in a small developing economy, such a loss would be catastrophic. Industrial economies can afford – both absolutely and as a proportion of GDP – resource misallocations, resource non-utilisation, and shocks to stability very much greater than can very poor economies. The impact of a very poor harvest on the USSR economy and on that of Mali are so different as to be almost incomparable. The effect of terms of trade shifts (positive or negative) for the United States *can* be significant, witness the 1972–3 impact of swings in food export prices on its balance of payments and domestic food prices; but it hardly compares with their impact on, say, Sri Lanka where they can cut real purchasing power of GDP by up to 20 per cent in one year.[11]

Finally, the peripheral economies have far fewer safety nets provided by the international system, if they slip, than do the metropolitan ones. True, a central economy can still approach the point of total international insolvency, as Italy is demonstrating. However, Italy is an exception and any peripheral economy with a similar record of non-government, economic instability, uncontrolled capital flight, and structural imbalance would have been 'taken in hand' by its creditors long ago. Central bank swaps, tacit or open offset agreements, emergency co-ordinated bolstering action of various types are all available to central, but *not* to peripheral, economies. The United Kingdom over 1966–74 (and perhaps longer) and the United States over 1970–3 have been able to pursue policies which would have led to universal obloquy and international 'corrective' action had any developing economy behaved similarly. Instead, the UK and USA (while ultimately under rather considerable international pressure) were viewed with some sympathy and, more critical, given massive support.

There is, of course, an obvious reason for this. The international economic system cannot survive the international insolvency of any of its largest members. Therefore, such insolvency must be averted at all costs. If the country in real danger of insolvency insists on pursuing internationally reckless economic policies for domestic reasons, it can be coaxed, prodded, bullied a little, but it *must* be helped to pull through, not pushed to the wall. No such instinct for systemic survival is operative for any one peripheral economy nor, to date, even for the poor economies as a group. The fate of the cautious, conservative, minimalism proposed in the Pearson Commission Report (1969)[12] is evidence enough of that. Whether the recent Special Session, the proposed but largely unfunded Emergency Fund and the World Food Conference represent a change remains, at the most optimistic, very much an open question.

If more flexibility and more risk together offered yet another unequal bargain to most poor economies over 1970–3 the situation became infinitely worse in 1974. The petroleum crisis threatened basic interests of the central economies. Because it affects the poor too, they are mentioned and their support against oil producers sought, but only as a tactical ploy or a secondary interest. Indeed, the reactions of virtually all major economies – export to safety, grab the floating oil reserves, negotiate bilateral oil for industry deals – give rise to doubts as to whether the centre and the system will hold. If they do not, monetary and capital transfer anarchy *will* be loosed upon the world. Even in small doses it would be very damaging indeed to the periphery long before it was equally draconic in its effects at the centre. True, it might keep real interest rates negative and 'legitimise' default but it would also deal much heavier blows to real terms of trade and real resource transfers.

Tanzanian Finance Minister C. D. Msuya summed the situation up in words which now look prophetic addressed to a European Ecumenical Seminar on EEC Policies and World Development, meeting in Brussels during February 1974:

I cannot accept that 'problems at home' prevent a serious consideration of global development needs by EEC. In the case of the current crisis – that of petroleum prices – I suggest that many poor countries are much worse affected than most if not all of the 9. In the case of Tanzania we find that our total (not just our fuel) import bill has been raised by over one-tenth and that – with only 6 to 8 per cent of our fuel used for pleasure driving and only about 12 to 14 per cent for passenger cars at all – we can save very little on quantity used without crippling cuts in rural health, agricultural extension, transport of staple foods, manufacture of textiles and similar key outputs. For us there can be no assumption that oil producer earnings will be spent on our machinery or invested in our capital markets to offset this higher import bill; for you there can. For you there is no danger that by high interest rates, reduced government spending, industrial confrontation, and import cutting we will destroy the prices obtained for your raw material exports; for Tanzania there is every danger that the EEC states severally and jointly will do exactly that (Msuya, 1974b, p. 4).

Tanzanian experience: 1967–73

Tanzanian international financial and resource flow policy from 1967 through 1973 can be considered under four headings: (1) the exchange rate; (2) reserve levels and management; (3) foreign resource procurement; and (4) the pursuit of a rather specially defined dynamic equilibrium in respect of international transactions.[13] The year 1967 is a convenient starting point because the 1966–7 initiation of a formal and explicit strategy of transition to socialism marks a significant shift from the 1961–7 institutional framework and much less systematised strategy framework.

1. *The exchange rate*

Tanzanian exchange rate strategy rests on several broadly agreed premises:

(*a*) no Tanzanian action on parity will significantly affect the import purchasing or external debt servicing capacity of any given level of exports because it will not affect their international price;

(*b*) *marginal* costs of different exports vary so widely with respect both to one another, and to *average* real resource costs of the same exports, that exchange rate policy is quite incapable of serving as a fine tuning device for export promotion;

(*c*) tariff changes can have the same impact as parity changes so far as imports are concerned, and are instruments better adapted to deal with *individual* (as opposed to overall) relative price shifts;

(*d*) reduction of absolute (and to a lesser extent relative) prices for exported agricultural products has undesirable production, income distribution and social implications; but it does not necessarily follow that (devaluation induced) price increases can be viewed with equanimity, unless it is assumed that devaluation implies sharp increases in domestic food crop prices to avoid an artificial shift to export crops which would be structurally and dynamically dubious (as well as quite mad in the present food crisis);[14]

(*e*) machinery for controlling price changes, and especially distribution margin changes, is limited and can be swamped by major parity alterations;

(*f*) price changes, in particular inflation, are largely imported, not domestically generated; thus a downward creeping parity is not self-evidently appropriate;

(*g*) rapid price changes (especially generalised inflation) are likely to result in undesired changes in income distribution, damage to the lower half of the distribution of rural and of urban workers (including self employed), near infeasibility of accurate medium term planning, and (given data collection, coverage and timing problems) a significant loss of accuracy and effectiveness in short term economic policy.

These initial assumptions have been analysed and tested by experience; indeed they have grown out of the two major (1967, 1971) parity change decisions. As is evident, they do *not* always lead to a commitment to avoid any parity change but do lead to an aversion to treating a large change as a minor and easily reversible decision.

In 1967 the decision (taken jointly by Kenya, Uganda, and Tanzania, but clearly not with Tanzania as a dissenting partner) not to devalue with sterling turned on two points. First, few export prices (tea and perhaps, at that point, tourism) were basically sterling-denominated so that maintaining the exchange rate did not force many export price reductions in domestic price terms. Second, devaluation would have had very serious inflationary implications, especially since Tanzania's new wages and salaries policy had only been put into formal operation a few months earlier and could hardly have stood up to the 10 per cent urban cost of living increase devaluation would have entailed. Further, unless domestic food prices were raised (worsening the inflationary spiral) devaluation would have had perverse implications for rural income distribution and resource allocation as between export and domestic crops.

In 1971 (and again in 1973) different conclusions were drawn because different circumstances prevailed. Again, the decisions to devalue along with the dollar were joint ones (although in 1971 Tanzania acted rather in advance of its partners), as were those to alter the operating peg from the pound to the dollar. It was believed that most export prices were basically dollar-determined and would stay relatively constant in dollars. Thus the effect of not devaluing would have been to force down rural prices with significant disincentive effects. The inflation danger was recognised but seen as un-avoidable, especially as in 1971 (though not in 1973) the balance of payments position counselled an increase in the cost of imported relative to domestic goods. In 1973, the need to limit imported inflation (and profit margin widening which had been notable in 1971–3, partly as a result of, and partly facilitated by, the 1971 devaluation) led to the creation of a comprehensive price planning mechanism to oversee producer, importer, distributor, and consumer prices of major products.

The other two changes – a 2.5 per cent revaluation against the dollar in early 1973, and a reverse 2.5 per cent devaluation later in the same year – were of a different nature. Because sterling had proven such an erratic currency to which to tie the shilling, the currency in which the central rate was expressed had been switched to the dollar. When the dollar fell to unreasonably low levels in 1973 while Tanzania's international balance was strong, the marginal adjustment sought to stabilise the shilling *vis-à-vis* third currencies. *Pari passu*, the dollar recovery led to a reversal.

On balance, the 1967, 1971 and 1973 decisions look correct in retrospect. Certainly none created uncontrollable international imbalance or domestic dislocation effects. Whether an independent devaluation would have been sound policy at any point (as was argued in some Tanzanian academic circles)[15] is less clear. It would have had to be massive (40 per cent was advanced as a proposal) to secure major resource shifts to exports (a policy objective which in any event had no significant backing). It could have done so only at the price of slowing of food production which barely exceeded population growth and of widening rural income inequality. The prices and incomes policy would have been a probable casualty, because machinery to calculate, guide, and control secondary and spread price effects of massive devaluation did not exist, and this would have led to a self-generating domestic inflationary process. The export impact might, in any case, have been slim, especially if domestic prices had spiralled autonomously, and far more costly to attain that way than by selective subsidies (for instance, for agricultural or manufacturing inputs) and the provision of infrastructure (to open new areas to the production of such crops as tea, tobacco, and cashew nuts).

On balance, the case for a major independent devaluation looks as weak in retrospect as it did in 1967 and 1972. It would become stronger, in a positive sense, if Tanzania acquired industrial and processing capacity based on domestic raw materials adequate to mount a major structural shift cum expansion of exports and if the bulk of these industries needed a 15 to 20 per cent shift in relative prices to make exports viable. In a negative sense, it would become stronger if domestic inflation or shifts in the terms of trade were seriously to erode real purchasing power of primary producers and this could not be offset by productivity-boosting input subsidies, or export tax reductions. In practice, the positive eventuality is unlikely for at least a decade, and the negative one may be little less so unless massive internally generated inflation occurs, since the room for the alternative policy steps cited is fairly large.

The argument that exchange rate alterations are more efficient than multiple intervention practices is of limited relevance because no *single* exchange rate would be optimal on the export side, given marginal/average and regional cost differentials. *Any* single rate would require detailed backup policies. A multiple exchange rate system, plus low export taxes and higher staple food prices, might well be preferable to tax/subsidy schemes but it would be no less complex.

2. *Reserve levels and management*

In respect of reserve level policy there have also been certain broad areas of agreement:

(*a*) reserves are needed partly for working balances and seasonal swings but, above all, to strengthen Tanzania's international economic independence by increasing its bargaining power and room for manoeuvre; reserves fulfil this purpose by buying time to respond to an external event, whether a withdrawal of aid or a drought;

(*b*) target reserve levels should therefore relate to possible deviations from trend levels of imports, exports and financial flows, not to currency in circulation;

(*c*) target levels – three months worth of imports (counting foreign currency, SDRs, and golde tranche as reserves) – are middle positions which will not be met at the end of a period of reserve use but should be exceeded at the end of any period of particularly favourable international economic circumstances.

There has been a lively, largely open debate on appropriate reserve levels. In both 1969 and 1973 reserve 'hoarding' was challenged – in the latter year even by the Bank of Tanzania. But over 1970–1 and in 1974 sharp reductions in reserves necessitated controls and suggested that those who argued that the 1969 and 1973 levels were prudent peak reserves and not evidence of trend hoarding were practically, if not necessarily analytically, correct.

Reserve management has aroused relatively little debate, except from a limited number of academic and journalistic advocates of holding gold.[16] The policy has been an insurance-oriented one. In 1967 reserves were diversified to New York, limiting the impact of sterling devaluation. Over 1967–74 the successive sterling guarantee agreements permitted allocation of reserves between New York and London to be determined largely on the basis of relative interest rates. Investments have been basically in Treasury Bills plus time and term deposits with banks of absolutely first rate reputation. No more adventurous policy was deemed prudent even if it might have led to marginal revenue gains.

In 1970–2 and again in 1974 the (state-owned) National Bank of Commerce was instructed to build up use of its bills with correspondent banks to soften downward reserve swings. This clearly would involve a net interest cost if the reserve swing, in the event, ended before a crisis level was reached. However, that cost was deemed worth paying as an insurance premium when large downward reserve swings for periods of three consecutive months or more were recorded.

3. *Foreign resource procurement*

Tanzania's foreign resource use strategy has been outlined particularly clearly by the Minister for Finance in a 1974 address to the TANU Youth League's Dar es Salaam branch (Msuya, 1974a):

(a) foreign aid is used to supplement domestic resources...

(b) foreign resources are almost entirely secured by the public sector for use by public sector governmental or parastatal units...

(c) foreign resources are used within (nationally) planned contexts to advance Tanzanian goals. Because it is possible today – to a degree we did not enjoy even four years ago – to secure foreign resources for almost all development sectors, there is no justification for the belief that such resources can be used to distort our development priorities. Where this has happened, it is essentially due to weaknesses on the part of our institutions or senior management, or lack of clearly defined policies...

(d) the price of dispensing with all foreign resources today would be significantly lower development and unemployment of considerable domestic resources plus a significant reduction in standards of consumption and public services to the mass of the people in the country...

(e) the Government is fully conscious of the problems which can be raised by indiscriminate use of or excessive reliance on (e.g. for 50 per cent of total investment) the use of foreign resources. In Tanzania the role of foreign aid is essentially augmentative. The main responsibility for development of Tanzania lies squarely with the Tanzanians themselves and their self-reliance. This fact is borne out by an analysis of the investments made during the last ten years...

(f) Tanzania has the policies, institutions and resolve to develop her economy on its declared socialist and self-reliant principles without waiver or favour (p. 5).

The record bears out these assertions (Green, 1972a; 1973a). Tanzania has consistently been willing to act as it believed correct at the cost of real or potential aid loss. A series of cases involving the Federal Republic of Germany, the USA, the UK, and the USSR can be cited. In none – even when apparently faced with a British organised veto of IBRD funding after landlord nationalisation – has Tanzania backed down. Equally, it has normally taken a firm line on what resources it wanted, for what purposes, and on what maximum terms, and left offers not consistent with it unused.[17]

The present debt service burden – after adjusting the government/national parastatal figure of Sh 200 million-odd for 1974 upward by Sh 40 million as Tanzania's share of East African Community and Corporation debt service – is 10 per cent of commodity exports. If one projects a (gross) flow of loans and grants rising 10 per cent a year from 1974 (say 5 per cent real and 5 per cent inflation) on terms similar to those of recent years, the cost would rise to Sh 450 million in the early 1980s and Sh 1,500 million in the early 1990s. Both figures are still in the 10 to 12 per cent of commodity exports range assuming a 10 per cent monetary growth in these as well. This type of projection cannot pretend to prophesy. What it does indicate is that with a rising net foreign resource inflow – but one falling as a share of gross investment which is likely to grow 6 to 7.5 per cent a year in real terms – Tanzania can avoid a debt service trap. Special borrowing over 1974–7 required, however the loans are formally described, to meet the foreign cost of staple food deficiencies, could raise the debt service ratio, reducing leeway, but still keeping it well below a 20 per cent average. Similarly, even with a 10 per cent annual growth rate in real foreign funding a gradual increase (under 0.5 per cent a year) in the ratio of savings to GDP will be sufficient to provide balance in that respect.

With the ratio of taxes and tax-like charges at 35 per cent of monetary GDP at market prices, and with the ratio of gross national saving to gross national product at 20 per cent, the use of foreign resources in Tanzania's case can hardly be deemed inconsistent with its stated policy of self-reliance. Few other poor countries have achieved a comparable tax effort and fewer still, with a comparable level of GDP *per capita* ($112.50 in 1973), an equal level of gross national saving. With gross domestic investment at about 27.5 per cent of GDP a net foreign inflow (excluding reserve changes) of one-quarter of gross investment is (in the absence of a food crisis) a complementary, not a dominant resource.

4. *International equilibrium*

Tanzania has consistently sought a rather special, and not very explicitly defined, type of dynamic international equilibrium. Because this has little in common with the standard free trade equilibrium construct, it is worth noting its conditions:

(*a*) a negative current account balance (excluding interest and grant aid) equal to and opposite to the level of foreign grant and loan transfers (net of service costs and payments for acquired foreign assets);

(*b*) the average terms of foreign resource procurement must not exceed about 3 per cent interest, and five years' grace plus a twenty year term for repayment;

(*c*) the foreign resources must be of a type and order of magnitude consistent with their being fitted into (as opposed to moulding) national planning objectives;

(*d*) on the domestic side, the combined foreign resource inflow and domestic savings must be adequate in amount, and appropriate in nature, to finance investment of at least 25 per cent of GDP in a non-inflationary manner.

These conditions seem to apply only taking one year with another. They do not exclude reserve swings around the normal prudent level. Over a twenty year time horizon, a fall in the ratio of the current account deficit (as defined) to investment would be posited as a goal – it is not normally seen as a short term condition.[18]

This definition of equilibrium, of course, is consistent with the attitude toward exchange rates analysed earlier. Because the economy is non-homogenous to the point of fragmentation (especially in the export sector) *no* single exchange rate is 'optimal' from the viewpoint of the current account balance, production incentives, or income distribution. Specific corrective action (export and import tax adjustments, internal prices diverging from export and import parity, 'shadow price' project analysis) will be necessary whatever exchange rate is set. Similarly, as even industrial economies now recognise, there is no guarantee that an exchange rate optimal on current account and factor price considerations would result in an appropriate rather than a perverse capital account balance.

In 1970–2 improved domestic credit planning and foreign exchange budgeting, institutional reform in the import/wholesale commerce sector and the external finance division of the Treasury, capital account exchange control (backed by inconvertibility of notes) within East Africa, and a one year pause in real growth in budgetary expenditure were undertaken to meet and reverse the growing international imbalance and to make subsequent maintenance of balance easier.[19] Over 1972–3 this package was highly effective, with domestic savings and foreign exchange reserves rising significantly and the reformed commercial and foreign finance procuring institutions turning in notably better performances. Real output growth held steady at the previous (1964–73) rate of 5 per cent a year over 1971–3, while rural reorganisation and income redistribution picked up momentum.

Tanzanian experience: 1973–4

The weakness in the underlying position was not clear in 1973 and, while early warnings appeared in the Minister's February speech in Brussels, it was not fully recognised as involving a horrifying Sh 1,000–1,200 million net deterioration on basic international account for 1974 as opposed to 1973 until May or June. What were the weaknesses and why the delay in identifying their significance?

First, over 1961–73 basic food output had a trend growth rate of only 3 per cent – barely above that of population – leaving no leeway for the back-to-back bad weather losses of 1973 and 1974. In respect of sugar, wheat and dairy products, very sharp increases in demand, arising from concentrating increases in real consumption power on lower income groups exacerbated the growth in net import demand. The explosive 1973–4 food price increases, linked to the high import demand, implied an increase of Sh 800 million in 1974 over 1972–3 average food imports.

Second, petroleum – and consequential plastics, fertiliser, and shipping – prices increased massively and steadily from mid-1973 through April 1974. The direct petroleum bill net additions totalled about Sh 350–400 million;[20] the indirect ones for fertiliser and plastics perhaps Sh 25 million; and that for freight as much as another Sh 200–225 million.

Third, demand growth fed by income redistribution had outstripped mass consumer good production capacity with textiles, garments, and yarn showing a Sh 140 million import increase over 1971–3; and imports of cement, other construction materials, and plastics showed similar trends. Thus real consumer goods imports appeared over 1971–3 to have reversed their fairly rapid 1966–71 downtrend.

Fourth, except for manufactured goods exports to Kenya, export volume experienced nearly total stagnation over 1966–74.

Fifth, general import price inflation (which caused a cumulative 1961–71 terms of trade loss of over Sh 2,000 million)[21] continued in 1974 and was no longer accompanied, as in 1972–3, by export price increases.

Until January 1974, most of the real terms of trade losses on food, petroleum, and freight (perhaps Sh 800–900 million) were *not* predictable. Faster and more detailed reviews might have revealed the impending crisis a few weeks earlier than the apparent March–April studies did; but the real lesson is how rapidly the combination of weather and international price changes can unleash a foreign balance crisis of tidal wave proportions on an extreme peripheral economy, even if it is following a relatively cautious external economic strategy backed by forward foreign exchange planning. By July 1974, reserves had fallen to Sh 600 million (seven weeks worth of estimated current imports) and a Sh 900 million 'emergency gap' (above normal foreign borrowing) was forecast for the year 1974–5.[22]

The basic Tanzanian strategy – taking domestic and external measures together – adopted in mid-1974 and now being followed sought:

(*a*) to cover the 'emergency' deficit by special funding;

(*b*) to seek to produce its way out of the special imbalance within three years;

(*c*) to avoid massive import or investment cutbacks which would destroy the momentum of development;

(*d*) to raise domestic prices to cover input cost increases and to bring staple foodstuff prices near import parity until basic self sufficiency is re-established;

(*e*) to raise (for the first time since independence) public sector salary scales as well as minimum wages to limit or avert purchasing power erosion, and to impose a one year wage and salary freeze from May 1974 through April 1975;

(*f*) to expand government finance from recurrent revenue for fixed investment in productive sectors and housing investment, but at the same time to limit additional taxation almost totally to export price windfall gains and to mass market amenities (beer, cigarettes);

(g) to aim for a continued 5 to 6 per cent annual real growth rate.

This was evidently a strategy which involved risks if the major industrial economies proceeded to create a recession combined with high inflation, a trade war, and monetary panic. On the other hand, as opposed to a strategy of retrenchment, it would preserve the development momentum built up over 1964–73.

The selective production expansion effort centres on basic foods, exports and mass consumer goods and building materials. An energy programme seems necessarily more long term, apart from oil savings resulting from a major dam completion in 1975; but, with significant potential in terms of coal and, probably, natural gas, it could be significant in the 1980s.

Production expansion in agriculture centres on maize, wheat, rice, sugar, milk and oilseeds. The build up in required institutions and input supplies has proceeded far enough that the main problem so far as surmounting the crisis is concerned is weather. Expansion of domestic manufacturing capacity is to be concentrated on textiles, garments, shoes and cement over 1974–7, and on integration of the iron and steel industry with a new 500,000 ton basic steel unit over the period to 1980. Export expansion, apart from marginal to moderate boosting of traditional agricultural exports and the possible addition of soybeans, is intended to concentrate on pre-export processing (sisal to twine, cashew nuts to kernels, hides to leather) and on finding foreign outlets for a portion of the output of basically domestic market oriented industries (textiles, garments, cement, steel and aluminium products, tyres and tubes) especially in the African regional and Indian Ocean markets.

A rough summary of the quantitative implications suggests possible improvements on external account by 1977–87 of:

(a) Sh 700 million on agricultural import reductions (grain, Sh 550 million; sugar, Sh 150 million);

(b) Sh 150 million on net import substitution and Sh 25–50 million in export expansion from the manufacturing sector;

(c) Sh 50–75 million export gains from processing and Sh 150 million from expanded traditional export quantities.

These total Sh 1,100 million, or more than the 1974–5 'emergency' estimate, but they could be reduced in terms of real import purchasing power if the 1974 pattern of worsening terms of trade is continued or exacerbated by collective recession in the industrial economies.

To meet the 1974–5 – 76–7 emergency gaps, Tanzania's strategy would require at least Sh 1,750 million special assistance disbursed promptly with half on grant or IDA terms. Late 1974 experience suggested that the required commitments might well be obtainable (including ones from oil producing states), but that prompt disbursements were less likely, even though the underlying requirement was for free foreign exchange to import staple foodstuffs.

The Tanzanian strategy has certain interesting aspects:

(*a*) it is based on the assumption that significant emergency finance and access to basic food supplies can be obtained for up to three years;

(*b*) in no way, however, does it include assumptions of basic structural reforms, such as the 'link' or an international commodity 'parity' scheme;

(*c*) it concentrates on adding to national integration (including export processing), both among economic sectors and between production and use, and is therefore clearly 'inward looking';

(*d*) but it does seek to break out of the 1966–73 export stagnation to increase capacity to import intermediate and capital goods;

(*e*) it is linked to poverty eradication and more even income distribution as an engine of growth as well as development;[23]

(*f*) it nevertheless appears almost ultra-orthodox in emphasising that the public productive sector must generate investible surpluses and the recurrent budget a surplus for investment.

Generalisations from Tanzanian experience

What does the Tanzanian experience and strategy suggest for the economies of the extreme periphery as a group? The possible elements fall into three clusters: (1) international system changes; (2) international crisis response mechanisms; (3) internal structural transformations.

In the first area there is little new to say. The top priorities surely remain: effective market access,[24] effective industrial economy support for the changes in global production location and trade patterns this implies, nearly totally grant or IDA-term multilateral and bilateral finance to the least developed with commercial capital markets made more available to the less underdeveloped by interest rate subsidies and guarantees, the SDR link (preferably in the form of 100 per cent initial allocation to developing economies with structural trade deficits so that everyone else could run a surplus at one and the same time),[25] new institutional structures (varying from commodity to commodity) to remove the present normal pattern of *de facto* unilateral buyer oligopsony during normal or slump periods.

This list is not unrealistic in the sense that its implementation would damage world economic efficiency even on the narrowest definition. It is, in fact, based on dynamic comparative advantage, with quite moderate egalitarian elements of redistribution plus introduction of a countervailing power check to existing unbalanced market power situations. However, only limited, if any, progress on these matters can be expected over any period of less than five years. That is no reason not to press such an agenda: sustained reiteration and argument have made it a little less of a daydream in 1974 than it looked in 1964.[26] But it does mean that the present crisis must be surmounted by other means.

Secondly, crisis response attitudes and mechanisms require complete overhaul so as to increase the speed and scale of response. While some of the smaller industrial economies (e.g. Sweden, Canada), the EEC, and certain of the OPEC states have acted, the attempts of the UN Special Assembly and the World Food Conference to secure co-ordinated, automatic, rapid and adequate resource flows (including food as well as funds) have not succeeded. The USA, USSR, Japan, and Federal Germany have either failed to realise the nature and scope of the need or have wilfully chosen to ignore it.

The need for continued co-ordinated pressure by the peripheral economies – including, if possible, the newly rich oil elite – is clear. The example of the associate/associable states' unity and clarity of aims in the 1973–5 talks with the EEC demonstrates that this is possible. In that sense, the OPEC also *does* offer a general lesson in strategy even if its tactical lessons are less clear-cut or general. The realisation that pooled power, even of small units, can have an impact whereas fragmented power on the periphery is ably played into cross-cancellation by the centre has now led, one must hope, to appropriate action conclusions.

One example is the proposed alteration in the IMF's articles of agreement. The developing countries have a blocking vote because two-thirds of all members as well as 80 per cent of all quotas are needed to ratify changes. They have every reason and every right to use this veto power to get an acceptable reform package, including a first instalment of the link, not merely yet another committee to talk about it. After all, the USA and the EEC have made it quite clear that *they* would use their quotas to 'veto' packages seen as inimical to their interests. Why should the poor meekly accept that it is either impossible or wrong to do likewise? Of course, the use of power requires bargaining and realism. But there is no bargain to be had *until* the power is organised and deployed. An immediate link, for example, could be traded off against pledges of, say, $5,000 million a year for 1975–6 through 1977–8 to the United Nations Emergency Programme. But no such counter-proposal can be tabled until it is clear that the requisite forty-five odd developing economies will refuse to ratify any IMF article changes unless the link is included or a substantial alternative funded before the vote.

The third, and most critical, cluster of responses is internal. Emergency international response can bridge a transitional gap but no more. Systemic changes at an adequate pace to fill the 'gap' are highly unlikely. Periphery responses must be primarily production-oriented and designed to reverse the temporary rise in dependence on external financial and resource transfers, to alter national systems, and to escape from permanent 'gappery'.

First, staple food production must be brought into both static and dynamic balance with a level of demand which is consistent with minimum acceptable consumption levels for all of the population of each developing economy. This implies reorientation of national and international provision of resources, research emphasis, and institutional development priorities. Among the primary needs are improved seeds and other inputs for food grown on dry, poor land; small scale irrigation; and effective credit and procurement systems reaching scattered populations. These are almost the inverse of the priorities of the 'Green Revolution'; the Gezira type of irrigation schemes; and the IBRD high income, export enclave, rural development projects. This is not to decry the latter group but to suggest that the partial success they have already attained and their limited potential for further application now render them of secondary urgency.

Second, mass market consumer goods manufacture and building material production based primarily on *domestic* inputs must be expanded at absolute rates more rapid than those of demand to achieve a significant saving in import requirements. In no other way can greater equality of income distribution and significant progress toward absolute poverty eradication be made consistent with greater national economic integration and the regaining of external balance.

Third, a reassessment of export strategies (including their absence) is needed to identify real *growth potential* areas (for example, perhaps grain, beef, sugar) and real *domestic linkage potential* ones (such as preprocessing of the exports and the building of manufacturing establishments with a view to export of initial-period excess capacity). Certainly 'more of the same' or 'diversify into somebody else's major export' strategies are unlikely to work and are still too common.[27]

Fourth, evaluation of genuine national and regional potential for integrated vectors, including capital goods or manufactured goods exports, is required. For example, a vector that could be constructed in East Africa consists of iron ore, limestone, coal, steel, coal chemicals, dyes, engineering industry products, structural steel, machine parts and simple machines; the plants could be spread among Kenya, Uganda, and Zambia as well as Tanzania, which has the best basic coal–iron ore combination. Alternatively, a purely Tanzanian vector with coal, coal chemicals, vanadium, and steel should prove viable.[28]

Fifth, emergency foreign resource transfers should be allocated nationally to construct internal economic structures less vulnerable to international disequilibria, with particular attention to reducing imbalances between sectoral production and use and increasing the linkages among domestic production sectors.

Sixth, strategy on exchange rates, reserve management, foreign resource procurement terms and debt service levels should be relatively insurance- (as opposed to Monte Carlo-) oriented.[29] The risks of an overtly gambling strategy are high and the possible losses outweigh the possible gains, as can be seen in the Ghanaian, Chilean, and Indonesian experiences.

It is fortunate that these internal changes *must* play a dominant role. They, and they alone, offer a route to economic independence based on balanced economic interdependence (Green, 1970 and 1973*b*; Saul, 1973). Integration into the world economy by the complete adoption of the agenda for systemic structural change would be far from an unmixed blessing. Exporting cheap labour in manufactured goods or tropical climates in tourism programmes is not necessarily a great advance on exporting raw materials. It is certainly arguable that it *increases* external dependency by its greater degree of urbanisation, alterations in consumption patterns, and use of externally controlled intermediary institutions and knowledge.

Thus, new difficulties and choices would confront extreme periphery economies if integration into a variant of the present international monetary, financial and trade system which was based on genuinely free trade and dynamic comparative advantage were on offer today. If such a variant emerges in a decade *after* internal structural changes have produced reintegration of their own fragmented economies, the results could be quite different (Green, 1968; Seers, 1963). It is not impossible for a relatively small, relatively late-starting economy (such as Finland) to build up economic independence and an increasingly interdependent international economic role, if a clear set of national goals, institutions and intersectoral linkages in production and use is developed.

Neither Tanzania's strategy nor this attempted generalisation from it is a strategy of integration into the world economic system on the *only* terms that are even partially on offer – in which the system's values and priorities are accepted in all major respects in return for acceptance as full members of its humbler classes. Such a strategy is bankrupt. Denying the doomsday ecologists' grosser visions of Armageddon is quite consistent with observing that European–North American patterns of resource use demand *per capita* levels of productive forces which few in the Third World and none on the extreme periphery can attain in a century. It is *doubly* bankrupt because were it to 'succeed', the implied international structure in the year 2070 would be characterised by the same basic hierarchy as that of today with some countries (e.g. Iran?) upclassed and some (e.g. the UK?) downclassed, but with no real alteration of the international class system nor of the psychological, intellectual and aspirational dependence of the 'proletarian nations'.

To paraphrase Malcolm X on the parallel issue of 'integration' of Black Americans, the starting point on the part of polities with low levels of productive forces and high levels of dependence must be to *assert* and to *believe*: the beauty, and the worth, of themselves, their people, their self-determined aspirations; the legitimacy of defending oneself, by any means including violence; the irrelevance of integration into the world socio-economic order for the poor and the self-loathing implied in begging for it; the necessity of confronting power with power; the urgency of the masses of the poor countries achieving control over their own communities and over the shaping of their own goals.

Self-determination, self-reliance, and self-acceptance are the only bases on which self-development and self-benefiting participation in the international monetary and economic system are possible. They are not the *fruits* of economic progress nor of less unequal exchange but their *preconditions*.

Notes

1   The analysis and views expressed in this paper are my personal responsibility and are not necessarily those of the Tanzania Treasury or of SIDA.
2   This is, of course, precisely the basis of the Chinese (and to a lesser extent the Yugoslav) ideological critique of Soviet relationships with, and attitudes toward, the poor countries.
3   The term is borrowed from Barbara Ward (1974). It identifies those poor countries who lack adequate quantities of scarce natural resources to achieve middle-income status prior to development. The international class system has never involved a simple two-way division; nor is lumping all socialist economies as a separate category universally helpful analytically. For example, a clear 'middle class' (including, on the one hand, the industrialised European socialist states and the smaller capitalist industrial economies and, on the other, semi-industrial economies like Brazil, Mexico, Singapore, South Africa, New Zealand and at least Iran of the oil rich) does exist in the international economic system (which is basically capitalist in structure and operation). Within each main class, major sub-categories may exist. This paper is particularly concerned with small economic units with high external trade to GDP ratios, e.g. Sri Lanka not Bangladesh, Tanzania not India, and, not insubstantially, Cuba not China. Further detailed conceptual analysis would require a separate paper.
4   Cost-efficient in the broad sense. Manpower for analysis and for diplomacy is limited. If deployed so as to achieve a series of marginal gains while leaving major battles unfought it has not been used cost-efficiently.
5   It is instructive to compare, for example, the preliminary report by Chairman Wardhana to the Nairobi annual meeting of the IMF and what the Group of Twenty actually agreed at its final meeting in mid-1974.
6   The 1970–4 period is not necessarily unique in that regard. Just as development analysis in general has been biased toward considering the Indian sub-continent as typical, assumptions about the price behaviour of poor countries has been biased by supposing that the dramatic Latin American inflators like Brazil, Argentina and Chile were typical.
7   No comment is intended on the ultimate justification for the project. On a narrow cost/benefit basis the IBRD is clearly right in rejecting the railway. However, part of Gabon's case is that the railroad is vital to creating the possibility for a national economy with some internal coherence, to supersede the present mélange of isolated export enclaves. Whether it would, in fact, do that is an open question but one the IBRD has really not directed its mind to answering, as opposed to pointing out that main initial users and beneficiaries would be foreign mining firms.
8   The tighter the present and short run future foreign exchange position of a country, the more difficult it will find it renewing loans. Only when it is in a position in which it could readily repay will it find the lender eager to extend the period!
9   Diaz-Alejandro draws the same conclusion (p. 194 above), suggesting resort to the commercial market for the richer of the poor (the middle-class aspirants) and concentration of truly concessional finance on the poorest (the extreme periphery).
10 Tanzanian experience in this field suggests two things. First, the task is not impossible – the Cotton and Coffee Authorities do a relatively good job of keeping abreast of world market trends and prospects and securing the best

possible prices at their auctions. Second, mistakes are easy – the Cashew Nut Authority, the Sisal Authority, and (on the buying side) the National Milling Corporation and National Sugar Board have made errors of judgement entailing very large losses to the national economy. Corrective measures have, in fact, been taken but learning in commodity markets has been demonstrated to be neither easy nor costless.

11 For example, if rice prices were to rise 100 per cent, petroleum prices 300 per cent, and other imports 15 per cent, while tea prices were to fall 10 per cent, and rubber prices 20 per cent, the *total* real purchasing power (not just import purchasing power) of Sri Lankan production would fall by 20 to 25 per cent. Except for the case of tea, the mid-1973 to mid-1974 record there was very like this example.

12 Cf. Green (1971*b*) and 'The Columbia Declaration' (an independent manifesto produced by eight 'scholars' including the author and signed by a majority of the Columbia Conference participants) in Ward *et al.* 1971, pp. 10–13, for a fuller exposition of this view of Pearson. See Ward, 1974, for a similar view on developments from 1970–4, albeit with a notably more optimistic picture of probable industrial and oil economy response in the next few years.

13 The general sources for this section are the *Annual Budget Speeches* 1967–8 through 1974–5, *Annual* and *Quarterly Reports of the Bank of Tanzania*, 1967–73, *Annual Plans* 1970–1 through 1974–5 (Government Printer, Dar es Salaam), and *Annual Trade Reports*, 1967 through 1973 (East African Customs and Excise Department, Mombasa, Kenya).

14 This conclusion is based on the interaction of ratchet effects, relative income considerations (i.e. best alternative crops and how distant the 'second best' is), and absolute reward-for-effort effects. (At some point the farmer quite rightly will think the return is too low to justify the extra work even though the return is still positive.) All seem to act more strongly in respect of absolute output price declines than in respect of relative price declines caused by increases in prices of other commodities, and *a fortiori*, than in respect of unilateral output price increases.

15 The debate was not on left–right or applied–theoretical divisions. In general, those most concerned with problems of individual project evaluation favoured devaluation while those most concerned with income distribution and problems of price control opposed it.

16 The journalistic side appears to be influenced by Tass correspondents quite legitimately promoting the USSR's interests as a net gold exporter. The academic case was based on safety and on the prospect of inflation of gold values exceeding interest on currency holdings. Practically speaking, since early 1972 (the point at which Tanzania's reserves touched a low point at which all were needed in immediately useable form) gold has not been available at official prices. Further, monetary gold inflows *de facto* came almost exclusively from South Africa which would raise distinct political problems for the Bank of Tanzania's adoption of a gold holding policy even if it bought from third parties itself.

17 Somewhat ironically, the bulk of Socialist European offers fall into this last category. In many cases they are 'plus capitaliste que les capitalistes' in terms, duration, and price inflation of tied goods. Tanzania has a most atypical aid procurement pattern: China first, Scandinavia second, IBRD–IDA third, smaller industrial economies (Canada, Netherlands) fourth, the USA fifth, Federal Germany sixth, Socialist Europe seventh. The revival of UK assistance (basically broken off since 1965) will probably move that source into fifth place.

18 A vocal, but very small, purist intellectual minority does demand more or less total severance of resource transfer links with non-socialist states. A broader criticism of the romantic and ahistoric elements in this group's overall analysis has been made by the author (Green, 1974). It is worth noting that the Dar es Salaam TANU Youth League Branch, one of the most radical and alert political groups in Tanzania, responded favourably to Minister Msuya's speech cited above.

19 For a more extended analysis see Green, 1971a.

20 The historical series pose problems because of the inter-mixing of Zambian imports (first of products, later of crude) with Tanzanian and because of the considerable exports of residual black oils. Imports, net of re-exports and finished product exports, seem to have been about Sh 190–200 million in 1973 and are likely to be about Sh 580 million in 1974.

21 Estimate prepared by the External Finance Section of the Treasury based on selected import prices. With the exception of sisal, Tanzania's export prices were – taken together – more or less static in monetary terms over 1961–71. The loss on sisal price declines was about Sh 500 million over the period.

22 The 1974–5 Budget Speech figure of Sh 1,000 million refers to calendar 1974. It is assumed that 1974–5 domestic grain purchases will be better than those of 1973–4 and that cutbacks on certain consumer goods imports will also help curb the gap.

23 Because a more equal income distribution – at least in Tanzania – concentrates demand growth both on a smaller number of goods and on items for most of which raw materials are or can be produced in Tanzania, it leads to both economies of scale and additional national economic integration through broader and deeper intrasectoral and intersectoral linkages.

24 Processed and manufactured goods exports are not irrelevant, even in the medium term, to countries like Tanzania. Sisal twine, vacuum packed roasted cashew nuts, leather, shoe parts, cotton yarn, cloth, specialty garments, parquet flooring, and other specialty timber products, pyrethrum preparations, tinned honey, beeswax products – the list is by no means inconsiderable in numbers, potential employment, value added, or export enhancement.

25 This is, of course, the same mechanism as that underlying the gold standard during its most successful period. Almost all additions to gold stocks were produced in then developing economies and earned by then industrialised economies by their running of trade surpluses with Australia, South Africa, Canada, the USA, etc. The analogy is not exact but is close enough to demonstrate that the idea is not inherently impracticable if accepted. The author owes this insight to Professor Peacock of Canada who was at the time advising the Commonwealth Secretariat on monetary reform.

26 For a distressing illustration of how little the main needs and obstacles have changed, cf. Green, 1967. However, some of the key themes do appear to have moved several steps closer to reality. The recent EEC-Associate discussions tackled the question of commodity stabilisation schemes which offer some insurance as to quantities and to prices relative to those of EEC exports, as well as merely unit commodity prices. What eventually was agreed was far from perfect but it is a matter of no little interest that serious negotiations were held on these lines and that some first steps toward a 'parity income' scheme were taken.

27 The present proposals for massive tourist facility expansion are yet a new illustration of this tendency.

28   Tanzania is committed to a regional approach if at all possible. As stated in its paper to the 1970 Lusaka Non-Aligned Summit (Tanzania, 1970) and as embodied in its membership in and commitment to the East African Community, Tanzania believes joint action by small, poor countries will yield more rapid and less costly advance. However, the East African Community is in grave danger of being eroded into a rather innocuous backwater so far as industrial development goes because of the continued lack of progress on joint industrial planning and allocation approaches (Green, 1972b). The dangers of erosion and attrition cited in 1972 are even more serious and time even more pressing in early 1975. This, not a 'crisis breakup', is the real threat to the future of the East African Economic Community. Like the EEC, the EAC does give an impression of successive unresolvable crises suddenly miraculously dissolved at the last minute. In both cases, reality is more complex than appearance, although in both, criticism of failure to hammer out agreements at earlier stages to avoid problem build-ups to real or apparent crisis proportions may well be justified.

29   Borrowing at negative real interest rates is clearly prudent (for the borrower who can make surplus generating use of the funds) if repayment is in domestic currency or if significant negative terms of trade shifts can be ruled out of consideration. Otherwise ability to repay in operating unit or government budget terms may not be matched by ability to transfer, e.g. if 'stagflation' or recession cum inflation in the industrial economies results in significant medium term falls and trend stagnation in import capacity. In principle, steadily rising borrowings could roll over such debts but in practice refinancing would be unlikely to be possible in such a setting.

References

Green, R. H., 1967. Unctad and after: anatomy of a failure. *Journal of Modern African Studies*, **5**, 243–67.

1968. *Stages in Economic Development: Changes in the Structure of Production, Demand and International Trade.* Khartoum: Bank of Sudan; and Yale University Economic Growth Center Paper 125.

1970. Political independence and the national economy: an essay on the political economy of decolonization. In *African Perspectives*, (ed.) C. Allen and R. W. Johnson, pp. 273–324. Cambridge: Cambridge University Press.

1971a. Resources, demands, investible surpluses and efficiency: certain pressing issues of freedom and necessity in the transition to socialism. *Taamuli* (Dar es Salaam), **2**, 9–18.

1971b. Anatomy of two assessments: Pearson, Jackson and development partnership. *African Review*, **1**, 44–5.

1972a. Foreign resources and the parastatal sector in a transition to socialism. In *The Use of Foreign Funds in the Development of the East African Countries.* Dakar: United Nations Institute for Economic Development and Planning.

1972b. East African economic integration: benefits, costs and priorities. Paper presented to East African Community Study Seminar, Kampala. Forthcoming from Dag Hammarskjöld Foundation.

1973a. Technical assistance and Tanzanian administration. In *Technical Assistance Administration in East Africa*, (ed.) Yashpal Tandon, pp. 29–64. Uppsala: Dag Hammarskjöld Foundation.

1973b. Economic independence and economic cooperation. In *Economic Indepen-*

dence in Africa, (ed.) D. P. Ghai, pp. 45–87. Nairobi: East African Literature Bureau.

— 1974. Relevance, efficiency, romanticism, and confusion in Tanzanian planning and management. Paper presented to conference on the problems of public sector management in Africa, Dar es Salaam. Forthcoming from Dag Hammarskjöld Foundation.

Mao Tse-tung, 1965. *Selected Works, Volume I*. Peking: Foreign Languages Press.

Msuya, C. D., 1974*a*. Foreign aid and Tanzanian development. *Rasilimali* (Dar es Salaam), January.

— 1974*b*. How the economic policy of the European Community appears to a developing country. Dar es Salaam: Treasury, unpublished.

Nyerere, Julius K., 1966. *Freedom and Unity*. London and Nairobi: Oxford University Press.

Pearson, L. B. *et al.* 1969. *Partners in Development, Report of the Commission on International Development*. New York: Praeger.

Saul, J. S., 1973. The political aspects of economic independence. In *Economic Independence in Africa*, (ed.) D. P. Ghai, pp. 123–50. Nairobi: East African Literature Bureau.

Seers, Dudley, 1963. The stages of economic development of a primary producer in the middle of the twentieth century. *Economic Bulletin of Ghana*, VII (no. 3) 57–69.

Tanzania, 1970. *Co-operation Against Poverty*. Dar es Salaam: Government Printer.

Ward, Barbara, 1974. First, second, third and fourth worlds. *Economist*, 18 May, 63–73.

Ward, Barbara, Runnalls, J. D. and d'Anjou, L. (eds.) 1971. *The Widening Gap: Development in the 1970s*. New York: Columbia.

12. International agencies: the case for proliferation

JOHN WHITE

Tasks and strategies

Efforts to reform the development agencies of the United Nations have generally had the aim of rationalising and consolidating these agencies within a single coherent structure. The Jackson Report, which constitutes perhaps the most thoroughgoing scheme for reform that has yet been proposed, is a notable example. In his summary statement of the Report's findings, Sir Robert Jackson declares: 'It must be emphasized that the major recommendations made by the Study are the minimum I consider essential to bring *system and order* into UN's development co-operation work and to permit it to expand steadily' (Jackson, 1969, p. 22). Generally speaking, the Jackson Report argues the case in terms of a need for greater efficiency. This is a characteristic, also, of other attempts at reform. Beyond a general presumption that a structure which reduces duplication and conflict will be less wasteful, the underlying reasons for wanting to rationalise and consolidate are seldom made clear. The Jackson Report, for instance, contents itself with restating the truisms of General Assembly resolution 2188 (XXI), to the effect that programmes should be 'relevant', should constitute 'a flexible, prompt and effective response', and should be efficiently administered, coherently planned and systematically evaluated (pp. 3–4). The Pearson Report, similarly, can be criticised for disguising, by means of a seemingly technocratic and efficiency-oriented approach, a rather strong bias in its view of the development process.[1]

Both of these reports exhibit a failure which is common to much of the literature emanating from or addressed to the official institutions of development – the failure to specify objectives except in terms so general and abstract as to be vacuous.[2] Seldom does this literature go much beyond stating the desirability of increases in aggregate GNP, and, more recently, in the welfare of the poorer sections of society. It would probably be generally agreed that these are indeed the objectives of the development process, so much so that the statement takes on the character of a definition. Significantly, statements along these lines tend to be associated with the question 'What is development?', not 'What are the key choices in development?'. As a definition, the kind of statement of objectives which recurs in the literature has very little bearing on questions of strategy.[3] The starting point of strategic thinking is the setting of objectives, by the exercise of a *choice*. Strategic thinking is not much concerned with forms of words. The most interesting and the most difficult strategic questions in the development process arise when one tries to translate the general objectives of economic growth and increased welfare into terms which make sense in the particular historical, social and cultural contexts of individual societies.

The starting point of the argument of this paper is the contention that the UN agencies, addressing themselves to a world-wide membership, are impeded in the setting of strategic objectives by the diversity of this membership. The UN agencies themselves tend to avoid the question of objectives, and the difficult political issues that it raises, by asserting that they exist to promote the objectives of their member states. This tendency has become more marked under the regime of 'country programming', but it will not serve. If the majority of member states has at least some objectives in common – i.e. if they have not only a common desire for 'development', but a common view of what it is, and of what is needed to achieve it – it should be possible to state these objectives as a basis for collective action. If, as seems more likely, they see themselves as pursuing differing ends along differing tracks, with a need to surmount differing obstacles, the possibility should at least be considered that no single piece of machinery can achieve 'a flexible, prompt and effective response' to such various demands, and that rationalisation and consolidation are the opposite of what is needed. Either way, objectives need to be stated. One cannot design a piece of machinery without knowing what it is for. What is missing in the discussion of reform of the UN machinery is a detailed specification of the tasks that this machinery is required to perform.

It is possible to see the tasks of UN development agencies in two quite different perspectives, with different and conflicting implications for any strategy of reform. First, the agencies may be seen as a set of discrete instruments for an astonishingly wide range of operational tasks, not all of which are necessarily closely interrelated. But it is equally possible to see the agencies, together with the central organs of the UN, as the components of a single world-wide 'system', providing the framework for a single world-wide strategy. It is only within the second of these perspectives that the case for rationalisation and consolidation seems self-evident. Indeed, a focus on strategy requires, not only consolidation, but also a higher degree of political control and accountability than most agencies would regard as practicable, and perhaps a closer degree of harmony than their members have yet achieved. A focus on operational tasks, in contrast, suggests a high degree of autonomy for each agency, to let it get on with the job allotted to it, unhampered by the necessarily cumbersome procedures of co-ordination and the retarding processes of complex intergovernmental negotiation. Within this perspective, overlap and duplication are not a serious issue. Indeed, a little healthy competition might be a spur to efficiency. There is enough work for all.

Historically, it is the acquisition of new tasks that has been the principal feature in the agencies' expansion. One would therefore expect a task-oriented perspective to be the one emphasised in proposals for reform; and one would expect such a perspective to be promoted by the agencies themselves, on the ground that it would strengthen the case for their autonomy, something which virtually all agencies tend to regard as desirable. Yet it has not been so. Since the early 1960s, the dominant language of reform has been the language of grand decennial strategies, world-wide in their intended scope.

Clearly, there are some tasks which are indeed best tackled on a world-wide basis, tasks in which the effective operational decisions are not within the power of any one country or group of countries. International monetary reform is perhaps the most conspicuous current example. Other obvious tasks of this kind are those which relate to the world as a single physical unit, such as exploitation of the seabed or the use of satellite communications. But most of the tasks which preoccupy strategists in developing countries, and to which the operational programmes of UN agencies are largely addressed, are not of this kind, and it is far from self-evident that a set of world-wide agencies offers the best design of machinery to help in their performance. The argument of this paper, quite simply, is that it does not.

In particular, there is one task which has stood in the forefront of debates concerning world-wide strategy, for which, in the view presented here, a more diversified set of institutions and arrangements needs to be considered – the task of mobilising external resources for development, or 'aid'.

It should be clear that the central organs of the UN do not remotely resemble a system of world government, and that the specialised agencies do not remotely resemble the departments of such a government. Indeed, it is precisely because the UN has neither the power to tax nor the power to direct its constituents into required activities that it has tended to develop operational programmes of its own; and in this sense it is moving further and further away from the political ideals which its Charter professes, and equally from the capacity to serve its member states in such ways as they may require. At the political level, it is best seen, perhaps, not as some sort of higher authority, but as a convenient framework for the resolution of conflicts between sovereign entities. In the context of development, the one major potential source of conflict which embraces all arises from the confrontation of rich and poor. But this is a *political* perception, which does not necessarily have any bearing on the operational programmes of UN agencies as technical bodies at the service of their clients. To the extent that conclusions are drawn, illegitimately, for the UN as a set of operational agencies, the inevitable outcome is the acquisition of a leadership role by the World Bank, as the principal mechanism for the transfer of resources at the world level. In arguing the case for a greater number and greater diversity of agencies, operating for the most part at a lower level and with more narrowly defined objectives, one is implicitly also arguing a case for a narrower definition of the tasks to be performed at the world level. This argument applies with especial force to the operations of the World Bank.

Evaluating the agencies' performance

Imprecision in the specification of tasks and objectives makes it difficult to assess the agencies' present and past performance. If one is not sure what an agency is supposed to have done, one cannot say whether it has done it.

Where tasks are precisely specified, there are tests that can be applied, as a basis for reform. Generally speaking, the tests to which the record of an enterprise may be submitted are of three main kinds:

(a) if it represents a particular set of interests, it may be judged by its success in defending or promoting those interests against competitors;

(b) if it has to compete for business, it may be judged by the measure of continuing demand for its services or its product;

(c) if its activities are measurable against some positive standard such as profitability, it can be judged by the success of its undertakings.

Unless some such test of utility can be found, by which the performance of the UN agencies can be judged, the case for alternative or additional institutions and arrangements is difficult to assess. By the same token, it would be difficult to assess the case for the UN agencies' continued survival.

At the operational level, UN agencies, being world-wide in their scope, do not represent any particular set of interests, except perhaps their own. There are two components within the UN system which have traditionally had a more representative character – UNCTAD, which has tended to offer itself as representing developing countries' interests rather than as a framework for conflict resolution, and the regional commissions – and it is significant that neither of these components has been allowed to acquire significant operational powers. Without operational powers, UNCTAD would perhaps be able to take greater advantage of its own universality if it saw itself exclusively as a framework for conflict resolution. For the major specialised agencies of the UN, that alternative perception is not possible, since it points towards a political function which is not related to the type of large operational programme which most of them have developed. The first test cannot be applied, and the implications of that inapplicability cannot be drawn.[4]

In principle, there is no reason why the UN agencies should not be required to compete for business with other agencies operating at different levels, including bilateral agencies. Indeed, for those who believe in the bracing influence of competition, the case for proliferation could be argued largely in these terms. For the agencies themselves, however, to encourage the application of such a test might be seen as compromising their claim to universality. In practice, it is resisted. Paradoxically, the agency which has been harshest in its application of market tests to some of the enterprises it supports, the World Bank, has also been the most dourly resistant to any competitive application of such tests to its own operations and the most ardent in its claim to universality.

Success in the undertakings of an enterprise is something that can be tested in many different ways, with very wide applications. In economic activity, the most familiar of such tests is profitability. Because both agencies themselves and most of the activities they support are not intended to show a profit, it is sometimes argued that they are not amenable to simple tests of success or failure. Against that line of defence, two attacks are possible.

First, profitability is not the only test. The bridge that falls down, the patient who dies, the puzzle that remains unsolved; all of these represent failures. All that is required is a statement of what was to be achieved. Both Escott Reid (1973, p. xiv) and, more substantially, Mason and Asher (1973, p. 232) have noted the resistance of the World Bank to review of its activities in these terms, and it is generally true that UN agencies are resistant to such positive evaluation. It is significant that such resistance is less marked among agencies which have to compete, or which have to satisfy a specific group of clients. The Asian Development Bank, for instance, which of all the regional banks most closely resembles the World Bank in its operational policies and preferences, has initiated a wide-ranging and very hard-edged review of its success or failure in a number of undertakings.

Secondly, there is some evidence to suggest that agencies tend to *avoid* enterprises in which profitability is a criterion, precisely because it would lead to a very clear test of their performance. International development finance institutions, for instance, tend to avoid industrial projects, and indeed the productive sectors as a whole, as Table 1 shows. Industrial financing up to 1972 ranged from 14.0 per cent for IBRD/IDA to 24.7 per cent for the Asian Development Bank. The proportion of industrial financing by the World Bank would be greater, of course, if the International Finance Corporation were included, but most observers are agreed that the IFC remains, significantly, the disregarded sister of the World Bank group (Mason and Asher, 1973, p. 745). The claim that such avoidance arises from an ideological view that industry belongs to the private sector looks less and less convincing in the climate of the 1970s. A more satisfactory explanation is the desire to avoid embarrassment.

Lacking, or resisting, a *test* of their performance, UN agencies need a *claim* on the resources of their member countries which does not depend on any test of performance for its substantiation. The easiest claim to establish, and the hardest to refute, is a moral claim. The organs and agencies of the UN are portrayed as the intermediate embodiment of an ultimate ideal of global harmony, or even of world government. Their claim on their members' resources is based, not on assessment of their record, but on their inherent virtue as the earthly representative of the ideal, and their opponents are manoeuvred into the position of seeming to be on the side of sin.

The claim manifests itself most clearly in the tendency to distinguish between multilateral and bilateral *channels* for the transmission of resources, rather than between international and national institutions. The agencies of

Table 1. *Sectoral distribution of loans by IBRD/IDA,[a] IADB,[b] AfDB[c] and AsDB,[d] cumulative to 1972*

	IBRD/IDA[a] (%)	IADB[b] (%)	AfDB[c,e] (%)	AsDB[d] (%)
Economic infrastructure	58.8	35.4	58.0	50.0
Productive sectors	26.1	38.6	32.2	37.8
Other	15.1	26.0	9.8	12.2
Total	100.0	100.0	100.0	100.0

[a] International Bank for Reconstruction and Development/International Development Association (World Bank).
[b] Inter-American Development Bank.
[c] African Development Bank.
[d] Asian Development Bank.
[e] Cumulative to end of 1971.
SOURCE: Annual Reports for 1971–2.

the UN, however, are not multilateral except in the trivial sense of being owned by more than two countries. These 'owners' do not participate substantially in operational decisions, but are provided with reserved areas within the traffic system, in which they may air their views. When this traffic system tries to *operate* multilaterally, it drifts away from actions into forms of words. When the agencies act, they do so in their own right and in pursuit of their own objectives, and in this sense are indistinguishable from any other agency. The multilateral label, however, enables them to claim for their operations the sanction of immanent virtue, and thus to avoid the normal tests of performance.

The claim to virtue deepens the resistance to competition, or to the creation of any parallel or alternative set of agencies. The world-wide agencies' status as the embodiment of the ultimate ideal would be much less usable as the basis for a claim on resources if there were, in fact, rival claimants to this position. Any alternative, however uncompetitive, constitutes a potential threat to the world-wide agencies, for the existence of an alternative gives greater weight to assessment of the agencies' record, relative to assumptions about their virtue, in appraisal of their utility.

The agencies and their clients

As the single embodiment of a single ideal, the community of UN agencies needs a dogma, and this constitutes an obstacle to discussion of the policy alternatives open to different countries or groups of countries as they confront their special problems. Most of the fashions in development studies have originated in the organs and agencies of the UN, or in the associated traffic; and the tendency of these fashions to take the form of an emphasis on one sector or another can be explained in terms of the sectoral organisation of the specialised agencies, each of which has an interest in promoting its own area of responsibility as the focus of attention. These fashions are damaging, for the advent of a new fashion tends to be accompanied by the overthrow of the accumulated lessons of experience, the most conspicuous current example being the way in which discussion of developing countries' employment problems has involved the rejection of economic growth as a major objective, rather than a more refined discussion of the distribution of the fruits of growth. The tendency towards universal application, also, is damaging, diverting attention from the many different problems that policymakers in different countries face.

This tendency, which emanates from the existence of a single dominant set of agencies, has been observable since the early 1960s, i.e. the beginning of the First Development Decade. The superstructure has now become so large that one sometimes forgets that the UN agencies were relatively late entrants to the set of relationships within which developed and developing countries act upon each other. So far as aid in the narrow sense is concerned, i.e. the primary transmission of resources by entities called 'aid agencies', the main elements of the pattern were set in the late 1950s, and the pattern has survived with only minor modifications into the 1970s. The events which precipitated the new pattern were the emergence of the Soviet Union as an alternative to Western, especially US, bilateral aid, the emergence of new candidates for aid in Africa and Latin America, following the earlier concentration first on Europe and then on Asia, and the Indian foreign exchange crisis of 1957–8. Its main elements were:

(a) the diffusion of aid to a wide range of developing countries, and ultimately to virtually all of them, and hence a diminishing concentration by donors on a small group of selected client states;

(b) a presumption on the part of developing countries that aid would be forthcoming, and hence a closer integration of aid into their policymaking processes;

(c) specification of the end-uses of aid;

(d) identification of these end-uses on the basis of a view that the intermediate function of aid, at least, was to provide support for development strategy (i.e. aid was not advertised as being *solely* for the promotion of exports or the maintenance of military alliances);

(e) the beginnings of a debate on alternative development strategies, conducted at first rather crudely in terms of East–West rivalries;

(f) diversification of the sources of aid, and hence a diminution of the capacity of both donors and recipients to exert leverage on each other;

(g) the beginnings of an attempt by the agencies which continued to provide more than 90 per cent of total aid – i.e. international agencies and the Western bilateral donors – to co-ordinate their efforts;

(h) increased use of loans instead of grants;

(i) a rapid increase in the volume of what was called 'aid' (using DAC definitions and figures), at an annual rate of 13 per cent in the late 1950s (a rate which was not attained again, even for a single year, throughout the 1960s).

It was a pattern not all the features of which were desirable from all developing countries' point of view, but it was at least highly dynamic. The main unit in the pattern was the nation state. It was given its first collective expression, not in the global system, but in one group of countries, the members of the North Atlantic Treaty Organisation, and this section of the pattern was subsequently transferred to the Organisation for European Economic Cooperation (OEEC), which in 1961 became the Organisation for Economic Cooperation and Development (OECD). The OECD's Development Assistance Committee remained one of the principal sources of collective operational initiatives throughout the subsequent decade.

The superimposition of a UN 'strategy' on this pattern at the beginning of the First Development Decade, after a period in which UN agencies had been confined to the fulfilment of relatively minor technical functions, is best seen as an attempt, by the developing countries and by an international bureaucracy which saw itself as acting in everybody's best interests, to wrest from the developed countries control of an evolutionary process which had already begun, and which this bureaucracy had not itself initiated. In doing so, it very nearly stopped that evolutionary process dead.

The capacity to respond to specific situations, used in the context of varied and often conflicting operational objectives, had been in the 1950s a powerful stimulus to action. At the global level, the need for consensus vitiated that stimulus. Objectives were replaced by targets, and in particular a target for the volume of aid. Instead of a continuing debate on the many different things that different countries might do in specific situations, the developed countries were given an instruction as to how *much* they were expected to do in total. The measurement of achievement, or rather of many different achievements, was replaced by the measurement of effort. Aimed at ironing out the abuses and inequalities of the pattern that began to evolve in the 1950s, the UN 'strategy' also ironed out the principal forces making for operational innovation. Competitive bargaining gave way to the fixed postures and portmanteau resolutions of UNCTAD. Successive UNCTAD conferences institutionalised the mendicant role of the developing countries, and in doing so they also institutionalised the propensity of the developed countries to say 'no'. By setting themselves up as the front runners in a single world-wide struggle for development, the world-wide agencies ensured that the pace would be desperately slow.

To the middle level operator in the traffic associated with the programmes of UN agencies – typically, say, an economic 'advisor' addressing himself directly to governments – this interpretation of the impact of the 'strategy' may seem exaggerated. He may well share the scepticism expressed here concerning the substance behind that endless succession of documents propounding 'new approaches' at the global level, but he might argue that it is irrelevant, and that under all the words is a massive collection of operational units, each of which is trying to get on with its own particular job. In arguing thus, he would be only half right. The fact is that the middle level staff of the world-wide agencies spend a high proportion of their time moulding, bending and twisting their proposals to fit whatever fashion the current strategy dictates, and they will normally try to persuade their local associates to do likewise. The strategy distorts, vitiates and corrupts, in a way that seeps into the farthest corners that the traffic reaches.

A strong case can be made for the view that the UN agencies, by virtue of their universality, have a central role to play in their respective fields. There is a strong case, also, for the view that among the UN agencies a special role of leadership falls naturally to the World Bank. The case is well made by Mason and Asher (1973), who are careful to specify what kind of leadership they have in mind: the Bank 'may not be a leader in development thought, but it has become a leader among development institutions in applying the available techniques to an analysis of the development problems of particular countries' (p. 469); and again, it may be, 'if not a leader of developmental thought, at least the main repository of what has in fact been learned' (p. 475).

The case becomes much weaker, however, if it is interpreted as giving the UN agencies a leadership role in determining the direction and objectives of development efforts. The leading personalities in the UN agencies some-times act as if this were their role, showing a propensity for stirring calls and prophetic utterances. Their right to use their positions for such purposes is questionable. Undoubtedly, the leading ranks of the UN community contain a high proportion of people who are more dedicated to the cause of development, and have a broader view of the development process, than the political leaders of some, perhaps many, developing countries; but few of them are elected, none of them is elected by a process which is even remotely representational, and there is no supreme political authority in whose name they act. The leaders of such agencies are ill advised, when indulging their propensity for prophetic utterances, to forget their status as hired functionaries. To keep his vision clear the prophet stands apart. When the practical administrator adopts the tone of the prophet, he is always vulnerable to the charge that his real aim is to promote his own programme, or that he is using the power that his programme gives him to promote his own perception.

The literature of development is replete with cases of UN agencies and the personnel at their disposal failing to understand or respond adequately to local conditions and local problems. Partly, this is attributable to the need of any world-wide organisation or world-travelling 'expert' for a universal model and universal prescriptions. If that were the whole problem, the solution would lie in decentralisation, since one could assume that the regional economic commissions, at present generally regarded as one of the more unsatisfactory segments of the UN community, would change their character markedly under the stimulus of real operational responsibility. But the problem is both deeper and simpler than that. An agency which is overwhelmingly the leading source of resources or services in its own particular field is under no great pressure to please the client. That, at its simplest, is the case for proliferation.

A new situation?

Whatever the differences between one group of developing countries and another, it was possible in the 1960s to see them all as having a common interest in securing a transfer of resources from the developed countries, and more generally in tilting the balance of international economic relationships in their own favour. The processes of the UN community of development agencies evolved in response to, and helped to sustain, what appears retrospectively as a relatively simple international economic order, arranged round a perception of three clearly separated groups of countries – West, East and South, or, in the jargon, developed market economies, centrally planned economies, and the variously named 'Third World'.

Has this simple view been rendered irrelevant by the financial and economic turbulence of 1973–4? It is convenient to see 1973 as the year in which what appears to be a fundamental change in the relationships began to materialise, if only because this change is most dramatically exemplified in the success of the oil exporting countries, and of the Arab oil exporters in particular, in organising themselves collectively to alter the balance of economic power in their favour. But it would be a mistake to see the oil exporters' coup as an isolated event. The more general though less dramatic rise in commodity prices in 1973, especially mineral prices, could in the long run be at least as significant as the rise in oil prices, for it suggests a wider application of the selective use of bargaining power. Diversity has been increased, also, by the rise in market interest rates and inflation. It is arguable that developing countries should now be using a discount rate in the region of 20 per cent, rather than the conventionally accepted 10 per cent. At such a rate, the crude distinction between 'official development assistance' and commercial lending breaks down, and needs to be replaced by a more carefully graduated continuum. A seven year export credit at 8 per cent, for instance, carries a grant element of between 29 per cent and 43 per cent, depending on the amortisation schedule, which is comparable to the grant element, at a discount rate of 10 per cent, of much of what has previously passed for aid.

With the advantage of hindsight, one can see that there were earlier and more general indications of the change. One sign, the full significance of which was perhaps not appreciated at the time, was the attention given by the UN itself to the classification of certain countries as being the 'least developed'. The concept of 'least developed' countries subsequently gave way, under the impact of the commodities boom, to the more emotive concept of a 'Fourth World'. The countries of the 'Fourth World' do not have minerals or other desirable natural resources, and they do not have the capacity to organise themselves to their own advantage. They are at the bottom. What was perhaps not fully appreciated was that the identification of a 'Fourth World', consisting of the minority of countries which are virtually destitute, implies the existence of a 'Third World', consisting of the *majority* of countries, which are not destitute, are not at the bottom, do have minerals or other desirable natural resources, and do have the capacity to organise themselves to their own advantage. As clients, they can afford to choose.

There are sound arguments for concentrating the international development and aid effort on the least developed countries, especially if the definitions are not manipulated to ensure that India, and even more casuistically Bangladesh, are excluded. But the corollary needs to be bluntly stated. In a world in which rich countries are increasingly unwilling to meet every new demand with a simple addition to their existing undertakings, such a concentration of effort means that countries other than those in the 'Fourth World' will increasingly be left to look after themselves. There are signs that some countries already see themselves as having this measure of independence, and are increasingly unwilling to adopt the mendicant posture thrust upon them by UN processes. Few would go so far as to admit that they attach diminishing importance to aid, relative to other external sources of finance, since to do so would be needlessly to throw away the chance of cheap money. Nevertheless, one gains a general impression in conversation, which could probably be documented with case studies of some recent visiting missions, that those countries which do have some room for manoeuvre are increasingly unconvinced of the need to go out of their way to satisfy the representatives of external development agencies, and are becoming increasingly competent in measuring the true worth of alternative sources of finance and advice, and in making selective use of them.

In operational terms, this trend seems likely to manifest itself in four ways.

First, to the extent that what might be called intermediate countries see a need for collective organisation, they are likely to identify such a need in terms of specific institutions, or agencies, to fulfil specific functions on their behalf. This could be a significant change. Because of the weakness of the control structure over the UN agencies, these agencies have a propensity to develop their own programmes and preferences, which then have to be sold to their member countries. Institutions established to meet some clearly perceived need are likely, for their own survival, to pay closer attention to the preferences of their clients. Perhaps the day of the preacher is over.

Secondly, the need for collective organisation is likely to be most strongly felt among groups of countries with substantial common or complementary interests which can best be served within an institutional framework. Collective organisation to serve a limited and specific common purpose seems to have greater practical potential as a way of realising the strength of numbers than more comprehensive and therefore more contentious schemes of economic integration, and certainly greater potential than putting all interests and purposes, however conflicting, into a single framework. The relationship between strength and numbers is not linear. When applicants come in crowds, they tend to be left milling at the door.

Thirdly, the growth of purpose-built agencies to serve the requirements of limited groups of countries will reduce the need of these countries for an all-purpose intermediary in their relations with the external world. In particular, an increase in the number of countries capable of going directly to the world's capital markets will reduce the need for external co-ordination of a special kind of resource called 'aid'. Rightly or wrongly, numerous countries have already exhibited a belief that they have that capacity, as is demonstrated by the rapid rise in borrowing of Eurocurrencies by developing countries, which in gross terms is now comparable to total aid, and which took place *before* the rise in oil prices had increased the pressure on oil importers to raise whatever finance they could, as a short term expedient. On a country-by-country basis, it would be worth investigating whether there is an association between the rise of commercial borrowing and an observable loss of interest in some of the World Bank's consultative groups. These groups were established partly with the objective of limiting the recipients' capacity to shop around among competing aid agencies, i.e. to *reduce* diversity. To the extent that developing countries now succeed in diversifying their sources of external capital again, by breaking away from an exclusive dependence on aid, it becomes more difficult for any external agency to maintain a dominant position in its own field. Increased competition becomes self-reinforcing.

Fourthly, increased diversity in the sources of external capital is likely to be accompanied by a sectoral shift in the focus of attention in the developing countries' relations with external agencies generally. Intermediate countries, by definition, have flourishing productive sectors. In general, both international and bilateral development agencies have given less attention to the productive sectors, and certainly less to productive sectors which are not in some sense ailing, than to social and economic infrastructure.

The UN agencies will have difficulty in responding to this trend, except possibly in agriculture, where considerable efforts are being made. Their past neglect of the productive sectors is reflected in their organisational structure; their rather leisurely pace is unsuited to a field in which speed of decision taking is often crucial; and they simply are not accustomed to living with the uncomfortably conspicuous difference between success and failure which is inherent in entrepreneurial activity.

There is a *prima facie* case for supposing that the UN community, and in particular UNCTAD as the central arena of debate, will have a more general difficulty in responding to the trend of events. As foreseen here, the trend may be summarised as a growing demand for institutions to serve the specific needs of limited groups of intermediate countries which have some room for manoeuvre, and therefore some capacity to exercise the client's normal right of choice in determining the service that he gets. It is not a general trend. It is not even a single trend, but rather a shift of emphasis to a level at which different groups of countries will exploit the resources at their command in varying ways and with varying degrees of success. There will be losers as well as winners, and the trend may be crudely expressed as one that favours institutions for winners. The institutions of the global development effort, in their rhetoric at least, are institutions for losers, but in order to render themselves attractive to a majority of their members they have to encourage their members in the misleading belief that the term 'losers' covers most of them. Comprehensive in their membership, the UN agencies are committed to the ideal of universal consensus on a strategy for universal progress. It is not a bad ideal, but it fails to meet the reality of the present situation. The agencies have no mechanism for developing an alternative set of ideals, each of which promises benefits only to some. Lacking such a mechanism, they lack also the capacity to identify those limited areas in which the scope for action lies.

Perhaps, in view of the extent to which some developing countries have been worse hit than others by rising oil prices, the UN community will be forced to become selective at last. There are some signs that this is already happening, but it may be doubted whether the constraints of UN politics will allow the process to go very far, or to achieve a significant impact. In particular, one should question any assumption that the new surplus countries will be any more willing than their predecessors, or even as willing, to shoulder the 'burden' of international development finance, or that a way can be found of channelling the bulk of the new surpluses through the existing global institutions. After all, one of the principal factors in the acquisition of these surpluses has been a rejection of the rules by which these institutions operate. Gestures, in the form of a fund of a few billion dollars here, a few hand-outs there, may be possible, but the really large sums will go through other channels; and the countries which succeed in diverting these channels to themselves will be those which can offer something in return.

If this forecast is correct, then the need to use the UN agencies more selectively will become overwhelming. There will be a role for them, still, in urgent relief operations, and in countries for which aid as traditionally conceived is the most sensible and obvious strategy, even in the long term. In other words, they will be needed, mainly, in the countries which have nothing, or very little, to offer in return. These countries are more numerous than those listed in the UN category of 'least developed' countries. The new situation suggests a division of effort which might even free the agencies of the international aid effort, and the developed countries behind them, to get down to the serious business of helping the countries of the South Asian sub-continent. It is not self-evident, however, that the developed countries will want to take advantage of that opportunity.

The agencies that the clients want

The establishment of a new agency at any intermediate level between the global and the national levels usually requires justification in highly specific terms. The question has to be answered: Why is it desirable to establish this particular agency at this particular level? An important element in the establishment of such an agency, therefore, is the identification of a group of named countries which have an interest in its creation.

Any agency at an intermediate level is exclusive as well as inclusive. In its title and given functions, it postulates a membership which leaves some countries out. The countries that constitute its membership, therefore, are likely to consider what binds them as well as what divides them. With that consciousness of a positive relationship, they are likely to seek participation in the agency's operational processes, and to engage in continuing assessment of the utility of its services.

The momentum behind the demand for services may be political, technical or competitive. Politically, there may be a desire for an agency simply as the outward and visible sign of a more general sense of common identity. Technically, there may be a feeling that a group of countries needs a particular service, or a particular adaptation of a service, which is not available from existing sources. Competitively, a group of countries may require collective organisation in its own best interests *vis-à-vis* other countries.

Competitive momentum is inherently perhaps the strongest of the three. It was a major factor, for instance, in the establishment of the three big regional banks, each of which was seen as having a potential capacity to attract additional resources to its region, if necessary by diversion from other regions; and it is always the main factor, of course, in the creation of military alliances.

In relation to national developmental activities, the services that international agencies may be required to perform can be divided into six main types:

(i) providing a framework for the resolution of conflicts between member states;

(ii) promoting joint activities between member states, which reap the advantages of scale, e.g. under complementarity or production sharing agreements;

(iii) providing assistance in the mobilisation of resources;

(iv) providing advice in fields which require specialised technical skills;

(v) providing assistance in the recruitment of personnel or organisations to perform specified tasks, e.g. engineering contractors, or managing agents;

(vi) acting on member countries' behalf in negotiations with external organisations, e.g. foreign private investors, or aid agencies.

Not all of these services, however, are likely to form the basis of a demand for the creation of *new* agencies.

Providing a framework for the resolution of conflicts is only useful to countries which are in conflict. Obstacles to reaching agreement on the creation of new agencies are likely to be greater among such countries than among countries which are not in conflict. Conflict resolution is a service which extant agencies may acquire, but it usually impedes their evolution rather than promoting it, the EEC being an obvious example.

The promotion of collectively beneficial activities is sometimes treated as a variant of conflict resolution. The tendency is especially marked in the literature of economic integration, which talks in terms of trade-off and the need for mutual concessions. To that extent, the same reasoning applies as above, though the demand for agencies to perform this service may be effective where the collective benefit is obvious and relatively sure, and the element of trade-off relatively small, as appears to be the case, for instance, with the organs of the Andean Group.

In any field in which a country needs external advice, it is likely also to need advice on what sort of advice it needs. There is something very odd in the notion of a group of countries setting up an advisory agency to advise itself. It is more likely to look to extant external agencies for such a service. Even for extant agencies, the advisory function presents problems. The need for advice about the kinds of advice needed means that extant agencies are continually drawn forward into pressing advice upon their clients. At the consultant level, this may be regarded as a legitimate effort to get business. At the more pretentious level of international agencies, however, it shades into the dangerous area of policy prescription. National governments are more likely to want external advice in limited areas in which their policy objectives are already reasonably precise and clear than advice on what their policy objectives should be. The authors of heavy mission reports are usually satisfied if some, at least, of their recommendations are taken up on a selective basis, failing to recognise that this represents quite a different use of the report from the use implicit in the spirit in which it was written.

One is left, then, with resource mobilisation, recruitment and negotiation as three services which deserve scrutiny as the basis for creating new agencies. Strangely, all three are areas in which the global system is weak.

With a few exceptions, such as the IFC, international agencies do not regard resource mobilisation on behalf of their clients as their principal function. They are more concerned with resource mobilisation for themselves, which they then transmit to their clients at their own discretion. The point is made by Mason and Asher, in their observation that the World Bank has never fulfilled what was originally seen as its principal role, namely the provision of an underwriting and guarantee facility which would enhance the independent borrowing capacity of its clients (1973, pp. 26, 107). The most plausible explanation of this avoidance does not lie in any accident of the World Bank's evolution, but in the inherent conflict between helping its clients to borrow and borrowing for itself, since both increase its total exposure. The claim that the World Bank's success with its own bond issues has increased the total resources available to its developing member countries must be regarded at best as not proven, when set against the alternative that was open to it. It should be noted, also, that the IFC, as the most conspicuously client-oriented agency at the global level, is crippled by a charter which restricts it too narrowly on the issue of who its clients should be.

The principle that technical assistance should be advisory rather than operational impedes the recruitment of operational personnel or organisations. The World Bank's obsession with competitive bidding, which provides rather weak protection for the client but rather strong protection for the World Bank against charges of favouritism, is directly opposed to the recruitment function. There is no reason why developing countries should not hire people or organisations to do certain jobs for them. The Arab oil exporters, as the leading exponents of a more independent line, do it all the time. But the rhetoric of the UN community condemns it as showing a lack of self-reliance.

The need for assistance in negotiation is increasingly recognised, and UNCTAD, in particular, has made some attempt to develop a service of this type; but to develop such a service effectively requires an agency which does not suffer from the ambiguities and conflicts of interest which are inherent in the structure of a world-wide membership.

The identification of groups of countries which might develop the momentum for the creation of new institutions points in three main directions: (a) integrated regional groups; (b) non-integrated regional groups, requiring collective institutions for specific and limited purposes; (c) producer groups. In looking for the areas in which the creation of new agencies would be most beneficial to the largest possible number of developing countries, one needs to consider which of these three directions is most likely to meet the dual requirement of a high degree of momentum and the widest possible geographical spread.

Integration, while no doubt highly desirable, typically has a very large element of trade-off. It lacks the initial momentum required for the creation of new institutions. Among those few groups of countries in which the drive towards integration is strong, the collective institutions, also, tend to be strong – e.g. the Central American Bank for Economic Integration (CABEI) in association with the Central American Common Market. Where, however, the drive is not strong, to create institutions with the promotion of integration as one of their principal functions is to create institutions in the form in which the probability of failure is highest. For most regional groups, integration is a distant objective. The journey towards one's destination is not helped by one's assuming that one is already there.

The precedent of the oil exporters suggests that the potential momentum of producer groups is far greater. But it is as well to be clear about the direction of that momentum. It is a direction which carries the notion of institutions for winners to extremes. Producer organisations will favour those countries which have natural resources, especially minerals, that are crucial to modern technology. There is a significant difference between a producer organisation which realises the advantage of possession of a commodity which is in great demand and a producer organisation which does little more than preserve an organised market for a commodity for which there are competitive substitutes. Producer organisations for jute and tea will not significantly change the world. Producer organisations for minerals which enjoy the same sort of demand as oil, even if not in the same degree, could indeed change the world; but in some respects it would be a change for the worse, in terms of the potentiality for conflict, and of the damage inflicted on very poorly endowed countries as well as on the developed countries whose economic dominance would thus be eroded.

A better spread of benefits will be secured if groups can be identified which link relatively well endowed countries with the poorly endowed. Among such groups integration will be exceptionally difficult, because of the fears induced by the inherent inequality of the relationship. For some time to come, therefore, it would seem prudent to put the main emphasis on institutions performing specific and limited services for non-integrated regional groups. If the services required are resource mobilisation, recruitment and negotiation, the search for a feasible alternative can be narrowed down to financial intermediaries at the regional and subregional levels, since the second and third of these services, as well, obviously, as the first, are most effectively provided by agencies which command some measure of financial power.

In recent years, a conspicuous element in the growth of new international institutions outside the global system has been the growth of regional and subregional development banks. While regional banks constitute a partial realisation of the case for proliferation, at least in the field in which the need for duplication, competition and a stronger client-orientation would appear greatest, they do not necessarily meet that part of the case for proliferation which rests on the need for adaptability to local conditions. At the regional level – i.e., as the term is used in UN parlance, at the continental level – development banks have been established to perform essentially the same function as the World Bank, acting as a multilateral channel for the transmission of resources. To this end, the three big regional banks are closely modelled on the World Bank. Two of them have developed countries among their members, but this is less significant in shaping their operations than the fact that all three of them have the aim of mobilising resources for themselves, from the same group of developed countries, which they then transmit to their developing country members at their own discretion. The Asian Development Bank, in which developed countries have a majority of the voting power, has explicitly modelled its loan policy on that of the World Bank. But the African Development Bank, which has no developed countries as members, has in practice tended to operate in the same way, because it still needs to satisfy developed countries of its respectability as a channel for resources. Paradoxically, it is the acquisition of a soft fund financed and partially controlled by developed countries which may now drive the African

Development Bank into a more experimental line, by shifting the focus from resource mobilisation to resource deployment.

At the subregional level, there has been rather more innovation and a rather more entrepreneurial spirit, with the Caribbean Development Bank as perhaps the most conspicuous example. There has also been a greater effort to escape from the obsessions of the aid-dependent mentality and the ambivalence to which these obsessions give rise. At the extreme, there is the Arab Fund for Economic and Social Development, which hardly needs to look for external sources of support, having had the distinction of multiplying its authorised capital before making a single loan. But the Andean Development Corporation, also, is relatively unequivocal in its capital structure and in its relations with external sources of support.

While further structural and operational innovations are to be expected in the creation of new subregional development banks in the next few years, they constitute only one of several possible lines of advance. The utility of development banks, as conventionally established, is limited by two constraints.

First, as typically constituted, a development bank's borrowing capacity is related to the backing of callable capital rather than to the strength of its balance sheet. This imposes a formal ceiling. It is rare for an international development bank to achieve a gearing of more than 1:1 (the CABEI being the most conspicuous exception), and less than 0.5:1 is not uncommon, as compared with the conventional banking rule of thumb allowing a ratio of 10:1.

Secondly, the fact that a development bank ultimately has only its subscribed capital to fall back on tends to make it exceptionally cautious, and to take a narrow view of what projects it will finance. The 'banking mentality' attributed to institutions such as the World Bank is not typical of banking, which can be a rather adventurous activity, but of *development* banking. It arises, not, as is sometimes claimed, from the need to go to the market for funds, but from the firmness with which these institutions are tied to their capital base. Some groups of countries have already appreciated these limitations, and set up complementary financial institutions which are capable of greater operational flexibility, e.g. the Caribbean Investment Bank.

The establishment of a relatively flexible institution, paying more attention to the mobilisation of resources directly on behalf of its clients, and concentrating on the productive sectors for which resources can be mobilised from a wide range of sources, requires a smaller initial capital than a comparable development bank, if only because it is likely to end up with a healthier portfolio. There are few conceivable collections of developing countries which could not finance the establishment of such institutions for themselves, without waiting for the sanction of external support.

The significance of creating a larger number *and variety* of relatively small new financial agencies, serving limited groups of countries for limited purposes, is greater than it might seem. True, it is not a grand decennial strategy. That is indeed its significance, for it constitutes a first step in quite another direction. The creation of agencies which see themselves as mobilising resources on their clients' behalf and at their clients' direction, as recruiting personnel to work in their clients' employment, and as negotiating on behalf of their clients in a context of undivided loyalty; these are developments which would constitute a major enhancement of the developing countries' capacity to exercise choice. Anyone who would deny them that choice, on the ground that many of their governments would use their resources unwisely, needs to be very sure of the basis of his own superior authority. In the case of a bilateral agency, that basis is the ownership of the resources deployed; an international agency cannot claim the same. If a proliferation of international agencies does materialise in the next few years, there will be some cases, no doubt, in which new agencies are established for no clear reason other than the propensity of bureaucracies to breed, and which will be open to criticism on the familiar ground of duplication and waste. More generally, however, such a trend should be read as a sign of determination on the part of sovereign societies to choose their own prescriptions, and not to submit to the prescriptions of those who claim too much power and who admit too little responsibility; and it should be welcomed accordingly.

Notes

1   This was one of the main themes in the generally critical reviews that the Report received. See, in particular, Patel, 1971 and Byres, 1972.
2   I have argued this point more fully elsewhere (White, 1974, chapter 11).
3   For a particularly clear instance of the genre, see Seers, 1970.
4   For UNCTAD, at least, it is possible to take this analysis to a positive conclusion (Lipton, 1972).

References

Byres, T. J. (ed.), 1972. *Foreign Resources and Economic Development: A Symposium on the Report of the Pearson Commission.* London: Frank Cass.
Jackson, Sir Robert, 1969. *A Study of the Capacity of the UN Development System.* Geneva: United Nations.
Lipton, Michael, 1972. Unctad Schmunctad? *Bulletin, Institute of Development Studies* (University of Sussex), **5**, 30–41.
Mason, Edward S. and Asher, Robert E., 1973. *The World Bank Since Bretton Woods.* Washington: The Brookings Institution.
Patel, I. G., 1971. Aid relationship for the seventies. In *The Widening Gap*, (ed.) Barbara Ward, J. D. Runnalls and L. d'Anjou, pp. 295–311. New York: Columbia University Press.
Reid, Escott, 1973. *Strengthening the World Bank.* Chicago: Adlai Stevenson Institute.
Seers, Dudley, 1970. The meaning of development. *Institute of Development Studies, Communications*, no. 44, Brighton.
White, John, 1974. *The Politics of Foreign Aid.* London: Bodley Head.

Index

abaca, 34, 59–60
Abs, Hermann, 212
Abu Dhabi, 78, 130, 244
Adam, G., 117
Adelman, M. A., 53
adjustment assistance, 88
Adler, J., 232
advertising, 81, 136, 168
Afghanistan, 115
African Development Bank, 280, 291–2
aid, *see* official development assistance
Alcoa, 133
Algeria, 42, 115, 134, 189–90, 193
aluminium, 61, 63, 69, 73, 130, 133
Andean Group, 10, 26, 86, 139, 147, 289, 292
Argentina, 119, 139, 182, 187, 211, 232
Arrow, K., 221
Asian Development Bank, 279–80, 291
Australia, 44, 48, 66, 73, 74, 132–3
Avramovic, D., 207, 215

Bahrein, 115
balance of payments problems, 177–88, 210–13, 216–17, 221, 230–1, 263
bananas, 10, 22, 41, 42, 46, 47, 49, 53, 57, 59–60, 130, 135–6
Bangladesh, 24, 66, 177, 194, 285
bankruptcy, 220–1, 235–6
bargaining, 12–15, 19–20, 23, 34, 38, 47, 49, 77–88, 121, 141, 151–3, 156, 161, 163, 171
Barnet, R. S., 119
bauxite, 10, 41, 42, 49, 53, 60, 62–3, 66, 67, 73, 130, 132–5
beef, 57
Belgium, 54, 115, 181
Bhagwati, J. N., 230
Bolivia, 115, 194
Botswana, 115
Boumedienne, President, 253
Braden Company, 128
brain drain, 128
Brazil, 81, 119, 139, 184, 187, 189, 193, 194, 211, 226, 232
Bucharest, 9
buffer stocks, 44–6, 134–5

Bulgaria, 190
Burenstam-Linder, S., 96, 98
Burma, 115
Burundi, 115

Calvo doctrine, 137
Cameroun, 115
Canada, 66, 71, 73, 74, 122, 123, 182, 187, 266
capital markets, 177, 185, 188–98, 220–2, 231, 234, 286
Caribbean Development Bank, 292
Central African Republic, 115
Central American Bank for Economic Integration, 290, 292
Ceylon, 81; *see also* Sri Lanka
Chad, 48, 115, 178
Chile, 73, 115, 116, 128, 134, 211, 232, 267
China, 140
chromium, 83
CIPEC, 72–3, 130, 134–5
cocoa, 10, 32–3, 41, 43, 45, 46, 53, 56, 57, 60, 61–3, 211
coconut oil, 60–1, 67
codes of conduct, 124
coffee, 10, 22, 32–3, 41, 43, 46, 53, 57–8, 60, 61–3, 78, 81, 85, 211
Colombia, 115, 116, 184, 187, 190
commodity agreements, 5, 14, 32–3, 37, 41–5
commodity cartels, 15, 19, 40–1, 53–75, 77–85, 290–1
Communist Manifesto, 88
consumption patterns, 96, 99–102, 113, 127–8
co-operation
    Third World, 14–15, 20–1, 25–6, 39, 45, 49, 53–68, 77–88, 194
    developed and less developed, 8, 12–16, 43, 85, 222
copper, 10, 41, 47, 53, 56–8, 60, 62–3, 67–74, 130, 133–5, 154, 211
copra, 46, 60–1, 67
Corden, M., 179
Costa Rica, 115
Cotonfran, 48
cotton, 34, 39, 46, 56, 57, 59–60
Council of the Americas, 123

[295]